Symbol	Meaning
$>$	Is greater than
$\not>$	Is not greater than
$\geq$	Is greater than or equal to
J	The set of integers
^-a	The additive inverse of a
$\|x\|$	Absolute value of the number x
g.c.d.	Greatest common divisor
l.c.m.	Least common multiple
$\equiv$	Is congruent to
$\cong$	Is equivalent to; is congruent to
$\left[\dfrac{a}{b}\right]$	Equivalence class of ordered pairs
x^{-1}	The multiplicative inverse of x
R	The set of rational numbers
$\approx$	Is approximately equal to
$\%$	Percent
$\sqrt{x}$	The positive square root of x
$\overleftrightarrow{AB}$	Line AB
$\overline{AB}$	Line segment AB
$\overset{\circ\!\!\!\!-\!\!\!\!\circ}{AB}$	Open line segment AB
$\overset{\circ\!\!\!\!-\!\!\!\!\bullet}{AB}$	Half-open line segment AB
$\overleftrightarrow{AB}$	Half-line AB
$\overrightarrow{AB}$	Ray AB
$\|$	Is parallel to
$\angle ABC$	Angle ABC
$m(A)$	The measure of set A
$\triangle ABC$	The triangle with vertices A, B, and C
$\sim$	Is similar to
$P(A)$	The probability of A
$P(\overline{A})$	The probability of not-A

Modern Elementary Mathematics

MODERN

ELEMENTARY MATHEMATICS

MALCOLM GRAHAM

University of Nevada, Las Vegas

 HARCOURT, BRACE & WORLD, INC.

New York   Chicago   San Francisco   Atlanta

Modern Elementary Mathematics, Malcolm Graham

ISBN: 0-15-561037-6

Library of Congress Catalog Card Number: 73-105693

Printed in the United States of America

Drawings by Graphic Presentation Services, Inc.

Dedicated to Carolyn, Joyce, and John

Preface

This text is designed to provide elementary teachers and others with a modern approach to mathematics. It is written for those who plan to teach or are teaching in the elementary school, and it may also be used as a text for those desiring to study mathematics as a part of their general education. Many students will find the material of this text more relevant to their educational program and more interesting to study than a traditional course in algebra and trigonometry. The recommendations of the Committee on the Undergraduate Program in Mathematics (CUPM), as well as various publications of the National Council of Teachers of Mathematics, were used in selecting material for the text.

The first three rather short chapters deal with sets, operations with sets, and relations. These concepts lead logically into the study of numbers and number systems discussed in succeeding chapters. The nature of mathematical proof is first introduced in Chapter 6, with frequent exposure to simple proofs thereafter.

The text places emphasis not only on understanding some basic concepts of mathematics, but also on being able to use these concepts in problem solving. Chapters 11 and 13 are largely devoted to problems of application. A few introductory concepts in statistics and probability are presented in Chapter 14.

My aim has been to write a text which is mathematically sound but at the same time reasonably easy for students to read and study.

The material of the text is adequate for a two-semester sequence of courses of three credits each, or the equivalent. Chapters 1–8 contain approximately half the content of the text and Chapters 9–14 the remainder. For a shorter course, the following parts of the text are recommended: Chapters 1–7, Sections 1–7 of Chapter 8, Sections 1–6 of Chapter 9, Sections 1–10 of Chapter 10, and Sections 1–5 of Chapter 11. Depending upon the depth of coverage, this material should be sufficient for a one-semester course of three to five credits, or the equivalent.

Rather than include more exercises than most students have time to work—which burdens the instructor with the chore of selection for assignments—I have chosen to include a moderate number of appropriate exercises at the end of major text sections. Students should be able to work all or nearly all the exercises. Answers to most of them are given in the back of the book. Review exercises, for which answers are not supplied, are included at the end of each chapter.

I would like to express my appreciation to the University of Nevada for granting me a sabbatical leave to begin work on this book. Many helpful suggestions were offered by various mathematicians and mathematics educators; in particular, I am grateful for the useful criticisms of Professor Robert Arnold, Fresno State College; Professor Robert Pruitt, San Jose State College; and my wife, Mrs. Carolyn L. Graham, Clark County School District, Las Vegas, Nevada. I would also like to thank Mr. Paul L. Wegkamp; Dr. John M. Kingston, University of Washington; and Dr. George Monk, University of Washington, for their critical reading of the manuscript.

Malcolm Graham

Contents

Modern Elementary Mathematics

Chapter One

An Introduction to Sets

Some things occur in nature while others are made by man. For example, gold and silver are already in existence and may be discovered; rockets, automobiles, and mathematical systems, however, come into being as inventions of man. Of course, an automobile is a physical object that we can see and touch while mathematics is essentially an abstract set of ideas, but mathematics has its roots in the physical world about us and many of its applications are found in the environment in which we live.

Elementary mathematics probably began with attempts to answer such questions as, How many sheep do I own? How many people are in this room? and How many brothers and sisters do you have? Basically these questions are asking, How many elements are in a particular set of objects? The process used to determine the number of elements in a set is called counting. In Chapters 1 and 2 we shall develop ideas and vocabulary concerning sets which will later be applied to number concepts.

The meaning of the word set in mathematics is essentially the same as in everyday language. We all know what is meant when we speak of a set of books, a set of dishes, or a salt and pepper set. A set is a collection. In mathematics the members of a set are also called the elements of the set. For example, if a certain set is the states of the United States of America whose official names begin with the letter C, its members, or elements, are California, Colorado, and Connecticut.

The elements of a set may be physical objects, letters of the alphabet, numbers, poems, or anything we wish to consider. A football team is a set (of players). A herd of sheep is a set (of sheep). The telephones in the United States constitute a set (of telephones).

A set in mathematics should be carefully and clearly defined to avoid ambiguity. Care taken in defining a set will assist in determining the members of the set. Examples of sets whose members are easily determined are:

1. The set whose members are past presidents of the United States of America.

2. The set whose elements are the first ten letters of our alphabet.

3. The 1969 graduating class of the University of Nevada, Las Vegas.

Note that in each of the above examples it would be possible to determine whether or not any given element is a member of the set in question.

Examples of sets that are not clearly defined and whose membership would be difficult to establish are:

1. The set of all intelligent people.

2. The set whose elements include all interesting novels.

3. The set of all good-looking girls.

It would be impossible to get general agreement on whether certain elements belong or do not belong to each of these sets.

1.3
Notation
for Sets

One way to indicate a set is to list the names of the elements in roster form and enclose them in a pair of braces. For example, the set whose elements are 1, 3, 5, and 7 may be indicated as $\{1, 3, 5, 7\}$. Note that the names of the elements are separated by commas. The order in which the elements of a set are listed makes no difference except possibly as a matter of convenience. In the above example the set could have been indicated as $\{3, 5, 7, 1\}$ or $\{7, 1, 3, 5\}$ or in any other way obtained by reordering the elements.

If we do not wish to list all the elements of a set, we can let a capital letter such as A, B, or C represent the set. $A = \{1, 3, 5, 7\}$ is read, "A is equal to the set whose elements are 1, 3, 5, and 7." While capital letters are used to represent sets, lowercase letters are frequently used to represent elements of a set. If we wish simply to identify a set of any four elements, we might use $A = \{a, b, c, d\}$. If we then wish to identify some other set containing three elements, we can let $B = \{e, f, g\}$.

Confusion can sometimes arise in identifying the elements of a set where some of the elements are similar or identical. For example, suppose we wish to identify the letters of the alphabet used in writing the word *alfalfa*. Since our alphabet has but one *a*, one *l*, and one *f*, the set of letters would be $\{a, l, f\}$. If we were designing a typewriter to write the word *alfalfa*, it would need a set of only three keys. However, if we asked for the set of elements needed to print the word *alfalfa* for this text, we would need seven elements: three elements of *a*, two of *l*, and two of *f*. We could identify this set by using subscripts and writing $\{a_1, a_2, a_3, l_1, l_2, f_1, f_2\}$ which is read, "the set whose elements are *a* sub-one, *a* sub-two," and so forth.

As another example, suppose a woman gives birth to twins. Even though they may be identical, the twins are a set of two elements rather than one. (Try to convince the mother otherwise!)

Another important symbol in dealing with sets is $\in$, which is read "is an element of." For example, $3 \in A$ is read, "3 is an element of set A" or "3 is a member of set A." A slanted bar / through a symbol generally negates it. $9 \notin A$ is read, "9 is not an element of set A."

Sometimes it is convenient or even necessary to describe the elements of a set rather than to list them in roster form, particularly if there are many elements in the set. For this purpose we use what is commonly known as set-builder notation. $A = \{x \mid x$ has a certain property$\}$ is read, "A is equal to the set of all elements x such that x has a certain property." The vertical bar is the only new symbol we have used and in this context it is read "such that." The set $\{1, 3, 5, 7\}$ could be indicated by writing $\{x \mid x$ is an odd number less than 8$\}$; this is read, "the set of all elements x such that x is an odd number less than 8." The set of all odd numbers can be indicated by simply writing $\{x \mid x$ is an odd number$\}$; this is read, "the set of all elements x such that x is an odd number." Note that the restrictions placed on the elements of the set follow the vertical bar. It should be emphasized that there is no single correct method for defining a set using set-builder notation; several different and perhaps equally useful methods for identifying any given set may be formulated.

EXERCISE 1.3

1. In which of the following sets are the members easily determined?
   (a) Great novels of the eighteenth century.
   (b) Positive integers greater than 12 but less than 20.
   (c) Positive integers greater than 12.
   (d) Three consecutive large numbers.
   (e) The wealthy people of the world.

2. Indicate each of the following sets by listing the elements in roster form:
   (a) The first four letters of our alphabet. $\{a, b, c, d\}$
   (b) The odd numbers with only one digit. $\{1, 3, 5, 7, 9\}$
   (c) All positive integers whose square is 25. $\{5\}$
   (d) The months of the year whose names begin with the letter J.
   (e) The great living men of today.

3. Express each of the following sets in as many ways as possible by changing the order of the elements:
   (a) $\{a, b\}$ (b) $\{a, b, c\}$
   (c) $\{2, 3, 4\}$ (d) $\{7\}$

4. Write in words the meaning of the following:
   (a) $A = \{8, 9, 10\}$
   (b) $8 \in A$

    (c) $\{x \mid x = \text{a whole number}\}$
    (d) $\{x \mid x \text{ is an integer greater than 5}\}$
    (e) $B = \{x \mid x \in A \text{ and } x \text{ is greater than 8}\}$
    (f) $K = \{b, c, 5\}$
    (g) $5 \notin K$

5. Use mathematical symbols to indicate the following:
    (a) C is equal to the set whose elements are 5, 10, and 15. $C = \{5, 10, 13\}$
    (b) 5 is a member of set C. $5 -$
    (c) 7 is not an element of set C.
    (d) The set of all elements x such that x is an even integer.
    (e) The set of all elements y such that y is an odd number greater than 7.

6. Use set-builder notation to indicate each of the following sets:
    (a) $\{1, 2, 3, 4, 5, 6, 7, 8, 9, 10\}$ (b) $\{1, 3, 5, 7, 9\}$
    (c) $\{4, 6, 8, 10, 12\}$ (d) $\{a, b, c, d, e, f, g\}$
    (e) $\{s, t, u, v, w, x, y, z\}$

$\{x \mid x \text{ is an even number greater than 3 } \& \text{ less than } 13\}$

1.4 Equal Sets

Sometimes sets that are defined differently may actually have the same elements. In this event the sets are said to be *equal*.

DEFINITION 1.4.1

If every element of set A is an element of set B and if every element of set B is an element of set A, then set A is equal to set B.

We denote that set A is equal to set B by writing $A = B$. At first it may seem a waste of time to denote A as one set and B as another set if they are indeed the same set. However, in working with two sets it may not be immediately apparent that they are the same set. Note that by definition equal sets contain exactly the same elements and that A and B are two *names* for the same set.

Example 1. Suppose set A contains every student in a class who owns an automobile and set D contains every student who has a driver's license. If every student who owns an automobile has a driver's license and if every student with a driver's license has an automobile, then set A is equal to set D.

1.5 The Empty Set

A set may be defined but contain no elements; such a set is called *the empty set*. The set of children in a given family, for example, may be the empty set. Another way in which a set may be defined such that the empty set results is $\{x \mid x$ is a man 200 feet tall$\}$. Many other examples can be given.

DEFINITION 1.5.1

The set containing no elements is called the empty set.

The empty set is denoted by the symbol $\varnothing$. It may also be denoted by a pair of empty braces $\{\ \}$, but the symbol $\varnothing$ is usually preferred and is easier to write. Note that the empty set is *not* designated by $\{\varnothing\}$; this notation would represent a set containing one element $\varnothing$ rather than the set with no elements. Similarly, the set $\{0\}$ contains the element zero and hence is not the empty set.

Since any two empty sets would have to be equal by Definition 1.4.1, there is only one empty set. Hence the expression "*the* empty set" is used rather than "*an* empty set." The empty set may also be called the *null set* or the *void set*.

1.6
Subsets

Sometimes we find that every member of one set is also a member of some other set. If such a relation exists, the one set is said to be a *subset* of the other. For example, the set of insects is a subset of the set of all animals in the world.

DEFINITION 1.6.1

If every element of set A is also an element of set B, then set A is a subset of set B.

We indicate that A is a subset of B by writing $A \subseteq B$. This may be read, "A is a subset of B," or "A is included in B," or "A is contained in B." The symbol $\subseteq$ may be reversed; thus, $B \supseteq A$ is read "B contains A" and means the same as $A \subseteq B$.

Example 1. If $A = \{a, b\}$ and $B = \{a, b, c\}$, then $A \subseteq B$ since every element in A is also an element in B. The fact that A is a subset of B may also be expressed by writing $\{a, b\} \subseteq \{a, b, c\}$.

Example 2. If $C = \{a, d\}$ and $A = \{a, b, c\}$, then C is not a subset of A since $d \in C$ but $d \notin A$. We can then write $C \not\subseteq A$ which is read, "C is not a subset of A."

Note that by Definition 1.6.1 every set is a subset of itself. Also observe that, since the empty set contains no elements, it is necessarily true that there are *no* elements in the empty set which are *not* members of every other set; hence, the empty set is a subset of every other set, including itself. Problem 3 of Exercise 1.7 further clarifies this situation.

1.7
Proper Subsets

We frequently wish to refer to part of a set but not the entire set. In this case we are dealing with a set known as a *proper subset* of the original set.

DEFINITION 1.7.1

If every element of set A is an element of set B but not every element of set B is an element of set A, then set A is a *proper subset* of set B.

The fact that A is a proper subset of B is denoted by writing $A \subset B$. This may be read, "A is a proper subset of B," or "A is properly included in B," or "A is properly contained in B." The symbol $\subset$ may be reversed; thus, $B \supset A$ is read "B properly contains A" and means the same as $A \subset B$.

Note that every subset of B, including the empty set, is a proper subset of B except B itself. Incidentally, some authors prefer to classify both the set itself and the empty set as improper subsets of a given set. From our definitions, however, the empty set is a *proper subset* of every set *except* itself, and a *subset* of every set *including* itself. The student should verify these statements by using Definition 1.7.1 to test a few specific examples.

Example 1. If $S = \{a, b, c\}$, the subsets of S are $\{a, b, c\}$, $\{a, b\}$, $\{a, c\}$, $\{b, c\}$, $\{a\}$, $\{b\}$, $\{c\}$, and $\varnothing$. By definition, all these are proper subsets of S except S itself or $\{a, b, c\}$.

Now that we have defined equal sets, subsets, and proper subsets, it is interesting to note the relationship that exists between the symbol $\subseteq$ and the symbols $\subset$ and $=$. The symbol $\subseteq$, used to indicate that one set is a subset of another, is a combination of $\subset$, the symbol for a proper subset, and $=$, the symbol for equals. Since a subset is either a proper subset of a given set or equal to the given set, this symbolism is quite appropriate.

⊂ *Proper subsets are contained in a given set.*
⊆ *Subsets are equal to or contained in a " ".*

EXERCISE 1.7   *Improper only when equal - all the rest are proper*

1. Define each of the following terms:
   (a) equal sets   (b) the empty set
   (c) subset   (d) proper subset

2. Which of the following sets are equal?
   $A = \{1, 3, 5, 7\}$
   $B = \{2, 4, 6, 8\}$
   $C = \{x \mid x \text{ is an odd number and } x \text{ is less than } 9\}$
   $D = \{5, 3, 7, 1\}$

3. Given $A = \{a, b, c, d\}$ and the empty set $\varnothing$:
   (a) Is every element in $\varnothing$ in A? (If your answer is "no," name an ele-
       ment in $\varnothing$ that is not in A.)
   (b) Is every element in A in $\varnothing$?
   (c) Is $\varnothing$ a proper subset of A by Definition 1.7.1?

4. Explain the difference between $\varnothing$ and $\{\varnothing\}$.

5. Which of the following sets are subsets of $\{a, b, 7, \Delta\}$?
   (a) $\{a, \square\}$ (b) $\{7\}$
   (c) $\{5, 7\}$ (d) $\{a, b, 7, \Delta\}$
   (e) $\varnothing$ (f) $\{\varnothing\}$
   (g) $\{\Delta, a, 7\}$ (h) $\{\Delta, b, 7, a\}$
   (i) $\{a, b, \varnothing\}$ (j) $\{\ \}$

6. Which of the sets in problem 5 are proper subsets of the given set? *b c g j*

7. State the number of elements in each of the following sets.
   (a) $\{7, a, \square, \varnothing\}$ (b) $\{a, \square, \varnothing\}$
   (c) $\{\square, \varnothing\}$ (d) $\{\varnothing\}$
   (e) $\varnothing$

8. What is the difference in meaning between $\{a\}$ and a?

9. State two methods of symbolism that can be used to show that every element of A is a member of B but that B contains at least one element that
   is not in A. $A \subset B$ $B \supset A$

1.8

The
Power Set

It is possible to have a set whose elements are themselves sets. For
example, the set of all the subsets of $A = \{d, e, f\}$ is $S = \{\{d, e, f\},$
$\{d, e\}, \{d, f\}, \{e, f\}, \{d\}, \{e\}, \{f\}, \varnothing\}$.

DEFINITION 1.8.1

A set whose elements are all the subsets of a given set A is said to be the
power set of A.

In the above example, S is the power set of A since its members are all the subsets of A. A question with an interesting answer is, How many elements are there in the power set of a given set? First, we shall develop a general principle to be used in answering this question.

Suppose a person has three different suits and four different neckties. In how many ways can he dress? With each suit he can wear four different neckties so the answer is $4 + 4 + 4 = 3 \times 4 = 12$. Suppose he also has five different pairs of shoes. Then each pair of shoes can be worn with each of the previous 12 ways of dressing, making $12 + 12 + 12 + 12 + 12 = 5 \times 12 = 60$ different ways of dressing; or the number of ways of dressing is $3 \times 4 \times 5$. In general, if there are a choices for doing one thing, b choices for doing another, c choices for another, and so forth, then *together* they may be done in $a \times b \times c \times \cdots$ different ways.

Now let us consider an example that is slightly different from the one above but where the same principle applies. Suppose a married couple has four children. If they are going to take a trip, how many different sets of their children can they take with them? In this case there are exactly two choices for each child—either he is accepted or he is not accepted for the trip. Therefore, there are two choices for the first child, two choices for the second child, and so on, and the total number of possible ways of selecting children for the trip is $2 \times 2 \times 2 \times 2 = 2^4 = 16$.

We shall now return to the original question concerning the number of subsets of a given set containing n elements. It is obvious that there are exactly two choices for each element; either an element is selected to be in a particular subset or it is *not* selected to be in a particular subset. If a set contains three elements, for example, there are two choices in selecting or not selecting each of the three elements to be in a particular subset, thus making the number of possible subsets equal to $2 \times 2 \times 2 = 2^3 = 8$. In general, the number of subsets in a set containing n elements is n factors of 2, or 2^n. Therefore, the number of elements in the power set of a set of n elements is 2^n. Note that if every element is rejected, the empty set is obtained and if every element is selected, the set itself is obtained. The number of *proper* subsets is $2^n - 1$ since the power set includes the set itself.

EXERCISE 1.8

$3 \times 5 \times 4 = 6\emptyset$

1. Define:
   (a) subset   (b) power set

2. A college girl has three sweaters, five skirts, and four pairs of shoes. If she wears one of each, in how many ways can she dress?

3. In buying an automobile there are ten optional extras, such as radio, air conditioner, and power steering. How many different sales orders are possible?

4. A restaurant menu lists six different items. If you choose *at least one* item, in how many different ways can you place an order?

5. (a) Identify the power set of $\{a, b, 8\}$ by the roster method.
   (b) How many elements does the power set contain?
   (c) How many proper subsets does $\{a, b, 8\}$ have?

6. If A and B are sets and $A = B$, which of the following statements are true?
   (a) $A \subset B$ (b) $A \subseteq B$
   (c) $B \subseteq A$ (d) $B \subset A$
   (e) $A \supseteq B$ (f) $B \supseteq A$

7. What is the relation between A and B if $A \subseteq B$ and $B \subseteq A$?

8. Given $A = \{a, b, c, d\}$:
   (a) Is $\emptyset \subset A$? Explain.   (b) Is $\emptyset \in A$? Explain.
   (c) Is $0 \subset A$? Explain.   (d) Is $\{0\} \subset A$? Explain.

REVIEW EXERCISES

1. Express $\{3, 6, 9\}$ in as many ways as possible by changing the order of the elements.

2. Write in words the meaning of $\{x \mid x \in A$ and $x \notin B\}$.

3. Use set-builder notation to indicate $\{20, 21, 22, 23, 24\}$.

4. Name each of the subsets of $\{j, k, r\}$.

5. Does $\{\emptyset\} = \emptyset$? Explain.

6. Given $A = \{0, 1, 2, 3, 4\}$:
   (a) Identify a proper subset of A.   (b) Is $\emptyset \subset A$?
   (c) Is $\emptyset \in A$?   (d) Is $\{0\} \subset A$?
   (e) Is $\{\emptyset\} \subset A$?

7. If A is a set of elements:
   (a) Is $A \subseteq A$? Explain.
   (b) Is $A \subset A$? Explain.
   (c) Is $A = A$? Explain.

8. How many elements are in the power set of $\{7, 8, 9\}$? Name them.

9. Define the following terms and give an example of each:
   (a) equal sets   (b) subset
   (c) proper subset   (d) empty set
   (e) power set

10. Using set-builder notation, identify three sets equal to the empty set.

Chapter Two

Venn Diagrams and Operations with Sets

2.1
Introduction

In this chapter, additional concepts concerning sets are introduced. Selected operations on sets as well as some of their properties are discussed. The reader will probably notice that some of the properties of operations with sets are the same as the properties of operations with numbers. However, we shall not be concerned with any formal treatment of numbers and their operations at this time.

Venn diagrams (discussed in Section 2.2) frequently help us to understand and develop concepts concerning sets and operations on sets.

2.2
Venn
Diagrams

Diagrams of the type used in this section and some of the following sections are named after John Venn (1834–1923), an English logician. Venn diagrams are also called *Euler diagrams* in honor of the mathematician Leonard Euler (1707–1783). In Venn diagrams, elements of a set are represented by that part of a plane inside or on a simple closed curve. Sometimes specific elements of a set are indicated by letters or other symbols within the simple closed curve.

Example 1. Represent the set *B* as a proper subset of set *A* by using a Venn diagram.

Solution: Any of the diagrams in Figure 2.2.1 would be satisfactory.

FIGURE 2.2.1

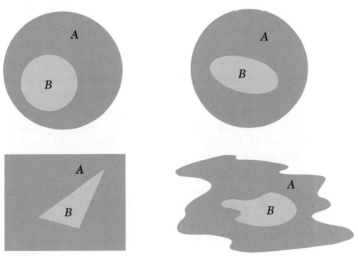

The important thing is that all of region B is contained in region A, but since B is a *proper* subset of A, not all of region A is contained in region B.

Example 2. Let $G = \{a, b, c\}$ represent members of a basketball team who wear glasses and let $T = \{a, b, c, d, e\}$ represent the team. Illustrate with a Venn diagram.

Solution: The solution is Figure 2.2.2.

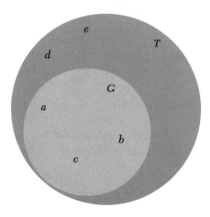

FIGURE 2.2.2

2.3 Universal Sets

It is usually necessary to restrict the elements from which a given set may be chosen. For example, in a sociological study it might be desired to select a family from a given geographic region, income level, occupation, or racial group. The set of elements from which a given set may be chosen is known as the universe or the universal set for that particular situation. The letter U may be used to represent the universe unless some other letter is more appropriate.

If the basketball team in Example 2 of Section 2.2 were selected from Columbia College, then the universe would be the students of Columbia College and the situation could be illustrated by the Venn diagram in Figure 2.3.1.

It can be seen that $G \subset T \subset C$ (the universe). If we wished to consider T as the universe, we could simply omit the rectangle from the diagram and show $G \subset T$. Some authors follow the convention of always representing the universe with a rectangle. If we followed this convention for $G \subset T$, T would be shown as a rectangle.

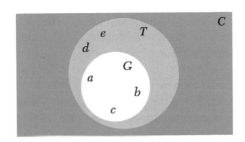

FIGURE 2.3.1

2.4 DEFINITION 2.4.1

The
Complement
of a Set

If U is the universal set and if A is a subset of U, then the set of all elements of U that are not elements of A is the complement of A. The complement of A is indicated by A'.

Example 1. If $U = \{0, 1, 2, 3, 4\}$ and $A = \{2, 3\}$, then the complement of A is $A' = \{0, 1, 4\}$.

Example 2. Given that the universe T is the set of tenth grade boys in a certain school and that G is the set of those who play the guitar, draw a Venn diagram, shading in G'.

Solution: See Figure 2.4.1.

Example 3. Given that U is the set of all boys in a school, T is the boys in the tenth grade, and G is the tenth grade boys who play the guitar, draw a Venn diagram, shading in G'.

Solution: The solution is Figure 2.4.2.

FIGURE 2.4.1   FIGURE 2.4.2

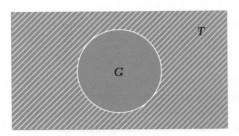
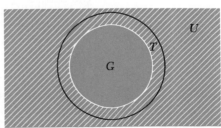

In comparing Examples 2 and 3 note that the complement of a given set is determined by the set chosen as the universe. In Example 2 the complement of G is all the boys in T (the tenth grade) who do not play the guitar, and we say that G' is the complement of G with respect to T. In Example 3 the complement of G is all the boys in U (the school) who do not play the guitar, and we say that G' is the complement of G with respect to U.

EXERCISE 2.4

1. Define the *complement* of a set.
2. Draw a Venn diagram showing that:
   (a) The set of all cats is a subset of the set of all animals.
   (b) $\{2, 3, 4\}$ is a subset of $\{2, 3, 4, 5\}$.
   (c) The set of female cats is a subset of all cats, which in turn is a subset of all animals.
3. If the universal set $U = \{0, 1, 2, 3\}$, tell which of the following are subsets of U.
   (a) $\{0, 3\}$ (b) $\{3, 2\}$
   (c) $\{3, 2, 1, 0\}$ (d) $\varnothing$
   (e) $\{3, \varnothing\}$ (f) $\{0\}$
   (g) $\{3, 4\}$ (h) $\{\varnothing\}$
4. If $U = \{a, b, c, d, e\}$, what is the complementary set of each of the following?
   (a) $\{a, b, c\}$ (b) $\{a\}$
   (c) $\{e, a\}$ (d) $\{b, d, a, c, e\}$
   (e) $\varnothing$ (f) $\{c, a, b\}$
5. Given that U is the universe and $A \subset B \subset U$, illustrate this with a Venn diagram.
6. Draw another Venn diagram exactly like the one in answer to question 5, but in addition shade A' with horizontal parallel lines and B' with vertical parallel lines.
7. (a) What does $(C')'$ equal?
   (b) Simplify $((C')')'$.
   (c) If C is the complement of D, what is the complement of C?

2.5
The Meaning of Two New Symbols: $\vee$ and $\wedge$

We have already used symbols such as $\in$, $\subseteq$, $\subset$, $\not\subset$, and $\varnothing$ to abbreviate certain mathematical expressions. We shall now add two more symbols to our list.

The symbol for *or* is $\vee$. In everyday language, the word *or* has two possible meanings. In some particular situation, a or b might mean either a or b but not both; in some other situation it might mean either a or b or both. For example, "I shall go to the movies or stay home" would mean that I shall either go to the movies or stay home but not both, whereas "Do you like golf or tennis?" is probably asking whether you like either golf or tennis or both. To avoid the possibility of misinterpretation in mathematics, *a* or *b* (written $a \vee b$) is defined to mean *either a or b or both*.

Example 1. Given $A = \{a, b, 3\}$ and $B = \{a, 3, 5, 7\}$, the set of all elements in A or B is $\{a, b, 3, 5, 7\}$. We could write $\{x \mid (x \in A) \vee (x \in B)\} = \{a, b, 3, 5, 7\}$.

The symbol for *and* in mathematics is $\wedge$. If we say *a* and *b* (written $a \wedge b$), we mean both *a* and *b*.

Example 2. Given $A = \{a, b, 3\}$ and $B = \{a, 3, 5, 7\}$, the set of all elements in both A and B is $\{a, 3\}$. This could be written as $\{x \mid (x \in A) \wedge (x \in B)\} = \{a, 3\}$.

2.6
The Union of Sets

In this section we shall learn how two sets can be used in some way to identify a unique (exactly one) third set. In other words, we shall perform some *operation* on two sets to determine a third set. Since the operation is on only two sets at a time, it is called a binary operation. A formal definition of a binary operation will be given later; at this time, however, the treatment will be informal.

The first binary operation on sets to be discussed is *union* (or set-theoretic sum). The symbol for the union of sets is $\cup$ (not to be confused with the capital letter U which is often used for a universal set). Union, of course, implies a uniting or joining together.

DEFINITION 2.6.1

The union of two sets A and B is the set containing all elements that belong to A or B. In abbreviated form we write $A \cup B = \{x \mid (x \in A) \vee (x \in B)\}$.

Note that the operation union is a binary operation (on two sets only) and that by using the definition for this operation we identify a unique set associated with A and B. Since $A \cup B$ is a single set, a single letter such as C can be used to name this set and we may write $C = A \cup B$.

Example 1. If $A = \{2, 3, 4\}$ and $B = \{3, 4, 5, 6\}$, then $A \cup B = \{2, 3, 4, 5, 6\}$.

Example 2. If a Venn diagram is used to identify $A \cup B$ in the previous problem, we could first shade in A horizontally and then shade in B vertically as in Figure 2.6.1. But, since any shaded region in A *or* B contains elements in $A \cup B$, $A \cup B$ could be better shown by making a drawing like Figure 2.6.2, where all the shading is in the same direction. From Figure 2.6.2 we can readily see that $A \cup B = \{2, 3, 4, 5, 6\}$.

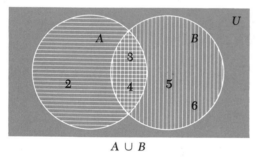
$A \cup B$

FIGURE 2.6.1

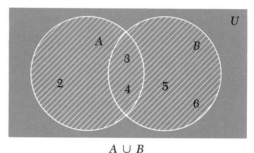
$A \cup B$

FIGURE 2.6.2

2.7
The Intersection of Sets

Another important binary operation on sets is that of *intersection* (or set-theoretic product). The symbol for the intersection of sets is $\cap$.

DEFINITION 2.7.1

The intersection of two sets A and B is the set containing all elements that belong to both A and B. In abbreviated form we write $A \cap B = \{x \mid (x \in A) \wedge (x \in B)\}$.

Observe the similarity between the symbols $\cap$ and $\wedge$ as well as between the symbols $\cup$ and $\vee$, which were used in the previous section.

Using the same sets that were used in Section 2.6, we shall now find their intersection rather than their union.

Example 1. If $A = \{2, 3, 4\}$ and $B = \{3, 4, 5, 6\}$, then $A \cap B = \{3, 4\}$.

Example 2. If a Venn diagram were used to identify $A \cap B$, could first shade in A with horizontal stripes and then shade in with vertical stripes as in Figure 2.7.1. The region that is striped both directions contains elements in $A \cap B$ since it is in A an in B. Again we see that $A \cap B = \{3, 4\}$. An alternative diagram is Figure 2.7.2.

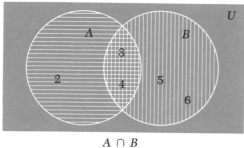

$A \cap B$

FIGURE 2.7.1

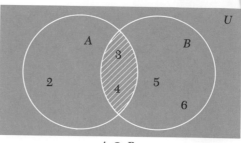

$A \cap B$

FIGURE 2.7.2

Example 3. Given $A = \{a, b, c, d\}$, $B = \{c, d, e\}$, and $U = \{a, b, c, d, e, f, g, h\}$, find $A' \cap B'$ without Venn diagrams.

Solution: Since $A' = \{e, f, g, h\}$ and $B' = \{a, b, f, g, h\}$, $A' \cap B' = \{e, f, g, h\} \cap \{a, b, f, g, h\} = \{f, g, h\}$.

Example 4. Solve Example 3 using Venn diagrams.

Solution: See Figure 2.7.3. A' is represented by the region with horizontal parallel lines and B' is represented by the region with vertical parallel lines. $A' \cap B'$ is the region with both horizontal and vertical lines and is the set containing three elements $\{f, g, h\}$.

FIGURE 2.7.3

FIGURE 2.7.4

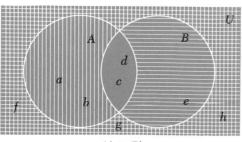

$A' \cap B'$

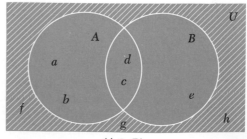

$A' \cap B'$

A simplified diagram for $A' \cap B'$ is shown in Figure 2.7.4. Note that $A' \cap B' = (A \cup B)'$.

DEFINITION 2.7.2

If the intersection of two sets A and B is the empty set, then the sets are *disjoint*.

Example 5. If $A = \{a, b, c\}$ and $B = \{d, e\}$, then $A \cap B = \varnothing$ and A and B are said to be disjoint sets. The situation is illustrated by the Venn diagram in Figure 2.7.5. Note that no region is shared by A and B.

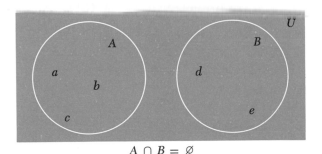

$$A \cap B = \varnothing$$

FIGURE 2.7.5

Although many different binary operations on sets may be defined, our discussion will be confined to three of the more common and frequently used operations: union and intersection, which have already been defined, and the Cartesian product, which will be discussed in Chapter 3.

EXERCISE 2.7

1. We refer to the states of the United States of America as the *Union*. How does this use of the word union relate to our discussion?

2. Draw a diagram to show the *intersection* of Main Street and Fifth Avenue. Use your pencil to shade the intersection. Is the shaded region "Main or Fifth" or "Main and Fifth"?

3. (a) What does *a or b* mean in mathematics?
   (b) What does *a and b* mean in mathematics?

4. Given $A = \{a, b, c\}$ and $B = \{c, d, e\}$:
   (a) Indicate in roster form $\{x \mid (x \in A) \vee (x \in B)\}$.
   (b) Indicate in roster form $\{x \mid (x \in A) \wedge (x \in B)\}$.

5. Define the terms:
   (a) union   (b) intersection
   (c) disjoint

6. What is meant when we say that union and intersection are *binary* operations on sets?

7. Given $A = \{a, b, c, d\}$, $B = \{c, d, e\}$, and $U = \{a, b, c, d, e, f, g\}$, use Venn diagrams to show:
   (a) $A \cup B$ (b) $A \cap B$

8. Using the sets given in problem 7, identify by the roster method each of the following sets:
   (a) $A \cup B$ (b) $A \cap B$
   (c) A' (d) B'
   (e) $A' \cup B$ (f) $A \cup B'$
   (g) $A' \cap B'$ (h) $A' \cup B'$

9. Given $A = \{2, 3, 4\}$, $B = \{4, 5, 6\}$, and $U = \{1, 2, 3, 4, 5, \ldots\}$, show by Venn diagrams:
   (a) $A \cup B$ (b) $A \cap B$

10. Given two intersecting sets A and B, use Venn diagrams similar to Figure 2.7.4 to show:
    (a) A' (b) B'
    (c) $A \cup B$ (d) $A \cap B$
    (e) $A' \cup B$ (f) $A \cup B'$
    (g) $A' \cap B$ (h) $A \cap B'$
    (i) $A' \cup B'$ (j) $A' \cap B'$

2.8
Some Properties of Union and Intersection

Many binary operations are defined in mathematics. For example, the addition of numbers is a binary operation in which we associate with two given numbers a unique number called their *sum*. In this chapter, of course, we are dealing with sets rather than numbers and our concern is with the operations of union and intersection. These operations have some very interesting properties.

(1) $A \cup B = B \cup A$

You have probably already observed that the order in which sets are joined does not affect the result. For example, $\{1, 2, 3\} \cup \{3, 4, 5\} = \{1, 2, 3, 4, 5\}$ and $\{3, 4, 5\} \cup \{1, 2, 3\} = \{1, 2, 3, 4, 5\}$. In general, then, $A \cup B = B \cup A.$ Since A and B may be interchanged or *commuted*, we say that the union of sets is commutative.

(2) $A \cap B = B \cap A$

Using the same sets as above, note that $\{1, 2, 3\} \cap \{3, 4, 5\} = \{3\}$ and that $\{3, 4, 5\} \cap \{1, 2, 3\} = \{3\}$ or, in general, $A \cap B = B \cap A$. Noting once again that A and B may be commuted, we say that the intersection of sets is commutative. Statements (1) and (2) may also be verified by using Venn diagrams.

(3) $(A \cup B) \cup C = A \cup (B \cup C)$

If three or more sets are to be united, they must be joined two at a time since union is a *binary* operation. It can be readily verified by using an example, or by using Venn diagrams, that it makes no difference which two sets are united first. In general, then, $(A \cup B) \cup C = A \cup (B \cup C)$, and we say that the union of sets is associative. The parentheses indicate the two sets on which the operation is to be performed first; however, since it makes no difference which two sets are united first, we may write $A \cup B \cup C$ without ambiguity.

Example 1. Let $A = \{2, 3, 4\}$, $B = \{3, 4, 5\}$, and $C = \{5, 6\}$. We shall show that $(A \cup B) \cup C = A \cup (B \cup C)$.

$$\begin{aligned}
(A \cup B) \cup C &= (\{2, 3, 4\} \cup \{3, 4, 5\}) \cup \{5, 6\} \\
&= \{2, 3, 4, 5\} \cup \{5, 6\} \\
&= \{2, 3, 4, 5, 6\} \\
A \cup (B \cup C) &= \{2, 3, 4\} \cup (\{3, 4, 5\} \cup \{5, 6\}) \\
&= \{2, 3, 4\} \cup \{3, 4, 5, 6\} \\
&= \{2, 3, 4, 5, 6\}
\end{aligned}$$

Since $(A \cup B) \cup C$ and $A \cup (B \cup C)$ both equal $\{2, 3, 4, 5, 6\}$, they are names for the same set and we may write $(A \cup B) \cup C = A \cup (B \cup C)$.

(4) $(A \cap B) \cap C = A \cap (B \cap C)$

As with the union of sets, it may be readily verified by an example or by a Venn diagram that the intersection of sets is associative. Symbolically, $(A \cap B) \cap C = A \cap (B \cap C)$. Since it makes no difference on which two sets the operation of intersection is performed first, we may write $A \cap B \cap C$ without ambiguity.

(5) $A \cup (B \cap C) = (A \cup B) \cap (A \cup C)$

(6) $A \cap (B \cup C) = (A \cap B) \cup (A \cap C)$

The parentheses in (5) and (6) indicate that the operations within them should be performed before the remaining operations. For example, $A \cup (B \cap C)$ means that we must first find the set resulting from the intersection of B and C and then join A with this set.

Note that in (5) and (6) we are dealing with two operations rather than with only one. The properties stated in (5) and (6) are generally known as the *distributive properties*. In (5) we say that union is distributive over intersection and in (6) that intersection is distributive over union. (Incidentally, in arithmetic, multiplication is distributive over addition: $2 \cdot (3 + 5) = (2 \cdot 3) + (2 \cdot 5)$; however, addition is not distributive over multiplication: $2 + (3 \cdot 5) \neq (2 + 3) \cdot (2 + 5)$.) Examples 2 and 3 will verify that intersection is distributive over union.

Example 2. Given $A = \{2, 3, 4\}$, $B = \{3, 4, 5\}$, and $C = \{5, 6\}$, it can be verified that $A \cap (B \cup C) = (A \cap B) \cup (A \cap C)$. Note that we say *verify* rather than *prove*, since one example does not constitute a general proof.

$$A \cap (B \cup C) = \{2, 3, 4\} \cap (\{3, 4, 5\} \cup \{5, 6\})$$
$$= \{2, 3, 4\} \cap \{3, 4, 5, 6\}$$
$$= \{3, 4\}$$
$$(A \cap B) \cup (A \cap C) = (\{2, 3, 4\} \cap \{3, 4, 5\}) \cup (\{2, 3, 4\} \cap \{5, 6\})$$
$$= \{3, 4\} \cup \varnothing$$
$$= \{3, 4\}$$

Since $A \cap (B \cup C)$ and $(A \cap B) \cup (A \cap C)$ are names for the same set $\{3, 4\}$, $A \cap (B \cup C) = (A \cap B) \cup (A \cap C)$.

Example 3. With Venn diagrams for any sets A, B, and C, it may be shown that $A \cap (B \cup C) = (A \cap B) \cup (A \cap C)$. The left-hand diagram in Figure 2.8.1 illustrates $A \cap (B \cup C)$. $(B \cup C)$ is striped horizontally and A is striped vertically. The crosshatched region is contained in A *and* in $(B \cup C)$ and therefore represents $A \cap (B \cup C)$. The right-hand diagram of Figure 2.8.1 represents $(A \cap B) \cup (A \cap C)$. $(A \cap B)$ is striped horizontally and $(A \cap C)$ is striped vertically. The region that is striped horizontally *or* vertically (or both) is in $(A \cap B)$ *or* $(A \cap C)$ and represents $(A \cap B) \cup (A \cap C)$.

In summary, then, some of the properties implied by the definitions of the union and intersection of sets are:

1. $A \cup B = B \cup A$ (Union is commutative.)
2. $A \cap B = B \cap A$ (Intersection is commutative.)

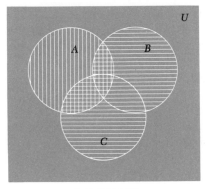
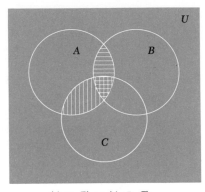

$A \cap (B \cup C)$ $(A \cap B) \cup (A \cap C)$

FIGURE 2.8.1

3. $(A \cup B) \cup C = A \cup (B \cup C)$ (Union is associative.)
4. $(A \cap B) \cap C = A \cap (B \cap C)$ (Intersection is associative.)
5. $A \cup (B \cap C) = (A \cup B) \cap (A \cup C)$ (Union is distributive over intersection.)
6. $A \cap (B \cup C) = (A \cap B) \cup (A \cap C)$ (Intersection is distributive over union.)

EXERCISE 2.8

1. Express in roster form $\{x \mid (x \in A) \wedge (x \in B)\}$ if $A = \{2, 3, 4, 5\}$ and $B = \{4, 5, 6, 7\}$.

2. Express in roster form $\{x \mid (x \in A) \vee (x \in B)\}$ if $A = \{2, 3, 4, 5\}$ and $B = \{4, 5, 6, 7\}$.

3. Given $A = \{a, b, c\}$, $B = \{c, d, e, f\}$, and $C = \{a, e, f, g\}$, use a method similar to Example 2 of Section 2.8 to verify:
   (a) $A \cup B = B \cup A$
   (b) $A \cap B = B \cap A$
   (c) $A \cap (B \cup C) = (A \cap B) \cup (A \cap C)$
   (d) $A \cup (B \cap C) = (A \cup B) \cap (A \cup C)$

4. Rely on the definitions of union and intersection to complete the following:
   (a) $A \cup \emptyset = ?$ (b) $A \cup A = ?$
   (c) $A \cap \emptyset = ?$ (d) $A \cap A = ?$
   (e) If $A \subseteq B$, then $A \cup B = ?$
   (f) If $A \subseteq B$, then $A \cap B = ?$
   (g) If A and B are disjoint (contain no common elements), then $A \cap B = ?$

5. Using Venn diagrams with three intersecting sets similar to those of Figure 2.8.1, verify that $A \cup (B \cap C) = (A \cup B) \cap (A \cup C)$.

6. Use Venn diagrams to determine whether or not $(A \cup B) \cap C$ is equal to $A \cup (B \cap C)$.

REVIEW EXERCISES

1. What is meant by the term *universal set?*

2. If $U = \{2, 4, 6, 8, 10\}$, what is the complementary set of $\{6, 10\}$?

3. Use a Venn diagram to illustrate the situation described in problem 2. Shade in the complement of $\{6, 10\}$.

4. If $A = \{1, 2, 3\}$, $B = \{1, 2, 3, 4, 5, 6\}$, and $U = \{1, 2, 3, 4, 5, 6, 7\}$:
   (a) Identify A' by the roster method.
   (b) Identify B' by the roster method.
   (c) If B is considered to be the universe, identify A' by the roster method.

5. If $A = \{2, 3, 4, 5\}$ and $B = \{5, 6, 7\}$, express in roster form:
   (a) $\{x \mid (x \in A) \wedge (x \in B)\}$
   (b) $\{x \mid (x \in A) \vee (x \in B)\}$

6. Given $A = \{2, 4, 6, 9\}$ and $B = \{6, 9, 12\}$, complete the following statements by indicating the sets in roster form:
   (a) $A \cup B = ?$ (b) $A \cap B = ?$
   (c) $A \cup \varnothing = ?$ (d) $A \cap \varnothing = ?$

7. Given $A = \{a, b, c, d\}$ and $B = \{a, b, x, y\}$, complete the following statements by indicating the sets in roster form:
   (a) $A \cap B = ?$ (b) $A \cup B = ?$
   (c) $A \cup \varnothing = ?$ (d) $A \cap \varnothing = ?$
   (e) $B \cup B = ?$

8. If $C = \{1, 2, 3, 4\}$ and $D = \{1, 2, 8, 9\}$, indicate which of the following are true and which are false.
   (a) $C \subset D$ (b) $\{0\} \subseteq D$ (c) $\{2, 4\} \subset C$
   (d) $\{\varnothing\} \subset C$ (e) $\varnothing \subset D$ (f) $D \subset (C \cup D)$

9. In a fraternity with 40 members, 21 have a class in mathematics, 5 have classes in both mathematics and biology, while 10 have classes in neither mathematics nor biology.
   (a) Draw a Venn diagram to illustrate this situation.
   (b) How many members have a class in mathematics but not in biology?
   (c) How many have a class in biology but not in mathematics?

10. Given $A = \{0, 1, 2\}$, $B = \{2, 3, 4, 5\}$, and $D = \{4, 5, 6\}$, express in roster form:
    (a) $A \cap (B \cup C)$
    (b) $(A \cap B) \cup C$
    (c) Does $A \cap (B \cup C) = (A \cap B) \cup C$?

Chapter Three

Cartesian
Product Sets
and Relations

3.1
Introduction

In defining the Cartesian product of two sets it is necessary to understand what is meant by an ordered pair of elements. As discussed in Chapter 1, if a set is identified by listing its elements, order is not important; for example, $\{a, b\} = \{b, a\}$. In some situations, however, the order of elements can be very important. For example, in using the numbers 2 and 7 in a fraction, order is important since $\frac{2}{7} \neq \frac{7}{2}$. When we wish to indicate an ordered pair of elements we write (a, b). Note that parentheses (not braces) are used to indicate an ordered pair. In general, $(a, b) = (c, d)$ if and only if $a = c$ and $b = d$.

Once two elements a and b have been ordered, they may be thought of either as two separate elements or as a single element. This would be similar to thinking of a husband and wife as two people or as one married couple. A set whose elements are three ordered pairs may be indicated by writing $\{(a, b), (c, d), (e, f)\}$.

3.2
Cartesian Products

We must understand the concept of a *Cartesian product* to understand the formal definition of a relation. Cartesian products (sometimes called simply *product sets*) are so named in honor of the famous French mathematician, René Descartes (1596–1650).

DEFINITION 3.2.1

The Cartesian product of set A and set B, denoted by $A \times B$, is the set of all ordered pairs (a, b) such that $a \in A$ and $b \in B$.

This could be expressed in set notation by writing $A \times B = \{(a, b) \mid (a \in A) \wedge (b \in B)\}$. In general, $(a, b) \neq (b, a)$; for example, $(3, 8) \neq (8, 3)$. However, if $a = b$, then $(a, b) = (b, a)$, as in the case of $(3, 3) = (3, 3)$.

Note that the cross symbol $\times$ is used in mathematics in two distinct situations. It is used to indicate the Cartesian product of two sets, and it is also used to indicate the multiplication of two numbers. Hence we may write $A \times B$, read "A cross B," and we may also write 2×7, read "2 times 7." There is little chance for confusion since a Cartesian product is always indicated when the cross $\times$ appears between the symbols for two sets, while a product is always indicated when the cross appears between the symbols for two numbers.

Example 1. If $A = \{a, b, c\}$ and $B = \{2, 3\}$, then $A \times B = \{(a, 2), (a, 3), (b, 2), (b, 3), (c, 2), (c, 3)\}$. The first element of each ordered pair is a member of set A and the second element is a member of set B. Since there are three choices for the first element and two choices for the second, the number of ordered pairs is $3 \times 2 = 6$. Each ordered pair of elements constitutes a *single* element of the Cartesian product set.

Example 2. Using the sets given in Example 1, $B \times A = \{(2, a), (2, b), (2, c), (3, a), (3, b), (3, c)\}$. Again there are six elements in the Cartesian product set but not the same six that were identified as elements of $A \times B$ in Example 1.

The ordered pairs or elements of a Cartesian product set may be easily found by making a table. For any element (a, b), a is called the first component and b is called the second component of the ordered pair. In making a table, it is customary to list the first components horizontally and the second components vertically.

If $A = \{d, e, f\}$ and $B = \{1, 2, 3, 4\}$, the tables for $A \times B$ and $B \times A$ are as illustrated in Figures 3.2.1 and 3.2.2.

b			
4	$(d, 4)$	$(e, 4)$	$(f, 4)$
3	$(d, 3)$	$(e, 3)$	$(f, 3)$
2	$(d, 2)$	$(e, 2)$	$(f, 2)$
1	$(d, 1)$	$(e, 1)$	$(f, 1)$
	d	e	f	a

$A \times B$

FIGURE 3.2.1

a			
f	$(1, f)$	$(2, f)$	$(3, f)$	$(4, f)$
e	$(1, e)$	$(2, e)$	$(3, e)$	$(4, e)$
d	$(1, d)$	$(2, d)$	$(3, d)$	$(4, d)$
	1	2	3	4	b

$B \times A$

FIGURE 3.2.2

EXERCISE 3.2

1. Define *Cartesian product*.
2. Given $A = \{2, 3, 4\}$ and $B = \{7, a\}$:
   (a) Find $A \times B$.
   (b) Find $B \times A$.
   (c) How many elements are in the Cartesian product set $A \times B$?
   (d) How many elements are in the Cartesian product set $B \times A$?
   (e) How many elements in $A \times B$ are also in $B \times A$?

3. Given $C = \{4, 5, 6\}$ and $D = \{5, 6, 7\}$:
   (a) Find $\{(c, d) \mid (c \in C) \wedge (d \in D)\}$.
   (b) Find $\{(d, c) \mid (d \in D) \wedge (c \in C)\}$.
   (c) How many elements are in the Cartesian product $C \times D$?
   (d) How many elements are in the Cartesian product $D \times C$?
   (e) How many elements in $C \times D$ are also in $D \times C$?

4. If $A = \{a, b, c\}$ and $B = \{f\}$:
   (a) Find $\{(x, y) \mid (x \in A) \wedge (y \in B)\}$.
   (b) Find $\{(y, x) \mid (y \in B) \wedge (x \in A)\}$.
   (c) How many elements are in $A \times B$?
   (d) How many elements are in $B \times A$?
   (e) How many elements in $A \times B$ are also in $B \times A$?

5. Given $A = \{2, 3, 4\}$ and $B = \emptyset$:
   (a) How many elements are in set A?
   (b) How many elements are in set B?
   (c) Find $\{(a, b) \mid (a \in A) \wedge (b \in B)\}$.
   (d) Find $\{(b, a) \mid (b \in B) \wedge (a \in A)\}$.
   (c) How many elements are in $A \times B$?
   (f) How many elements are in $B \times A$?

6. If $U = \{1, 2, 3, \ldots, 10\}$, $A = \{1, 2, 3, 4, 5, 6\}$, and $B = \{8, 9\}$:
   (a) Find A' (the complement of A).
   (b) Find B'.
   (c) Find $B \times A'$.
   (d) Find $A' \times B$.
   (e) Find $B \times B$.

7. If $A = \{1, 2, 3\}$, find $A \times A = \{(a, b) \mid (a \in A) \wedge (b \in A)\}$.

8. If $A = \{a, b\}$ and $B = \{a, b\}$:
   (a) Find $A \times B$.
   (b) Find $B \times A$.
   (c) Find $A \times A$.
   (d) Find $B \times B$.
   (e) Why does $A \times B = B \times A = A \times A = B \times B$?

9. If $A = \emptyset$ and $B = \emptyset$, find $A \times B$.

3.3
Introduction to the Relation Concept

In this section the notion of a *relation* is developed but a precise definition is reserved for Section 3.4. A relation provides a means of comparing or associating elements of one set with elements of another set (or the same set). The elements to be compared or related may be numbers, people, colleges, ideas, automobiles, or anything we wish to consider. We might even compare or relate elements that are themselves sets.

Usually, there is a method or rule by which we can tell whether two elements are related in some particular way. For example, consider the relation "is taller than." By a process of measurement we could determine whether or not John is taller than Mary. If John is taller than Mary, then we say that John is related to Mary for the relation "is taller than." The symbol $\mathcal{R}$ or $\circledR$ is frequently used to represent a relation. "John $\mathcal{R}$ Mary" is read, "John is related to Mary." For specific relations, however, more appropriate symbols may be used. If T is the relation "is taller than," "John T Mary" would be read, "John is taller than Mary." For brevity, "John T Mary" may be read, "John is T to Mary."

Some other examples of relations are:

(a) is the father of   (b) is the son of

(c) is younger than   (d) is equal to

(e) is less than   (f) is a friend of

(g) is a multiple of   (h) is a subset of

(i) is a student of

Example 1. Consider the sets $A = \{$Carson City, Sacramento, Trenton, Albany$\}$ and $B = \{$California, Florida, New Jersey, Nevada$\}$. The elements of set A that are related to elements of set B by the relation $\mathcal{R}$, "is the capital of," are as follows:

Sacramento $\mathcal{R}$ California
Carson City $\mathcal{R}$ Nevada
Trenton $\mathcal{R}$ New Jersey

Note that order makes a big difference here. California is not the capital of Sacramento, but Sacramento is the capital of California. Hence, for the relation "is the capital of," California is *not* related to Sacramento even though Sacramento is related to California.

As we shall see in Section 3.4, the relation "is the capital of" could be expressed simply as a set of ordered pairs. In fact, we may consider the set of ordered pairs to be the relation and write $\mathcal{R} = \{$(Sacramento, California), (Carson City, Nevada), (Trenton, New Jersey)$\}$. Note that this set of ordered pairs is a subset of $A \times B$ and that the first component of each ordered pair is related to the second component. Some other relation would result in a different subset of ordered pairs in $A \times B$.

3.4

**Definition
of a
Relation**

DEFINITION 3.4.1

Given two sets A and B, a relation in $A \times B$ is any subset $\mathcal{R}$ of $A \times B$.

It is important to understand that by Definition 3.4.1, *any* subset of $A \times B$, including $A \times B$ itself and the empty set, is a relation in $A \times B$. Furthermore, since any subset of a Cartesian product set is a set of ordered pairs, it follows that a relation in $A \times B$ will be a set of ordered pairs such that the first component of each ordered pair is an element of set A and the second component is an element of set B.

A symbol such as $\mathcal{R}$ is used to name a relation (a set of ordered pairs) as well as to state that an element a is related to an element b (written $a \mathcal{R} b$). Hence, if $a \mathcal{R} b$, then $(a, b) \in \mathcal{R}$. In other words, the ordered pair (a, b) tells us that a is related to b.

If set A is equal to set B, then $A \times B = A \times A$. In this case we can identify relations in $A \times A$, and any relation $\mathcal{R}$ in $A \times A$ is a subset of $A \times A$: $\mathcal{R} \subseteq A \times A$. Sometimes a relation in $A \times A$ is referred to simply as a relation in A.

Example 1. Let A be the set of all cities in the United States of America and let B be the set of all states in the United States of America. The Cartesian product $A \times B$ is the set of all ordered pairs whose first component is a city and whose second component is a state. (a) The set of ordered pairs whose first component is a capital city and whose second component is the state of which the first is the capital is a relation in $A \times B$. (b) The set of ordered pairs—first the most populous city of a state and then the state to which the city belongs—is also a relation in $A \times B$. (c) The set of ordered pairs—first a city with over 1,000,000 people and then the state to which it belongs—is another relation in $A \times B$.

Each relation in Example 1 is a subset of $A \times B$. The relations defined could be identified in abbreviated form as $\mathcal{R}_1$, $\mathcal{R}_2$, and $\mathcal{R}_3$.

Example 2. Let A be the set of all states in the United States of America. The Cartesian product $A \times A$ is the set of all ordered pairs of states. Examples of relations in $A \times A$ are: (a) the set of all ordered pairs of states such that the first component is larger in area than the second component; (b) the set of all ordered pairs of states such that the first component borders on the second component; (c) the set of all ordered pairs of states such that the first component has a higher mountain than the second component; (d) the set of all ordered pairs of states such that the first component has a larger population than the second component.

Each relation defined in Example 2 is a subset of $A \times A$. For brevity these relations could be identified as $\mathcal{R}_1$, $\mathcal{R}_2$, $\mathcal{R}_3$, and $\mathcal{R}_4$.

Using set-builder notation, a relation $\mathcal{R}$ defined in $A \times B$ can be identified as $\{(a, b) \mid (a, b) \in A \times B \text{ and } a \mathcal{R} b\}$. If $\mathcal{R}$ is defined in $A \times A$, then the set can be written $\{(a, b) \mid (a, b) \in A \times A \text{ and } a \mathcal{R} b\}$.

3.5
Identifying
Relations

Given $A = \{1, 2, 3\}$ and $B = \{1, 2, 3, 4\}$, a table of the ordered pairs of the Cartesian product $A \times B$ appears in Figure 3.5.1.

Recall that by definition any subset of $A \times B$ is a relation and is called a *relation in* $A \times B$. In any relation the set of first components of the ordered pairs is called the domain of the relation and the set of second components of the ordered pairs is called the range of the relation.

Each of the following examples refers to the Cartesian product $A \times B$ illustrated in Figure 3.5.1.

b			
4	$(1, 4)$	$(2, 4)$	$(3, 4)$
3	$(1, 3)$	$(2, 3)$	$(3, 3)$
2	$(1, 2)$	$(2, 2)$	$(3, 2)$
1	$(1, 1)$	$(2, 1)$	$(3, 1)$
	1	2	3	a

$$A \times B$$

FIGURE 3.5.1

Example 1. Let us identify a relation in $A \times B$ such that a is related to b if a "is greater than" b. The "is greater than" relation in $A \times B$ is the set $\{(2, 1), (3, 1), (3, 2)\}$. Note that the first component of each ordered pair is greater than the second. The domain of this relation is $\{2, 3\}$ and the range is $\{1, 2\}$.

Example 2. Now we shall find the elements of the relation in $A \times B$ identified as $\{(a, b) \mid (a, b) \in A \times B$ and $a \,\Re\, b$ if a is less than $b\}$. The relation expressed in roster form is $\{(1, 2), (1, 3), (1, 4), (2, 3), (2, 4), (3, 4)\}$. The domain is $\{1, 2, 3\}$ and the range is $\{2, 3, 4\}$.

Example 3. If we define $a \,\Re\, b$ to mean $a = b$, then the relation in $A \times B$ would be $\{(1, 1), (2, 2), (3, 3)\}$. The domain is $\{1, 2, 3\}$ and the range is $\{1, 2, 3\}$.

Example 4. If $a \,\Re\, b$ is defined to mean $a = 8 \times b$, then there are no elements in set A related to those of set B. Therefore, the relation in $A \times B$ is the empty set, and we may write $\Re = \varnothing$.

EXERCISE 3.5

1. Define *relation*.

2. If set A contains 3 elements and set B contains 4 elements:
   (a) How many ordered pairs are in $A \times B$?
   (b) How many subsets are in $A \times B$?
   (c) How many relations are in $A \times B$?

3. Given $A = \{1, 2\}$ and $B = \{1, 2, 3, 4, 5\}$, make a table of $A \times B$ similar to the one shown in Figure 3.5.1. With the help of the table, identify by the roster method the following relations in $A \times B$:
   (a) $\{(a, b) \mid a \text{ is less than } b\}$
   (b) $\{(a, b) \mid a = b\}$
   (c) $\{(a, b) \mid a \text{ is greater than } b\}$
   (d) $\{(a, b) \mid b = a^2\}$
   (e) $\{(a, b) \mid a = b^2\}$

4. What are the domain and range of each of the five relations identified in problem 3?

5. Given set $A = \{a, b\}$, $B = \{a, b, c\}$, $C = \{b, c\}$, and $D = \{c\}$, indicate which sets are related by the inclusion relation $\subseteq$.

6. Given $A = \{4, 5\}$ and $B = \{1, 2, 3, 4, 5\}$, identify by the roster method each of the following:
   (a) The product set $A \times B$.
   (b) The product set $B \times A$.
   (c) The relation $\Re_1$ in $A \times B$ such that $a \,\Re_1\, b$ if a is less than b.
   (d) The relation $\Re_2$ in $B \times A$ such that $b \,\Re_2\, a$ if b is less than a.
   (e) The relation $\Re_3$ in $A \times A$ such that $a \,\Re_3\, b$ if b is greater than a.
   (f) The relation $\Re_4$ in $B \times A$ such that $b \,\Re_4\, a$ if b is equal to a.

7. If A contains three elements and B contains four elements:
   (a) How many distinct relations are there in $A \times B$ (including the empty set)?
   (b) How many distinct relations are there in $B \times A$ (including the empty set)?

8. Given $A = \{1, 2\}$ and $B = \{7, 8, 9\}$, identify $\{(a, b) \mid (a, b) \in A \times B \wedge a = b\}$.

3.6
Some Properties of Relations in $A \times A$

If a relation $\mathcal{R}$ is defined in $A \times A$, then $\mathcal{R}$ is a subset of $A \times A$. Such relations may have certain properties. Three of these, the *reflexive*, *symmetric*, and *transitive* properties, are discussed in this section.

DEFINITION 3.6.1

If a relation $\mathcal{R}$ is defined in $A \times A$ and if $a \, \mathcal{R} \, a$ for every $a \in A$, then $\mathcal{R}$ is reflexive.

The definition says in effect that *every* element in A must be related to itself if the reflexive property holds for a given relation $\mathcal{R}$.

Example 1. Consider a set of people A and the relation "is the same height as" in $A \times A$. It is true that each person is the same height as himself. Then, by definition, "is the same height as" is a reflexive relation and $a \, \mathcal{R} \, a$ holds for every $a \in A$.

Example 2. Let $B = \{1, 2, 3, 4\}$ and consider the relation "is less than" in $B \times B$. It is not true that every element is less than itself. As a matter of fact, $a \, \mathcal{R} \, a$ does not hold for any element in this case. The "is less than" relation is not reflexive.

DEFINITION 3.6.2

If a relation $\mathcal{R}$ is defined in $A \times A$ and if $a \, \mathcal{R} \, b$ implies $b \, \mathcal{R} \, a$, then $\mathcal{R}$ is symmetric.

Note that the definition does not require that any given element a be related to b; however, *if a is related to b, then b* must be related to a for the relation to be symmetric.

Example 3. Consider a set of people A and the relation "is the same height as" in $A \times A$. It is true that if a "is the same height as" b, then b "is the same height as" a. Since $a \mathcal{R} b$ implies $b \mathcal{R} a$, the relation "is the same height as" is symmetric.

Example 4. Let $B = \{1, 2, 3, 4\}$ and consider the relation "is less than" in $B \times B$. Then a "is less than" b does not imply b "is less than" a. Since $a \mathcal{R} b$ does not imply $b \mathcal{R} a$, the relation "is less than" is not symmetric.

DEFINITION 3.6.3

If a relation $\mathcal{R}$ is defined in $A \times A$ and if $a \mathcal{R} b$ and $b \mathcal{R} c$ imply $a \mathcal{R} c$, then $\mathcal{R}$ is <u>transitive</u>.

The definition of the transitive property does not require that a be related to b or that b be related to c; however, *if* a is related to b and b is related to c, *then* a must be related to c for the relation to be transitive.

Example 5. Consider a set of people A and the relation "is the same height as" in $A \times A$. If a is the same height as b and b is the same height as c, then a is the same height as c. Hence, "is the same height as" is a transitive relation.

Example 6. Consider the set $B = \{1, 2, 3, 4\}$ and the relation "is less than" in $B \times B$. If a is less than b and b is less than c, then it is implied that a is less than c. Hence, "is less than" is transitive. Although the "is less than" relation is transitive, it is neither reflexive nor symmetric, as we discovered in Examples 2 and 4.

3.7
Equivalence Relations

We noted in the previous section that the relation "is the same height as" is reflexive, symmetric, and transitive. Such a relation is said to be an *equivalence relation*. The relation "is less than" is transitive but neither reflexive nor symmetric; hence it is not an equivalence relation.

DEFINITION 3.7.1

A relation defined in $A \times A$ with the reflexive, symmetric, and transitive properties is an equivalence relation.

Example 1. Let A be a set of line segments in a given plane. The relation "is the same length as" is reflexive, symmetric, and transitive. By definition, then, "is the same length as" is an equivalence relation in $A \times A$. "Is perpendicular to" is not an equivalence relation since it is symmetric but neither reflexive nor transitive.

Example 2.   Let A be the set of people living in Charleston. The relations, "is the same age as," "has the same address as," and "is the same height as," are equivalence relations in $A \times A$.

Examples of relations that are not equivalence relations are: "is the mother of," "is the brother of," "is greater than," and "is a divisor of."

3.8
Equivalence Classes

A prime feature of an equivalence relation in $S \times S$ is that the relation *partitions* the set S into disjoint subsets known as *equivalence classes*. A set of equivalence classes of a set S is called a partition of S. Before we formally define an equivalence class, we shall examine an equivalence relation defined in a set and identify the equivalence classes of the partition. Recall that a relation in $S \times S$ may be referred to simply as a *relation in S*.

Consider the set $S = \{Ann, Bob, Carolyn, Don, Esther\}$ and the relation "is the same sex as." Clearly this is an equivalence relation since the reflexive, symmetric, and transitive properties hold: a is the same sex as a; if a is the same sex as b, then b is the same sex as a; if a is the same sex as b and b is the same sex as c, then a is the same sex as c. The equivalence classes of S determined by the relation "is the same sex as" are $\{Ann, Carolyn, Esther\}$ and $\{Bob, Don\}$. Note that these sets are disjoint and that every member in an equivalence class is related to every other member in its class.

Another equivalence relation defined in S, such as "is the same age as," might partition S into only one equivalence class (if all five persons have the same age) or into as many as five equivalence classes (if all five persons have different ages). In each case, however, the sets of the partition will be disjoint.

DEFINITION 3.8.1

If $\mathcal{R}$ is an equivalence relation defined in S and $a \in S$, then the equivalence class of a, denoted by $[a]$, is equal to $\{x \mid (x \in S) \wedge (x \, \mathcal{R} \, a)\}$.

From Definition 3.8.1 we see that an equivalence class may be named by enclosing *any one* of its members in *brackets*. Using the definition of an equivalence class and the properties of an equivalence relation, we shall show in the following discussion that an equivalence relation partitions the set in which it is defined into disjoint subsets.

1. Every element of S belongs to an equivalence class since $a \, \mathcal{R} \, a$ implies $a \in [a]$.

2. If $a \in [b]$, then $b \in [a]$ since $a \, \mathcal{R} \, b$ implies $b \, \mathcal{R} \, a$.

3. If $c \in [a]$ and $c \in [b]$, then $[a] = [b]$. We can prove this by using the transitive property, since if $c \in [a]$ and $c \in [b]$, then $c \, \mathcal{R} \, a$ and $c \, \mathcal{R} \, b$ both hold. Of course, if $c \, \mathcal{R} \, a$ is true, $a \, \mathcal{R} \, c$ holds by the symmetric property. Then we have $a \, \mathcal{R} \, c$ and $c \, \mathcal{R} \, b$, which imply $a \, \mathcal{R} \, b$ by the transitive property of equivalence. But if $a \, \mathcal{R} \, b$, then $[a] = [b]$ is implied since the transitive property can be used to show that every element of $[a]$ is in $[b]$ and that every element of $[b]$ is in $[a]$.

We can see from the above discussion that if two equivalence classes have one element in common, they contain all the same elements and are equal. Otherwise the sets are disjoint, and the statement that an equivalence relation partitions a set in which it is defined into disjoint subsets (called *equivalence classes*) is indeed true.

Example 1. Find the equivalence classes of the set {*big, large, small, great, yellow, little*} for the relation "can mean the same as."

Solution: The partition contains three equivalence classes: (1) {*big, large, great*}, (2) {*yellow*}, (3) {*small, little*}. We could identify the first equivalence class as [*big*], [*large*], or [*great*]; the second equivalence class as [*yellow*]; and the third equivalence class as [*small*] or [*little*].

EXERCISE 3.8

1. Define *relation*.

2. Define the *reflexive* property of a relation in $A \times A$.

3. Define the *symmetric* property of a relation in $A \times A$.

4. Define the *transitive* property of a relation in $A \times A$.

5. Define an *equivalence relation* in $A \times A$.

6. Given the following five relations defined in the set of all people, draw a table and check the properties of each relation. Also check the appropriate space if the relation is an equivalence relation.

$\mathcal{R}_1$ "is as tall as"
$\mathcal{R}_2$ "is shorter than"
$\mathcal{R}_3$ "lives in the same country as"
$\mathcal{R}_4$ "is the mother of"
$\mathcal{R}_5$ "is a cousin of"

The relation	$\mathcal{R}_1$	$\mathcal{R}_2$	$\mathcal{R}_3$	$\mathcal{R}_4$	$\mathcal{R}_5$
Reflexive					
Symmetric					
Transitive					
Equivalence relation					

7. Which of the properties—reflexive, symmetric, and transitive—apply to the relations below? Note that some of the relations could be defined in sets of elements where the elements themselves are sets.
   (a) $\subset$ (is a proper subset of)
   (b) $\subseteq$ (is a subset of)
   (c) $=$ (is equal to)
   (d) is perpendicular to
   (e) is the spouse of

8. Given $A = \{1, 2, 3\}$ and $B = \{1, 9\}$, find the subsets $\mathcal{R}_1$, $\mathcal{R}_2$, $\mathcal{R}_3$, $\mathcal{R}_4$, and $\mathcal{R}_5$ in $A \times B$ that constitute each relation defined below:
   (a) $(a, b) \in \mathcal{R}_1$ if a is less than b.
   (b) $(a, b) \in \mathcal{R}_2$ if a is greater than b.
   (c) $(a, b) \in \mathcal{R}_3$ if $a = b$.
   (d) $(a, b) \in \mathcal{R}_4$ if $a = \sqrt{b}$.
   (e) $(a, b) \in \mathcal{R}_5$ if $b = \sqrt{a}$

9. Using sets A and B . problem 8, find the relations in $B \times A$ such that:
   (a) $(b, a) \in \mathcal{R}_1$ if b is less than a. (11) 12 13 91 92
   (b) $(b, a) \in \mathcal{R}_2$ if b is greater than a.
   (c) $(b, a) \in \mathcal{R}_3$ if $b = a$.
   (d) $(b, a) \in \mathcal{R}_4$ if $b = \sqrt{a}$.

10. Find the equivalence classes of the set $\{2, 3, \frac{1}{2}, (1 + 1), \frac{2}{4}, (2 + 1), \frac{6}{2}, 9\}$ for the relation "is equal to."

11. Give an example of a relation that is transitive but neither reflexive nor symmetric.

12. Give an example of a relation that is neither reflexive nor symmetric nor transitive.

3.9

Functions

Suppose a relation consists of a set of ordered pairs such that the first component of each ordered pair is a year in history and the second is the population (in thousands) of the town Springfield in that year. This relation might be {(1910, 7), (1920, 12), (1930, 16), (1940, 18), (1950, 16), (1960, 24)}. The population in both 1930 and 1950 was 16,000 so there are two ordered pairs with the same second component. However, at any given time there could not be two different populations for Springfield; hence this relation could not have two ordered pairs with the same *first* component. A relation such as this is called a *function*.

A function is sometimes called a *single valued relation* since each element in the domain is matched with exactly one element in the range.

DEFINITION 3.9.1

Def

A relation $\mathfrak{R}$ in $A \times B$ is a function if for each element a of the domain there is a unique (exactly one) element b in the range satisfying $a \mathfrak{R} b$.

This is equivalent to saying that no two ordered pairs of a relation which is a function may have the same first component.

Example 1. The relation $\mathfrak{R}_1 = \{(a, 2), (b, 2), (c, 3), (d, 4)\}$ is a function since for each component of the domain there is a unique second component. Note that the relation is a function even though the *second* component 2 has two different first components, a and b.

Example 2. The relation $\mathfrak{R}_2 = \{(a, 2), (a, 3), (b, 5)\}$ is not a function since the first component a is related to both 2 and 3. The second component of a is not unique.

Example 3. The relation $\mathfrak{R}_3 = \{(x, y) \mid (y = 2x)$ and $(x = 1, 2, 3, \ldots)\}$ is a function since for each first component x of $\mathfrak{R}_3$, there is a unique second component. This function with infinitely many ordered pairs could be written as $\{(1, 2), (2, 4), (3, 6), \ldots, (x, 2x), \ldots\}$. The general element of the function is indicated by $(x, 2x)$.

3.10
Inverse
Relations

If we reverse the order of each of the components of a given rela-
tion $\mathcal{R}$, we get another relation which is called the *inverse relation* of $\mathcal{R}$.
The inverse relation of $\mathcal{R}$ is denoted by $\mathcal{R}^{-1}$ (read "R inverse").

DEFINITION 3.10.1

Given the relation $\mathcal{R}$ in $A \times B$, the inverse relation of $\mathcal{R}$, $\mathcal{R}^{-1}$, is the relation in $B \times A$ consisting of all ordered pairs (b, a) such that $a \, \mathcal{R} \, b$.

From Definition 3.10.1 it can be seen that $b \, \mathcal{R}^{-1} \, a$ means $a \, \mathcal{R} \, b$.
The domain of $\mathcal{R}$ is the range of $\mathcal{R}^{-1}$, and the range of $\mathcal{R}$ is the domain
of $\mathcal{R}^{-1}$. If $\mathcal{R}$ is a relation in $A \times B$, then $\mathcal{R}^{-1}$ is a relation in $B \times A$.

Example 1. The inverse relation of $\mathcal{R}_1 = \{(1, 4), (2, 3), (5, 6)\}$ is
$\mathcal{R}_1{}^{-1} = \{(4, 1), (3, 2), (6, 5)\}$.

Example 2. The inverse relation of $\mathcal{R}_2 = \{(a, 1), (b, 2), (c, 9)\}$ is
the relation $\mathcal{R}_2{}^{-1} = \{(1, a), (2, b), (9, c)\}$.

Example 3. The inverse relation of $\mathcal{R}_3 = \{(1, 2), (2, 4), (3, 6), \ldots,$
$(x, 2x), \ldots\}$ is $\mathcal{R}_3{}^{-1} = \{(2, 1), (4, 2), (6, 3), \ldots, (2x, x), \ldots\}$.

EXERCISE 3.10

1. Which of the following relations are functions?
   (a) $\mathcal{R}_1 = \{(1, 6), (2, 7), (3, 8), (4, 9)\}$
   (b) $\mathcal{R}_2 = \{(2, 3), (5, 9), (6, 9)\}$
   (c) $\mathcal{R}_3 = \{(1, 1), (2, 2), (3, 3), (4, 4)\}$
   (d) $\mathcal{R}_4 = \{(1, 9), (1, 10), (2, 3), (4, 5)\}$
   (e) $\mathcal{R}_5 = \{(1, 7), (2, 7), (3, 7), (4, 7)\}$
   (f) $\mathcal{R}_6 = \{(8, 7), (8, 6), (8, 5)\}$

2. Which of the following relations are functions?
   (a) $\mathcal{R}_1 = \{(x, y) \,|\, (x = 1, 2, 4) \wedge (y = 3x)\}$
   (b) $\mathcal{R}_2 = \{(x, y) \,|\, (x = 1, 3, 5) \wedge (y = x^2)\}$
   (c) $\mathcal{R}_3 = \{(x, y) \,|\, (x = 1, 2, 3, \ldots) \wedge (y = x + 2)\}$

3. Indicate by the roster method the relations in problem 2.

4. (a) Write the inverse relation for each of the relations given in problem 1.
   (b) Which of the inverse relations are functions?

5. (a) Write the inverse relation for each of the relations given in problem 2. Use the roster method.

(b) Which of the inverse relations are functions?

3.11
The Graphing of Relations

A graph may be thought of as a picture of a relation. Frequently, a graph helps us to better understand a relation and its properties. You will recall that the Cartesian product was named after René Descartes. The Cartesian coordinate system of graphing relations is also named in Descartes' honor. This coordinate system of graphing is illustrated in Figure 3.11.1 for the relation $\mathcal{R} = \{(x, y) \mid (y = 2x) \land (x = 1, 2, 3)\}$.

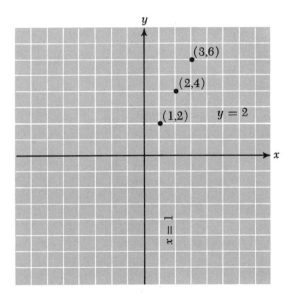

FIGURE 3.11.1

In graphing relations, each ordered pair is represented by a point. To illustrate, consider the ordered pair $(1, 2)$. The ordered pair $(1, 2)$ is represented by the intersection of the graph of $x = 1$ and the graph of $y = 2$. Note that the graph of $x = 1$ is a line 1 unit to the right of the y-axis and parallel to it; the graph of $y = 2$ is a line parallel to the x-axis and 2 units above it. The numbers 1 and 2 are called the coordinates of the point $(1, 2)$. The two axes are called the coordinate axes, and their point of intersection $(0, 0)$ is called the origin.

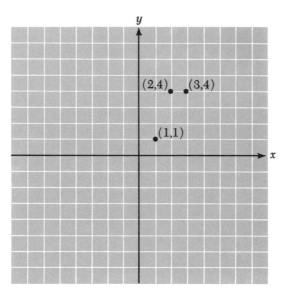

FIGURE 3.11.2

Example 1.   The graph of $\mathcal{R}_1 = \{(1, 1), (2, 4), (3, 4)\}$ appears in Figure 3.11.2. The coordinates of all three points are labeled.

This relation is a function, since the first component of each ordered pair has a unique second component. The inverse relation $\mathcal{R}_1{}^{-1} = \{(1, 1), (4, 2), (4, 3)\}$ is not a function, however, since the second component of 4 is not unique. The fact that 4 is related to both 2 and 3 for $\mathcal{R}_1{}^{-1}$ is apparent from the graph of $\mathcal{R}_1{}^{-1}$ since one point is directly above another. See Figure 3.11.3.

The Cartesian approach to graphing ordered pairs of numbers as points is an extremely simple concept; in fact, its effectiveness probably results from its simplicity. Any relation whose elements are ordered pairs of numbers may be represented by a Cartesian graph—even relations with infinitely many elements.

EXERCISE 3.11

1. Express in roster form the inverse relation for each of the following relations:
   (a) $\mathcal{R}_1 = \{(1, 2), (2, 3), (3, 5), (4, 5)\}$
   (b) $\mathcal{R}_2 = \{(2, 1), (3, 1), (4, 2), (5, 1)\}$
   (c) $\mathcal{R}_3 = \{(1, 1), (2, 2), (5, 3)\}$
   (d) $\mathcal{R}_4 = \{(2, 1), (2, 3), (4, 5)\}$

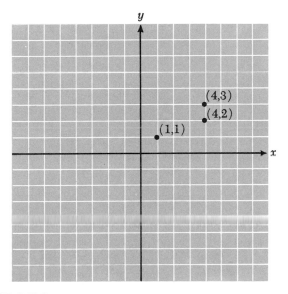

FIGURE 3.11.3

2. Graph each of the relations of problem 1 separately, using a dot to identify the location of each point. On each of these four graphs plot the coordinates of the inverse relation by using a small cross to identify each point. If you have made no mistakes, each pair of graphs should be symmetrical about a line from the origin making a 45° angle with the x-axis.

3. (a) Which of the relations of problem 1 are functions?
   (b) Which of the inverse relations of problem 1 are functions?

4. If $\mathcal{R}^{-1}$ is the inverse relation of $\mathcal{R}$, what is the inverse of $\mathcal{R}^{-1}$?

5. If $\mathcal{R} = \{(2, 3), (a, 7)\}$, what does $(\mathcal{R}^{-1})^{-1}$ equal?

6. What can be said about the ordered pairs of a relation that is its own inverse?

7. Under what condition will the inverse of a function also be a function?

REVIEW EXERCISES

1. If $A = \{a\}$ and $B = \{1, 2, 3\}$:
   (a) Identify by the roster method $\{(x, y) \mid (x \in A) \wedge (y \in B)\}$.
   (b) Identify by the roster method $\{(y, x) \mid (y \in B) \wedge (x \in A)\}$.

2. Given $M = \{a, b, c\}$ and $T = \{0, 1\}$, identify the following sets by the roster method:
   (a) $M \times T$ (b) $T \times M$
   (c) $M \times M$ (d) $T \times T$
   (e) $T \times \varnothing$

3. If $A = \{1, 2, 3\}$ and $B = \{2, 3, 4\}$, use the roster method to name:
   (a) $A \times B$ (b) $B \times A$
   (c) $(A \times B) \cap (B \times A)$ (d) $(A \times B) \cup (B \times A)$

4. Given $A = \{a, b, c\}$, $B = \{1, 2\}$, and $U = \{a, b, c, d, e, 1, 2, 3\}$:
   (a) Identify A'.
   (b) Identify B'.
   (c) Identify $A' \times B'$.

5. What is a relation in $A \times B$?

6. What is a relation in $A \times A$? In A?

7. If A has five elements, how many possible relations may be identified in $A \times A$?

8. Is the relation "has the same initial digit as" defined in $\{64, 22, 26, 13, 11\}$:
   (a) reflexive?
   (b) symmetric?
   (c) transitive?

9. Is the relation "has a smaller initial digit than" defined in $\{64, 22, 26, 13, 11\}$:
   (a) reflexive?
   (b) symmetric?
   (c) transitive?

10. Given the relation $\{(1, 1), (2, 8), (3, 8), (4, 64), (5, 125)\}$:
    (a) Identify its domain.
    (b) Identify its range.
    (c) Is the relation a function? Explain.
    (d) Is the inverse relation a function? Explain.

11. If $C = \{1, 2, 3, 4, 5\}$ and $D = \{a, b, c\}$:
    (a) How many elements are in $C \times D$?
    (b) How many subsets has $C \times D$?
    (c) How many distinct relations may be defined in $C \times D$?
    (d) How many elements are in $D \times C$?
    (e) How many subsets has $D \times C$?
    (f) How many distinct relations may be defined in $D \times C$?

12. Which of the following relations are functions?
    (a) $\mathcal{R}_1 = \{(2, 3), (4, 9), (5, 3), (6, 0)\}$
    (b) $\mathcal{R}_2 = \{(1, 4), (1, 5), (2, 4), (3, 9)\}$
    (c) $\mathcal{R}_3 = \{(2, 7), (6, 3), (7, 3)\}$
    (d) $\mathcal{R}_4 = \{(5, 7), (6, 7)\}$
    (e) $\mathcal{R}_5 = \{(7, 5), (7, 6)\}$
    (f) $\mathcal{R}_6 = \{(1, 2), (3, 4), (5, 6), (8, 8), (9, 9)\}$

13. Refer to problem 12 and:
    (a) Identify by the roster method the inverse relation of each function.
    (b) Tell which of the inverse relations are functions.

14. Tell which of the properties—reflexive, symmetric, and transitive—
    apply to the relations below. Assume each relation is defined in the set
    of all people.
    (a) is a sister of
    (b) lives sixteen miles from
    (c) has the same color hair as
    (d) is shorter than
    (e) is older than
    (f) is the father of
    (g) is the daughter of

15. Which of the relations in problem 14 are equivalence relations?

16. If neither A nor B is the empty set and $A \times B = B \times A$, what is the
    relation of set A to set B?

Chapter Four
Correspondences, Numbers, and Numerals

4.1
Introduction

We have discussed sets and operations with sets, but very little has been said about numbers and their operations. In this chapter the concept of number will be introduced through the use of sets, and the representation of numbers by number symbols or numerals will be discussed. First, however, we must define and discuss some new terms.

4.2
Correspondences

The elements of one set may usually be assigned arbitrarily or by some rule to those of another and in various ways. The resulting set of ordered pairs is, of course, called a relation. The pairing of elements from one set to another may also be called a correspondence. If a correspondence is such that each element of the first set is matched with exactly one element of the second set, the correspondence is a *single-valued relation* or *function;* it may also be called a *mapping*.

Several types of correspondences are illustrated in Figure 4.2.1. The correspondences in (a) and (b) are functions; however, those in (c) and (d) are relations that are not functions since some of the elements of set A, in this case r and t, are assigned to more than one element of set B.

It is interesting to explore the various ways in which elements of one set may be assigned to elements of another set, but at this time we

FIGURE 4.2.1

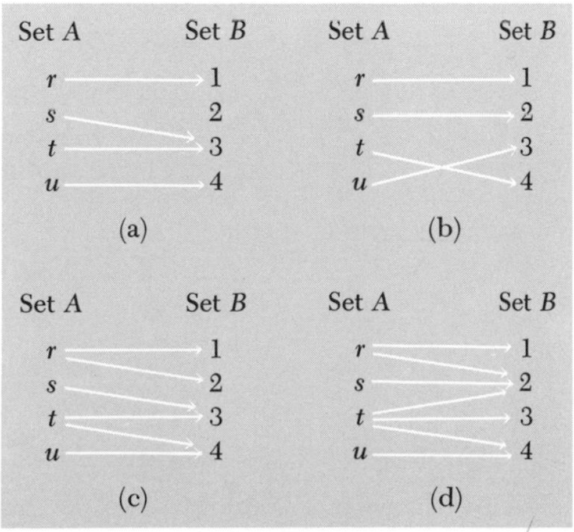

Set A   Set B   Set A   Set B
  r ────────→ 1   r ────────→ 1
  s ─────── 2   s ─────── 2
  t ─────── 3   t ─────── 3
  u ─────── 4   u ─────── 4
        (a)   (b)

Set A   Set B   Set A   Set B
  r ─────── 1   r ─────── 1
  s ─────── 2   s ─────── 2
  t ─────── 3   t ─────── 3
  u ─────── 4   u ─────── 4
        (c)   (d)

are primarily interested in a particular type of correspondence between the elements of two sets known as a *one-to-one correspondence* (abbreviated 1–1).

4.3

One-to-One Correspondences and Equivalent Sets

DEFINITION 4.3.1

The elements of two sets A and B are said to be in a one-to-one correspondence if each member of A is paired with exactly one member of B and if each member of B is paired with exactly one member of A in such a way that the two sets of ordered pairs are inversely related functions.

Many examples of sets whose elements can be placed in a one-to-one correspondence may be found. A shoe salesman should find a one-to-one correspondence between the elements of the set of left shoes and the elements of the set of right shoes in his store. In a theater there should be a one-to-one correspondence between patrons and tickets sold. A one-to-one correspondence should exist between husbands and wives in a monogamous society.

In Figure 4.3.1, (a) and (b) are one-to-one correspondences since they each satisfy Definition 4.3.1. Note that arrows go from elements of set A to elements of set B and also from elements of set B to elements of set A. By using double-headed arrows, we see that the two sets of

FIGURE 4.3.1

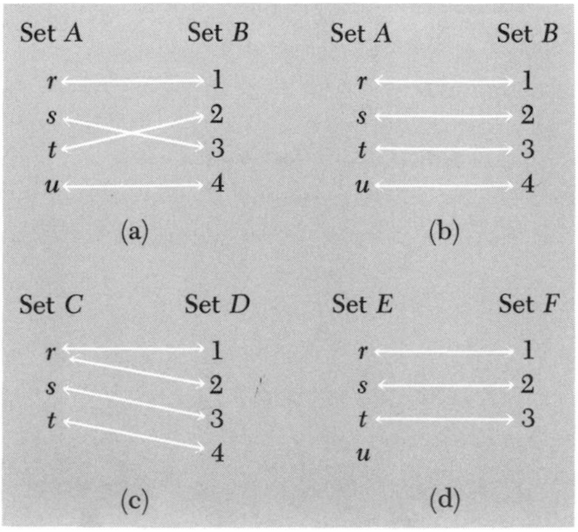

ordered pairs of elements that result are functions that are the inverses
of each other. The inversely related functions resulting from the one-to-
one correspondence in part (a) of Figure 4.3.1 are $\{(r, 1), (s, 3), (t, 2), (u, 4)\}$
and $\{(1, r), (3, s), (2, t), (4, u)\}$. Part (c) is not a one-to-one correspondence
since two elements of set D are paired with r, and part (d) is not a
one-to-one correspondence since u is not paired with any element
of set F.

It is interesting to note that the elements of some sets can be
paired in many different ways to produce a one-to-one correspondence.
Each correspondence results in another pair of inversely related functions.
Elements of sets A and B in Figure 4.3.1 are paired in two different ways,
but they could be paired in $4 \times 3 \times 2 \times 1 = 24$ different ways. Why?
(See Section 1.8 if necessary.)

DEFINITION 4.3.2

If the elements of two sets A and B can be placed in a one-to-one
correspondence, the sets are said to be equivalent (or *matched*).

Note that when two sets are equivalent, we have one *set* related
to another *set*. To be sure, it is only when the *elements* of two sets can
be placed in a one-to-one correspondence that the sets are related—but
it is the *sets* (not the elements) which are said to be equivalent. To call
the sets equivalent is quite appropriate since the matching relation
for sets is an equivalence relation—it is reflexive, symmetric, and
transitive.

The matching relation satisfies the reflexive property since the
elements of set A can be placed in a one-to-one correspondence with the
elements of itself $(A \, \mathcal{R} \, A)$. The symmetric property is satisfied since
the elements of set B can be placed in a one-to-one correspondence
with the elements of set A if the elements of set A can be placed
in a one-to-one correspondence with the elements of set B (if $A \, \mathcal{R} \, B$, then
$B \, \mathcal{R} \, A$). And finally, the transitive property holds since $A \, \mathcal{R} \, B$ and $B \, \mathcal{R} \, C$
imply $A \, \mathcal{R} \, C$. The reader is asked to verify the transitive property
for the matching relation in problem 8 of Exercise 4.3.

EXERCISE 4.3

1. Define *one-to-one correspondence*.
2. Define *equivalent sets*.
3. Identify the inversely related functions resulting from the one-to-one
   correspondence in part (b) of Figure 4.3.1.

4. Explain the difference between equivalent sets and equal sets. Refer to Section 1.7 if necessary.

5. (a) Are equal sets equivalent?
   (b) Are equivalent sets equal?

6. Given:
   $A = \{a, b, c\}$
   $B = \{c, a, b\}$
   $C = \{1, 2, 3\}$
   $D = \{b, a, c\}$
   $E = \{4, 5, 6\}$
   (a) Which sets are equal?
   (b) Which sets are equivalent?

7. Using $\{a, b, c, d\}$, verify that the matching relation is reflexive.

8. Given $A = \{a, b, c\}$, $B = \{d, e, f\}$, and $C = \{g, h, i\}$, verify that the matching relation is transitive.

9. (a) In how many ways can the elements of $\{a, b, c\}$ be placed in a one-to-one correspondence with the elements of $\{1, 2, 3\}$?
   (b) Show all possible one-to-one correspondences.

10. In how many ways can $\{a, b, c, d, e\}$ be placed in a one-to-one correspondence with itself?

4.4
Cardinal Numbers

Since the matching relation for sets is an equivalence relation, it partitions all sets into equivalence classes. For example, $\{a, b, c\}$, $\{4, 7, 9\}$, $\{\Delta, 2, f\}$, and $\{\text{cat, horse, ox}\}$ are equivalent sets and belong to the same equivalence class. The property that these equivalent sets have in common is called their *cardinal number*. We happen to give the cardinal number of these sets the name "three." Similarly, the sets $\{b, a\}$, $\{6, 4\}$, and $\{\Delta, e\}$ are members of the same equivalence class and we say that each of these sets has the cardinal number "two."

DEFINITION 4.4.1

The property that is possessed by all members of a class of equivalent sets is the cardinal number of each of the sets.

Other definitions of cardinal numbers have been used by various authors, but this one will suit our purposes. The important result of our definition is that any two sets that are equivalent have the same cardinal number. A *number* is an abstraction and should not be confused with a *name* for the number. A name or symbol for a number is called a numeral.

Both III and 3 are numerals for a certain number. Many different numerals can be invented for any given number.

To designate the cardinal number of a set A, we use the symbol $n(A)$. For example, if $A = \{a, b, c\}$, we can write $n(\{a, b, c\}) = 3$ or $n(A) = 3$. In saying that $n(\{a, b, c\}) = 3$, it has been assumed that the reader can *count*. But what is counting? This question will be answered in the next section.

4.5
Standard Sets and the Natural Numbers

The elements of sets such as $\{a\}$, $\{b\}$, $\{\square\}$, and $\{k\}$ can be placed in a one-to-one correspondence; the sets are, therefore, equivalent to each other and have the same cardinal number. We use the symbol 1 (the numeral 1) to name the cardinal number of each of these sets as well as the cardinal number of each of the other members of the equivalence class to which these representative sets belong. We can also identify a set containing only the element 1 denoted by $\{1\}$. We call this particular representative set the standard set for the class of sets that are equivalent to it. Similarly, $\{a, 1\}$, $\{\square, k\}$, and $\{\triangle, t\}$ are representatives of another equivalence class of sets, and we name the cardinal number of each of these sets 2. By using all the elements of the previous standard set $\{1\}$ (there is a single element in this case) together with the element 2, we can generate a standard set $\{1, 2\}$ for this class. In the same way we can form sets $\{1, 2, 3\}$, $\{1, 2, 3, 4\}, \ldots,$ $\{1, 2, 3, 4, 5, \ldots, n\}$. Each time we generate another standard set, we use all the elements of the previously formed standard set together with one more element. Note that sets formed in this way are ordered and that the cardinal number of each set is the last-named element of the set: $n(\{1\}) = 1$, $n(\{1, 2\}) = 2$, $n(\{1, 2, 3\}) = 3, \ldots,$ and $n(\{1, 2, 3, \ldots, k\}) = k$.

If the set $\{1, 2, 3, 4, 5, 6, \ldots\}$ is continued without termination, as indicated by the dots, it is said to be an infinite set and to contain infinitely many elements. This set is called the set of natural numbers or counting numbers and is designated as $N = \{1, 2, 3, \ldots\}$.

Note that the standard sets used to represent sets belonging to the same equivalence class are initial subsets (occur at the beginning) of the natural numbers. This means that the cardinal number of any finite set, except the empty set, may be found by placing the elements of the set in a one-to-one correspondence with the elements of an initial subset of the natural numbers. The last named natural number in the correspondence will name the cardinal number of the set. This process is called counting. When a child counts "one, two, three" on his fingers, he is putting his fingers in a one-to-one correspondence with the elements of an initial subset of the natural (or counting) numbers.

Example 1.   Find the cardinal number of $\{a, b, \square, k, \triangle\}$.

Solution: First establish a one-to-one correspondence between the given set and an initial subset of the natural numbers:

$$\{a, b, \square, k, \triangle\}$$
$$\updownarrow \;\; \updownarrow \;\; \updownarrow \;\; \updownarrow \;\; \updownarrow$$
$$\{1, 2, \;\; 3, \;\; 4, \;\; 5, \;\; 6, 7, \ldots\}$$

Since the elements of the given set can be placed in a one-to-one correspondence with the elements of the standard set $\{1, 2, 3, 4, 5\}$, and since the last named element of this set is 5, we know that $n(\{a, b, \square, k, \triangle\}) = n(\{1, 2, 3, 4, 5\}) = 5$.

Again we emphasize that ordinary counting (such as counting the number of people in your mathematics class) is a simple but very specific process. We place the elements of the given set in a one-to-one correspondence with the elements of an initial subset of the natural (counting) numbers. The last named element in the correspondence names the cardinal number of the given set. Almost any child can count, but analyzing the procedure provides a better understanding of the process.

4.6
If and Only If

The expression "if and only if" is frequently used in mathematics, but it can be a source of mystery if the student does not understand its meaning. Since we shall use the expression in the next section, we shall introduce it at this time. "*A* if and only if *B*" is equivalent to making two statements: (1) "If *B*, then *A*" and (2) "If *A*, then *B*." In other words, not only does the truth of *B* imply that *A* is true, but the truth of *A* implies that *B* is true. For example, if the statement "George wears his raincoat if and only if it is raining" is true, we can be sure of two things: (1) If it is raining, then George wears his raincoat, and (2) If George wears his raincoat, then it is raining.

In many cases statement *A* will imply *B*, but statement *B* will not imply *A*. If you own a Chevrolet, then you own an automobile; but if you own an automobile, then you may or may not own a Chevrolet (since you might own a Ford, Plymouth, Rambler, etc.). Hence the statement "You own an automobile if and only if you own a Chevrolet" is false.

The expression "if and only if" is frequently abbreviated as "iff." "A if and only if B" can be written "A iff B."

EXERCISE 4.6

1. Define *cardinal number*.

2. Find the number of elements in $\{a, \triangle, 4, \phi, 8\}$ by placing the elements of the set in a one-to-one correspondence with the elements of an initial subset of the natural (counting) numbers.

3. Identify the standard set that is equivalent to each of the following sets and give the name of the cardinal number of each set
   (a) $\{2, 1, 0\}$ (b) $\{a, b\}$
   (c) $\{3, 6, 9, 12, 15\}$ (d) $\{g\}$
   (e) $\{\varnothing, A, 7, 9\}$

4. Explain what is meant by "counting" the elements of a set.

5. Given $A = \{a, b, c, d\}$ and $B = \{1, 2, 3\}$, complete the following:
   (a) $n(A) = ?$ (b) $n(\{1, 2, 3\}) = ?$
   (c) $n(B) = ?$ (d) $n(A \cup B) = ?$
   (e) $n(B \cup A) = ?$ (f) $n(A \times B) = ?$
   (g) $n(B \times A) = ?$ (h) $n(A \cap B) = ?$

6. Given $A = \{a, b, c, d\}$ and $B = \{c, d, e\}$, complete the following:
   (a) $n(A) = ?$ (b) $n(B) = ?$
   (c) $n(A \cup B) = ?$ (d) $n(A \cap B) = ?$
   (e) $n(\{c, d, e\}) = ?$ (f) $n(A \cup \{8\}) = ?$
   (g) $n(B \cup \varnothing) = ?$ (h) $n(B \cup \{0\}) = ?$

7. (a) Why do you suppose the natural numbers are called natural numbers?
   (b) Why do you suppose the natural numbers are also called the counting numbers?

8. What is meant by "C if and only if D"?

9. Tell which of the following statements are false *and explain why*.
   (a) You are a woman if and only if you are a human being.
   (b) Three sides of a triangle are equal if and only if the three angles are equal.
   (c) A filled bucket is heavy if and only if it is filled with lead.

4.7   DEFINITION 4.7.1

Finite and Infinite Sets   A nonempty set is finite if and only if its elements can be put in a one-to-one correspondence with the elements of a standard set $\{1, 2, 3, \ldots, n\}$. The empty set is also said to be finite.

DEFINITION 4.7.2

If a set is not finite, it is infinite

DEFINITION 4.7.3

A set is denumerable if and only if its elements can be put in a one-to-one correspondence with the natural numbers $\{1, 2, 3, \ldots\}$.

DEFINITION 4.7.4

A set is countable if it is either finite or denumerable.

Now that we have defined four terms, an example of each will be given.

Example 1.   The set $\{a, b\}$ is a *finite* set since its elements can be put in a one-to-one correspondence with the elements of the standard set $\{1, 2\}$.

Example 2.   The set $\{3, 6, 9, 12, \ldots\}$ is an *infinite* set since its elements cannot be put in a one-to-one correspondence with the elements of a standard set $\{1, 2, 3, \ldots, n\}$. The set of natural numbers $\{1, 2, 3, \ldots\}$ is also infinite. Why?

Example 3.   The set $\{3, 6, 9, 12, \ldots\}$ is *denumerable* since its elements can be put in a one-to-one correspondence with the natural numbers as follows:

$$\{3, 6, 9, \ldots, (3n), \ldots\}$$
$$\updownarrow \updownarrow \updownarrow \qquad \updownarrow$$
$$\{1, 2, 3, \ldots, \quad n, \ldots\}$$

Example 4.   The set $\{a, b\}$ is *countable* since it is finite, and the set $\{3, 6, 9, \ldots, (3n), \ldots\}$ is *countable* since it is denumerable.

The reader should not conclude that all infinite sets are denumerable; many are not. For example, the set of all subsets of the natural numbers is infinite but not denumerable. The set of all points on a line segment is infinite but not denumerable.

It is interesting to note that the elements of some proper subsets of a denumerable set may be put in a one-to-one correspondence with the elements of the set itself. For example, the even numbers $\{2, 4, 6, \ldots\}$

may be put in a one-to-one correspondence with the natural numbers $\{1, 2, 3, \ldots\}$; therefore, by Definition 4.4.1 the two sets have the same cardinal number. It may be difficult to realize that a proper subset of an infinite set can have the same cardinal number as the entire set since this is not true for finite sets. It is not possible to establish a one-to-one correspondence between a proper subset of a finite set and the set itself. Hence, any proper subset of a finite set has a cardinal number different from (smaller than) that of the original set.

EXERCISE 4.7

1. Define a finite and one an unample.
2. Define an *infinite set*. Give an example.
3. Define a *denumerable set*. Give an example.
4. Define a *countable set*. Give an example.
5. Is the set of natural numbers denumerable? Explain.
6. If a set is denumerable, must it be infinite?
7. If a set is infinite, must it be denumerable?
8. What is wrong with the statement, "A set is denumerable if and only if it is infinite"?
9. Tell which of the terms—*finite, infinite, denumerable,* and *countable*—apply to each of the following sets:
   (a) $\{a, b, c\}$ (b) $\{1, 2, 3\}$
   (c) $\{1, 2, 3, \ldots\}$ (d) $\{a, b, c, \ldots, r\}$
   (e) $\{1, 2, 3, \ldots, n\}$ (f) $\{1, 2, 3, \ldots, n, \ldots\}$
   (g) $\{2, 4, 6, \ldots, (2n)\}$ (h) $\{2, 4, 6, \ldots, (2n), \ldots\}$
   (i) the hairs of your head   (j) registered Republicans
                                                  in the U.S.A.
   (k) molecules of water on   (l) the points of a line segment
       the earth
   (m) the points on a circle   (n) fish in the oceans
10. Show that the set $\{10, 20, 30, \ldots, (10n), \ldots\}$ is denumerable.
11. Show that the even numbers constitute a denumerable set.
12. Show that the odd numbers constitute a denumerable set.
13. (a) Show that $\{4, 8, 12, \ldots, (4n), \ldots\}$ is equivalent to the set of natural numbers.
    (b) Is $\{4, 8, 12, \ldots, (4n), \ldots\}$ equal to the set of natural numbers? Explain.
14. (a) May a finite set and one of its proper subsets be equivalent?
    (b) May an infinite set and one of its proper subsets be equivalent?

(c) Name a proper subset of $\{7, 14, 21, \ldots, (7n), \ldots\}$ that is equivalent to it.

(d) Name a proper subset of $\{7, 14, 21, \ldots, (7n), \ldots\}$ that is not equivalent to it.

4.8

The Whole Numbers

Until now the cardinal number of the empty set has been avoided. We avoid it no longer and define the cardinal number of the empty set to be 0 (zero) and write $n(\varnothing) = 0$. If we take the set of natural numbers, $N = \{1, 2, 3, \ldots\}$, and include zero with it, the resulting set is the whole numbers, W. Symbolically, $\{0\} \cup \{1, 2, 3, \ldots\} = \{0, 1, 2, 3, \ldots\} = W$.

4.9

The Ordinal Use of Numbers

Although a technical distinction can be made between cardinal and ordinal numbers, we will place our emphasis on the ways in which they are used. A cardinal number can be used to answer questions such as, How many elements are in a set? How large is the set? or What is the size of the set?

The standard sets, $\{1\}$, $\{1, 2\}$, $\{1, 2, 3\}, \ldots$, which are initial subsets of the natural or counting numbers, have been used to identify the cardinal numbers of other sets. However, since these standard sets are ordered, they can also be used to establish an order in another set or to determine the nature of the ordering in another set which has already been ordered. For example, if we wish to establish an order for the members of family A according to height (assuming no two are the same height), we can make a one-to-one correspondence between elements representing the members of the family and the elements of an initial subset of the counting numbers in such a way that the element representing the tallest member is associated with 1, the next tallest with 2, and so on:

$$A = \{a,\ b,\ c,\ d\}$$
$$N = \{1,\ 2,\ 3,\ 4,\ 5,\ 6, \ldots\}$$

From the correspondence we see immediately that there are four members of the family (the cardinal use of 4). But upon rearranging the elements of A in the order of the counting numbers assigned to each element, we establish an *order* according to height.

$$A = \{c,\ a,\ b,\ d\}$$
$$N = \{1, 2, 3, 4, 5, 6, \ldots\}$$

The tallest member of the family is c, the next tallest is a, and so on. If the elements of A were placed in a one-to-one correspondence with the elements of an initial subset of N according to the age of each member of the family, some other ordering of the elements might possibly result.

If the elements of a given set are already ordered, the position of each element within the given set can be determined by placing the elements of this set in a one-to-one correspondence with the elements of an initial subset of the counting numbers. For example, the letters of our alphabet constitute an ordered set. From the correspondence below we see that a is "letter 1" of the alphabet or the *first* letter, b is "letter 2" of the alphabet or the *second* letter, and so on. What is the *sixth* letter of the alphabet? Obviously, it is f. This is an example of using numbers in the ordinal sense.

$$\{a, b, c, d, e, f, g, h, \ldots, z\}$$
$$\updownarrow \updownarrow \updownarrow \updownarrow \updownarrow \updownarrow \updownarrow \quad\quad \updownarrow$$
$$\{1, 2, 3, 4, 5, 6, 7, 8, \ldots, 26\}$$

Other statements illustrating the ordinal use of numbers are: (1) John is in the eighth grade; (2) Joyce finished fifth in the swimming race; (3) Turn to page 93 of the text; (4) She was the first-born child; (5) The fifth letter of the word *mathematics* is an e.

4.10
Numbers for Identification

Sometimes numbers are assigned for purposes of identification and may or may not have cardinal or ordinal implications. Examples are: army serial numbers for soldiers, license tag numbers, locker numbers, social security numbers, and zip code numbers. You can probably think of many others. A number, however, may be used for identification and also have ordinal or cardinal implications. For example, numbering the seats in a theater may order the seats, identify the (cardinal) number of seats, and identify the seat in which the purchaser of a given ticket is entitled to sit.

EXERCISE 4.10

1. What is the cardinal number of the empty set?
2. Why is the cardinal number of the empty set zero?
3. Show that the set of whole numbers is denumerable.
4. Use a standard set to order $\{4, 2, 7, 5, 6, 10\}$ so that the largest number is first, the next largest is second, and so on.

5. Use a standard set to order $\{4, 2, 7, 5, 6, 10\}$ so that the smallest number is first, the next smallest is second, and so on.

6. Write three sentences illustrating the cardinal use of the number 5.

7. Write three sentences illustrating the ordinal use of the number 5.

8. Give an example of a number that you use for the purpose of identification.

9. Given $A = \{a, b, c\}$ and $B = \{b, c, d, e\}$:
   (a) $n(A \cup B) = ?$
   (b) Show that $n(A \cup B) = n(A) + n(B) - n(A \cap B)$.
   (c) $A \times \varnothing = ?$
   (d) $n(A \times \varnothing) = ?$

10. Given $C = \{0, 1, 2\}$ and $D = \{0\}$, complete the following:
    (a) $n(C) = ?$ (b) $n(D) = ?$
    (c) $n(C \cup D) = ?$ (d) $n(C \cup \varnothing) = ?$
    (e) $n(C \cap D) = ?$ (f) $n(C \times D) = ?$
    (g) $n(D \times C) = ?$ (h) $n(C \times \varnothing) = ?$

REVIEW EXERCISES

1. In how many ways can $\{a, b, c, d\}$ be placed in a one-to-one correspondence with $\{1, 2, 3, 4\}$?

2. In how many ways can the elements of $\{1, 2, 3, 4, 5, 6\}$ be matched with themselves?

3. Given $A = \{a, b, c, d, e\}$ and $B = \{a, b, c\}$:
   (a) How many elements are in $A \times B$?
   (b) How many subsets are in $A \times B$?

4. Given $A = \{a, b, c, d, e\}$ and $B = \{c, d, e, f, g, h\}$, complete the following:
   (a) $A \cup B = ?$ (b) $A \cap B = ?$
   (c) $n(A \cup B) = ?$ (d) $n(A \cap B) = ?$
   (e) $n(A \cup \varnothing) = ?$

5. If $A = \{l, m, n, o, p\}$ and $B = \{1, 2, 3\}$, complete the following:
   (a) $n(A \times B) = ?$ (b) $n(B \times A) = ?$
   (c) $n(B \times \varnothing) = ?$ (d) $n(\varnothing \times B) = ?$
   (e) $n(A \times \varnothing) = ?$

6. Complete the following:
   (a) $n(\varnothing) = ?$ (b) $n(\{\ \}) = ?$
   (c) $n(\{0\}) = ?$ (d) $n(\{\varnothing\}) = ?$
   (e) $n(\{0, \varnothing\}) = ?$

7. (a) Identify in roster form $\{x \mid 4 \text{ is greater than } x \text{ and } x \in W\}$.
   (b) Identify in roster form $\{x \mid 4 \text{ is less than } x \text{ and } x \in W\}$.

8. Name the next three terms of each of the following infinite sets:
   (a) $\{0, 1, 2, 3, \ldots\}$ (b) $\{0, 1, 4, 9, 16, \ldots\}$
   (c) $\{0, 1, 3, 6, 10, 15, \ldots\}$ (d) $\{1, 1, 2, 3, 5, 8, 13, \ldots\}$

9. How does the cardinal number of $\{1, 2, 3, 4, \ldots, n, \ldots\}$ compare with the cardinal number of $\{11, 22, 33, 44, \ldots, 11n, \ldots\}$? Explain.

10. (a) Give three examples of finite sets.
    (b) Give three examples of infinite sets.
    (c) Give three examples of denumerable sets.
    (d) Give three examples of finite countable sets.
    (e) Give three examples of infinite countable sets.

Chapter Five
Systems
of Numeration

5.1 Introduction

In Chapter 4 the concept of a cardinal number was discussed, and the cardinal number of a given set was defined as that property possessed by all members of the class of equivalent sets to which the given set belongs (Definition 4.4.1). The name or symbol for a number is called a numeral. A plan by which symbols of a given set are used separately or in combination to form numerals is called a system of numeration. In this chapter we will be concerned with some of the systems of numeration that have been developed for the natural and whole numbers. Although many systems of numeration have been invented, we will mention only a few. Additional information on numeration systems may be found in various encyclopedias as well as in books on number systems and the history of mathematics. After studying this chapter, the reader may find it interesting to try to originate a system of numeration.

5.2 The Tally Numeral System

One of the earliest systems of numeration (probably the earliest) was the *tally system*. This system, which was only one easy step beyond making a one-to-one correspondence between such things as pebbles and sheep, consisted merely of making strokes in the sand or in clay such that they were in a one-to-one correspondence with the members of a flock of sheep, a group of warriors, a herd of cattle, or some other set. Even today we sometimes make tally marks to record such simple things as the score in a game or the number of persons enrolling in a course.

In Egyptian and Grecian lands primitive numerals appeared as |, | |, | | |, and so forth, while in the Far East the tally system appeared as —, =, ≡, and so on. Today we frequently group at five as a matter of convenience, and write the numeral twelve, for example, as ⊥⊥⊤ ⊥⊥⊤ | |.

Originally, the word "tally" referred to a stick with cross notches on it indicating the amount of a debt. The stick would be split lengthwise with one half going to the debtor and the other half to the creditor. The two halves could then be matched at any future time to verify the amount of the debt.

5.3 The Egyptian Numeral System

One of the earliest systems of numeration on record is the *Egyptian system*, which dates back as far as 3000 B.C. A chart of early Egyptian hieroglyphic (picture) symbols used in their numeration system is shown in Figure 5.3.1 and compared with the equivalent Hindu-Arabic numerals that we use.

In studying Figure 5.3.1 you will see that a single symbol is used for each number that is a power of ten: 1, 10, 100, 1000, and so forth. Numerals other than powers of ten are formed simply by repeating a symbol and using the *additive* principle. For example, thirty-two may be written ∩∩∩ǀǀ. Numerals from one to twenty are shown in Figure 5.3.2, and other selected numerals are shown in Figure 5.3.3. Since only the additive principle is involved in writing Egyptian numerals, the arrangement of the symbols for any given number is simply a matter of convenience. For example, fifteen may be written as shown in Figure 5.3.2 or as ∩ǀǀǀǀǀ, or ǀǀǀǀǀ∩, or ǀǀ∩ǀǀǀ, and so on.

The Egyptian system of numeration had two distinct disadvantages. It contained no numeral for zero, and place value was not used. By place value we mean the modification of a symbol's value according to its location or place in a numeral. In our system of numeration, for example, $52 \neq 25$ even though the same symbols, 2 and 5, are used in each numeral. However, since place value was not a feature of the Egyptian system, the order in which symbols appeared in a numeral was immaterial.

Although we are not prepared to discuss fractions to any extent in this chapter, it seems worth mentioning that the Egyptians did use fractions with numerators of one (called *unit fractions*). The numeral for a unit fraction was formed by placing the symbol ⌢ over the symbol for the denominator. For example, $\frac{1}{3}$ was written ⌢ǀǀǀ and $\frac{1}{12}$ was written ⌢∩ǀǀ. A special symbol [was used for $\frac{1}{2}$, and ⬦ was used

FIGURE 5.3.1

Hindu-Arabic Numeral	Egyptian Numeral	Description of Symbol
1	ǀ	Stroke
10	∩	Heel bone
100	℮	Scroll
1,000	𝕩	Lotus flower
10,000	⌒	Bent finger
100,000	⋈	Tadpole
1,000,000	𝕏	Astonished man

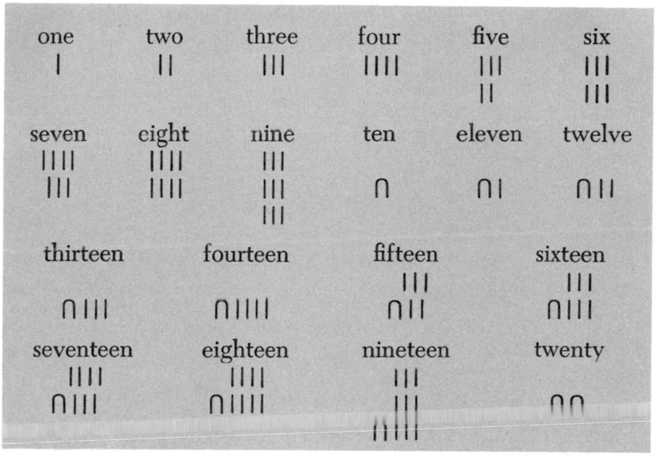

one	two	three	four	five	six
I	II	III	IIII	III II	III III

seven	eight	nine	ten	eleven	twelve
IIII III	IIII IIII	III III III	∩	∩I	∩II

thirteen	fourteen	fifteen	sixteen
∩III	∩IIII	III ∩II	III ∩IIII

seventeen	eighteen	nineteen	twenty
IIII ∩IIII	IIII ∩IIII	III III IIIII	∩∩

FIGURE 5.3.2

for $\frac{2}{3}$. Other fractions between zero and one were expressed as sums of unit fractions. For example, $\frac{2}{5}$ would be written as $\frac{1}{3} + \frac{1}{15}$ or $\overline{III}$ $\overline{\underset{II}{\cap III}}$; note that $\frac{1}{3}$ is the largest unit fraction less than $\frac{2}{5}$. Similarly, the Egyptians would have written $\frac{5}{7}$ as the sum $\frac{1}{2} + \frac{1}{5} + \frac{1}{70}$. Note once again that $\frac{1}{2}$ is the largest unit fraction that does not exceed $\frac{5}{7}$, $\frac{1}{5}$ is the next largest that may be added to $\frac{1}{2}$ such that the sum does not exceed $\frac{5}{7}$, and $\frac{1}{70}$ finally gives us the sum $\frac{5}{7}$. It is interesting to know that every

FIGURE 5.3.3

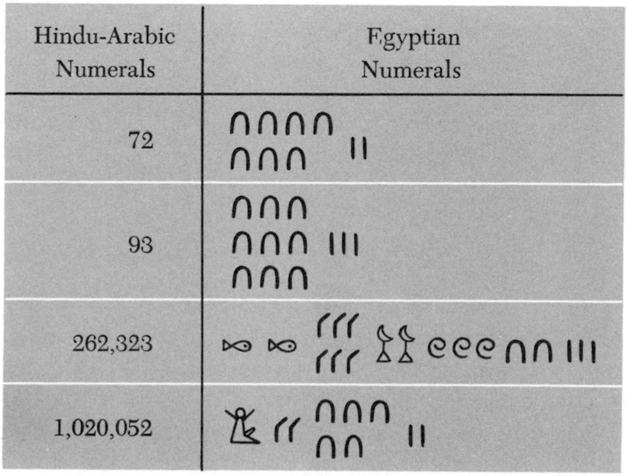

Hindu-Arabic Numerals	Egyptian Numerals
72	∩∩∩∩ ∩∩∩ II
93	∩∩∩ ∩∩∩ III ∩∩∩
262,323	∞ ∞ ⌒⌒⌒ ⌒⌒⌒ ⌢⌢ ℓℓℓ ∩∩ III
1,020,052	𝕏 ⌒⌒ ∩∩∩ ∩∩ II

fraction may be written in this way as the sum of unit fractions. This was proved by the English mathematician James Joseph Sylvester (1814–1897).

EXERCISE 5.3

1. Do you believe it is likely that the tally system of numeration was invented independently by different people? Explain.

2. Write an Egyptian numeral for each of the following:
   (a) 43   (b) 3628
   (c) 2,300,562   (d) 50,235
   (e) 64,107   (f) 1,234,123

3. How does the number represented by the Egyptian numeral ℮ (‖ ∞ compare with the number represented by ∞ (℮ ‖?

4. Using our system of numeration, write the equivalent of each of the following Egyptian numerals:

   (a) ⟮⟮ ∩∩∩ ∩∩∩ ‖‖   (b) 𝕶 ∞ ∩∩∩∩∩ ∩∩∩∩ ‖‖‖ ‖‖‖

   (c) ‖‖‖∩∩ ‖‖‖ ∩∩ ⟮⟮⟮ ⁇⁇ ℮℮℮   (d) ℮℮℮ ⟮⟮⟮ ‖‖‖

   (e) ∞ ‖‖‖ ℮℮℮ ℮℮℮   (f) ℮℮℮ ℮℮℮ ℮℮℮ ⁇⁇ ‖‖‖‖ ‖‖‖

5. Referring to problem 4, write in Egyptian numerals:
   (a) The sum of (a) and (b).
   (b) The sum of (d) and (e).
   (c) The sum of (c) and (f).

6. Referring to problem 4, use our system of numeration to write:
   (a) The sum of (a) and (b).
   (b) The sum of (d) and (e).
   (c) The sum of (c) and (f).

5.4
The Babylonian Numeral System

The early *Babylonian system of numeration* dates back to about the same time as the Egyptian system (3000 B.C.). Babylonian writings have been preserved in clay that was baked in the sun or in kilns. Numerals in the Babylonian system were formed with cuneiform (wedge-shaped) symbols. Like the Egyptian system, the Babylonian system had an

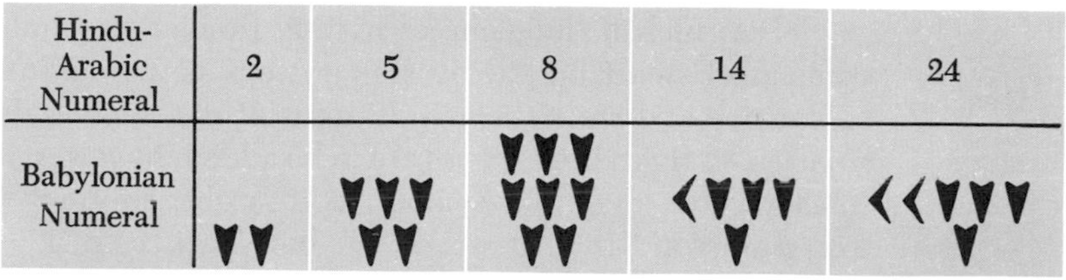

Hindu-Arabic Numeral	2	5	8	14	24
Babylonian Numeral	▼▼	▼▼▼ ▼▼	▼▼▼ ▼▼▼ ▼▼	❮▼▼▼ ▼	❮❮▼▼▼ ▼

FIGURE 5.4.1

additive property. However, only two symbols were used: ▼ for one and ❮ for ten. Certain selected numerals are shown in Figure 5.4.1.

The Babylonian numeral system also had a *place value* property which led to its designation as a sexagesimal system. The place of the symbol in the numeral determined the power of sixty by which its value was multiplied. Beginning at the right, the various groups of symbols would be multiplied by 60^0, 60^1, 60^2, 60^3, and so on. (Incidentally, we shall show later that $60^0 = 1$.) The numeral ▼▼ ❮ ▼▼▼, for example, would have the value $(2 \cdot 60^2) + (10 \cdot 60^1) + (3 \cdot 1)$, which we would write as $7200 + 600 + 3 = 7803$. Although we have appropriately spaced the symbols in the Babylonian numeral above, this was frequently not done by the Babylonians, and only the context of the writing could be used to tell which symbols belonged in the units place, the 60's place, the $(60 \cdot 60)$'s place, and so on. As a result, several interpretations were frequently possible.

Even though the Babylonian numeration system was frequently ambiguous, had no symbol for zero, and was awkward to use in many ways, it was a great step forward because of its place value characteristic. Clay tablets of the Babylonians with their cuneiform symbols are displayed in some of our museums and are worth a visit. We can probably thank the stable nature of the clay tablets and the dry climate of Babylonia for their preservation.

5.5
The Roman Numeral System

Other than the Hindu-Arabic system of notation, the *Roman system* is probably the most familiar. It uses letters as numerals. Single symbols are used for some numbers that are multiples of five as well as for those that are powers of ten. Basic symbols are given below with the corresponding Hindu-Arabic (decimal) symbol:

I	V	X	L	C	D	M
1	5	10	50	100	500	1000

The rules of the game of writing Roman numerals are somewhat complex. Essentially the Roman system is an *additive* system with *subtractive* and *multiplicative* features. If the symbols decrease in value from left to right, their values are to be added; however, if a symbol has a smaller value than the symbol to its right, subtraction is indicated. For example, XI = 10 + 1 = 11, but IX = 10 − 1 = 9. In general, not more than four identical symbols are used in succession since a new symbol can replace them. For example, IIIII is not used for 5 since V can be used instead. In fact, usually not more than three identical symbols are used in succession since the subtractive property is available: 4 is written as IV rather than IIII, and 90 is XC rather than LXXXX.

In applying the subtractive feature of the Roman numeral system, only symbols representing numbers that are powers of ten (I, X, and C) can be written to the left of symbols representing larger numbers. Furthermore, a symbol can only be written to the left of symbols for the next two larger numbers having distinct symbols. Hence, only subtraction combinations of IV, IX, XL, XC, CD, and CM are found in Roman numerals, while combinations such as IL and XD are not used. Note that there are never more than two symbols involved in a subtraction combination. Without definite rules for the subtractive feature, ambiguous situations would result. For example, what number would be represented by IVX, 6 or 4?

As an alternative to making new symbols for very large numbers, the multiplicative property is used. One bar over a numeral multiplies its value by 1000, and two bars over a numeral multiplies its value by 1000 · 1000 or 1,000,000. For example, $\overline{V}$ = 5 · 1000 = 5000; $\overline{\overline{IX}}$ = 9 · 1,000,000 = 9,000,000; and $\overline{CCCDCII}$ = 300 · 1000 + 500 + 100 + 1 + 1 = 300,602.

The Roman numeral system, because of the influence of the Roman Empire and the fact that the system was as good or better than most other systems that had been developed, held a strong position for nearly 2000 years in commerce and in scientific and theological literature. The Hindu-Arabic system finally replaced the Roman system because of its overwhelming superiority, but it was a bitter battle which was not easily won. The Hindu-Arabic system has been in general use only about 400 years, which historically is a very short time.

EXERCISE 5.5

1. Write Babylonian numerals for the following:
   (a) 7   (b) 35   (c) 604

2. Name at least two ways in which the Babylonians could have corrected the ambiguity of interpretation inherent in their numeral system.

3. Which basic property of the Babylonian numeral system is not found in the Roman system?

4. Write decimal numerals for the following Roman numerals:
   (a) XXIV   (b) LXXXVII   (c) CCXXIV
   (d) DCCLXXXII   (e) MMVI   (f) MLVIII
   (g) $\overline{\text{V}}$CCLXXX   (h) $\overline{\text{XD}}$XXV   (i) $\overline{\overline{\text{XXX}}}$DLIX

5. Write Roman numerals for each of the following:
   (a) 245   (b) 1492
   (c) 1066   (d) 1952
   (e) 123,456   (f) 2,000,017

6. Write the three Roman numerals immediately following DCXLVIII.

7. Referring to problem 4, use the Roman numeral system to find:
   (a) The sum of (a) and (b).
   (b) The sum of (c) and (d).
   (c) The sum of (e) and (f).

8. Remembering that the Roman numeral system has no place value:
   (a) Multiply XXIII by II.
   (b) Multiply XXIV by VI.

9. How could the Roman system of numeration be modified to make multiplying easier?

5.6
Exponents

Before discussing the Hindu-Arabic numeral system (with which you are already familiar) and other systems with the place value property, it will be helpful to review some concepts concerning the use of *exponents*.

You will probably recall that we can write $5 \cdot 5 \cdot 5$ as 5^3, and $6 \cdot 6 \cdot 6 \cdot 6$ as 6^4. In general, $a^n = a \cdot a \cdot a \ldots$ to n factors of a. The a is called the base and the superscript n is called the exponent of a or the power to which a is raised. A common error is to say that a^n means that a is multiplied by itself n times. This is not true, for with n factors the operation of multiplication is performed not n but $(n - 1)$ times.

Example 1. $2^5 = 2 \cdot 2 \cdot 2 \cdot 2 \cdot 2 = 32$. Note that the operation of multiplication is performed four times, *not* five times.

The following statements or theorems will not be proved, but examples will be given to illustrate the statements and make them plausible.

(a) $a^b \cdot a^c = a^{b+c}$, $a \neq 0$.

Example 2. $3^2 \cdot 3^4 = (3 \cdot 3)(3 \cdot 3 \cdot 3 \cdot 3) = (3 \cdot 3 \cdot 3 \cdot 3 \cdot 3 \cdot 3)$
$$= 3^6 = 729,$$
or $3^2 \cdot 3^4 = 3^{2+4} = 3^6 = 729.$

Example 3. $10^2 \cdot 10^3 = (10 \cdot 10)(10 \cdot 10 \cdot 10)$
$$= (10 \cdot 10 \cdot 10 \cdot 10 \cdot 10) = 10^5 = 100{,}000,$$
or $10^2 \cdot 10^3 = 10^{2+3} = 10^5 = 100{,}000.$

(b) $(a^b)^c = a^{b \cdot c}$, $a \neq 0$.

Example 4. $(4^2)^3 = 4^2 \cdot 4^2 \cdot 4^2 = (4 \cdot 4)(4 \cdot 4)(4 \cdot 4)$
$$= (4 \cdot 4 \cdot 4 \cdot 4 \cdot 4 \cdot 4) = 4^6 = 4096,$$
or $(4^2)^3 = 4^{2 \cdot 3} = 4^6 = 4096.$

(c) $\dfrac{a^b}{a^c} = a^{b-c}$, $a \neq 0$.

In this situation we have three possibilities worthy of note: (1) b is greater than c, (2) b is equal to c, or (3) b is less than c.

Case 1.   If b is greater than c, we have no special problem.

Let $\dfrac{a^b}{a^c} = \dfrac{a^5}{a^2}.$

Then $\dfrac{a^5}{a^2} = \dfrac{a^3 \cdot a^2}{a^2} = a^3 \cdot \dfrac{a^2}{a^2} = a^3 \cdot 1 = a^3,$

or $\dfrac{a^5}{a^2} = a^{5-2} = a^3.$

Case 2.   If b is equal to c, we get a^0.

Let $\dfrac{a^b}{a^c} = \dfrac{a^7}{a^7}.$

Then $\dfrac{a^7}{a^7} = a^{7-7} = a^0.$

But we know that a^7 divided by a^7 must equal 1. For this and other reasons, we define $a^0 = 1$ if $a \neq 0$.

Case 3. If b is less than c, we get a negative exponent.

Let $\dfrac{a^b}{a^c} = \dfrac{a^2}{a^5}$.

Then $\dfrac{a^2}{a^5} = a^{2-5} = a^{-3}$.

But we know that

$$\frac{a^2}{a^5} = \frac{a^2}{a^2 \cdot a^3} = \frac{a^2}{a^2} \cdot \frac{1}{a^3} = 1 \cdot \frac{1}{a^3} = \frac{1}{a^3},$$

and we therefore define $a^{-3} = \dfrac{1}{a^3}$, or in general

$a^{-p} = \dfrac{1}{a^p}$ if $a \neq 0$.

For each of the above statements, (a), (b), and (c), we have the restriction $a \neq 0$. Without this restriction we would have the possibility of an indicated division by zero, and division by zero is not defined. For example, $0^2 \cdot 0^{-5}$ would result in the following:

$$0^2 \cdot 0^{-5} = 0^{-3} = \frac{1}{0^3} = \frac{1}{0}.$$

Later we shall say more about barring division by zero and about the use of negative numbers.

The reader should be certain to remember that by definition $a^0 = 1$ if $a \neq 0$. One reason for this definition was indicated in discussing Case 2 above.

EXERCISE 5.6

1. How many times is the operation of multiplication performed in finding the value of 64^3?

2. Simplify each of the following:
   (a) $2^3 \cdot 2^2$ (b) $2^0 \cdot 2^5$ (c) $(a^2)^3$
   (d) $x^7 \cdot x^2$ (e) $3^7 \cdot 3^{-5}$ (f) $5^7 \cdot 5^{-7}$
   (g) $x^{100} \cdot x^5$ (h) $(x^{100})^5$ (i) 3^{-2}

3. Simplify each of the following:
   (a) $\dfrac{2^7}{2^4}$ (b) $\dfrac{3^5}{3^5}$ (c) $\dfrac{6^0}{2}$

   (d) $\dfrac{2^4}{2^7}$ (e) $\dfrac{10^{12}}{10^9}$ (f) $\dfrac{10^2}{10^5}$

4. Simplify each of the following:
   (a) $10^2 \cdot 10^3$ (b) $10^7 \cdot 10^{-4}$
   (c) $10^6 \cdot 10^{-8}$ (d) $4^2 \cdot 4^3$
   (e) $4^5 \cdot 4^7$ (f) $4^4 \cdot 4^{-1}$

5. Simplify each of the following:
   (a) $10^2 \cdot 2^3$ (b) $2^4 \cdot 3^2$

   (c) $\dfrac{2^3}{7^2}$ (d) $\dfrac{2^5 \cdot 10^3}{2^3 \cdot 10^2}$

   (e) $(3 \cdot 2)^5$ (f) $3 \cdot 2^5$

5.7
The Hindu-Arabic Numeral System

The system of numeration that is commonly used in most of the world today is the *Hindu-Arabic system.* It is also referred to as the *decimal system* because of the unique role of ten in its structure (*decem* is the Latin word for ten).

Like most numeral systems, the Hindu-Arabic system went through a long metamorphic period. Although the Hindus are given credit for the primary development of the system, some of its features apparently originated with other peoples. In writings prior to the time of Christ there is no evidence that the Hindus used either zero or place value. It is possible that they obtained the idea of the zero symbol from the Greeks and the concept of place value from the Babylonians. In any event, the Hindus eventually incorporated both features into their numeral system, which was then carried into Europe, probably by traders and other travelers. It is known that the Arabs invaded North Africa and Spain and brought the Hindu numerals with them. The symbols gradually changed from generation to generation, but with the invention of the printing press in the fifteenth century they became fairly well standardized. The symbols we use today are much like those used in the fifteenth and sixteenth centuries. Some variations, however, may be seen on bank checks and on the ticker tape in a stockbroker's office. Perhaps electronic devices will cause another modification of our numerals.

The ten basic symbols in our decimal system of notation are 0, 1, 2, 3, 4, 5, 6, 7, 8, 9. Each of these symbols is called a digit. Digits are used separately or in combination with other digits to form numerals, just as letters are used separately or in combination with other letters to form words. For example, the numeral 6352 has four digits.

The decimal system has a *place value property* such that the value of each digit in a numeral is multiplied by some power of ten according to the position of the digit in relation to a *reference point.* This reference point is called the decimal point of the numeral. The value of each digit is multiplied by the appropriate power of ten, and these terms are then added together. This means that the system also has an *additive property*.

Example 1. $2059.74 = 2 \cdot 10^3 + 0 \cdot 10^2 + 5 \cdot 10^1 + 9 \cdot 10^0 + 7 \cdot 10^{-1} + 4 \cdot 10^{-2}$. Note that the reference (decimal) point is indicated by a dot on the line between the digits 9 and 7. The power of ten used as a factor begins with zero for the digit immediately to the left of the decimal point and increases one unit for each digit as we progress to the left. As we progress to the right, the exponent of ten decreases one unit for each digit. The value of the entire numeral is then found by adding the terms as indicated.

A numeral such as 2059.74 is said to be expressed in standard form. In the equation of Example 1, 2059.74 has been rewritten in what is called expanded form or polynomial form. Since $10^3 = 1000$, $10^2 = 100$, and so forth, we could have used any of several expanded forms of notation such as the following:

$$2059.74 = 2000 + 0 + 50 + 9 + .7 + .04$$
$$= 2(1000) + 0(100) + 5(10) + 9(1) + 7(.1) + 4(.01)$$
$$= 2(1000) + 0(100) + 5(10) + 9(1) + 7(\tfrac{1}{10}) + 4(\tfrac{1}{100})$$
$$= 2(10^3) + 0(10^2) + 5(10^1) + 9(10^0) + 7(10^{-1}) + 4(10^{-2}).$$

Observe that if there is no symbol of operation between two numerals, the numbers they represent are to be treated as factors and multiplied. For example, $2(1000) = 2 \times 1000 = 2 \cdot 1000 = 2000$.

Actually, the Hindu-Arabic system of numeration does have a multiplicative feature, but the factor by which any given digit is multiplied is (as explained above) determined by the *place* of the digit in relation to the decimal point. Consequently, the best name for this property seems to be place value. Recall that the Roman system has a multiplicative feature not determined by the location of a symbol but rather by the placement of one or two bars over a given symbol. Since the Roman system has no symbol for zero, the Romans could not use a place value system in the same way we do. How could the numeral for five hundred six (506) be written using a place value system if we had no symbol for zero?

EXERCISE 5.7

1. What is a digit?
2. What is a numeral?

3. What are the ten basic symbols of the Hindu-Arabic numeral system?

4. Why is the Hindu-Arabic system of numeration sometimes referred to as the decimal system?

5. What is meant when we say that the Hindu-Arabic numeral system has a place value property?

6. What is the purpose of a decimal point in a numeral?

7. Rewrite the standard numeral 643.56 using three different expanded forms of notation.

8. Rewrite each of the following standard numerals in expanded form using exponential notation:
   (a) 943   (b) 2342
   (c) 105   (d) 94.2
   (e) 0.007 (f) 100.234

9. Write the standard numeral for each of the following:
   (a) $4(10^3) + 3(10^2) + 7(10^1) + 6(10^0)$
   (b) $4(10^5) + 6(10^3) + 3(10^0) + 2(10^{-2})$
   (c) $7(10^{-3}) + 8(10^{-5}) + 9(10^{-7})$

10. Why is a numeral for zero important in a numeral system having a place value property?

5.8
Reading and Writing Decimal Numerals

There are certain arbitrary conventions in reading and writing decimal numerals. The place values to the left of the decimal point are named *units, tens, hundreds, thousands, ten thousands, hundred thousands, millions, ten millions,* and so on; those to the right of the decimal point are named *tenths, hundredths, thousandths, ten-thousandths, hundred-thousandths, millionths,* and so forth. For ease in reading, the digits to the left of the decimal point are usually separated into groups or periods of three by commas and are read accordingly. For example, 24,635,943 is read as though it were $24(1,000,000) + 635(1000) + 943(1)$ or "twenty-four million, six hundred thirty-five thousand, nine hundred forty-three." It is *not* read: "two ten million, four million, six hundred thousand, three ten thousand, five thousand, nine hundred, four tens, and three." About the only exceptions to reading numerals in terms of ones, thousands, millions, billions, and so forth, are the four-digit numerals. For example, the numeral 6400 is sometimes read as "sixty-four hundred" $(64 \cdot 100)$ rather than "six thousand, four hundred" $(6 \cdot 1000 + 400)$.

Figures 5.8.1 and 5.8.2 summarize and help clarify place value names and period value names.

When a decimal point is not shown in a numeral, the numeral is

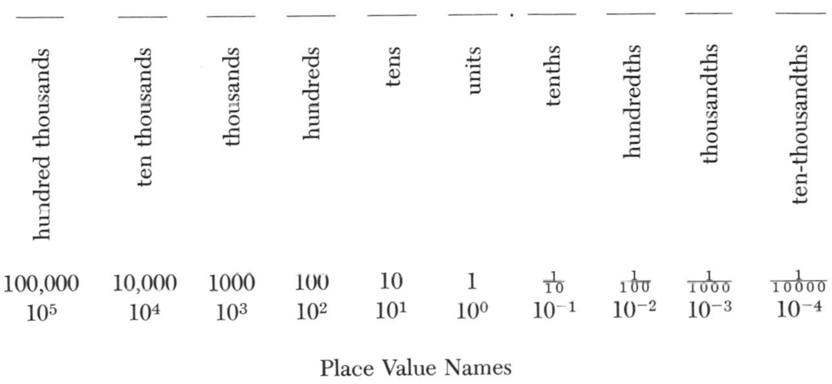

hundred thousands	ten thousands	thousands	hundreds	tens	units	tenths	hundredths	thousandths	ten-thousandths
100,000	10,000	1000	100	10	1	$\frac{1}{10}$	$\frac{1}{100}$	$\frac{1}{1000}$	$\frac{1}{10000}$
10^5	10^4	10^3	10^2	10^1	10^0	10^{-1}	10^{-2}	10^{-3}	10^{-4}

Place Value Names

FIGURE 5.8.1

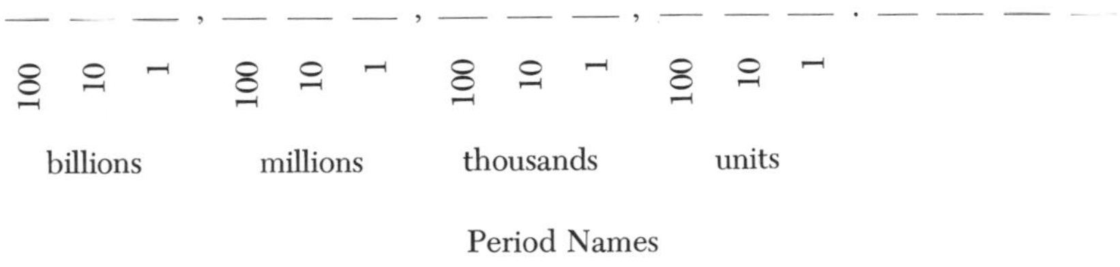

100	10	1	100	10	1	100	10	1	100	10	1
billions			millions			thousands			units		

Period Names

FIGURE 5.8.2

read as though a decimal point followed the last digit. So "63" and "63." are two numerals for the same number and are both read "sixty-three."

The word "and" is not used in reading numerals such as 24,635,943. However, if there are digits following the decimal point in a numeral, the decimal point is read as "and." For example, 34.5 is read "thirty-four *and* five tenths." Incidentally, it is common practice to use the word "and" for the decimal point when writing bank checks in amounts such as "thirty-six and $\frac{75}{100}$ dollars."

The hyphen is used for the word forms of the numerals twenty-one through ninety-nine (excluding, of course, those that name multiples of ten). The hyphen is also used with words such as "ten-thousandths." As an example, 2.0004 is written "two and four ten-thousandths."

Although the digits to the left of the decimal point are read according to their separation by commas into periods, those to the right are read only in terms of the smallest unit of measure. For example, 0.016147 is read "sixteen thousand, one hundred forty-seven millionths" rather than "sixteen thousandths, one hundred forty-seven millionths." In other words, it is read in terms of the whole number of millionths.

EXERCISE 5.8

1. Write the following using standard Hindu-Arabic notation:
   (a) two thousand sixty-five
   (b) twenty-four million, fifty thousand, one hundred forty-two
   (c) fifteen and five hundred forty-two ten-thousandths   15. 0542
   (d) one hundred and sixteen millionths
   (e) one hundred sixteen millionths   .00116

2. Why is it important not to use the word "and" when reading a numeral such as 0.3014?

3. Write each of the following numerals in words:
   (a) 5280   (b) 94
   (c) 7,006,005   (d) 7.008
   (e) 16.0054   (f) 0.000012
   (g) 500.017   (h) 0.517

5.9
Scientific Notation

In writing numerals for very large and very small numbers, it is convenient to use what is called *scientific notation*. For example, if we wish to write the numeral 6,000,000,000,000, it is easier to write 6×10^{12}; or if we wish to write 0.0000073, it is easier to write 7.3×10^{-6}. If a large number such as $6 \times 10^{3,500,000}$ were written in standard notation, it would occupy this entire book!

In using scientific notation, only one digit is placed to the left of the decimal point. This number is then multiplied by the appropriate power of ten. For example, if the distance to the sun measured to the nearest million miles is 93,000,000, we would write 9.3×10^7. Note that the exponent of 10, in this case 7, indicates that the numeral 9.3×10^7 may be renamed in standard form as 93,000,000 by moving the decimal point of 9.3 seven places to the right. Similarly, in cases where a negative exponent of 10 is involved, the standard numeral is found by moving the decimal point the appropriate number of places to the left. For example, the standard notation for 8.135×10^{-6} is .000008135.

In addition to making it easy to write numerals for very large and very small numbers, such as 6.5×10^{50} or 7.43×10^{-18}, scientific notation is used to show the unit of measure. For example, if we measure the diameter of the earth using thousands of miles as the unit of measure and find it closer to 8 thousand than to 7 thousand or 9 thousand, we shall write 8×10^3 miles as the diameter of the earth. If, however, the diameter of the earth is measured in hundreds of miles and found to be closer to 80 hundred than to 79 hundred or 81 hundred, we write 8.0×10^3 showing that both the 8 and the first zero are significant in our measurement. (Actually, the diameter of the earth is closer to 79 hundred miles or 7.9×10^3 miles.) Without the use of scientific notation we could not be certain whether a measurement of 8000 miles was measured to the nearest thousand miles, hundred miles, ten miles, or perhaps to the nearest mile; however, we would probably assume the zeros were not significant digits.

In numerals with values less than 1, such as 0.0075, it is common to place a zero before the decimal point to help make the decimal point conspicuous. The zeros following the decimal point are not significant digits since their only purpose is to give the 7 and 5 the proper place value. If, however, we have a zero following the 5 making the numeral 0.00750, this zero *is* a significant digit indicating that the measurement is made to the nearest hundred-thousandth of a unit rather than to the nearest ten-thousandth of a unit. We would read 0.00750 as "seven hundred fifty hundred-thousandths," not as "seventy-five ten-thousandths." Using scientific notation, $0.00750 = 7.50 \times 10^{-3}$.

Example 1. The following numerals are rewritten using scientific notation:
(a) $63,000 = 6.3 \times 10^4$
(b) $914,600,000 = 9.146 \times 10^8$
(c) $0.000715 = 7.15 \times 10^{-4}$
(d) $0.000080 = 8.0 \times 10^{-5}$

Example 2. The following numerals are rewritten using standard notation:
(a) $5.9 \times 10^5 = 590,000$
(b) $9.32 \times 10^7 = 93,200,000$
(c) $8.58 \times 10^{-6} = 0.00000858$
(d) $8.70 \times 10^{-4} = 0.000870$

EXERCISE 5.9

1. Write numerals for the following numbers using scientific notation:
   (a) 75,000,000,000   (b) 0.00000006
   (c) 642,000   (d) $0.00007 = 7 \times 10^{-5}$
   (e) $0.000072 = 7.2 \times 10^{-5}$ (f) $0.000070 \quad 7 \times 10^{-5}$
   (g) eight ten-thousandths   (h) eighty hundred-thousandths

2. Write standard numerals for the following:
   (a) 7.5×10^7 (b) 7.623×10^6
   (c) 4.3×10^{-7} (d) 8.23×10^{-6}
   (e) 7×10^{-5} (f) 7.00×10^{-5}

3. Compute the following and indicate the results in scientific notation:
   (a) $(2 \cdot 10^5)(4 \cdot 10^4)$ (b) $(2 \cdot 10^{18})(2 \cdot 10^{-14})$
   (c) $(3 \cdot 10^{17})(2 \cdot 10^{-12})$ (d) $(3 \cdot 10^5)(3 \cdot 10^{-7})$

5.10
Numeral Systems with Bases Other Than Ten

We say that our numeration system has a base of ten because the value of each of the digits in a numeral is multiplied by a power of ten: 10^0, 10^1, 10^2, and so forth. About the only obvious reason for using a base of ten in our system of numeration is that we have ten fingers. The fact that humans have ten fingers is probably the reason that so many systems have special features involving ten. If man had eight fingers, we would probably use a base of eight. The Mayan Indians, who once lived in southeastern Mexico and Central America, had a highly developed civilization long before they were discovered by Europeans in the sixteenth century. Their numeration system used a base of twenty. Perhaps they used their toes as well as their fingers for counting!

As noted earlier, the Hindu-Arabic system uses a set of ten basic symbols or digits—zero through nine. There is no need to invent an entirely new symbol for ten since we have a place value system. We can write ten as 10 using a combination of two symbols from the ten basic symbols. The situation would be similar if we used any base other than ten. With a base of eight, for example, we would need eight basic symbols—zero through seven. In general, n symbols are required for a base of n in a place value system.

Using a base of four the basic symbols are $\{0, 1, 2, 3\}$, and we group at four, writing 10 (read as "one four"). Figure 5.10.1 compares counting in base four with counting in base ten. In a base four numeral, the digits are multiplied by increasing powers of four as we progress to the left: $(four)^0$, $(four)^1$, $(four)^2$, and so forth. If there are digits to the right of a reference point, they are similarly multiplied by $(four)^{-1}$, $(four)^{-2}$, $(four)^{-3}$, and so on. In general, for any base n, the place values are powers of n: n^0, n^1, n^2, and so on to the left of the reference point, and n^{-1}, n^{-2}, n^{-3}, and so forth to the right of the reference point. Note that we do not call the reference point in base four a decimal point, for this would imply a base of ten.

If we are using base four, it is important to read 32 as "three fours and two" or as "three-two, base four," *not* as "thirty-two" (which

	Base Ten		Base Four
1	one	1	one
2	two	2	two
3	three	3	three
4	four	10	one four
5	five	11	one four and one
6	six	12	one four and two
7	seven	13	one four and three
8	eight	20	two fours
9	nine	21	two fours and one
10	ten (one ten and zero)	22	two fours and two
11	eleven (one ten and one)	23	two fours and three
12	twelve (one ten and two)	30	three fours
13	thirteen (one ten and three)	31	three fours and one
14	fourteen (one ten and four)	32	three fours and two
15	fifteen (one ten and five)	33	three fours and three
16	sixteen (one ten and six)	100	one four-fours
17	seventeen (one ten and seven)	101	one four-fours, zero fours, and one
18	eighteen (one ten and eight)	102	one four-fours, zero fours, and two
19	nineteen (one ten and nine)	103	one four-fours, zero fours, and three
20	twenty (two tens)	110	one four-fours, one four, and zero
21	twenty-one (two tens and one)	111	one four-fours, one four, and one

FIGURE 5.10.1

would mean three tens and two). In order to show that we are using base four in the numeral 32, we can write 32_{four}. If a numeral has no subscript, it is assumed to be written in base ten unless a specific statement is made to the contrary.

By regrouping the elements of a representative set S, it is possible to show that a numeral in a given base is equivalent to some other numeral in another base. Some examples follow.

Example 1. By regrouping the elements of a representative set S, show that 32_{four} is equivalent to 14_{ten}.

Solution (Note that, for simplicity, commas are omitted in the sets below):

Set S	$n(S)$
$\{[a\ b\ c\ d][e\ f\ g\ h][i\ j\ k\ l]\ m\ n\}$	32_{four}
$\{[a\ b\ c\ d\ e\ f\ g\ h\ i\ j]\ k\ l\ m\ n\}$	14_{ten}

Note that we commonly refer to the cardinal number of

set S as "fourteen." However, another name for this same cardinal number is 32_{four}, and we may write $14_{ten} = 32_{four}$.

Example 2. By regrouping the elements of a representative set S, show that $23_{five} = 16_{seven}$.

Solution:

Set S	$n(S)$
$\{[a\ b\ c\ d\ e][f\ g\ h\ i\ j]\ k\ l\ m\}$	23_{five}
$\{[a\ b\ c\ d\ e\ f\ g]\ h\ i\ j\ k\ l\ m\}$	16_{seven}

Example 3. By regrouping the elements of a representative set S, show that $14_{ten} = 112_{three}$.

Solution:

Set S	$n(S)$
$\{[a\ b\ c\ d\ e\ f\ g\ h\ i\ j]\ k\ l\ m\ n\}$	14_{ten}
$\{[[a\ b\ c][d\ e\ f][g\ h\ i]][j\ k\ l]\ m\ n\}$	112_{three}

In translating a numeral from base ten to some other base, or from some other base to base ten, we can avoid the cumbersome (but meaningful) method of regrouping by using our knowledge of the decimal system. In base four, for example, we know that the first digit to the left of the reference point (perhaps we could call it a "fours point" instead of a "decimal point") is in the units position ($4^0 = 1$). The next digit to the left is in the fours position ($4^1 = 4$); the next, the sixteens position ($4^2 = 16$); the next, the sixty-fours position ($4^3 = 64$); and so on. To the right of the reference point (fours point) would be the digit representing the number of fourths ($4^{-1} = \frac{1}{4}$); the next, the number of sixteenths ($4^{-2} = \frac{1}{16}$); and so on. See Figure 5.10.2.

FIGURE 5.10.2

10^3	10^2	10^1	10^0	10^{-1}	10^{-2}	10^{-3}	} Base four notation
4^3	4^2	4^1	4^0	4^{-1}	4^{-2}	4^{-3}	
64	16	4	1	$\frac{1}{4}$	$\frac{1}{16}$	$\frac{1}{64}$	} Decimal notation

Place Values in Base Four

The preceding paragraph illustrates the fact that the language we use in discussing other bases is still the language of base ten. For example, in the fours system we have no name for the (four)^3 place except the decimal name, the sixty-fours place. We are in the habit of thinking in the decimal system; however, if we were to regularly use some other system, we would undoubtedly develop a suitable vocabulary for it.

The following examples illustrate how our knowledge of computation in the decimal system can be used to translate a numeral from some other base to base ten, or vice versa.

Example 4. Write the numeral in base ten that is equivalent to 312_{four}.

Solution:

$$
\left.
\begin{aligned}
312_{\text{four}} &= 3 \cdot 4^2 + 1 \cdot 4^1 + 2 \cdot 4^0 \\
&= 3(16) + 1(4) + 2(1) \\
&= 48 + 4 + 2 \\
&= 54_{\text{ten}}
\end{aligned}
\right\}
\begin{aligned}
&\text{Expanded form using base ten} \\
&\text{or decimal numerals}
\end{aligned}
$$

Example 5. Translate 2014_{five} into a decimal numeral.

Solution:

$$
\left.
\begin{aligned}
2014_{\text{five}} &= 2 \cdot 5^3 + 0 \cdot 5^2 + 1 \cdot 5^1 + 4 \cdot 5^0 \\
&= 2(125) + 0(25) + 1(5) + 4(1) \\
&= 250 + 0 + 5 + 4 \\
&= 259_{\text{ten}}
\end{aligned}
\right\}
\text{Decimal numerals}
$$

Example 6. Translate 26_{ten} into a base three numeral.

Solution: We know that $3^0 = 1, 3^1 = 3, 3^2 = 9, 3^3 = 27, 3^4 = 81$, and so on. The largest of these numbers that is less than or equal to the given number 26_{ten} is 9. This means that the first digit of our numeral in base three will be in the 9, or 3^2, position. So we find the greatest multiple of 3^2 or 9 that is less than 26, the greatest multiple of 3^1 that is less than the remainder, and so on as indicated below:

$$
\left.
\begin{aligned}
26_{\text{ten}} &= 2(3^2) + 8 \\
&= 2(3^2) + 2(3^1) + 2 \\
&= 2(3^2) + 2(3^1) + 2(3^0) \\
&= 222_{\text{three}}
\end{aligned}
\right\}
\begin{aligned}
&\text{Expanded form using base} \\
&\text{ten numerals}
\end{aligned}
$$

Example 7. Rename 67_{ten} as a numeral in base seven.

Solution:

$$\left. \begin{aligned} 67_{ten} &= 1(7^2) + 18 \\ &= 1(7^2) + 2(7^1) + 4 \\ &= 1(7^2) + 2(7^1) + 4(7^0) \end{aligned} \right\} \quad \text{Decimal numerals}$$
$$= 124_{seven}$$

The smallest number we can use for a base in a place value system is *two.* If we try to use a base of *one,* we simply end up with a tally numeral system! Using a base of two, we need a set of only two basic symbols, 0 and 1, as opposed to ten symbols in the decimal system. Of course, this makes many numerals quite long. For example, the binary numeral for 99 is 1100011. The first eleven numerals in base two are: 0, 1, 10, 11, 100, 101, 110, 111, 1000, 1001, 1010.

The invention and increased use of electronic computers have aroused considerable interest in the base two or binary system of numeration. Since an electrical circuit in a computer is either opened or closed, two alternatives are automatically present to represent the digits 0 and 1. However, the dichotomy of an open or closed circuit not only can be used to represent 0 and 1, but also to answer *yes* or *no, true* or *false,* and so on. Thus the logic inherent in a wide variety of problems can be preserved in the machine in the same way as 0 and 1, and everything in a problem is reduced to a sequence of two characters.

If a base larger than ten is used in a place value numeration system, it is necessary to invent new symbols. In base twelve, for example, we would need unique symbols for ten and eleven. We might represent the numerals of base twelve as follows: 0, 1, 2, 3, 4, 5, 6, 7, 8, 9, T, E, 10, 11, 12, 13, 14, 15, 16, 17, 18, 19, 1T, 1E, 20, 21, and so on. In base twelve numerals, of course, each digit is multiplied by the appropriate power of twelve. The base twelve system is known as the *duodecimal system* since the Latin word for twelve is "duodecim" which means two plus ten.

Example 8. Represent 101101_{two} as a numeral in base ten.

Solution:

$$\left. \begin{aligned} 101101_{two} &= 1 \cdot 2^5 + 0 \cdot 2^4 + 1 \cdot 2^3 + 1 \cdot 2^2 \\ &\quad + 0 \cdot 2^1 + 1 \cdot 2^0 \\ &= 1(32) + 0(16) + 1(8) + 1(4) \\ &\quad + 0(2) + 1(1) \\ &= 32 + 0 + 8 + 4 + 0 + 1 \end{aligned} \right\} \quad \text{Decimal numerals}$$
$$= 45_{ten}$$

Example 9. Rename $2E7_{twelve}$ as a numeral in base ten.

Solution:

$$
2E7_{twelve} = 2 \cdot 12^2 + E \cdot 12^1 + 7 \cdot 12^0 \\
= 2(144) + 11(12) + 7(1) \\
= 288 + 132 + 7 \\
= 427_{ten}
$$

Decimal numerals

EXERCISE 5.10

1. (a) What do you suppose people mean when they say numbers like twenty and thirty are "nice round numbers"?
   (b) If we used a base of four, what numbers would be "nice round numbers"?

2. By regrouping the elements of a representative set S, show that 15_{ten} is equivalent to 21_{seven}.

3. By regrouping the elements of a representative set S, show that 32_{four} is equivalent to 112_{three}.

4. How many basic symbols are needed in a place value numeral system:
   (a) in base seven?
   (b) in base fifteen?
   (c) in base k?

5. Write each of the following numerals in words.
   (a) 43_{seven}
   (b) 265_{seven}
   (c) 304_{seven}

6. Write the numerals from one to fifteen in base seven.

7. Why cannot 273 be a numeral in base six?

8. Why does $3_{four} = 3_{five} = 3_{six} = 3_{seven}$, and so forth?

9. Using a base twelve (duodecimal) system, rename each of the following:
   (a) 17   (b) 38
   (c) 167   (d) 131

10. Rename each of the following using decimal numerals:
   (a) 25_{seven} (b) 34_{five}
   (c) 123_{four} (d) 201_{seven}
   (e) $2T4_{twelve}$ (f) $T0E_{twelve}$

11. Rename the following using a base five numeral system:
   (a) 3   (b) 5
   (c) 7   (d) 18
   (e) 25   (f) 31
   (g) 99   (h) 125
   (i) 130   (j) 634

12. Rename the following using base seven numerals:
    (a) 23_{four}
    (b) 34_{five}
    (c) 78_{nine}

REVIEW EXERCISES

1. Write an Egyptian numeral and a Roman numeral for each of the following:
    (a) 32   (b) 475
    (c) 642   (d) 1892
    (e) 5280   (f) 29,523

2. Write a Babylonian numeral for each of the following:
    (a) 23
    (b) 124
    (c) 341

3. Translate each of the following into a decimal numeral:
    (a) MCMLVI   (b) ∞∩∩∩⌇℮℮℮‖
    (c) 524_{seven} (d) ▼ ⟨⟨ ▼▼▼▼
    (e) 101101_{two} (f) $T3E_{twelve}$

4. Discuss the statement: 2^5 means that 2 is to be multiplied by itself 5 times.

5. Rewrite each of the following standard numerals in expanded form using exponential notation:
    (a) 432   (b) 6245
    (c) 7009   (d) 87.3
    (e) 0.3009   (f) 280.345

6. Write each of the following in words:
    (a) 245   (b) 309
    (c) 23,439   (d) 206
    (e) 0.206   (f) 200.006

7. Use exponential notation to express the following in simplified form:
    (a) $7 \times 7 \times 7 \times 7 \times 7 \times 7$ (b) $8 \times 8 \times 8 \times 5 \times 5$
    (c) $8^6 \times 8^4$ (d) $47^8 \div 47^5$
    (e) $5^0 \times 5^7$

8. Using a base of three, write numerals for the numbers from zero to ten.

9. Write a numeral for each of the following numbers using scientific notation:

(a) 239,000   (b) 93,000,000

(c) 865,742   (d) 0.00093

(e) 0.000930   (f) 672.0

10. Write standard numerals for each of the following:

(a) 8.3×10^8 (b) 4.32×10^7

(c) 6.3×10^{-3} (d) 8.35×10^{-7}

(e) 6.40×10^5 (f) 6.40×10^{-5}

Chapter Six

The System
of Whole Numbers

6.1
Introduction

We have discussed such topics as the nature of sets, equal and equivalent sets, and relations in Cartesian product sets. We have also defined the whole numbers and identified several systems of numeration. In this chapter we shall be concerned with a number system—the system of whole numbers. A *number system* should not be confused with a *system of numeration*, which is used in naming numbers.

A number system consists of a set of elements called numbers and operations defined for these numbers. The system will have various properties in accordance with the way in which the elements for the system are chosen and the way in which the operations of the system are defined.

Before discussing the essential features of the system of whole numbers, a few comments will be made on mathematical reasoning, the nature of proof, and the equals relation for numbers. After treating operations on the whole numbers and the properties of the operations, the chapter concludes with a short discussion of order relations.

6.2
Mathematical Reasoning and Proofs

Although at times it may seem otherwise, mathematics is an area of study in which creativity may be expressed to a high degree. Mathematics is created by man, and the rate at which it is being created has been greatly accelerated in recent times. More mathematics has been produced since 1900 than in all previous time. In most instances, however, the student must learn a vast amount of mathematics before he can add new knowledge to the mathematics that has already been developed.

How, then, can mathematics be a creative subject for the elementary school student or even the college student? Each may solve problems independently which have already been solved by someone else, pose new problems for solution, and perhaps attempt to solve some of the classical problems. The satisfaction of climbing a mountain that you have never climbed may be little diminished by the fact that others have climbed it. Many people enjoy working a crossword puzzle knowing full well that the answer is provided on the next page. Solving a problem in mathematics without assistance can be equally rewarding.

What sort of activity is the "doing" of mathematics? In mathematics an attempt is made to prove certain things concerning numbers, points, lines, planes, and so forth. We are frequently interested in how these results might apply to situations in other areas of study, such as physics, chemistry, biology, engineering, the social sciences, business, and economics. In attempting to prove things in mathematics, two types of reasoning are usually used—*inductive* and *deductive*.

Inductive reasoning is a method of arriving at what seems to be a reasonable conclusion based on experimentation and observation of what happens in a number of similar situations. Even intuition resulting from a variety of past experiences may be of assistance in the inductive process. As an example of inductive reasoning, let us consider the set of odd numbers $\{1, 3, 5, 7, \ldots\}$ and observe that $1 = 1^2$, $(1 + 3) = 4 = 2^2$, $(1 + 3 + 5) = 9 = 3^2$, and $(1 + 3 + 5 + 7) = 16 = 4^2$. By induction it appears that $1 + 3 + 5 + 7 + 9$ will equal 5^2 and, in general, that $1 + 3 + 5 + \ldots$ to n addends will be equal to n^2. In this case our induction is correct, and we could prove that it is correct by deductive reasoning, which is described later in this section.

Consider $\{x \mid x = (n^2 - n + 17) \wedge (n = 1, 2, 3, \ldots)\}$. Here we find that x has the values 17, 19, 23, 29, 37, 47, 59, 73, and 89, respectively, when n has the values 1, 2, 3, 4, 5, 6, 7, 8, and 9. Inductive reasoning may lead us to believe that x will be a prime number for all natural numbers n. However, our induction is false since for $n = 17$, we get $x = 289 = 17 \cdot 17$.

Since inductive reasoning can be unreliable, we depend upon other methods of proof. But we do not discard a beautiful thing like inductive reasoning simply because it sometimes leads us astray. In fact, more often than not, induction tells us what might be true and worthy of an attempted proof. Frequently, having arrived at a tentative conclusion based on induction, we use *deductive reasoning* to prove (or disprove) our hypothesis or tentative conclusion.

In a deductive proof we start with certain undefined terms, definitions, and basic assumptions which we believe or assume to be true. From these we then make assertions which the accepted basic assumptions seem to imply. When our assertions lead us in some logical way to a general principle, we say that this principle has been proved and call it a theorem. It would be wise not to consider this description to be a definition of a proof, for the methods of proof in mathematics are varied. But, varied as the methods may be, a proof must above all consist of *convincing* arguments. A proof may be convincing to a grade school child and not to a college student; a proof that was convincing in 1950 may not, in the light of new knowledge, be convincing today!

The most useful type of mathematical proof is the deductive proof which shows that a principle holds in general rather than in a limited number of instances. However, when the number of cases is small, a statement may be shown to be true by testing every case. A statement may also be proved *not* to hold in general simply by showing one case in which it is false. This is known as a proof by counterexample.

Proofs may be written in formal outline form with numbered statements and reasons, or they may be written in much the same style as the exposition of this text. Since some proofs will soon be given in the text, no sample proofs will be given at this time.

6.3
The Equals Relation for Numbers

Before discussing operations in the system of whole numbers, we must define the *equals* relation for the whole numbers. The equals relation has already been defined for sets. A single definition for equals could be used with reference to both sets and numbers, for if two symbols such as a and b are names for the same object (whether it be a physical object or an abstract concept), a and b are said to be equal and we write $a = b$. However, defining equals separately for each of several different situations helps to set up criteria for judging whether two symbols are indeed names for the same object. For example, it may be immediately apparent that $(9 + 3)$ and 12 are names for the same number but without some criteria for making a judgment it is not quite so obvious that $\frac{3}{7}$ and $\frac{51}{119}$ are names for the same number. For this reason we shall again discuss equals when rational numbers are considered.

The following definition is quite general and applies to all numbers, including the whole numbers.

DEFINITION 6.3.1

Two numbers a and b are equal and we write $a = b$ if and only if a and b are names for the same number.

Regardless of whether equals is defined for numbers or sets, it is an equivalence relation and therefore has the following properties:

1. For every a, $a = a$ (reflexive property).
2. If $a = b$, then $b = a$ (symmetric property).
3. If $a = b$ and $b = c$, then $a = c$ (transitive property).

EXERCISE 6.3

1. (a) What is a numeration system? Refer to Section 5.1 if necessary.
   (b) What is a number system? Refer to Section 6.1.

2. Describe briefly what is meant by inductive reasoning.

3. Describe briefly what is meant by deductive reasoning.

4. If a conclusion based on inductive reasoning can be false, what useful purpose can be served by this type of thinking?

5. What is a theorem?

6. (a) Describe briefly what is meant by a proof.
   (b) Why is it difficult to define the word "proof"?
   (c) Is a proof absolute? Does it establish the truth of a statement in such a way that it need never be reconsidered?

7. Give a general definition of equals for numbers.

6.4
Addition in the Whole Numbers

In this section the operation of addition on the whole numbers will be defined. Since addition, as well as some other operations on numbers, is classified as a *binary operation*, we shall first define the term binary operation.

DEFINITION 6.4.1

A binary operation on a set S, denoted by $\star$, associates with each ordered pair (a, b) of elements in $S \times S$ a *uniquely* determined (exactly one) element $a \star b$.

Ordinarily an operation will be denoted by some familiar symbol such as $+$ or $\cdot$ rather than by $\star$. However, the above definition is written to refer to any binary operation.

If each ordered pair of elements (a, b) in $S \times S$ can be associated with some uniquely determined element $a \star b$ *in* S, this fact is expressed by saying that S is closed under the operation $\star$, or by saying that the operation $\star$ in S has the property of closure. We can say, then, that the set of whole numbers is closed under the operation of addition since each ordered pair of whole numbers (a, b) has associated with it a uniquely determined whole number $a + b$ called the *sum*. For example, the ordered pair $(2, 4)$ has the uniquely determined (exactly one) sum $2 + 4$ or 6. The operation of subtraction, however, does not associate any whole number with certain ordered pairs such as $(4, 7)$, and $4 - 7$ is, therefore, undefined in the set of whole numbers. Similarly, $5 \div 8$ is undefined in the whole numbers. Hence we say that the set of whole numbers is *not closed* under the operations of subtraction and division. Although there are many ordered pairs of whole numbers (a, b) not associated with any whole number by the operations of subtraction or division, when $a - b$ and $a \div b$ do exist, they are *unique* and therefore useful.

In advanced mathematics it is common to require the closure property as part of the definition of a binary operation. However, since it is convenient in elementary mathematics to refer to subtraction and division in the whole numbers as operations, we shall not require closure in our definition of a binary operation.

Having discussed operations on numbers in a general way, we are prepared to define specific operations in the whole numbers. The set of whole numbers $W = \{0, 1, 2, 3, \ldots\}$ has already been defined in terms of sets. We now define the addition of whole numbers in terms of sets. Addition is an operation on numbers, whereas union and intersection are operations on *sets*.

DEFINITION 6.4.2

If A and B are disjoint sets $(A \cap B = \varnothing)$ such that $a = n(A)$ and $b = n(B)$, then the binary operation of addition $(+)$ assigns to the ordered pair (a, b) a whole number $a + b$ equal to $n(A \cup B)$.

When a and b are added to produce the number $a + b$, a and b are called addends and $a + b$ is called their sum.

Example 1. Suppose $A = \{a, b, c\}$ and $B = \{d, e, f, g\}$. If the elements of A and B are each put in a one-to-one correspondence with the elements of an initial subset of the counting numbers, we find that $n(A) = 3$ and $n(B) = 4$. But $A \cup B = \{a, b, c, d, e, f, g\}$ and $n(A \cup B) = 7$; therefore, the sum $3 + 4 = 7$ by Definition 6.4.2.

Definition 6.4.2 for the sum of two numbers does not preclude the possibility that the numbers a and b may be the same number $(a = b)$. For example, if $a = 4$ and $b = 4$, we may conclude from the definition that $4 + 4 = 8$.

Although the above definition is awkward to use directly in finding the sum of two large numbers, its application is probably the best way to teach children the meaning of the operation of addition for the whole numbers. The definition also serves as the foundation for determining the *properties* of the operation of addition which are discussed next.

6.5
The Closure Property for Addition in W

The closure property for addition in W means that for any two elements a and b in the whole numbers, there *exists* a *unique* (exactly one) element $a + b$ in W, which we call the sum. Note that closure has two requisites: *existence* and *uniqueness*. In saying that a and b are any two elements contained in W, we note once again the possibility that $a = b$. For example, the sum $7 + 7$ is a uniquely determined whole number which may be written in standard form as 14. The fact that the closure property holds for addition in the whole numbers is sometimes expressed in mathematics by saying that "the set of whole numbers is closed under addition."

By examining the definition of addition in W, we can easily see that if $A \cup B$ did not exist as a unique set, the sum $a + b$ would not exist uniquely. Therefore, the closure property for the addition of whole numbers depends upon the assumption that the closure property holds for the union of sets. Although we did not list closure as one of the properties of the operation of union, we could have done so, for it is tacitly assumed in the definition of union. Not only does the set $A \cup B$ *exist* for any two sets A and B, but it is *unique,* and the two requisites of closure are satisfied.

> **Example 1.** Is the set of prime numbers $\{2, 3, 5, 7, 11, 13, 17, \ldots\}$ closed under addition? (A whole number is prime if it has exactly two distinct factors.)
>
> *Solution:* If the set of prime numbers is closed under addition, the sum of any two primes would have to be another prime. However, $5 + 7 = 12$, and 12 is not prime since it has more than two distinct factors (the factors of 12 are 1, 2, 3, 4, 6, and 12). Therefore the closure property does not hold for the set of prime numbers.

EXERCISE 6.5

1. Define the operation of addition for the whole numbers.

2. Suppose $A = \{a, b, c\}$ and $B = \{b, c, d, e\}$. We find $n(A) = 3$ and $n(B) = 4$. $A \cup B = \{a, b, c, d, e\}$ and $n(A \cup B) = 5$. However, $3 + 4 \neq 5$ even though $n(A \cup B) = 5$. Why not?

3. As we have seen, $n(A \cup B) = n(A) + n(B)$ when $A \cap B = \varnothing$.
   (a) Try to find a general formula for $n(A \cup B)$ that holds when $A \cap B \neq \varnothing$. Use a Venn diagram to aid your thinking.
   (b) Does your formula from part (a) hold when $A \cap B = \varnothing$?

4. State the closure property for addition in the whole numbers.

5. What is meant by the statement, "The closure property of addition has two requisites, *existence* and *uniqueness*"?

6. Given two whole numbers such as 14,605 and 2,831,469, what does the closure property for addition tell us about their sum?

7. Using *inductive* reasoning, decide whether you believe the closure property of addition holds for each of the following sets:
   (a) $\{2, 4, 6, 8, 10, \ldots\}$ (b) $\{10, 20, 30, 40, 50, \ldots\}$
   (c) $\{1, 3, 5, 7, 9, \ldots\}$ (d) $\{3, 6, 9, 12, 15, \ldots\}$

**6.6
The
Commutative
Property
of Addition
in *W***

For any two elements a and b contained in the set of whole numbers, $a + b = b + a$. This is a statement of the commutative property of addition.

A proof of the commutative property of addition in the whole numbers is given below. Since this is the first formal proof of this text, the implications from step to step will be minimal. A proof with fewer steps in which several reasons are given for each step follows the first proof. There is no unique way for writing any proof, but there are certain general techniques which are commonly used.

Given: Sets A and B where $A \cap B = \varnothing$ and $a = n(A)$ and $b = n(B)$
To prove: $a + b = b + a$

Assertions	Reasons
1. $a = n(A)$	1. Given
2. $b = n(B)$	2. Given
3. $a + b = n(A \cup B)$	3. Definition of addition in W
4. $b + a = n(B \cup A)$	4. Definition of addition in W
5. $n(B \cup A) = n(A \cup B)$	5. $B \cup A = A \cup B$
6. $b + a = n(A \cup B)$	6. Transitive property of the equals relation applied to steps 4 and 5
7. $n(A \cup B) = b + a$	7. Symmetric property of equals
8. $a + b = b + a$	8. Transitive property of equals applied to steps 3 and 7

The proof above could be shortened by making assertions of greater magnitude. However, if the advancement from one step to the next is too great, it may be difficult to completely justify each assertion. For comparative purposes, a shorter proof of the commutative property for addition in the whole numbers is given below.

Given: Sets A and B where $A \cap B = \varnothing$ and $a = n(A)$ and $b = n(B)$

To prove: $a + b = b + a$

Assertions	*Reasons*
1. $a + b = n(A \cup B)$ and $b + a = n(B \cup A)$	1. Given facts and definition of addition in W
2. $n(A \cup B) = n(B \cup A)$	2. $A \cup B = B \cup A$
3. $a + b = b + a$	3. Symmetric and transitive properties of the equals relation

Example 1. Is the operation of division commutative?

Solution: $8 \div 2 = 4$ but $2 \div 8 \neq 4$. Therefore $8 \div 2 \neq 2 \div 8$, and the operation of division is not commutative.

6.7 The Associative Property of Addition in W

Since addition is defined as a binary operation, we can add two and only two numbers at a time. We shall therefore define the sum of three addends, $a + b + c$, to be equal to $(a + b) + c$. The parentheses indicate that we are first to add a and b. This is possible by the closure property for addition in W. The single number $(a + b)$ can then be added to c, and again there exists a unique number for this sum by the closure property of addition.

The above generalizations are exemplified in finding the sum $3 + 4 + 5$ by the following method: $3 + 4 + 5 = (3 + 4) + 5 = 7 + 5 = 12$. Note that the operation of addition has been performed on exactly two numbers at a time. Using the concepts that have been developed, we now state and discuss the associative property of addition.

The **associative property of addition** states that for any elements a, b, and c in W, $(a + b) + c = a + (b + c)$. In other words, if we are given three addends, we may initially add either the first two or the last two. A proof is not given for the associative property of addition, but its justification will be found to depend upon the fact that the operation of union is associative for sets: $(A \cup B) \cup C = A \cup (B \cup C)$.

A question frequently asked by students is, "Can we initially add the first and last numbers, a and c?" It is, of course, true that $(a + b) + c = (a + c) + b$. However, we need not *assume* that this statement is true since it can be *proved* by using the commutative and associative properties of addition. The proof follows.

Assertions	*Reasons*
1. $(a + b) + c = a + (b + c)$	1. Associative property of addition
2. $a + (b + c) = a + (c + b)$	2. Commutative property of addition
3. $a + (c + b) = (a + c) + b$	3. Associative property of addition
4. $(a + b) + c = (a + c) + b$	4. Transitive property of equals (applied twice)

By a similar line of reasoning it can be proved that for any finite number of addends, any two may be added first, then any other addend may be added to this result, and so on, until the final sum is determined.

Example 1. Verify the associative property for addition by showing that $(3 + 4) + 9 = 3 + (4 + 9)$.

Solution:

$(3 + 4) + 9 = 7 + 9 = 16$, and

$3 + (4 + 9) = 3 + 13 = 16$.

Therefore, $(3 + 4) + 9 = 3 + (4 + 9)$.

Example 2. Show by an example that the associative property does not hold for subtraction.

Solution:

$(8 - 4) - 2 = 4 - 2 = 2$.

$8 - (4 - 2) = 8 - 2 = 6$.

But $2 \neq 6$. Therefore, $(8 - 4) - 2 \neq 8 - (4 - 2)$.

6.8
The Identity Element for Addition in *W*

There exists a unique number in the set of whole numbers such that when it is used as an addend with any other whole number a, the sum is a. This number is 0 (zero) and is called the identity element for addition in *W*. We express this idea by writing

$$a + 0 = 0 + a = a \quad \text{for every } a \text{ in } W.$$

By using previous definitions and assumptions, we write the following in proving the *existence* of 0 as the identity element for addition in W:

$$a + 0 = n(A) + n(\varnothing) = n(A \cup \varnothing) = n(A) = a.$$

Then by the repeated use of the transitive property for equals, we conclude that $a + 0 = a$; and since addition is commutative, $a + 0 = 0 + a = a$. Note that we proved the *existence* of an identity element but not its *uniqueness*.

It will now be shown that the identity element for addition is *unique* (that is, 0 is the only identity element). Let us suppose there is another identity element for addition which we shall represent with the symbol x. Then, by definition of an identity element for addition, it must be true that $x + 0 = x$ (since 0 is an identity element) and it must also be true that $x + 0 = 0$ (since x is an identity element). But if $x = x + 0$ and $x + 0 = 0$, then $x = 0$ by the transitive property of equals, and we see that any other identity element x must simply be another name for zero. Hence zero is *unique* and our proof is complete.

Zero may be called either the *identity element for addition* or simply the additive identity. Zero is the additive identity for every whole number including itself since $0 + 0 = n(\varnothing) + n(\varnothing) = n(\varnothing \cup \varnothing) = n(\varnothing) = 0$.

EXERCISE 6.8

1. (a) State the commutative property of addition in the whole numbers.
   (b) Give an example verifying the commutative property of addition in W.
2. (a) Prove the commutative property of addition in W with the assistance of your text.
   (b) Prove the commutative property of addition in W without any assistance.
3. Using $A = \{a, b\}$ and $B = \{c, d, e, f\}$, prove that $2 + 4 = 4 + 2$. Show that $n(A \cup B) = n(B \cup A)$ as part of your proof.
4. State the associative property of addition in the whole numbers.
5. Use the associative property of addition to find the sum $6 + 9 + 4$ in two different ways.
6. What is meant by saying that there is an identity element for addition in the whole numbers?
7. (a) Prove the *existence* of zero as an identity element for addition in W.
   (b) Prove that zero is *unique* as an identity element for addition in W. Write a formal proof by listing assertions and reasons.

8. Which property (or properties) of addition is applied in each of the following?
   (a) $72 + 34 = 34 + 72$
   (b) $(7 + 5) + 2 = 7 + (5 + 2)$
   (c) $(3 + 4) + 7 = (4 + 3) + 7$
   (d) $34{,}920 + 0 = 34{,}920$
   (e) $(3 + 4) + 5 = 3 + (5 + 4)$
   (f) $a + x = x + a$
   (g) $x + 0 = x$
   (h) $(9 + 2) + 3 = 9 + (3 + 2)$

6.9
Multiplication in the Whole Numbers

Most of us have learned that in finding the product of two whole numbers such as 3×4, we may use 4 as an addend 3 times. Thus $3 \times 4 = 4 + 4 + 4 = 12$. This is probably one of the most meaningful ways of teaching the concept of multiplication, provided sets of physical objects are used to assist in the learning process.

DEFINITION 6.9.1

If a and b are in W, the binary operation of multiplication ($\cdot$ or $\times$) assigns to the ordered pair (a, b) a whole number indicated by $a \cdot b$ equal to $b + b + b + \ldots$ to a addends.

The number $a \cdot b$ is called the product of the factors a and b. It is also said to be a multiple of both a and b. The product of the factors a and b may be indicated by $a \cdot b$ or $a \times b$ or simply ab with no symbol between the a and b. However, when specific numbers are used as factors, such as 3 and 4, they cannot be written without a symbol between them. If 3 and 4 were written as factors with no symbol between them, the numeral for thirty-four (34) would be indicated. Some alternative ways of writing the product of 3 and 4 are: $3 \cdot 4 = 3 \times 4 = 3(4) = (3)4 = (3)(4) = 12$. It is important that the reader not confuse the cross symbol ($\times$) used between *numbers* to indicate the operation of multiplication with the same or similar symbol used between *sets* to indicate a Cartesian product.

The above definition for the product of two whole numbers a and b does cause a problem if the first factor happens to be zero. For example, if we have the product $0 \cdot 42$, what does it mean to use 42 as an addend zero times and what number is indicated by so doing?

If we use the somewhat more sophisticated set-theoretic approach to multiplication, as we did with addition, the above problematical situation is avoided. The set-theoretic approach is certainly not superior in all respects to the repeated addend approach, but it does have some advantages. Once again we define multiplication, but this time in terms of the Cartesian product of sets (see Section 3.2 for a review of the Cartesian product).

DEFINITION 6.9.2

If A and B are sets with $a = n(A)$ and $b = n(B)$, then the binary operation of multiplication ($\cdot$ or $\times$) assigns to the ordered pair (a, b) a whole number $a \cdot b$ equal to $n(A \times B)$.

In the definition of addition it was necessary that $A \cap B = \varnothing$. This is not required in the definition of multiplication since the number of elements in $A \times B$ is not affected by whether A and B are disjoint sets.

The relation between the repeated addend approach and the Cartesian product approach to multiplication may easily be seen by referring to Figure 6.9.1. This illustration shows the Cartesian product

b				
3	(1, 3)	(2, 3)	(3, 3)	(4, 3)
2	(1, 2)	(2, 2)	(3, 2)	(4, 2)
1	(1, 1)	(2, 1)	(3, 1)	(4, 1)
	1	2	3	4	a

$A \times B$

FIGURE 6.9.1

$A \times B$ where $A = \{1, 2, 3, 4\}$ and $B = \{1, 2, 3\}$. It is readily seen in the repeated addend approach that the product $4 \cdot 3 = 3 + 3 + 3 + 3 = 12$. In the Cartesian product approach there are 4 columns of ordered pairs with each column containing 3 elements, and $n(A) \cdot n(B) = 4 \cdot 3 = n(A \times B) = 12$.

Example 1. Using the sets $A = \{a, b\}$ and $B = \{a, b, c\}$, find the product $2 \cdot 3$.

Solution:

$n(A) = 2$ and $n(B) = 3$.

$2 \cdot 3 = n(A \times B) = n(\{(a, a), (a, b), (a, c), (b, a), (b, b), (b, c)\}) = 6$.

Therefore, $2 \cdot 3 = 6$.

In the repeated addend approach to multiplication, we have difficulty in finding a product such as $0 \cdot 3$ since using 3 as an addend zero times is conceptually vague. The best way to sidestep the issue would probably be to say that by the commutative property (discussed later) $0 \cdot 3 = 3 \cdot 0$. Then, using zero as an addend three times, we get $0 + 0 + 0 = 0$. However, the reader will discover in Example 2 that in using the Cartesian product approach to multiplication, no difficulty is encountered in finding the product $0 \cdot 3$.

Example 2. Using the sets $A = \varnothing$ and $B = \{a, b, c\}$, find the product of 0 and 3.

Solution:

$n(A) = 0$ and $n(B) = 3$.

$0 \cdot 3 = n(A \times B) = n(\varnothing \times B) = n(\varnothing) = 0$.

Therefore, $0 \cdot 3 = 0$.

In general, $0 \cdot a = n(\varnothing) \cdot n(A) = n(\varnothing \times A) = n(\varnothing) = 0$, and in the special case when $a = 0$, we get $0 \cdot 0 = n(\varnothing) \cdot n(\varnothing) = n(\varnothing \times \varnothing) = n(\varnothing) = 0$. Similarly, it may be shown that $a \cdot 0 = 0$. We may summarize by stating that: $0 \cdot a = a \cdot 0$ for all a in W. (The reader should try to give reasons for each step in Examples 1 and 2 above.)

It is easy to see that we would not wish to find the product 634×538 by a direct application of either of the given definitions of multiplication. However, the definitions serve as the foundation for more sophisticated techniques for finding products. By using a definition of multiplication and the properties of multiplication discussed below, it is quite easy to find the product of any two whole numbers. Note that the word "multiplication" is used to refer to both the process of finding a product and the binary operation of multiplication. Analogous statements can be made for addition, subtraction, and other mathematical operations.

6.10
The Closure Property for Multiplication in W

The closure property for multiplication in W states that for any two elements a and b in W, there exists a unique element $a \cdot b$ in W, which we call the product of a and b. As in the case of addition, we do not preclude the possibility that $a = b$. For example, $7 \cdot 7$ is a uniquely determined whole number which may be written in standard form as 49.

The fact that the closure property holds for multiplication in W may be expressed by saying that "the set of whole numbers is closed under multiplication." By examining the definition of multiplication expressed in terms of the Cartesian product set, it is evident that the closure property for the multiplication of whole numbers depends upon the *existence* of a *unique* Cartesian product $A \times B$ for any two sets A and B. In other words, we have assumed the closure property for the Cartesian product set $A \times B$.

Example 1.   Is the set of prime numbers, $\{2, 3, 5, 7, 11, 13, 17, \ldots\}$, closed under multiplication?

Solution: If the set of prime numbers is closed under multiplication, then the product of any two primes would have to be another prime. However, $2 \cdot 3 = 6$, and 6 is not prime since it has more than two distinct factors. As a result, we can state that the set of prime numbers is not closed under multiplication.

Example 2.   Is the set of even numbers closed under multiplication?

Solution: Since an even number is a whole number with at least one factor of 2, the product of any two even numbers may be expressed as $(2a) \cdot (2b) = 4ab$, where a and b are in W. But the product $4ab = 2(2ab)$, which has a factor of 2, and hence is an even number. Therefore, the set of even numbers is closed under multiplication.

EXERCISE 6.10

1. Define multiplication, using the repeated addend approach.
2. Define multiplication, using the Cartesian product approach.
3. Using Definition 6.9.1, find the product $4 \cdot 2$.
4. Using Definition 6.9.2 and the sets $A = \{a, b, c, d\}$ and $B = \{1, 2\}$, find the product $4 \cdot 2$ by counting the elements in the product set $A \times B$.
5. Using set $A = \{a, b, c\}$ and set $B = \varnothing$, prove that $3 \cdot 0 = 0$.
6. State the closure property for multiplication in the whole numbers.
7. Using *inductive* reasoning, decide whether you believe the closure property of multiplication holds for each of the following sets:
   - (a) $\{2, 4, 6, 8, 10, \ldots\}$
   - (b) $\{10, 20, 30, 40, 50, \ldots\}$
   - (c) $\{1, 3, 5, 7, 9, \ldots\}$
   - (d) $\{1, 2, 4, 8, 16, 32, \ldots\}$
   - (e) $\{0, 1\}$
   - (f) $\{0, 1, 2\}$
8. If $ab = 0$, what conclusions can you make concerning possible values of a and b?

6.11
The Commutative Property of Multiplication in W

For any two elements a and b in W, $a \cdot b = b \cdot a$. This is a statement of the commutative property of multiplication. Since the reader is already familiar with this property, we proceed directly to its proof.

Given: Sets A and B such that $a = n(A)$ and $b = n(B)$ with a and b in W.

To prove: $a \cdot b = b \cdot a$

Assertions	Reasons
1. $a = n(A)$ and $b = n(B)$	1. Given
2. $a \cdot b = n(A \times B)$	2. Definition of multiplication in W
3. $b \cdot a = n(B \times A)$	3. Definition of multiplication in W
4. $n(A \times B) = n(B \times A)$	4. $A \times B$ and $B \times A$ are equivalent (not equal) sets
5. $a \cdot b = n(A \times B) = n(B \times A) = b \cdot a$	5. Steps 2, 4, and 3 (and symmetric property of equals)
6. $a \cdot b = b \cdot a$	6. Transitive property of equals

6.12
The Associative Property of Multiplication in W

Since multiplication is a binary operation, we shall define $a \cdot b \cdot c$ to be equal to $(a \cdot b) \cdot c$. You will recall that we defined $a + b + c$ to mean the same as $(a + b) + c$ in considering the associative property for addition. By defining $a \cdot b \cdot c$ to mean $(a \cdot b) \cdot c$, we can use the binary operation of multiplication and find products such as $3 \cdot 4 \cdot 7 = (3 \cdot 4) \cdot 7 = 12 \cdot 7 = 84$. Note that only *two* numbers at a time have been used as factors.

The associative property of multiplication states that for any elements a, b, and c in W, $(a \cdot b) \cdot c = a \cdot (b \cdot c)$. It is easy to see that: $(a \cdot b) \cdot c = n(A \times B) \cdot n(C) = n[(A \times B) \times C]$, and $a \cdot (b \cdot c) = n(A) \cdot n(B \times C) = n[A \times (B \times C)]$. The associative property of multiplication is, therefore, a consequence of the fact that $n[(A \times B) \times C] = n[A \times (B \times C)]$.

Example 1. Verify the associative property of multiplication by showing that $(3 \cdot 4) \cdot 6 = 3 \cdot (4 \cdot 6)$.

Solution:

$(3 \cdot 4) \cdot 6 = 12 \cdot 6 = 72$, and

$3 \cdot (4 \cdot 6) = 3 \cdot 24 = 72$.

Therefore, $(3 \cdot 4) \cdot 6 = 3 \cdot (4 \cdot 6)$.

Example 2.   Use the associative property of multiplication to find the product $2 \times 6 \times 9 \times 3$.

Solution:

$$
\begin{aligned}
2 \times 6 \times 9 \times 3 &= (2 \times 6) \times 9 \times 3 \\
&= [(2 \times 6) \times 9] \times 3 \\
&= (12 \times 9) \times 3 \\
&= 108 \times 3 \\
&= 324.
\end{aligned}
$$

Using the associative property, we can prove that the product of any finite number of factors may be found by multiplying any two factors initially, and then multiplying this product by any other factor, and so on.

EXERCISE 6.12

1. State the commutative property for multiplication in W.
2. Verify the commutative property by finding the product 7×35 and comparing it with the product 35×7.
3. Using $A = \{a, b\}$ and $B = \{1, 2, 3\}$, prove that $2 \cdot 3 = 3 \cdot 2$ by showing $n(A \times B) = n(B \times A)$ as part of your proof.
4. State the associative property for multiplication in W.
5. Using $A = \{a, b\}$, $B = \{k\}$, and $C = \{1, 2, 3\}$, prove $(2 \cdot 1) \cdot 3 = 2 \cdot (1 \cdot 3)$ by showing that $n[(A \times B) \times C] = n[A \times (B \times C)]$.
6. In each of the following, one or more of the properties of addition or multiplication is exemplified. Tell which property (or properties) is being applied:
   (a) $3 + 4 = 4 + 3$ (b) $3 \times 27 = 27 \times 3$
   (c) $xy = yx$ (d) $(3 + 5) + 5 = 3 + (5 + 5)$
   (e) $6(4 + 5) = (4 + 5)6$ (f) $8 + n = n + 8$
   (g) $a + (b + 8) = a + (8 + b)$ (h) $(xy)z = x(zy)$
   (i) $(a + x) + 2 = a + (x + 2)$ (j) $7[(4 + 5) + 6] = 7[4 + (5 + 6)]$
7. Use the associative property of multiplication to find the product $2 \times 3 \times 5 \times 4$.

6.13
The Identity Element for Multiplication in W

There exists a unique number in the set of whole numbers such that when it is used as a factor with any other whole number a, the product is a. This number is 1 (one) and is called the identity element for multiplication in W. We express this idea by writing

$$a \cdot 1 = 1 \cdot a = a \quad \text{for every } a \text{ in } W.$$

Using previous definitions and assumptions, we write the following to show the *existence* (but not the *uniqueness*) of 1 as the identity element for multiplication:

> Assume $a = n(A)$ and let $\{k\}$ be a representative set containing one element. Then $a \cdot 1 = n(A \times \{k\}) = n(A) = a$. By use of the transitive property, $a \cdot 1 = a$; and since multiplication is commutative, $a \cdot 1 = 1 \cdot a = a$.

In the above discussion, it may not be immediately obvious that $n(A \times \{k\}) = n(A)$. However, suppose $A = \{a_1, a_2, a_3, \ldots, a_r\}$; then $n(A) = r$. But $A \times \{k\} = \{(a_1, k), (a_2, k), (a_3, k), \ldots, (a_r, k)\}$. It is now seen that the elements of $A \times \{k\}$ and the elements of A may be placed in a one-to-one correspondence and, therefore, $n(A \times \{k\}) = n(A)$.

The number 1 may be called either the *identity element for multiplication* or simply the multiplicative identity. Note that 1 is the multiplicative identity for every element including itself since $1 \cdot 1 = n(\{k\} \times \{k\}) = n(\{(k, k)\}) = 1$. In considering $n(\{(k, k)\})$, note that (k, k) is only *one ordered pair* in the Cartesian set.

The uniqueness of 1 as the identity element for multiplication may be proved by a method analogous to the method that was used in showing the uniqueness of 0 as the additive identity. Refer to Section 6.8.

6.14
The Distributive Property of Multiplication over Addition in W

Before discussing the distributive property of multiplication over addition, it is appropriate to mention that by convention the operations of *multiplication* and *division* take precedence over the operations of *addition* and *subtraction* unless indicated to the contrary. For example, in the expression $2 + 5 \cdot 3$ we multiply before adding and get $2 + 5 \cdot 3 = 2 + 15 = 17$. However, if we specifically desire addition to take precedence over multiplication, we may so indicate with the use of parentheses and write $(2 + 5) \cdot 3 = 7 \cdot 3 = 21$. Similarly, $2 \cdot 5 + 2 \cdot 3 = 10 + 6 = 16$, while $2 \cdot (5 + 2) \cdot 3 = 2 \cdot 7 \cdot 3 = 42$. Note how the precedence of operations applies in the following discussion of the distributive property.

By saying that multiplication is distributive over addition, we mean that for all a, b, and c in W, $a(b + c) = ab + ac$ and $(b + c)a = ba + ca$. The relation $a(b + c) = ab + ac$ is called the left distributive property since the factor a is to the left of the factor $(b + c)$, which has two addends. Similarly, the right distributive property states that $(b + c)a = ba + ca$. Since both the left and right distributive properties hold for multiplication over addition, we shall, as a matter of convenience, use the expression the distributive property to include both. Some authors state the distributive property as $a(b + c) = (b + c)a = ab + ac$. This can be justified since the expression $ba + ca$ from the right distributive property is equal to $ab + ac$ by the commutative property of multiplication.

To justify the left distributive property for the whole numbers, we can use the fact that the Cartesian product operation is distributive over union. Although we did not prove this relation, it may be easily verified for sets with small numbers of elements. For sets A, B, and C, we can write: $A \times (B \cup C) = (A \times B) \cup (A \times C)$. This equation is true in general, but we are interested in the case where $B \cap C = \varnothing$ since addition in the whole numbers is defined in terms of the union of disjoint sets. Assuming, then, that $B \cap C = \varnothing$, $a = n(A)$, $b = n(B)$, and $c = n(C)$, we see:

1. $a(b + c) = n(A)[n(B) + n(C)] = n(A) \cdot n(B \cup C)$
   $= n[A \times (B \cup C)]$ and

2. $ab + ac = n(A) \cdot n(B) + n(A) \cdot n(C) = n(A \times B) + n(A \times C)$
   $= n[(A \times B) \cup (A \times C)]$.

But $n[A \times (B \cup C)] = n[(A \times B) \cup (A \times C)]$ since $A \times (B \cup C) = (A \times B) \cup (A \times C)$, and we conclude that $a(b + c) = ab + ac$.

The right distributive property may be easily proved by using the left distributive property and the commutative property for multiplication.

Example 1. Verify the truth of the distributive property of multiplication over addition by showing that $3(4 + 5) = 3 \cdot 4 + 3 \cdot 5$.

Solution:

$3(4 + 5) = 3 \cdot 9 = 27$, and

$3 \cdot 4 + 3 \cdot 5 = 12 + 15 = 27$.

Therefore, $3(4 + 5) = 3 \cdot 4 + 3 \cdot 5$.
(Note that $3(4 + 5) \neq 3 \cdot 4 + 5$.)

The validity of the distributive property is illustrated in an interesting way by using an array of dots as shown in Figure 6.14.1. First

$$4 \cdot (3 + 5)$$

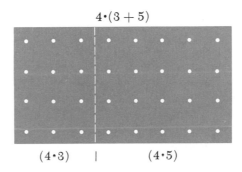

$$(4 \cdot 3) \quad | \quad (4 \cdot 5)$$

FIGURE 6.14.1

consider the array in its entirety in representing $4 \times (3 + 5) = 4 \times 8 = 32$. Then consider the array as divided in representing $(4 \times 3) + (4 \times 5)$. Note that the dots in the array could be placed in a one-to-one correspondence with the elements in the Cartesian product $A \times (B \cup C) = (A \times B) \cup (A \times C)$, where $4 = n(A)$, $3 = n(B)$, $5 = n(C)$, and $B \cap C = \emptyset$.

If $a(b + c) = ab + ac$, then by the symmetric property of equals, $ab + ac = a(b + c)$. The distributive property is frequently used in this "reverse" way, particularly in simplifying algebraic expressions.

Example 2. Rename $3 \cdot 4 + 3 \cdot 8$ by using the distributive property.

Solution: $3 \cdot 4 + 3 \cdot 8 = 3(4 + 8)$.

Example 3. Rename $ax + bx$ by using the distributive property.

Solution: $ax + bx = (a + b)x$.

Example 4. Rename $8 + 12 + 20$ by using the distributive property.

Solution: $8 + 12 + 20 = (8 + 12) + 20 = 4(2 + 3) + 20 = 4[(2 + 3) + 5] = 4(2 + 3 + 5)$. (Some steps may be omitted.)

EXERCISE 6.14

1. What is meant by saying there is an identity element for multiplication in *W*?

2. (a) Prove the *existence* of 1 as the identity element for multiplication in W.

(b) Prove the *uniqueness* of 1 as the identity element for multiplication in W. (See the uniqueness of 0 proof in Section 6.8.)

3. (a) Verify the left distributive property by showing that $6(8 + 3) = 6 \cdot 8 + 6 \cdot 3$.

(b) Using the same factors, verify the right distributive property.

4. Assume the left distributive property to be true and prove the right distributive property.

5. Use the distributive property to find the standard numeral for each of the following:

(a) $2(3 + 5)$ (b) $(6 + 9)3$
(c) $2(30 + 4)$ (d) $2(34)$
(e) $(40 + 3)2$ (f) $(43)2$
(g) $3[(4 + 5) + 7]$ (h) $5(3 + 4 + 2)$

6. Rename each of the following by using the distributive property. (There may be more than one possible result.)

(a) $7(a + n)$ (b) $(x + y)a$
(c) $ax + ay$ (d) $a \cdot 10^2 + 10$
(e) $k^2x + k^2y$ (f) $4xay + kx$
(g) $ax + ay + az$ (h) $6 + 9 + 12$
(i) $ax + a$ (j) $ax^3 + x^3 + bx^3 + cx^3$

7. (a) Prove that $7x + 3x = 10x$.
(b) Prove that $3x + x = 4x$.

8. In proving that $a(b + c) = ab + ac$, it is necessary that $A \times (B \cup C) = (A \times B) \cup (A \times C)$. Verify that $A \times (B \cup C) = (A \times B) \cup (A \times C)$ by listing the ordered pairs of $A \times (B \cup C)$ and those of $(A \times B) \cup (A \times C)$ if $A = \{d, e\}$, $B = \{f, g, h\}$, and $C = \{i, j, k, l\}$.

6.15
The Substitution and Cancellation Properties

In mathematical expressions we may substitute a number for its equal. This property is frequently referred to as the substitution property. The justification for substituting a number for its equal may depend on the symmetric or transitive properties of equals. However, where sums and products are involved, the justification depends on the closure property for the particular operation with which we are concerned.

In each of the following theorems, the property of closure for an operation is used in the proof. However, as noted, in each case we could think of substituting some number for its equal.

THEOREM 6.15.1

If a, b, and c are in W and $a = b$, then $a + c = b + c$.

Proof: By definition of equals, a and b are names for the same number.

This means that the numerals $a + c$ and $b + c$ represent the same sum. By the closure property for addition in W, the sum of any two whole numbers exists and is unique. Therefore, $a + c = b + c$.

We may also think of substituting b for its equal a in the expression $a + c$ with the result $a + c = b + c$.

THEOREM 6.15.2

If a, b, and c are in W and $a = b$, then $a \cdot c = b \cdot c$. The proof is similar to the proof of Theorem 6.15.1 and is left as an exercise for the student. We may also think of substituting b for a (its equal) and getting $a \cdot c = b \cdot c$.

THEOREM 6.15.3

If a, b, c, and d are in W with $a = b$ and $c = d$, then $a + c = b + d$. The proof depends on the property of closure for addition and is similar to the proofs of Theorems 6.15.1 and 6.15.2. Again we may think in terms of substitutions. If b and d are substituted for their equals a and c, the result is $a + c = b + d$.

Henceforth, when a number in a mathematical expression is replaced by its equal, we may refer to the substitution property as justification.

Example 1.   If $y = 7 + 5a$ and $a = 4$, express y as a whole number.

Solution:

1. $y = 7 + 5a$ 1. Given
2. $y = 7 + 5 \cdot 4$ 2. Substitution property (or closure for multiplication)
3. $y = 7 + 20$ 3. Multiplication fact
4. $y = 27$ 4. Addition fact

We have shown that if $a = b$, then $a + c = b + c$. It has also been stated that if $a = b$, then $ac = bc$. Does it not seem reasonable that the converse statements might be true? That is, if $a + c = b + c$, then $a = b$; and if $ac = bc$, then $a = b$. The converse statements *with one restriction* are true and can be proved. However, since the principle of the existence of additive and multiplicative inverses can be used so conveniently in the proofs and since we have not yet discussed inverse elements, we shall simply state the two theorems and delay their proofs until additive and multiplicative inverses are discussed. Theorems 6.15.4 and 6.15.5 are referred to as the cancellation properties of addition and multiplication.

THEOREM 6.15.4

If a, b, and c are in W and $a + c = b + c$, then $a = b$.

THEOREM 6.15.5

If a, b, and c are in W, $c \neq 0$, and $ca = cb$, then $a = b$.

The restriction in Theorem 6.15.5 stating $c \neq 0$ is obviously necessary if we consider an example such as $0 \cdot 5 = 0 \cdot 7$. Without this restriction, we would conclude that $5 = 7$.

Example 2.   Express x as a whole number if $7x + 4 = 39$.

Solution:

1. $7x + 4 = 39$	1. Given
2. $7x + 4 = 35 + 4$	2. Addition fact
3. $7x = 35$	3. Cancellation property of addition
4. $7x = 7 \cdot 5$	4. Multiplication fact
5. $x = 5$	5. Cancellation property of multiplication

Example 3.   If $3x = 8 + 4$, express x as a whole number.

Solution:

1. $3x = 8 + 4$	1. Given
2. $3x = 12$	2. Addition fact
3. $3x = 3 \cdot 4$	3. Multiplication fact
4. $x = 4$	4. Cancellation property of multiplication

EXERCISE 6.15

1. (a) Prove Theorem 6.15.2. (The proof is similar to the proof of Theorem 6.15.1.)
   (b) Prove Theorem 6.15.3.
   (c) If a, b, c, and d are in W with $a = b$ and $c = d$, prove $ac = bd$.

2. State the *cancellation property of addition.*

3. State the *cancellation property of multiplication.*

4. If $xy = xz$, then $y = z$. For what value of x is this statement false?

5. Use the substitution property to express x as a whole number if $x = 3y + 7$ and $y = 4$.

6. Use the cancellation property of addition to express x as a whole number if $x + 3 = 17$.

7. Justify the expressions, "If equals are added to equals, their sums are equal," and "If equals are multiplied by equals, their products are equal."

8. Find the value of x if $3x + 4 = 52$. Use the cancellation properties in the solution.

9. Find the value of x if $7x = 32 + 31$.

10. Find the whole number such that if it is multiplied by 6, the product will be 4 less than 136.

6.16
Subtraction in the Whole Numbers

Since the operation of subtraction may be defined in terms of addition, it is, from this point of view, not considered a fundamental operation. A definition of subtraction follows.

DEFINITION 6.16.1

If a, b, and k are in W and a is greater than or equal to b, then $a - b = k$ if and only if $a = b + k$.

In this definition of subtraction, the number a is called the minuend, b is called the subtrahend, and k the difference. Note that the definition is an "if and only if" statement. This means, for example, that *if* $7 - 2 = 5$, *then* $7 = 2 + 5$; and it also means that *if* $7 = 2 + 5$, *then* $7 - 2 = 5$. Since addition is commutative, we can see at once that if $7 = 2 + 5$, then it is also true that $7 = 5 + 2$; therefore, $7 - 5 = 2$ by the definition of subtraction. By similar reasoning we conclude, in general, that if $a = b + c$, then $a - b = c$ and $a - c = b$.

Subtraction may be thought of as finding a missing addend if one addend and a sum are known. For example, $8 - 5$ is that number which added to 5 will produce a sum of 8.

The operation of subtraction may also be interpreted in terms of sets. If $B \subseteq A$, $a = n(A)$, and $b = n(B)$, then $a - b$ is the number of elements that are in A but not in B. Let us consider the set $B = \{a, b, c\}$ and $A = \{a, b, c, d, e\}$. Referring to Figure 6.16.1, we see that $a =$

$n(A) = 5$, $b = n(B) = 3$, and $a - b = 2$, which is the number of elements that are in A but not in B. Therefore, $5 - 3 = 2$.

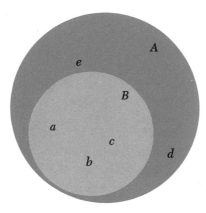

FIGURE 6.16.1

If set B is equal to set A, then $a = b$. In this case, the set of elements that are in A but not in B is the empty set $\varnothing$, and $a - b = 0$.

The restriction in the definition of subtraction requiring that a be greater than or equal to b is necessary since there is no whole number k such that $a - b = k$ if a is less than b. For example, $3 - 9 = k$ has no solution since $3 = 9 + k$ does not hold for any k in W. Since the operation of subtraction does not produce a whole number for *all* ordered pairs (a, b) in $W \times W$, the closure property does not hold for subtraction in W.

An example such as $5 - 3 \neq 3 - 5$ shows us that, in general, $a - b \neq b - a$ and subtraction is not commutative. Nor does the associative property hold for subtraction in W, for, in general, $(a - b) - c \neq a - (b - c)$. It is readily seen that $(8 - 5) - 2 \neq 8 - (5 - 2)$ since $(8 - 5) - 2 = 3 - 2 = 1$, while $8 - (5 - 2) = 8 - 3 = 5$.

With the properties of closure, commutativity, and associativity failing for subtraction in the whole numbers, it is somewhat refreshing to find that multiplication is distributive over subtraction. This property may be expressed by writing $a(b - c) = ab - ac$ and $(b - c)a = ba - ca$.

Example 1. Verify that the left distributive property holds for multiplication over subtraction by showing that $7(9 - 4) = 7 \cdot 9 - 7 \cdot 4$.

Solution:

$7(9 - 4) = 7 \cdot 5 = 35$, and

$7 \cdot 9 - 7 \cdot 4 = 63 - 28 = 35$.

Therefore, $7(9 - 4) = 7 \cdot 9 - 7 \cdot 4$.

The reader should be able to justify each of the above statements in the solution of Example 1 and also verify that the right distributive property holds for multiplication over subtraction.

EXERCISE 6.16

1. Define subtraction in the whole numbers.
2. (a) If $9 = 3 + 6$, what subtraction fact is determined by the definition of subtraction?
   (b) What other closely related subtraction fact may be determined by knowing that $3 + 6 = 6 + 3$?
3. Given set $A = \{a, b, c, d, e, f\}$ and set $B = \{a, b, c, d\}$, determine the value of $6 - 4$ by using a Venn diagram.
4. Closure does not hold for subtraction in W. What might be done to remedy the situation?
5. Give an example to show that the commutative property does not hold for subtraction.
6. Give an example to show that the operation of subtraction is not associative.
7. Illustrate by examples that both the left and right distributive properties hold for multiplication over subtraction.

6.17
Division in the Whole Numbers

As with subtraction, division may be defined in terms of another operation and, from this point of view, is not considered a fundamental operation. While subtraction is defined in terms of addition, division is defined in terms of multiplication.

DEFINITION 6.17.1

If a, b, and q are in W, and $b \neq 0$, $a \div b = q$ if and only if $a = bq$.

The expression $a \div b = q$ is read, "a divided by b is equal to q"; a is called the **dividend**, b the **divisor**, and q the **quotient**.

The restriction $b \neq 0$ in Definition 6.17.1 is quite necessary. First consider the case where $b = 0$ and $a \neq 0$. For example, when $a = 6$ we have $6 \div 0 = q$. By definition of division it is necessary that $6 = 0 \cdot q$ if the quotient q exists. However, there is no value for q satisfying this equation since $0 \cdot q = 0$ for all q, and it can be readily seen that $a \div 0$ is undefined for all $a \neq 0$.

Now suppose $a = 0$ and $b = 0$. Then $a \div b = 0 \div 0 = q$, and by the definition of division it is necessary that $0 = 0 \cdot q$ if q exists. But *all* whole numbers may be used as values of q in satisfying this equation, and the expression $0 \div 0$ is not uniquely determined. In fact, it could represent any whole number and hence has limited value. We say, therefore, that $a \div b$ is undefined if $b = 0$ and do not permit the operation of division by zero under any conditions. (Note, however, that $0 \div b = 0$ if $b \neq 0$. For example, $0 \div 5 = 0$.)

Frequently, $\frac{a}{b}$ or a/b is used to mean "a divided by b." For example, $8 \div 2 = \frac{8}{2} = 8/2 = 4$. We also say that 2 divides 8 since $8 = 2 \cdot 4$; "2 divides 8" may be written $2 \mid 8$. It should be emphasized that *divides* is a *relation* rather than an operation, even though it is defined in terms of an operation. Hence we may write $2 \mid 8$, but it is *incorrect* to write $2 \mid 8 = 4$. You will recall that the vertical bar $\mid$ is used in set notation to represent "such that." However, there should be no misunderstanding in also using the vertical bar to mean "divides" since the context in each case is quite different. The symbol $\nmid$ is read "does not divide."

DEFINITION 6.17.2

If $a \in W$ and $b \in N$, then b divides a, denoted by $b \mid a$, if and only if there exists a number c in W such that $a = bc$.

Although an extended definition may be given for the divides relation, we have purposely excluded $b = 0$ by saying $b \in N$. This means that $0 \nmid 0$ even though $0 = 0 \cdot c$. In this way the divides *relation* is consistent with the division *operation*. The divides relation is not symmetric, as will be seen by a single counterexample: $3 \mid 15$ but $15 \nmid 3$. Whether or not the divides relation is reflexive or transitive is left as an exercise for the reader.

In applying the definition of divides, we see that $3 \mid 12$ since $12 = 3 \cdot 4$, $6 \mid 6$ since $6 = 6 \cdot 1$, $4 \mid 0$ since $0 = 4 \cdot 0$, but $6 \nmid 17$ since $17 = 6 \cdot c$ is not satisfied for any c in W. Does $0 \mid 5$?

In studying the definition of division, it is seen that q exists for the equation $a = bq$ if and only if a is a multiple of b. For example, $16 = 5q$ has no solution for q in W because the multiples of 5 in W, $\{0, 5, 10, 15, 20, \ldots\}$, do not include the number 16. Since the operation of division does not assign a whole number to *all* ordered pairs (a, b) in $W \times W$, the closure property does not hold for division in W. Furthermore, $a \div b \neq b \div a$ except in special cases and hence division is not commutative. Is division associative? It is not, for in general, $(a \div b) \div c \neq a \div (b \div c)$. As an example, $(12 \div 6) \div 2 = 2 \div 2 = 1$, but $12 \div (6 \div 2) = 12 \div 3 = 4$. In summary, the properties of closure, commutativity, and associativity do not hold for division in the whole numbers.

Would you believe that the whole numbers have a right distributive property of division over addition? They do, but with rather severe restrictions and limitations. With the restriction $c \neq 0$, we can state that $(a + b) \div c = (a \div c) + (b \div c)$ *when division is possible*. The right distributive property of division over addition may also be written as

$$\frac{a + b}{c} = \frac{a}{c} + \frac{b}{c}$$

along with the appropriate restrictions and limitations.

Example 1.   Verify that the right distributive property of division over addition applies in the following case:

$$\frac{8 + 12}{4} = \frac{8}{4} + \frac{12}{4}.$$

Solution:

$$\frac{8 + 12}{4} = \frac{20}{4} = 5, \text{ and}$$

$$\frac{8}{4} + \frac{12}{4} = 2 + 3 = 5.$$

Therefore, $\dfrac{8 + 12}{4} = \dfrac{8}{4} + \dfrac{12}{4}.$

As mentioned, the right distributive property of division over addition has limitations when applied to the whole numbers. This may be illustrated by attempting to apply this property to the expression

$$\frac{9 + 3}{4} = \frac{9}{4} + \frac{3}{4}.$$

In so doing, we get

$$\frac{9+3}{4} = \frac{12}{4} = 3 \text{ and } \frac{9}{4} + \frac{3}{4} = ?$$

At this point we have some difficulty since the quotients $\frac{9}{4}$ and $\frac{3}{4}$ are not defined in W. However, if the number system is expanded to include the rational numbers (as discussed later), our problem is solved and we get: $\frac{9}{4} + \frac{3}{4} = \frac{12}{4} = 3$. By expanding our number system to include the rational numbers, we shall find that the right distributive property of division over addition holds with the sole restriction that the divisor $c \neq 0$.

EXERCISE 6.17

1. Define division in the whole numbers.

2. (a) Why do we bar division by zero when the dividend is not zero?
   (b) Why do we bar division by zero when the dividend is zero?
   (c) Under what conditions do we permit division by zero in the set of whole numbers?

3. What two different meanings have we given to the symbol $|$?

4. Which of the following properties hold for the operation of division in the whole numbers:
   (a) closure
   (b) commutativity
   (c) associativity

5. Which of the following ordered pairs are related by the "divides" relation?
   (a) $(2, 4)$ (b) $(4, 2)$
   (c) $(7, 7)$ (d) $(1, 1)$
   (e) $(3, 18)$ (f) $(0, 8)$
   (g) $(8, 0)$ (h) $(0, 0)$
   (i) $(0, 9)$ (j) $(9, 0)$

6. Prove whether or not the relation "divides" in the *natural* numbers is *reflexive, symmetric,* or *transitive.*

7. (a) Does $(6 + 12) \div 2 = (6 \div 2) + (12 \div 2)$?
   (b) Does $12 \div (2 + 4) = (12 \div 2) + (12 \div 4)$?

8. Give an example using whole numbers in which a *right* distributive property of division over addition is applicable.

9. Give an example using whole numbers in which a *right* distributive property of division over subtraction is applicable.

10. (a) Show by example that a *left* distributive property of division over addition does not hold.

    (b) Are there *any* whole numbers for which a left distributive property of division over addition would apply?

6.18
Properties
of Arbitrary
Binary
Operations

Having discussed some properties of specific binary operations, it seems appropriate to make a few general remarks concerning properties as they apply to arbitrary binary operations. Rather than considering familiar operations such as addition $(+)$ or multiplication $(\cdot)$, let us consider any two operations and call them "star" $(\star)$ and "triangle" $(\triangle)$. We shall also assume that $\star$ and $\triangle$ have been defined on an arbitrary set S. The reader's understanding of the following general definitions will be enhanced by his study of the preceding several sections of the text.

1. Closure

A set S is said to be *closed* under the binary operation $\star$ if, for any two elements a and b in S, there exists a unique element $a \star b$ in S.

2. The Commutative Property

The binary operation $\star$ is said to be *commutative* if $a \star b = b \star a$ for all a and b in S.

3. The Associative Property

The binary operation $\star$ is said to be *associative* if $(a \star b) \star c = a \star (b \star c)$ for all a, b, and c in S.

4. The Distributive Property

The binary operation $\star$ is said to be *distributive* over the binary operation $\triangle$ if $a \star (b \triangle c) = (a \star b) \triangle (a \star c)$ for all a, b, and c in S. This definition is known as the *left distributive property*. Similarly, $(b \triangle c) \star a = (b \star a) \triangle (c \star a)$ for all a, b, and c in S is called the *right distributive property*. As you know, both the left and right distributive properties hold for multiplication over addition.

5. The Existence of an Identity Element

The set S is said to contain an *identity element* with respect to the binary operation $\star$ if there is some element i in S such that $a \star i = i \star a = a$ for every a in S. In some systems, for a given operation, we may have a right or a left identity element, but not both. If a set S has a right identity element for the operation $\star$, then there is some element i

in S such that $a \star i = a$ for every a in S. Similarly, if a set S has a left identity element for the operation $\star$, then there is some element i in S such that $i \star a = a$ for every a in S.

6. Inverses

An element a in S is said to have an *inverse* with respect to the binary operation $\star$ if there is an element a^{-1} in S such that $a \star a^{-1} = a^{-1} \star a = i$. In this definition a^{-1} is read "a inverse," and the operation $\star$ assigns to the element and its inverse the identity element for that operation.

In general, members of the whole numbers have neither additive inverses nor multiplicative inverses. However, if we expand our number system to include negative numbers and rational numbers, we have both additive inverses and multiplicative inverses. For example, the additive inverse of 3 is $^-3$, and $3 + {}^-3 = 0$ (the additive identity). The multiplicative inverse of $\frac{2}{3}$ is $\frac{3}{2}$, and $\frac{2}{3} \cdot \frac{3}{2} = 1$ (the multiplicative identity). Inverse elements will be discussed further at the appropriate time.

EXERCISE 6.18

1. For the operation $\star$, define closure in the set S.

2. For the operation $\odot$, define the commutative property for the set A.

3. (a) State the left distributive property of multiplication over addition in W.
   (b) State the left distributive property of $\odot$ over $\star$ in W.

4. (a) What is meant by having an identity element for the operation of addition in W?
   (b) What is meant by having an identity element for the operation of $\triangle$ in W?

5. Is zero a right identity element for addition in W or a left identity element?

6. (a) Does the set of whole numbers have an identity element for the subtraction operation?
   (b) If so, what is the element?
   (c) Is the element a right or a left identity element?

6.19

The System

of

Whole Numbers

A number system consists of a set of elements called numbers and operations defined on the set of numbers. In accordance with the defined operations, various properties of the system may be deduced or in some way determined. In this chapter the *system of whole numbers* was established by defining operations on the set of whole numbers. The essential features of this system are summarized below.

DEFINITION 6.19.1

The system of whole numbers consists of the set $W = \{0, 1, 2, 3, 4, \ldots\}$ and the binary operations of addition $(+)$ and multiplication $(\cdot)$. The system has the following properties for any a, b, and c in W:

Closure Properties
1. There is a uniquely determined sum $a + b$ in W.
2. There is a uniquely determined product $a \cdot b$ in W.

Commutative Properties
3. $a + b = b + a$
4. $a \cdot b = b \cdot a$

Associative Properties
5. $(a + b) + c = a + (b + c)$
6. $(a \cdot b) \cdot c = a \cdot (b \cdot c)$

Distributive Property of Multiplication over Addition
7. $a \cdot (b + c) = a \cdot b + a \cdot c$ (left distributive property)
   $(b + c) \cdot a = b \cdot a + c \cdot a$ (right distributive property)

Identity Elements
8. There exists a unique element 0 such that for any a in W, $a + 0 = 0 + a = a$.
9. There exists a unique element 1 such that for any a in W, $a \cdot 1 = 1 \cdot a = a$.

EXERCISE 6.19

1. Describe briefly the meaning of the term *number system*.
2. (a) What two *fundamental* operations are defined in the set of whole numbers?
   (b) Why are subtraction and division not considered fundamental operations in the same sense as addition and multiplication? Refer back to Sections 6.16 and 6.17 if necessary.
3. Summarize the properties of the system of whole numbers, using a, b, c, and so forth to abbreviate your statements.
4. Indicate briefly the difference between a *numeration system* and a *number system*.

6.20
Order
Relations

If you have ever arranged a list of people's names in alphabetical order, you know that it can be done by comparing the names two at a time to determine which of each pair should come first. Eventually, by this process of finding the relationship between pairs, the entire set can be ordered. If the same set of names were arranged according to each person's height, age, or weight, rather than alphabetically, some other order for the same set would probably result. Different order relations may order the elements of a set in different ways.

In Chapter 3 we defined a relation as follows: Given two sets A and B, a relation in $A \times B$ is a subset of $A \times B$. However, if $A = B$, then we have a relation in $A \times A$ which may simply be called a relation in A. Some relations in A may order the elements of the set. Any relation that orders a set is called an order relation. A relation that orders a given set may or may not order some other set. For example, if we have three boys with the same names, no order would result if we were to try to order the boys in correspondence with an alphabetical listing of their names. However, this would not be the case with most sets of three boys.

Consider the set of numerals $A = \{21, 73, 459\}$. For a and b in A, $a \,\mathcal{R}\, b$ is defined to mean "a has a larger initial digit than b." The Cartesian product set $A \times A = \{(21, 21), (21, 73), (21, 459), (73, 21), (73, 73), (73, 459), (459, 21), (459, 73), (459, 459)\}$. The order relation $\mathcal{R}$ is the subset of $A \times A$ consisting of only those ordered pairs (a, b) in $A \times A$ that satisfy the relational phrase, "a has a larger initial digit than b." Hence $\mathcal{R} = \{(73, 21), (73, 459), (459, 21)\}$. The first ordered pair $(73, 21)$ tells us that 73 comes before 21, the next tells us that 73 comes before 459, and the last tells us that 459 comes before 21. With these restrictions, the elements of set A can be arranged from left to right in only one way, and we obtain the ordered set $(73, 459, 21)$. Parentheses, rather than braces, are used to indicate that the set is ordered. Note that the initial digit of any numeral in the ordered set is larger than the initial digit of every numeral to its right.

The reader certainly realizes by now that it is not necessary to write out in roster form the entire product set $A \times A$, or even the order relation set $\mathcal{R}$, to be able to order a set with a small number of elements. However, for illustrative purposes, these details were included in the discussion above.

Example 1. Given the set of people $S = \{a, b, c, d\}$, use the data of the chart below to order the set according to the given relations.

Person	Height	Weight	Age	Number of Children
a	62	110	28	4
b	60	115	26	1
c	63	120	18	0
d	68	140	20	1

(a) $x \mathcal{R} y$ if x is taller than y.

Solution: (d, c, a, b)

(b) $x \mathcal{R} y$ if x weighs less than y.

Solution: (a, b, c, d)

(c) $x \mathcal{R} y$ if x weighs more than y.

Solution: (d, c, b, a)

(d) $x \mathcal{R} y$ if x is younger than y.

Solution: (c, d, b, a)

(e) $x \mathcal{R} y$ if x has more children than y.

Solution: Since b and d have the same number of children, $b \not{\mathcal{R}} d$ and $d \not{\mathcal{R}} b$. We see that a precedes b and d and that b and d precede c. Neither b nor d comes first, however, since neither has more children than the other. Hence we can only "partially order" the set, and a diagram such as $a \overset{b}{\underset{d}{<{\;}>}} c$ may be used.

6.21
Ordering the Whole Numbers

The less than relation is an order relation for the whole numbers. Although we have assumed an intuitive comprehension of the concept of one number being less than another, a precise definition is needed. After defining "less than," we shall discuss some of its properties and implications for the whole numbers.

DEFINITION 6.21.1

If a and b are in W, a is less than b, denoted by $a < b$, if and only if there exists a natural number c such that $a + c = b$.

DEFINITION 6.21.2

If a and b are in W, a is greater than b, denoted by $a > b$, if and only if b is less than a.

Example 1. We can state that $7 < 10$ if there is a natural number c such that $7 + c = 10$. In this case such a number does exist since $7 + 3 = 10$, and the statement $7 < 10$ is true. From Definition 6.21.2, we may also state that $10 > 7$ since $7 < 10$.

Example 2. Since Definition 6.21.1 is an "if and only if " statement, we may reason as follows: If $8 + 2 = 10$, then $8 < 10$.

Example 3. In attempting to prove $8 < 8$, it must be shown that there exists a natural number c such that $8 + c = 8$. However, in this case $c = 0$ (the additive identity) and $c \notin N$. Therefore, $8 \not< 8$, but $8 = 8$.

It is seen from Definitions 6.21.1 and 6.21.2 that statements such as $2 < 7$ and $7 > 2$ are equivalent. If we combine the *equals* relation with the *less than* relation or with the *greater than* relation, we can find more equivalent statements. For example, $\leq$ is the "less than or equal to" relation, and $a \leq b$ means the same as $a \not> b$ or $b \not< a$ or $b \geq a$. We read $b \geq a$ as "b is greater than or equal to a."

The definitions for "less than," "equals," and "greater than" lead to an important property for the whole numbers called the *trichotomy law*. Each of the ordered pairs (a, b) in the product set $W \times W = \{(0, 0),$ $(0, 1), (0, 2), \ldots, (1, 0), (1, 1), (1, 2), \ldots, (2, 0), (2, 1), (2, 2), \ldots, (n, 0),$ $(n, 1), (n, 2), \ldots\}$ may be placed in exactly one of three disjoint subsets of $W \times W$ depending upon which one of the three relations $a = b, a < b$, or $a > b$ is satisfied. A formal statement of the trichotomy law follows.

The Trichotomy Law for Whole Numbers. For a and b in W, exactly one of the following is true:

1. $a = b$
2. $a < b$
3. $a > b$

In studying the "less than" relation for whole numbers together with the trichotomy law, it will be seen that the following properties hold for a, b, and c in W:

1. $a \not< a$ ($<$ is *irreflexive*).
2. If $a < b$, then $b \not< a$ ($<$ is *asymmetric*).
3. If $a < b$ and $b < c$, then $a < c$ ($<$ is *transitive*).
4. For distinct elements a and b in W, either $a < b$ or $b < a$ ($<$ is *connected*).

Since the reader is already familiar with the reflexive, symmetric, and transitive properties, the properties of the "less than" relation should be easily understood.

Example 4. Prove the transitive property for the relation $<$ defined in the whole numbers.

Given: $a < b$ and $b < c$

To prove: $a < c$

Proof:

1. $a + k_1 = b, \ k_1 \in N$	1. Definition of $<$
2. $b + k_2 = c, \ k_2 \in N$	2. Definition of $<$
3. $(a + k_1) + (b + k_2) = b + c$	3. Substitution property
4. $(a + k_1 + k_2) + b = c + b$	4. Commutative and associative properties of addition
5. $a + (k_1 + k_2) = c$	5. Cancellation and associative properties of addition
6. $k_1 + k_2 = m, \ m \in N$	6. Closure for addition in N
7. $a + m = c, \ m \in N$	7. Substitution property
8. $a < c$	8. Definition of $<$

Example 5. Using the $<$ relation, order the following subset of W: $\{12, 9, 10, 2, 7, 18\}$.

Solution: $(2, 7, 9, 10, 12, 18)$

The expression $a < b$ *and* $b < c$ may be abbreviated by writing $a < b < c$. In fact, using the order relation "less than," we may write $0 < 1 < 2 < 3 < 4 < 5 < 6 \ldots$ for the set of whole numbers.

A relation such as the less than relation for the whole numbers is said to linearly order the set on which it is defined. An order relation that linearly orders a set is irreflexive, asymmetric, transitive, and connected. In a linearly ordered set it is always possible to designate which of two distinct elements comes first. (Incidentally, there is not complete uniformity among authors in defining various types of order relations. Therefore, in reading other texts, it is important to check carefully the definitions being used.)

The word *linear* is, of course, derived from the word *line*. When members of the linearly ordered set $(0, 1, 2, 3, 4, \ldots)$ are placed in a one-to-one correspondence with "equally spaced" points on a line, we have what is called the number line, as illustrated below:

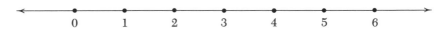

Zero is associated with some arbitrary point on the line, and 1 is associated with some convenient but arbitrary point to the right of 0. The number 2 is associated with a point to the right of 1 such that the distance from 1 to 2 is the same as the distance from 0 to 1. An analogous method is used to locate points corresponding to 3, 4, 5, and so on. Note that the word "distance" is left as an undefined term. The number line has many applications and will be used frequently throughout the text. Henceforth, we shall feel free to refer to any point on the number line in terms of the number with which it corresponds—the point 0, the point 1, the point 2, and so forth. A number k such that $a < k < b$ is said to be between a and b. On the number line, the point k will be to the right of a and to the left of b.

> **Example 6.** The set of numbers in W *between* 4 and 9 is $\{5, 6, 7, 8\}$. We can also write $4 < 5 < 6 < 7 < 8 < 9$.

In mathematics and in its applications to everyday problems, we are frequently interested in dealing with inequalities as well as with equalities. Certain basic theorems aid greatly in arriving at conclusions where inequalities are involved. A few such theorems are presented here. These theorems are exactly what we would expect to be true on the basis of inductive reasoning.

THEOREM 6.21.1

If a, b, and c are in W and if $a < b$, then $a + c < b + c$.

Proof:

1. $a < b$	1. Given
2. $a + k = b, k \in N$	2. Definition of $<$

3. $(a + k) + c = b + c$	3. Substitution property
4. $a + (k + c) = b + c$	4. Associative property of addition
5. $a + (c + k) = b + c$	5. Commutative property of addition
6. $(a + c) + k = b + c$	6. Associative property of addition
7. $a + c < b + c$	7. Definition of $<$

The converse of Theorem 6.21.1 is also true and will now be proved.

THEOREM 6.21.2

If a, b, and c are in W and if $a + c < b + c$, then $a < b$.

Proof:

1. $a + c < b + c$	1. Given
2. $(a + c) + k = b + c, k \in N$	2. Definition of $<$
3. $(a + k) + c = b + c$	3. Commutative and associative properties of addition
4. $a + k = b$	4. Cancellation property of addition
5. $a < b$	5. Definition of $<$

THEOREM 6.21.3

If a, b, and c are in W with $c \neq 0$ and $a < b$, then $ca < cb$.

Proof:

1. $a < b$	1. Given
2. $a + k = b, k \in N$	2. Definition of $<$
3. $c(a + k) = cb$	3. Substitution property
4. $ca + ck = cb$	4. Distributive property
5. $ck \in N$	5. Closure for multiplication in N
6. $ca < cb$	6. Definition of $<$

The converse of Theorem 6.21.3, which we state without proof, is also true. The proof will be given in the chapter on rational numbers.

THEOREM 6.21.4

If a, b, and c are in W with $c \neq 0$ and $ca < cb$, then $a < b$.

Example 7. Find the set of whole numbers for which $6 + n < 94$.

Solution:

1. $6 + n < 94$ 1. Given
2. $n + 6 < 94$ 2. Commutative property of addition
3. $n + 6 < 88 + 6$ 3. Addition facts
4. $n < 88$ 4. Theorem 6.21.2
5. Hence $n = 0, 1, 2, \ldots, 87$ 5. Definition of $<$
   or any of the elements of
   $\{n \mid 0 \leq n < 88\}$

EXERCISE 6.21

1. Define the order relation $<$ for the whole numbers.
2. Define the order relation $>$ for the whole numbers.
3. Given $S = \{a, b, c, d, e\}$, where $a = 5, b = 7, c = 9, d = 2$, and $e = 4$, order S if for x and y in S, $x \, \mathcal{R} \, y$ is defined as "x is less than y."
4. Order the set S in problem 3 if $x \, \mathcal{R} \, y$ is defined as "x is greater than y."
5. Order the set $S = \{7, 9, 25, 62, 4\}$ according to the relation $a \, \mathcal{R} \, b$ if $a \, \mathcal{R} \, b$ means that a is greater than b.
6. If $a \, \mathcal{R} \, b$ means that a has a larger terminal digit than b, order the set $C = \{7, 192, 43, 65, 49\}$.
7. (a) Can set C in problem 6 be linearly ordered according to the relation "is a larger number than"?
   (b) Can C be linearly ordered according to the relation "has a smaller initial digit than"? Explain.
8. Identify the set of whole numbers satisfying the following inequalities:
   (a) $x + 3 < 5$ (b) $x + 4 > 7$
   (c) $x + 2 < 40$ (d) $3x + 4 < 67$
   (e) $79 > 9x + 7$ (f) $8x + 4 < 28$
9. Given the set $A = \{(1, 3), (4, 2), (3, 3), (7, 5), (6, 2), (1, 1), (1, 7), (4, 9)\}$, use the roster method to identify the disjoint subsets A_1, A_2, and A_3, depending upon which one of the following three relations is satisfied for each ordered pair (a, b) in A: $a = b$, $a < b$, or $a > b$.
10. Which of the properties of an equivalence relation hold for the relation "greater than" defined on the whole numbers?

11. What are the elements of $\{n \mid (n \in W) \land (3 < n \leq 7)\}$?

12. How many solutions exist for the inequality $7 + n < 10$ if $n \in W$? If $n \subset N$?

13. (a) What is the largest whole number?
    (b) What is the smallest whole number?

14. For a, b, and c in W, prove that if $a < b$, then $a + c < b + c$.

15. For a and b in W and c in N, prove that if $a < b$, then $ac < bc$.

16. Which of the four properties—irreflexive, asymmetric, transitive, and connected—hold for the relation "comes before" as it is applied to the set of letters of our alphabet?

17. Show that the irreflexive and transitive properties of an order relation imply the asymmetric property. *Hint:* If a and b are in S and both $a \mathcal{R} b$ and $b \mathcal{R} a$ are assumed to hold for a relation in S, what does the truth of the transitive property imply?

REVIEW EXERCISES

1. Tell what is meant by inductive reasoning and give an example.

2. Can deductive reasoning lead to a false conclusion? Explain.

3. (a) What is a proof by counterexample?
   (b) Give a simple illustration.

4. (a) What conditions are necessary for an operation in a number system to have the property of closure?
   (b) Explain why the operation of subtraction in the whole numbers does not have the property of closure.

5. (a) Prove by using a counterexample that subtraction in the whole numbers is not commutative.
   (b) Prove by using a counterexample that subtraction in the whole numbers is not associative.

6. Show that 0 is unique as the additive identity element in the system of whole numbers.

7. Show that 1 is unique as the multiplicative identity element in the system of whole numbers.

8. Prove that if $a = b$, then $a + c = b + c$.

9. (a) Define $A \cup B$ if A and B are sets.
   (b) Define $A \times B$ if A and B are sets.
   (c) Define addition in the whole numbers.
   (d) Define subtraction in the whole numbers.
   (e) Define multiplication in the whole numbers.
   (f) Define division in the whole numbers.
   (g) Define the order relation $<$ for the whole numbers.

10. Outline briefly the system of whole numbers including its essential properties.

Chapter Seven

Algorithms for
the Whole Numbers

7.1
Introduction

In Chapter 6 we defined operations on the whole numbers and studied the properties of these operations. In this chapter we shall use these definitions and properties and our system of numeration to develop meaningful and efficient methods for finding sums, differences, products, and quotients. No attempt is made to consider all methods of manipulation, but it is hoped that the student will be reasonably able to justify certain arithmetical manipulations which are, due to practice and in the interest of speed, frequently performed by rote. We would not want to justify each step every time we find a product or a quotient, but it is heartening to be able to rationalize our actions.

The word algorithm refers to the particular method and symbolism used in performing an operation in mathematics. Many different algorithms have been developed for the same operation, and in many cases an algorithm is chosen as a matter of convenience or personal preference. The nature and types of algorithms that may be devised for performing operations in any mathematical system are determined primarily by the definitions of the operations, their properties, and the system of numeration that is used. As a result, the algorithms used in our decimal system can also be used in other place value systems analogous to it.

7.2
Algorithms of Addition

No special algorithms are needed for adding single-digit numbers since their sums are usually memorized or may be found by referring to a table of elementary facts such as Figure 7.2.1. The sums indicated in the addition table can be found by using the definition of addition given in terms of sets (Definition 6.4.2). The table, of course, could be enlarged to include sums of addends of two or more digits, but this is not necessary since we develop algorithms to perform such operations.

Instead of using sets to determine the sums, we could find sums by interpreting addition as measurement on the number line. In Figure 7.2.2, for example, the number line is used to determine the sum $4 + 3$. Note that the number 4 is represented by a distance of four units along the number line beginning at the point 0. The number 3 is represented by a distance of three units along the number line beginning at the point 4. Taken together, the distances extend from 0 to 7, and we conclude that $3 + 4 = 7$. The same technique could be used to find $32 + 57$ or $3429 + 2,735,524$, but the disadvantages of this method are apparent.

By using the properties of our decimal system of numeration (Section 5.7) and the properties of our number system (Section 6.19), we can

+	0	1	2	3	4	5	6	7	8	9
0	0	1	2	3	4	5	6	7	8	9
1	1	2	3	4	5	6	7	8	9	10
2	2	3	4	5	6	7	8	9	10	11
3	3	4	5	6	7	8	9	10	11	12
4	4	5	6	7	8	9	10	11	12	13
5	5	6	7	8	9	10	11	12	13	14
6	6	7	8	9	10	11	12	13	14	15
7	7	8	9	10	11	12	13	14	15	16
8	8	9	10	11	12	13	14	15	16	17
9	9	10	11	12	13	14	15	16	17	18

Addition Table

FIGURE 7.2.1

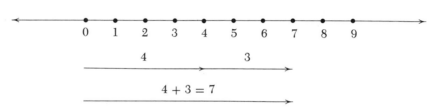

$$4 + 3 = 7$$

FIGURE 7.2.2

develop algorithms so that numbers of two or more digits can be added rapidly. We shall illustrate by finding the sum of 32 and 57.

Assertions and Reasons

1. $32 + 57 = (3 \cdot 10^1 + 2 \cdot 10^0) + (5 \cdot 10^1 + 7 \cdot 10^0)$ by the decimal system of numeration.

2. $(3 \cdot 10^1 + 2 \cdot 10^0) + (5 \cdot 10^1 + 7 \cdot 10^0) = (3 \cdot 10^1 + 5 \cdot 10^1) + (2 \cdot 10^0 + 7 \cdot 10^0)$ by the associative and commutative properties of addition.

3. $(3 \cdot 10^1 + 5 \cdot 10^1) + (2 \cdot 10^0 + 7 \cdot 10^0) = (3 + 5) \cdot 10^1 + (2 + 7) \cdot 10^0$ by the distributive property.

4. $(3 + 5) \cdot 10^1 + (2 + 7) \cdot 10^0 = 8 \cdot 10^1 + 9 \cdot 10^0$ by the table of elementary facts.

5. $8 \cdot 10^1 + 9 \cdot 10^0 = 89$ by the decimal system of numeration.

6. $32 + 57 = 89$ by the transitive property of equals.

The above statements justify the usual algorithm for addition in which the sums $2 + 7 = 9$ and $3 + 5 = 8$ are used to determine the sum of 32 and 57, as indicated below.

$$\begin{array}{r} 32 \\ 57 \\ \hline 89 \end{array}$$

In finding the sum $32 + 57$, there is no need to "carry" or *rename*. However, the usual algorithm for addition can also be justified where renaming certain numbers is involved. We shall find the sum of 64 and 29 as an example.

Assertions	*Reasons*
1. $64 + 29 = (6 \cdot 10^1 + 4 \cdot 10^0) + (2 \cdot 10^1 + 9 \cdot 10^0)$	1. System of numeration
2. $\quad = (6 \cdot 10^1 + 2 \cdot 10^1) + (4 \cdot 10^0 + 9 \cdot 10^0)$	2. Commutative and associative properties of addition
3. $\quad = (6 + 2) \cdot 10^1 + (4 + 9) \cdot 10^0$	3. Distributive property
4. $\quad = 8 \cdot 10^1 + 13 \cdot 10^0$	4. Table of elementary facts
5. $\quad = 8 \cdot 10^1 + (1 \cdot 10^1 + 3) \cdot 10^0$	5. System of numeration (renaming)
6. $\quad = 8 \cdot 10^1 + (1 \cdot 10^1) \cdot 10^0 + 3 \cdot 10^0$	6. Distributive property
7. $\quad = 8 \cdot 10^1 + 1 \cdot (10^1 \cdot 10^0) + 3 \cdot 10^0$	7. Associative property of multiplication
8. $\quad = 8 \cdot 10^1 + 1 \cdot 10^1 + 3 \cdot 10^0$	8. Law of exponents
9. $\quad = (8 + 1) \cdot 10^1 + 3 \cdot 10^0$	9. Distributive property
10. $\quad = 9 \cdot 10^1 + 3 \cdot 10^0$	10. Table of elementary facts
11. $\quad = 93$	11. System of numeration
12. $64 + 29 = 93$	12. Transitive property of equals

The above steps justify the conventional algorithm that follows:

"Carry" 1 (ten) or
rename $4 + 9 = 13$ as $10 + 3 \longrightarrow$ 1
64
29
―
93

Many teachers and authors use the words "rename" or "regroup" in place of "carry" since they seem to describe more accurately the computational procedure involved.

The method for finding the sum of two two-digit addends can readily be extended to find the sum of three or more addends with any number of digits and will not be discussed here.

EXERCISE 7.2

1. What is an algorithm?

2. Find each of the following sums by using a number line:
   (a) $3 + 5$
   (b) $4 + 1$
   (c) $4 + 1 + 2$

3. By using properties of the decimal system of numeration and properties of the system of whole numbers, justify the usual algorithm for finding the sum of $152 + 27$.

4. (a) In finding the sum $143 + 3 + 72{,}745 + 342$, why do we align the numerals on the right rather than on the left?
   (b) Find the sum indicated in part (a) and indicate the reasons underlying the process rather than responding purely by rote.

5. How can you justify having four addends in problem 4 if addition is a binary operation? (If necessary, refer to Section 6.7.)

7.3
Algorithms of Subtraction

The operation of addition assigns to an ordered pair of numbers a unique number called their sum. When a sum and one addend are given, the operation of finding the other addend is called subtraction. This concept is consistent with the formal definition of subtraction stated in Section 6.16.

If we limit our set of elements to the whole numbers, subtraction is possible only when the sum is greater than or equal to the given addend. Therefore, closure does not hold for subtraction in the whole numbers. As an example, $7 - 12$ is not associated with any whole number since no whole number added to 12 will produce a sum of 7. As noted earlier in the text, the commutative and associative properties also fail to hold for subtraction.

In a subtraction problem, the sum is called the minuend, the given addend is called the subtrahend, and the addend to be found is called the difference. As an example, in the statement $14 - 6 = 8$, 14 is the minuend, 6 is the subtrahend, and 8 is the difference. The conventional algorithm for finding the difference $65 - 42$ is shown below.

$$
\begin{array}{ll}
65 & \text{minuend (sum)} \\
42 & \text{subtrahend (known addend)} \\
\hline
23 & \text{difference (missing addend)}
\end{array}
$$

Note that in the above problem it is not necessary to know more than the basic facts and procedures for addition to find the difference 23. By answering the questions "What number added to 2 will produce 5?" and "What number added to 4 will produce 6?" we can find the difference 23. However, suppose we have a problem in subtraction such as the one below.

$$
\begin{array}{l}
\text{"Borrow" 1 (ten) or} \\
\textit{rename } 94 \text{ as } 80 + 14
\end{array}
\longrightarrow
\begin{array}{r}
8 \\
\cancel{9}{}^{1}4 \\
3\ 8 \\
\hline
5\ 6
\end{array}
$$

In this case there is no whole number which can be added to 8 to produce a sum of 4. We can, however, *rename* 94 (equal to $90 + 4$) as $80 + 14$; this process is sometimes referred to as "borrowing" 10 from the 90 and adding it to the 4. Then, noting that $8 + 6 = 14$ and $3 + 5 = 8$, we can determine that the missing addend is 56 (the difference). (The use of an *abacus* or *bead frame* is most helpful in learning and teaching the concepts of regrouping sets and renaming numbers.)

Addition and subtraction are called inverse operations because each "undoes" what the other "does." For example, if we start with an arbitrary number such as 14 and then add 5 and subtract 5 successively, the result of these operations is the original number, 14: $(14 + 5) - 5 = 14$; also, $(14 - 5) + 5 = 14$. In general, $(a + b) - b = (a - b) + b = a$. As you probably know, inverse operations are frequently used as checks on each other to identify possible computational errors.

The number line was used to identify the sum of two whole numbers. In a similar way it may also be used to find the difference of two whole numbers. Consider the difference $8 - 3$. Referring to Figure 7.3.1, we see that 8 is represented as measuring a distance of eight units along

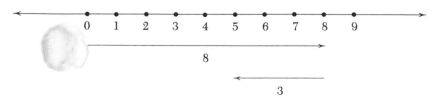

FIGURE 7.3.1

the number line beginning at the point 0 and moving to the *right*. Then, since 3 is to be subtracted from 8 (rather than added), we start at the point 8 and proceed three units to the *left* along the number line. The terminal point is observed to be 5 and we conclude that $8 - 3 = 5$. Obvious disadvantages result in using this technique with large numbers and we resort to using other, more productive, techniques as previously described.

  There are two common approaches to the operation of subtraction. For example, if we wish to find $8 - 3$, we may think of "taking away" 3 units from 8, or we may ask what number must be "added to" 3 to result in the sum of 8. In the text we have used the "additive" method of subtraction, but many problems lend themselves quite naturally to the "take away" interpretation. Both methods are referred to in the following exercises.

EXERCISE 7.3

1. A woman has $50 and spends $38 for a dress. She wishes to compute the amount of money she has left. Does this problem lend itself better to the "take away" or the "additive" interpretation of subtraction?

2. A man has $50. He wishes to know how much more money he needs in order to buy a radio costing $62. Does this problem lend itself better to the "take away" or the "additive" interpretation of subtraction?

3. Explain how a set of blocks or other objects might be used in teaching children the "additive" method of subtraction that is used in the text.

4. Explain how a set of blocks or other objects might be used in teaching children the familiar "take away" method of subtracting.

5. Evaluate each of the following, using a number line:
   (a) $5 - 3$ (b) $6 - 6$
   (c) $(8 - 4) - 2$ (d) $8 - (4 - 2)$
   (e) $(8 - 6) + 1$ (f) $(8 + 2) - 2$

6. Find the following differences and mentally justify each step in your algorithms.
   (a) $642 - 87$
   (b) $804 - 38$
   (c) $600,004 - 5648$

7. (a) Evaluate $(10 - 4) - 3$ and $10 - (4 - 3)$.

   (b) From part (a), what do you conclude concerning associativity for subtraction?

7.4

Algorithms
of
Multiplication

As in the case of addition, no special algorithms are needed for multiplying single-digit numbers since their products are usually memorized or may be found by referring to a table of elementary facts. Such a table appears in Figure 7.4.1.

·	0	1	2	3	4	5	6	7	8	9
0	0	0	0	0	0	0	0	0	0	0
1	0	1	2	3	4	5	6	7	8	9
2	0	2	4	6	8	10	12	14	16	18
3	0	3	6	9	12	15	18	21	24	27
4	0	4	8	12	16	20	24	28	32	36
5	0	5	10	15	20	25	30	35	40	45
6	0	6	12	18	24	30	36	42	48	54
7	0	7	14	21	28	35	42	49	56	63
8	0	8	16	24	32	40	48	56	64	72
9	0	9	18	27	36	45	54	63	72	81

Multiplication Table

FIGURE 7.4.1

Now let us examine the familiar multiplication algorithm and see what is involved in finding the standard numeral for a product such as $2 \cdot 36$.

Assertions	*Reasons*
1. $2 \cdot 36 = 2 \cdot (3 \cdot 10^1 + 6 \cdot 10^0)$	1. System of numeration
2. $= 2 \cdot (3 \cdot 10^1) + 2 \cdot (6 \cdot 10^0)$	2. Distributive property
3. $= (2 \cdot 3) \cdot 10^1 + (2 \cdot 6) \cdot 10^0$	3. Associative property of multiplication

	Assertions	*Reasons*
4.	$= 6 \cdot 10^1 + 12 \cdot 10^0$	4. Table of elementary facts
5.	$= 6 \cdot 10^1 + (10^1 + 2) \cdot 10^0$	5. System of numeration (renaming)
6.	$= 6 \cdot 10^1 + 1 \cdot 10^1 + 2 \cdot 10^0$	6. Distributive property
7.	$= (6 \cdot 10^1 + 1 \cdot 10^1) + 2 \cdot 10^0$	7. Associative property of addition
8.	$= (6 + 1) \cdot 10^1 + 2 \cdot 10^0$	8. Distributive property
9.	$= 7 \cdot 10^1 + 2 \cdot 10^0$	9. Table of elementary facts
10.	$= 72$	10. System of numeration
11.	$2 \cdot 36 = 72$	11. Transitive property of equals

Note that in the above proof only the principal reasons are given to justify each step. To justify step 6, for example, not only is the distributive property used but also the commutative property of multiplication and the fact that $10^0 = 1$. It is common in mathematics to omit writing some of the more obvious justifications for certain assertions. If such things as the commutative properties of addition and multiplication or the properties of equality were mentioned every time they were used in a text, it would make such a thick book and such dull reading that no one would want to either publish it or read it. Henceforth in this text it will be assumed that the reader will take the initiative in justifying some of the assertions in proofs.

Referring back to the proof above, we see that it justifies the common algorithm for multiplication, which appears below for $2 \cdot 36$.

$$\text{"Carry" 1 (ten) or}$$
$$\textit{rename } 2 \cdot 6 = 12 \text{ as } 10 + 2 \longrightarrow \quad \begin{array}{r} 1 \\ 36 \\ 2 \\ \hline 72 \end{array}$$

The common algorithm has the advantage of brevity, but the role of the distributive property is more evident if the following algorithm is written for the product $2 \cdot 36$.

$$36$$
$$\underline{2}$$
$$\overline{12} = 2 \times 6$$
$$\underline{60} = 2 \times 30$$
$$\overline{72} = 2 \times (30 + 6) = (2 \times 30) + (2 \times 6)$$

We shall want to examine the procedure for finding the product of two two-digit numbers, but first it is desirable to discuss the multiplication of a number by ten raised to some power: 10^1, 10^2, 10^3, and so forth. You are probably familiar with the method of multiplying a number by 10, 100, and so on, by annexing the appropriate number of zeros to its numeral. However, you should be able to justify this procedure. As an example, we shall show that $10 \cdot 438$ is equal to 4380.

Assertions	Reasons
1. $10 \cdot 438 = 438 \cdot 10$	1. Commutative property of multiplication
2. $= (4 \cdot 10^2 + 3 \cdot 10^1 + 8 \cdot 10^0) \cdot 10^1$	2. System of numeration
3. $= 4 \cdot 10^3 + 3 \cdot 10^2 + 8 \cdot 10^1$	3. Distributive property
4. $= 4 \cdot 10^3 + 3 \cdot 10^2 + 8 \cdot 10^1 + 0 \cdot 10^0$	4. $0 \cdot 10^0 = 0$, and 0 is the additive identity
5. $= 4380$	5. System of numeration
6. $10 \cdot 438 = 4380$	6. Transitive property of equals

The product $10 \cdot 438$ could have been determined simply by *annexing* a zero to 438. Note that we say *annex* and not *add,* for if zero is added to 438, the result is 438 since zero is the identity element for addition. Hence the word annex is used advisedly! By a similar line of reasoning it can be seen that a number may be multiplied by 100 by annexing two zeros to its numeral, by 1000 by annexing three zeros, and so on. We are now ready to examine the procedure for finding the product of two two-digit numbers, such as $43 \cdot 62$.

Assertions	Reasons
1. $43 \cdot 62 = (40 + 3) \cdot 62$	1. System of numeration
2. $= (40 \cdot 62) + (3 \cdot 62)$	2. Distributive property
3. $= [(10 \cdot 4) \cdot 62] + (3 \cdot 62)$	3. System of numeration

	Assertions	*Reasons*

4. $= [10 \cdot (4 \cdot 62)] + (3 \cdot 62)$ — 4. Associative property of multiplication

5. $= [10 \cdot 248] + 186$ — 5. Multiplication by a single-digit factor (previously justified)

6. $= 2480 + 186$ — 6. Multiplication by 10

7. $= 2666$ — 7. Addition algorithm

8. $43 \cdot 62 = 2666$ — 8. Transitive property of equals

From the steps above, we can readily justify the common algorithm for multiplication, as shown below, and see clearly the role of the distributive property in this operation.

$$
\begin{array}{r}
62 \\
43 \\
\hline
186 = 3 \times 62 \\
2480 = 40 \times 62 \\
\hline
2666 = (40 + 3) \times 62 = (40 \times 62) + (3 \times 62)
\end{array}
$$

Another algorithm that helps greatly in understanding the conventional algorithm is shown below on the left. Note that each pair of steps with braces is combined into a single step, resulting in the numbers 186 and 2480, as shown in the condensed algorithm on the right.

$$
\begin{array}{r}
62 \\
43 \\
\hline
6 = 3 \times 2 \ \Big\} \ 186 \\
180 = 3 \times 60 \\
80 = 40 \times 2 \ \Big\} \ 2480 \\
2400 = 40 \times 60 \\
\hline
2666
\end{array}
\qquad
\begin{array}{rl}
62 & \text{multiplicand} \\
43 & \text{multiplier} \\
\hline
186 \ \Big\} & \\
2480 \ \Big\} & \text{partial products} \\
2666 & \text{product}
\end{array}
$$

In the example above, the number 43 is called the multiplier, 62 the multiplicand, and, of course, 2666 the product. The numbers 186 and 2480 are called partial products. If we reverse the order of the factors and have 62 × 43, then 62 would be called the multiplier and 43 the multiplicand. Since multiplication is commutative, either of the two factors may be used as the multiplier. The number of digits in the multiplier determines the number of partial products in the algorithm. If you wished to find the product of 6243 and 73, which number would you use as the multiplier?

The justification of the procedure for multiplying numbers with more than two digits is similar to methods already described and will not be discussed further.

EXERCISE 7.4

1. (a) Why is it desirable to memorize the products of all numbers with single-digit numerals?
   (b) Why is it *unnecessary* to memorize the products of numbers with more than one digit in their numerals?
   (c) Why do you suppose the author of this text was required to memorize the products up to 12×12 when he was in grammar school?

2. (a) What is the effect of annexing a zero to a numeral in base ten?
   (b) What is the effect of annexing two zeros to a numeral in base ten?
   (c) What is the effect of annexing n zeros to a numeral in base ten?

3. Prove that if 34 is multiplied by 100, the result is 3400 (or 34 with two zeros annexed).

4. In discussing the procedure for multiplying 72 by 1000, why do we say "annex" three zeros to 72 rather than "add" three zeros to 72?

5. What would be the effect of annexing a zero to a numeral in base eight? In base six?

6. In finding the product 423×624, why can the zeros that are crossed off in the algorithm below be omitted?

$$\begin{array}{r} 624 \\ 423 \\ \hline 1872 \\ 1248\cancel{0} \\ 2496\cancel{0}\cancel{0} \\ \hline 263952 \end{array}$$

7. (a) Find the product of 6439 and 7 first by using 7 as the multiplier and then by using 6439 as the multiplier.
   (b) Which is easier? Explain.

8. (a) Find the product of 2437 and 2004 first by using 2004 as the multiplier and then by using 2437 as the multiplier.
   (b) When 2004 is used as the multiplier, are there any zeros in the partial products which may be omitted? Explain.
   (c) Which number is a better choice as a multiplier? Explain.

7.5
Algorithms of Division

In Section 6.17 it was mentioned that the closure property does not hold for the operation of division with whole numbers since, for a and b in W, $a \div b$ does not always exist as a whole number. It is necessary to expand the number system to include the rational numbers in order to even come close to having closure under division. Nevertheless, we do speak of dividing whole numbers and finding a "quotient" with a *remainder*. For example, we say that $17 \div 5$ has a quotient of 3 with a remainder of 2 since $17 = 5 \cdot 3 + 2$. However, it is only when the remainder in division is zero that we have a quotient as defined in Definition 6.17.1. If this is understood, there will be no misunderstanding of the way in which the word quotient is used in this section. It is undoubtedly a poor decision to use the word quotient in two different but closely related ways. However, we follow a long-standing practice in so doing.

Although the proof will not be given here, the following important theorem may be shown to be true. It is commonly referred to as the division algorithm.

THEOREM 7.5.1

For any two numbers a and b in W with $b \neq 0$, there exist whole numbers q and r such that $a = bq + r$ where $0 \leq r < b$.

In the division algorithm, a is called the dividend, b the divisor, q the quotient, and r the remainder.

Example 1. Referring to the division algorithm, if $a = 23$ and $b = 5$, then $23 = 5 \cdot 4 + 3$. Note that the remainder 3 is less than the divisor 5. The given example is commonly written:

$$
\begin{array}{r}
4 \\
5 \overline{)23} \\
20 \quad (5 \cdot 4) \\
\hline
3
\end{array}
$$

When we divide one number by another, we are trying to determine the largest value of q such that the product of the divisor and the quotient does not exceed the dividend. Referring to the above example, we note that $5 \cdot 0 = 0$, $5 \cdot 1 = 5$, $5 \cdot 2 = 10$, $5 \cdot 3 = 15$, $5 \cdot 4 = 20$, $5 \cdot 5 = 25$, and so forth; however, 4 is the desired value of q since $5 \cdot 4 = 20$ and $20 < 23$, while $5 \cdot 5 = 25$ and $25 > 23$. This process for determining q results in a value for r (the remainder) which is less than b (the divisor).

Inverse relationships exist between multiplication and division as well as between addition and subtraction. Therefore, division can be interpreted as the repeated subtraction of the divisor from the dividend just as multiplication was interpreted as the repeated addition of the same addend. For example, suppose we wish to divide 20 by 6. We successively subtract 6 from 20 until the remainder is less than 6:

$$
\begin{array}{rl}
20 & \\
-6 & \quad 1 \\
\hline
14 & \\
-6 & \quad 1 \quad 3 \quad \text{(quotient)} \\
\hline
8 & \\
-6 & \quad 1 \\
\hline
2 & \quad \text{(remainder)}
\end{array}
$$

It is readily seen that 6 may be subtracted from 20 three times and 2 remains. Hence the quotient is 3, the remainder is 2, and $20 = 6 \cdot 3 + 2$. This method, of course, would be rather cumbersome to use in finding the quotient $1031 \div 54$, so we resort to other methods.

The procedure below consists of the repeated guessing of *partial quotients*, multiplying, and subtracting as shown. In this case it seems best not to explain in detail what will be done, but simply to do it and then explain what has been done! Let us divide 1031 by 54.

$$
\begin{array}{r}
5 + 10 + 4 = 19 \\
\hline
54\overline{)\,1031} \\
270 \quad (54 \cdot 5) \\
\hline
761 \\
540 \quad (54 \cdot 10) \\
\hline
221 \\
216 \quad (54 \cdot 4) \\
\hline
5
\end{array}
$$

In the above problem the partial quotients 5, 10, and 4 were determined by random guessing and have a sum of 19. By applying the distributive property, we see that $54 \cdot (5 + 10 + 4) = 270 + 540 + 216 = 1026$; also, $54 \cdot (5 + 10 + 4) = 54 \cdot 19 = 1026$. The remainder is $1031 - 270 - 540 - 216 = 5$, which is the same as $1031 - 54 \cdot 19 = 5$, and we can write $1031 = 54 \cdot 19 + 5$. This verifies Theorem 7.5.1 (the division algorithm) and we note that the remainder 5 is less than the divisor 54.

Finally, the process can be refined until an algorithm is obtained in which each digit of the quotient is found directly without adding partial quotients. Using the same problem, $1031 \div 54$, we proceed. Note that the dividend has four digits; therefore, the quotient must have no more than four digits since the product of the quotient and the divisor must not exceed the dividend. The objective is to find the digits of the quotient and to immediately put each in its proper location. First, we see whether the quotient will have a digit in the thousands place. It cannot, since $54 \cdot 1000$ is equal to 54,000, which is greater than 1031. Next we try to find a digit for the hundreds place of the quotient, but $54 \cdot 100 = 5400$, which is also greater than 1031. Testing for the tens digit, it is seen that $54 \cdot 10 = 540$, which is less than 1031, and that $54 \cdot 20 = 1080$, which is greater than 1031, so the largest digit that can be in the tens position is 1. We then place the digit 1 above the tens position of the dividend and multiply as follows:

$$
\begin{array}{r}
1\cancel{0} \\
54\overline{)1031} \\
54\cancel{0}
\end{array}
$$

Note that it is not necessary to write the zeros. Subtracting, we have:

$$
\begin{array}{r}
1 \\
54\overline{)1031} \\
54 \\
\hline
491
\end{array}
$$

Looking for the digit for the units position, it is found that the largest number of units is 9 since $54 \cdot 9 = 486$, which is less than 491. Finally, we subtract 486 from 491, and our work is complete since the remainder 5 is less than the divisor 54.

$$
\begin{array}{r}
19 \\
54\overline{)1031} \\
54 \\
\hline
491 \\
486 \\
\hline
5
\end{array}
$$

The work can be checked for errors by seeing whether $54 \cdot 19 + 5$ is equal to 1031. Since the product of the divisor and quotient, plus the remainder, is equal to the dividend, evidently no error has been made.

In teaching "long division," studies have shown that it is best for students to learn to use an intermediate algorithm, which can be easily rationalized, prior to learning the commonly used algorithm discussed above. An algorithm of the intermediate variety which is quite easy to rationalize and which allows for some trial and error on the part of the student is the following:

$$
\begin{array}{r|l}
54)\overline{1031} & \\
\underline{540} & 10 \\
491 & \\
\underline{486} & 9 \\
\text{(remainder)}\ \ 5 & 19 \quad \text{(quotient)}
\end{array}
$$

Although the above method is less efficient than the more refined algorithm, it does have the advantage of making the basic notion of repeated subtraction more apparent to the learner. He can then proceed to the more refined algorithm in the interest of economy.

EXERCISE 7.5

1. (a) State Theorem 7.5.1 (the division algorithm).
   (b) Using a divisor of 7 and a dividend of 93, show that the division algorithm is true.

2. Use successive subtraction to find the quotient $74 \div 16$. What is the remainder?

3. Use three different algorithms similar to those of the text to find the quotient and remainder if the divisor is 68 and the dividend is 16,479. Do *not* successively subtract 68 from 16,479!

4. (a) Find the quotient and remainder of 144,173 divided by 24.
   (b) Check your results by using the division algorithm.
   (c) What error do you think is most likely to be made in a problem such as this?

5. Verify that the division algorithm $a = bq + r$ holds when the divisor is greater than the dividend by letting $a = 6$ and $b = 14$.

7.6
Computing in Place Value Systems with Various Bases

The algorithms developed for computing in our decimal system of numeration can also be applied to numeration systems with bases other than ten. Most adults have successfully mastered computing in base ten to the point where they perform the processes as automatically as a driver operates an automobile. Computing in nondecimal bases forces the student to reexamine the familiar algorithms and the principles underlying them. Some of the difficulties encountered by the adult in using nondecimal bases are the same as those experienced by the child in learning to use base ten. Students usually find computing in nondecimal bases enlightening as well as interesting and enjoyable.

It may now be desirable to review Section 5.10, in which numeration systems with various bases are discussed. Figure 5.10.1 compares base ten numerals with base four numerals. For example, $14_{\text{ten}} = 32_{\text{four}}$ and we read 32_{four} as "three fours and two." This name, though meaningful, is cumbersome. For this reason you may prefer to read 32_{four} as "three-two, base four." To cite another example, 231_{four} can be read "two-three-one, base four" rather than "two four-fours, three fours, and one." The important concept is that $32_{\text{four}} = [3(4) + 2]_{\text{ten}} = [12 + 2]_{\text{ten}} = 14_{\text{ten}}$ and $231_{\text{four}} = [2(4)^2 + 3(4)^1 + 1]_{\text{ten}} = [2(16) + 3(4) + 1]_{\text{ten}} = [32 + 12 + 1]_{\text{ten}} = 45_{\text{ten}}$. The reader should also be aware that if a numeral such as 231_{four} is written in expanded form in *base four numerals*, we have $231_{\text{four}} = [2(10)^2 + 3(10)^1 + 1]_{\text{four}}$, which is the same as $[2(4)^2 + 3(4)^1 + 1]_{\text{ten}}$.

7.7
Addition and Subtraction in Nondecimal Bases

In Section 5.10, particular attention was arbitrarily given to writing numerals in base four, so we shall begin here by adding in a base four system. As in base ten, it is necessary to memorize the sums of single-digit numbers in order to compute rapidly. However, speed is not our objective since we wish to devote our attention to understanding the basic principles of computation.

A knowledge of the base ten system can be used to find sums of single-digit numbers in base four. For example, suppose we wish to find the sum $3_{\text{four}} + 2_{\text{four}}$. Using base ten we find $3 + 2 = 5$, but we know that "five" is "*one* four and *one*"; hence $3_{\text{four}} + 2_{\text{four}} = 11_{\text{four}}$. The sums of other single-digit numbers in base four may be found in a similar way, and a base four addition table may be constructed as shown in Figure 7.7.1.

Note that if we were to use a base of four rather than a base of ten in our numeration system, it would be necessary to memorize only 4^2 or 16 basic addition facts instead of 10^2 or 100. How would we fare with base two or base twelve? See Figure 7.7.1.

Once the sums of single-digit numbers in a given base are found, the algorithms developed for base ten can be used to find any other sums in the given base. By renaming the numbers using base ten, the computation can be checked for possible errors as shown below. In checking, first write both the addends and their sum in base ten numerals. Then add using the base ten numerals and see if the sum is correct.

Base Four

+	0	1	2	3
0	0	1	2	3
1	1	2	3	10
2	2	3	10	11
3	3	10	11	12

Base Two

+	0	1
0	0	1
1	1	10

Base Twelve

+	0	1	2	3	4	5	6	7	8	9	T	E
0	0	1	2	3	4	5	6	7	8	9	T	E
1	1	2	3	4	5	6	7	8	9	T	E	10
2	2	3	4	5	6	7	8	9	T	E	10	11
3	3	4	5	6	7	8	9	T	E	10	11	12
4	4	5	6	7	8	9	T	E	10	11	12	13
5	5	6	7	8	9	T	E	10	11	12	13	14
6	6	7	8	9	T	E	10	11	12	13	14	15
7	7	8	9	T	E	10	11	12	13	14	15	16
8	8	9	T	E	10	11	12	13	14	15	16	17
9	9	T	E	10	11	12	13	14	15	16	17	18
T	T	E	10	11	12	13	14	15	16	17	18	19
E	E	10	11	12	13	14	15	16	17	18	19	1T

Addition Tables

FIGURE 7.7.1

Example 1. Find the sum $13_{four} + 33_{four}$.

Solution:

Base Four	*Check (Base Ten)*
1	1
13	7
33	15
112	22

Example 2. Find the sum $3_{\text{four}} + 13_{\text{four}} + 32_{\text{four}}$.

Solution:

Base Four	Check (Base Ten)
2	1
3	3
13	7
32	14
120	24

Example 3. Find the sum $1011_{\text{two}} + 101_{\text{two}}$.

Solution:

Base Two	Check (Base Ten)
1011	11
101	5
10000	16

In subtracting in various bases it is important to remember that when it is necessary to rename the minuend (borrow), the base determines the details of the renaming. Suppose, for example, we wish to use base four and find the difference $32_{\text{four}} - 13_{\text{four}}$. Using the conventional algorithm, we have:

$$\begin{array}{r} 32 \\ 13 \\ \hline \end{array}$$

In this case renaming is necessary since $3 > 2$. If one of the three fours of the minuend is added to the two ones, the result is "one four and two" or 12_{four}. Thus, we have renamed 32_{four} as $(20 + 12)_{\text{four}}$:

$$\begin{array}{r} 2 \\ \cancel{3}^{1}2 \\ 1\ 3 \\ \hline \end{array}$$

On subtracting "three" from "one four and two," we get "three" as shown in the completed solution below.

Base Four	Check (Base Ten)
2	
$\cancel{3}^{1}2$	14
1 3	7
1 3	7

Example 4.   Find the difference $3030_{four} - 233_{four}$.

Solution:

Base Four	Check (Base Ten)
2 3¹2	1 9
3̸ 0̸ 3̸¹0	2̸ 0̸¹4
2 3 3	4 7
2 1 3 1	1 5 7

Example 5.   Find the difference $642_{twelve} - 5E_{twelve}$.

Solution:

Base Twelve	Check (Base Ten)
5¹ 3	8
6̸ 4̸¹2	9̸¹1 4
5 E	7 1
5 T 3	8 4 3

EXERCISE 7.7

1. The following numerals are written in base seven. Rename them using base ten notation.
   (a) 14   (b) 35
   (c) 124   (d) 1243
   (e) 4006

2. Construct an addition table for base seven.

3. The following numerals are in base seven. Find the sums and check by using base ten numerals.

(a) 3	(b) 12	(c) 35	(d) 1233	(e) 26
4	34	34	435	53
				214

4. The following are base seven numerals. Find the differences and check by using base ten numerals.

(a) 4	(b) 31	(c) 212	(d) 242	(e) 2002
2	5	54	45	666

5. Find the base of the numeration system if:
   (a) $2 + 2 = 11$ (b) $6 + 5 = 14$
   (c) $7 + 9 = 12$ (d) $2 + 3 = 10$
   (e) $10 + 10 = 100$ (f) $4 + 4 = 12$

6. Find the base of the numeration system if:
   (a) $23 + 12 = 101$ (b) $65 + 55 = 142$
   (c) $78 + 38 = 127$ (d) $66 + 66 = 121$

7. Find the indicated sums and differences using the following base two numerals:

   (a)   1   (b)   11   (c)   101   (d)   1011   (e)   11101
       $+10$ -11 $+110$ -101 $+10111$

8. Find the indicated sums and differences using the following base twelve numerals:

   (a)   93   (b)   82   (c)   642   (d)   30T   (e)   TOT
       $+7$ $-T$ $+ET$ $-EE$ $+TOE$

7.8

Multiplication and Division in Nondecimal Bases

Let us begin by constructing a multiplication table in base four. As in constructing a base four addition table, a knowledge of base ten may be used. See Figure 7.8.1.

Base Four

·	0	1	2	3
0	0	0	0	0
1	0	1	2	3
2	0	2	10	12
3	0	3	12	21

Multiplication Table

FIGURE 7.8.1

The reader may wish to construct multiplication tables in base two and base seven as an aid in the study of some of the examples below.

Example 1.   Assuming the numerals are written in base four, find the product of the ordered pair (23, 31). Check by using base ten.

Solution:

Base Four	*Check (Base Ten)*
31	13
23	11
$\overline{213}$ = $2\times4^2 + 1\times4^1 + 3$	$\overline{13}$
122	13
$\overline{2033}$ = $2\times4^3 + 0\times4^2 + 3\times4 + 3$ $\overline{143}$	

$128 + 0 + 12 + 3$

In checking, write the original factors and their product in base ten numerals. Then multiply using the base ten numerals and see if the product is correct. Note that the two partial products in the base four multiplication do not equal the corresponding partial products in the base ten translation. Why not?

Example 2.   Assuming the numerals are written in base two, find the product $101 \cdot 1101$.

Solution:

Base Two	Check (Base Ten)
1101	13
101	5
1101	65
1101	
1000001	

Example 3.   Multiply 263_{seven} by 43_{seven}.

Solution:

Base Seven	Check (Base Ten)
263	143
43	31
1152	143
1445	429
15632	4433

Division is a more difficult operation to perform than the other operations that have been discussed. This is true whether a decimal or a nondecimal system of numeration is used. Below are two examples of division in base four, one with a single-digit divisor and the other with a two-digit divisor.

Example 4.   Divide 1311_{four} by 3_{four}.

Solution:

Base Four	Check (Base Ten)
213	39
3)1311	3)117
12	9
11	27
3	27
21	
21	

Example 5.   Divide 2033_{four} by 23_{four}.

Solution:

Base Four	*Check (Base Ten)*
31	13
$23)\overline{2033}$	$11)\overline{143}$
$\underline{201}$	$\underline{11}$
23	33
$\underline{23}$	$\underline{33}$

EXERCISE 7.8

1. Construct a multiplication table for a base two numeration system.

2. Construct a multiplication table for a base five numeration system.

3. The following shows two numbers multiplied to produce a product, first using base five numerals and then using base ten numerals.

Base Five	*Base Ten*
34	19
$\underline{32}$	$\underline{17}$
123	133
$\underline{2128}$	$\underline{198}$
2243	323

It will be seen that the factor $34_{five} = 19_{ten}$ and the factor $32_{five} = 17_{ten}$; also, the product $2243_{five} = 323_{ten}$.

(a) Referring to the given algorithms, does $123_{five} = 133_{ten}$?

(b) Does $2120_{five} = 190_{ten}$?

(c) Explain the reasons for the results in parts (a) and (b).

4. The following numerals are in base five. Find the products and check by using base ten numerals.

(a) 2 (b) 3 (c) 42 (d) 23 (e) 132
$\underline{2}$ $\underline{2}$ $\underline{3}$ $\underline{34}$ $\underline{23}$

5. Find the base of the numeration system if:

(a) $2 \times 4 = 13$ (b) $3 \times 4 = 20$
(c) $2 \times 2 = 11$ (d) $2 \times 7 = 13$
(e) $2 \times 7 = 16$ (f) $2 \times 7 = 10$

6. Write the numeral for the product 2×3 assuming a base of:

(a) four   (b) five
(c) six   (d) seven
(e) eight   (f) nine
(g) ten   (h) eleven

7. The following numerals are in base two. Find the products and check by using base ten numerals.

(a) 11
    1
    ̲

(b) 101
     11
    ̲̲

(c) 1011
      10
    ̲̲

8. (a) What is the effect of annexing a zero to a numeral in base ten?
   (b) What is the effect of annexing two zeros to a numeral in base ten?
   (c) What is the effect of annexing a zero to a numeral in base seven?
   (d) What is the effect of annexing two zeros to a numeral in base seven?
   (e) Change 23_{four} and 230_{four} to numerals in base ten and show that annexing a zero to 23_{four} has multiplied it by four.
   (f) What is the effect of annexing a zero to a numeral in base n $(n = 2, 3, 4, \ldots)$?

9. The following numerals are in base five. Find the quotients and remainders and check by using the division algorithm in base five.

(a) $3\overline{)124}$

(b) $4\overline{)232}$

(c) $12\overline{)342}$

10. (a) Prove by the use of base ten numerals that the following problem may have been written in either base four or base five notation.

$$
\begin{array}{r}
11 \\
12\overline{)132} \\
12 \\
\hline
12 \\
12 \\
\hline
\end{array}
$$

   (b) What other bases may have been used in the above example?
   (c) Why is three not a possible base in the example?

11. What base is being used in the following problem?

$$
\begin{array}{r}
13 \\
12\overline{)200} \\
12 \\
\hline
40 \\
40 \\
\hline
\end{array}
$$

REVIEW EXERCISES

1. (a) What is the value of memorizing the sums of numbers with single-digit numerals?
   (b) Why is it of limited value to memorize the sums of numbers with more than single-digit numerals?

2. (a) Construct an addition table using base three numerals.

(b) Construct a multiplication table using base three numerals.

3. (a) What would be some advantages of a base three system of numeration?

(b) What would be some disadvantages of a base three system of numeration?

4. The following numerals are written in base six. Rename them using base ten numerals.

(a) 25 (b) 54 (c) 243 (d) 4505 (e) 4004

5. The following numerals are written in base ten. Rename them using base five numerals.

(a) 12 (b) 39 (c) 60 (d) 125 (e) 264

6. The following numerals are in base four. Perform the indicated operations and check by using base ten numerals.

(a) $3202 + 313$ (b) $3122 + 3231$
(c) $2301 - 1232$ (d) $3202 - 2133$
(e) $3 \cdot 2301$ (f) $2 \cdot 233$
(g) $312 \div 2$ (h) $3212 \div 3$

7. (a) Add (express results in simplest form):

gallons	quarts	pints
6	3	1
2	1	3
1	2	1

(b) Subtract:

hours	minutes	seconds
4	20	5
2	30	21

(c) Explain how parts (a) and (b) above are related to systems of numeration. What "bases" are involved?

8. What base is used in the system of numeration if $389 + 279 = 635$?

9. Describe the role of the distributive property in finding the product 3×213.

10. Use two different algorithms to find the quotient $162,944 \div 67$.

11. What numeration base is used in finding the following product?

$$
\begin{array}{r}
432 \\
34 \\
\hline
1508 \\
1096 \\
\hline
12268
\end{array}
$$

12. What numeration base is used in finding the following quotient?

$$
\begin{array}{r}
24 \\
23\overline{)615} \\
46 \\
\hline
125 \\
125 \\
\hline
\end{array}
$$

13. Verify that the division algorithm $a = bq + r$ holds:
    (a) By letting $a = 34$ and $b = 6$.
    (b) By letting $a = 6$ and $b = 34$.
    (c) By letting $a = 52$ and $b = 4$.

14. The following numerals are in base four. Find the quotients and remainders and check by using the division algorithm in *base four*.

    (a) $3\overline{)213}$

    (b) $2\overline{)233}$

    (c) $3\overline{)203}$

Chapter Eight

The System
of Integers

8.1
Introduction

If a college student has $100 and spends $105, what is his net worth? Common responses to this question are "He is $5 in the hole," "He is $5 in the red," or "He is $5 in debt." In attempting to find the answer mathematically, it is necessary to find a number for $100 - 105$. However, since $100 < 105$, there is no whole number k such that $100 = 105 + k$, and hence subtraction in this case is impossible without extending the system of whole numbers.

Other examples from everyday life that show the need for extending our number system may be cited. Suppose a temperature reading is 60 degrees. What is the new reading if the temperature decreases 70 degrees? The answer might be "ten below zero" or "ten less than zero." In this type of situation, the best solution seems to be to invent new numbers. This is exactly what we do, and in representing a number ten less than zero we use the symbol $^{-}10$, which is read "negative ten," "the opposite of ten," or "the additive inverse of ten." We can then say that the temperature is $^{-}10$ (negative ten) degrees.

As was true for many other new concepts, negative numbers were not readily accepted—even by mathematicians. Diophantus of Alexandria (about A.D. 250) called an equation "absurd" if its roots were negative numbers. It was not until about the seventeenth century that negative numbers were generally accepted as "true" rather than "false" numbers.

8.2
The Set of Integers

It was mentioned in Section 8.1 that $^{-}10$ could be read "the additive inverse of ten." When we say that one number is the *additive inverse* of another, we mean that their sum is 0, the identity element for addition. Suppose, for example, we use the number 18 to represent the fact that a man earns $18. If he then spends $18, this expenditure could be represented by the number $^{-}18$. His net worth in this case is equal to 0, and we write $18 + {}^{-}18 = 0$. Similarly, we shall find it useful to define $1 + {}^{-}1 = 0$, $2 + {}^{-}2 = 0$, and so on. Note that in writing a negative number, such as $^{-}18$, the short horizontal line is part of the numeral and is elevated so that it will not be confused with the symbol used for the subtraction operation. There is inconsistency among authors in this respect, however, and some use the symbols $-1, -2, -3, \ldots$ rather than $^{-}1, {}^{-}2, {}^{-}3, \ldots$.

The *system of integers* is essentially an extension of the system of whole numbers, and the set of elements called the *integers* includes

151

the whole numbers as a proper subset. For each natural number n, we create a new unique number ^-n. The new numbers created are $^-1$, $^-2$, $^-3$, and so on. These numbers together with the whole numbers constitute the set of integers, which may be indicated as:

$$J = \{\ldots, {}^-3, {}^-2, {}^-1, 0, 1, 2, 3, \ldots\}$$

or

$$J = \{\ldots, {}^-3, {}^-2, {}^-1\} \cup \{0\} \cup \{1, 2, 3, \ldots\}$$

The elements of $\{\ldots, {}^-3, {}^-2, {}^-1\}$ are called the negative integers, and the elements of $\{1, 2, 3, \ldots\}$, which were previously called the natural numbers N, may also be called the positive integers.

Addition will be defined in the system of integers in such a way that $n + {}^-n = 0$. Thus, $1 + {}^-1 = 0$, $2 + {}^-2 = 0$, $3 + {}^-3 = 0$, and so on. In general, for any element a in J, there exists a unique number ^-a in J such that $a + {}^-a = {}^-a + a = 0$. The number ^-a is called the additive inverse of a. Note that the sum of an integer and its additive inverse is always equal to the additive identity element. In considering the set of integers J, the number a may be a positive integer, or a negative integer, or zero. If a is a positive integer, then its additive inverse is a negative integer; for example, the additive inverse of 5 is indicated by $^-5$, and $5 + {}^-5 = {}^-5 + 5 = 0$. If a is a negative integer, its additive inverse is a positive integer; for example, the additive inverse of $^-5$ may be indicated by $^{--}5$ or $^-({}^-5)$, and $^-5 + {}^{--}5 = 0$. However, we know that $^-5 + 5 = 0$, and since the additive inverse of a number is by definition unique, it must be true that $^{--}5 = 5$. In other words, 5 and $^-5$ are the additive inverses of each other. Similarly, the inverse of 6 is $^-6$ and the inverse of $^-6$ is $^{--}6$ or 6.

Finally, we must consider the additive inverse of 0. Suppose we indicate the additive inverse of 0 by writing $0 + {}^-0 = 0$. Since $0 + 0 = 0$, it follows that $0 + {}^-0 = 0 + 0$. Then, since 0 is the identity element, $^-0 = 0$. Hence, $^-0$ is simply another name for 0, and 0 is its own additive inverse. In fact, 0 is the only integer which is its own additive inverse.

An alternative to the additive inverse approach for constructing the integers is the concept of using equivalence classes of ordered pairs of whole numbers to represent the integers. The idea arises rather naturally in an attempt to establish closure for subtraction by extending the system of whole numbers. In the same way that 7, for example, may be used to represent the differences $(7 - 0)$, $(8 - 1)$, $(9 - 2)$, $(10 - 3), \ldots$, $^-7$ may be used to represent the differences $(0 - 7)$, $(1 - 8)$, $(2 - 9)$, $(3 - 10), \ldots$. If this approach is used in the construction of the set of integers from the whole numbers:

0 is identified with $\{(0 - 0), (1 - 1), (2 - 2), (3 - 3), \ldots\}$
1 is identified with $\{(1 - 0), (2 - 1), (3 - 2), (4 - 3), \ldots\}$
$^-1$ is identified with $\{(0 - 1), (1 - 2), (2 - 3), (3 - 4), \ldots\}$
2 is identified with $\{(2 - 0), (3 - 1), (4 - 2), (5 - 3), \ldots\}$
$^-2$ is identified with $\{(0 - 2), (1 - 3), (2 - 4), (3 - 5), \ldots\}$

$\vdots$

6 is identified with $\{(6 - 0), (7 - 1), (8 - 2), (9 - 3), \ldots\}$
$^-6$ is identified with $\{(0 - 6), (1 - 7), (2 - 8), (3 - 9), \ldots\}$

$\vdots$

It is interesting to find that either of the approaches that have been mentioned for constructing the set of integers is equally effective in extending the system of whole numbers in such a way that closure for subtraction is attained. Furthermore, both of these approaches result in the creation of new numbers that are less than zero.

EXERCISE 8.2

1. If you have $10 and spend $12, what integer can be used to represent your net worth?

2. Suppose you are playing a game and your score is 3. If on the next play you lose 5 points, what integer may now be used to represent your score?

3. If the temperature is 68 degrees and decreases 100 degrees, what integer can be used to represent the temperature?

4. Identify the set of integers, J.

5. What is meant by the *additive inverse* of an integer?

6. Why is $^-7$ the additive inverse of 7?

7. Why is 7 the additive inverse of $^-7$?

8. (a) What is the additive inverse of 17?
   (b) What is the additive inverse of the additive inverse of 17?
   (c) What is the additive inverse of the additive inverse of the additive inverse of 17?

9. Simplify the following:
   (a) $^{--}25$ (b) $^{---}25$ (c) $^{----}25$

10. What are the additive inverses of the following integers?
   (a) 7   (b) $^-3$
   (c) a (d) ^-b
   (e) $^-(x + y)$ (f) $a + b$
   (g) 0   (h) $^{--}23$

11. (a) Is 0 a positive number? Explain.
    (b) Is $^-0$ a negative number? Explain.
    (c) How are $^-0$ and 0 related?

12. What integer is represented by ^-x if:
    (a) $x = 3$ (b) $x = {}^-4$
    (c) $x = 7$ (d) $x = {}^-7$

8.3
The System of Integers

Essentially the *system of integers* will be treated as an extension of the system of whole numbers, and the same operations will be defined on the integers as were previously defined on the whole numbers. In so doing, the properties of closure, associativity, and so on, which applied to operations with the whole numbers, W, will also apply to operations with the integers, J. Zero (0) will continue as the additive identity and one (1) will maintain its status as the multiplicative identity for the set. In fact, in considering the whole numbers as a subset of the integers, their sums and products will remain the same as in the system of whole numbers. The only new basic property of J, not characteristic of W, is the existence of an *additive inverse* for each element in the system. The effects of this new property, however, are far-reaching.

The essential features of the system of integers are summarized below. It is interesting to compare Definition 8.3.1 with Definition 6.19.1 for the system of whole numbers.

DEFINITION 8.3.1

The **system of integers** consists of the set $J = \{\ldots, {}^-3, {}^-2, {}^-1, 0, 1, 2, 3, \ldots\}$ and the binary operations of addition $(+)$ and multiplication $(\cdot)$. The system has the following properties for any a, b, and c in J:

Closure Properties
1. There is a uniquely determined sum $a + b$ in J.
2. There is a uniquely determined product $a \cdot b$ in J.

Commutative Properties
3. $a + b = b + a$
4. $a \cdot b = b \cdot a$

Associative Properties
5. $(a + b) + c = a + (b + c)$
6. $(a \cdot b) \cdot c = a \cdot (b \cdot c)$

Distributive Property of Multiplication over Addition
7. $a \cdot (b + c) = a \cdot b + a \cdot c$ (left distributive property)
    $(b + c) \cdot a = b \cdot a + c \cdot a$ (right distributive property)

Identity Elements
8. There exists a unique element 0 in J such that for any a in J,
   $a + 0 = 0 + a = a$.
9. There exists a unique element 1 in J such that for any a in J,
   $a \cdot 1 = 1 \cdot a = a$.

Additive Inverses
10. For each a in J there exists a unique element ^-a in J such that
    $a + {}^-a = {}^-a + a = 0$.

8.4
**Addition
in the
Integers**

Our knowledge of the whole numbers enables us to add any two non-negative integers, and since zero is the identity element, no problem is encountered in finding the sum of a negative integer and zero. For example, $^-34 + 0 = {}^-34$, and $0 + {}^-17 = {}^-17$. However, in extending the binary operation of addition to include the negative integers, special attention must be given to finding the sum of an ordered pair of integers when one or both of the addends are negative. First, we shall consider the sum of two negative integers.

If \$3 is borrowed and then an additional \$2 is borrowed, it seems reasonable to represent the total debt by $^-3 + {}^-2 = {}^-(3 + 2) = {}^-5$. By using the definition of additive inverses and other properties of J, we shall prove that $^-3 + {}^-2 = {}^-(3 + 2) = {}^-5$.

Proof that $^-3 + {}^-2 = {}^-(3 + 2) = {}^-5$:

Let c represent the sum $^-3 + {}^-2$ by writing:

$$c = {}^-3 + {}^-2$$

Then,

$c + 2 = ({}^-3 + {}^-2) + 2$	Substitution property
$c + 2 = {}^-3 + ({}^-2 + 2)$	Associative property of addition
$c + 2 = {}^-3 + 0$	Additive inverse
$c + 2 = {}^-3$	Additive identity
$(c + 2) + 3 = {}^-3 + 3$	Substitution property
$(c + 2) + 3 = 0$	Additive inverse

$c + (2 + 3) = 0$	Associative property
$c = {}^-(2 + 3)$	Additive inverse
$c = {}^-(3 + 2)$	Commutative property of addition
$c = {}^-5$	Addition fact in W

Therefore,

$$ {}^-3 + {}^-2 = {}^-(3 + 2) = {}^-5 \qquad \text{Substitution and the transitive property of equals} $$

A proof similar to the one above shows that, in general, for any a and b in W, ${}^-a + {}^-b = {}^-(a + b)$.

Example 1.
(a) ${}^-5 + {}^-9 = {}^-(5 + 9) = {}^-14$.
(b) ${}^-12 + {}^-3 = {}^-(12 + 3) = {}^-15$.
(c) ${}^-20 + {}^-42 = {}^-62$ (omitting the intermediate step).

Next to be considered is finding the sum of two integers when one addend is positive and the other is negative. We shall again use the additive inverse property along with other properties of the integers to assist in finding these sums. When one addend is positive and the other negative, the sum may be zero, positive, or negative, depending on the particular addends involved.

If the addends are the additive inverses of each other, their sum, of course, is zero.

Example 2.
(a) ${}^-6 + 6 = 0$.
(b) $4 + {}^-4 = 0$.
(c) ${}^-2 + 2 = 0$.

In cases such as the following, the sums are positive integers:

Example 3.
(a) ${}^-6 + 8 = {}^-6 + (6 + 2) = ({}^-6 + 6) + 2 = 0 + 2 = 2$.
Note that 8 is renamed as the sum of two addends such that one of them is the additive inverse of ${}^-6$.
(b) ${}^-3 + 7 = {}^-3 + (3 + 4) = ({}^-3 + 3) + 4 = 0 + 4 = 4$.
(c) $7 + {}^-2 = (5 + 2) + {}^-2 = 5 + (2 + {}^-2) = 5 + 0 = 5$.

By methods similar to those used in Example 3 above, we may show that, in general, for any a and b in W, $a + {}^-b = {}^-b + a = (a - b)$ if $a > b$. Using this information, sums may be found quite rapidly. Alternative solutions to the problems of Example 3 are shown below.

Example 3. (Alternative Solutions)
(a) ${}^-6 + 8 = (8 - 6) = 2.$
(b) ${}^-3 + 7 = (7 - 3) = 4.$
(c) $7 + {}^-2 = (7 - 2) = 5.$

In cases such as the following, the sums are negative integers:

Example 4.
(a) ${}^-5 + 3 = ({}^-2 + {}^-3) + 3 = {}^-2 + ({}^-3 + 3) = {}^-2 + 0 = {}^-2.$
    Note that ${}^-5$ is renamed as the sum of two addends such that one of them is the additive inverse of 3.
(b) ${}^-6 + 2 = ({}^-4 + {}^-2) + 2 = {}^-4 + ({}^-2 + 2) = {}^-4 + 0 = {}^-4.$
(c) $4 + {}^-7 = 4 + ({}^-4 + {}^-3) = (4 + {}^-4) + {}^-3 = 0 + {}^-3 = {}^-3.$

By methods similar to those used in Example 4 above, we may show that, in general, for any a and b in W, $a + {}^-b = {}^-b + a = {}^-(b - a)$ if $a < b$. Using this information, sums may be found quite easily. Alternative solutions to the problems of Example 4 are shown below.

Example 4. (Alternative Solutions)
(a) ${}^-5 + 3 = {}^-(5 - 3) = {}^-2.$
(b) ${}^-6 + 2 = {}^-(6 - 2) = {}^-4.$
(c) $4 + {}^-7 = {}^-(7 - 4) = {}^-3.$

Below are two examples illustrating how addition in the integers may be used in solving equations.

Example 5. Find the value of x in each of the following equations:
(a) $x = 7 + {}^-4 + {}^-9$

Solution: (Note that some steps have been omitted.)

$$x = 7 + {}^-4 + {}^-9$$
$$x = (7 + {}^-4) + {}^-9$$
$$x = 3 + {}^-9$$
$$x = {}^-6$$

(b) $x + 2 = {}^-7$

Solution:

$$x + 2 = {}^-7$$
$$(x + 2) + {}^-2 = {}^-7 + {}^-2$$
$$x + (2 + {}^-2) = {}^-9$$
$$x + 0 = {}^-9$$
$$x = {}^-9$$

In Section 7.2, sums of whole numbers were found by interpreting addition as measurement on the number line. The sums of integers may be found in a similar way. Positive integers will be interpreted as referring to distances measured along the number line from left to right, while negative integers will measure distances in the opposite direction —from right to left. See the examples in Figure 8.4.1. Note that the number line has been extended so that the elements of $\{\ldots, {}^-3, {}^-2, {}^-1\}$ correspond to points to the left of zero in the same way that the elements of $\{1, 2, 3, \ldots\}$ correspond to points to the right of zero.

EXERCISE 8.4

1. What important property does the system of integers have that the system of whole numbers does not have?

2. What integer is equal to n if:
   (a) $n + 3 = 0$ (b) $n + {}^-5 = 0$
   (c) ${}^-13 + n = 0$ (d) $8 + n = 0$
   (e) $n + 3 = 2$ (f) $4 + n = 3$

3. (a) Show that $6 + {}^-5 = {}^-5 + 6$. What property is exemplified?
   (b) Show that $(7 + {}^-4) + {}^-9 = 7 + ({}^-4 + {}^-9)$. What property is exemplified?

4. Find the following sums:
   (a) $2 + {}^-7$ (b) ${}^-10 + 3$
   (c) ${}^-8 + {}^-7$ (d) ${}^-10 + 0$
   (e) ${}^-106 + 17$ (f) ${}^-63 + {}^-49$
   (g) $4 + ({}^-3 + {}^-7) + 9$ (h) $(4 + {}^-3) + ({}^-7 + 9)$
   (i) ${}^-5 + {}^-4 + 7 + {}^-6$ (j) $(a + b) + {}^-(a + b)$

5. Find the value of x for which each of the following equations is true:
   (a) $x + 2 = 7$ (b) $x + {}^-3 = {}^-7$
   (c) $5 + x = {}^-3$ (d) $x + a = 0$
   (e) $x + a = 3$ (f) ${}^-a + x = 7$

6. Find each of the following sums by interpreting addition as measurement on the number line. (See Figure 8.4.1.)

(a) $4 + 3$ (b) $5 + {}^-2$

(c) ${}^-3 + 7$ (d) ${}^-7 + {}^-2$

(e) $4 + {}^-4$ (f) ${}^-5 + 5$

$2 + 3 = 5$

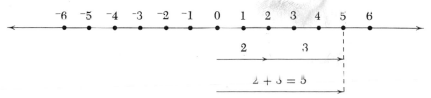

$^-3 + {}^-4 = {}^-7$

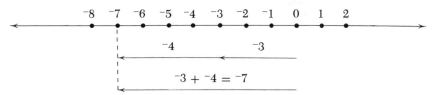

$^-3 + 7 = 4$

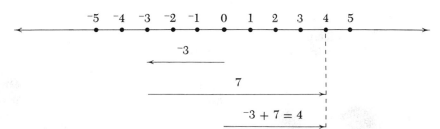

$4 + {}^-9 = {}^-5$

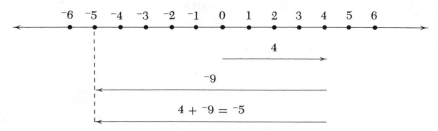

FIGURE 8.4.1

8.5
Subtraction in the Integers

As in the whole numbers, subtraction will be defined for the integers in terms of addition. From this point of view, subtraction is not considered a fundamental operation.

DEFINITION 8.5.1

If a, b, and k are in J, then $a - b = k$ if and only if $a = b + k$.

The definition of subtraction is used directly in the following examples. However, an alternative, and no doubt easier, method of finding differences will be discussed later in this section.

Example 1.
(a) $5 - 3 = 2$ since $5 = 3 + 2$.
(b) $6 - 8 = {}^-2$ since $6 = 8 + {}^-2$.
(c) $3 - {}^-7 = 10$ since $3 = {}^-7 + 10$.
(d) ${}^-7 - {}^-6 = {}^-1$ since ${}^-7 = {}^-6 + {}^-1$.
(e) ${}^-4 - 7 = {}^-11$ since ${}^-4 = 7 + {}^-11$.

As you will recall, the operation of subtraction in the whole numbers did not have the property of closure, and $a - b$ was defined only for $a > b$. This restriction has been removed in Definition 8.5.1 since the property of closure holds for subtraction in J. In fact, one of the principal reasons for expanding the number system to include the negative integers is to have closure under subtraction.

In examining Definition 8.5.1, it will be seen that closure for subtraction depends upon the *existence* of a *unique* integer k such that $a = b + k$ for all a and b in J. If this is the case, then by definition $a - b = k$.

First, we shall consider the *existence* of an integer k such that $a = b + k$. It is shown below that if $k = a + {}^-b$, the equation $a = b + k$ will be true. Hence the *existence* of k is proved. The reader should be able to justify each step in the following proof.

Proof that if $k = a + {}^-b$, then $a = b + k$:

Let $k = a + {}^-b$. Then,

$$b + k = b + (a + {}^-b)$$
$$= b + ({}^-b + a)$$
$$= (b + {}^-b) + a$$
$$= 0 + a$$
$$= a$$

Hence,
$$a = b + k \quad \text{if} \quad k = a + {}^-b.$$

Now that it has been shown that an integer k (equal to $a + {}^-b$) exists such that $a = b + k$, we must prove that k is *unique*. Suppose there is some other integer n such that $a = b + n$. Then $b + n = a = b + k$, and by the transitive property of equals, $b + n = b + k$. Finally, by adding b to each member of this equation, we see that $n = k$. Hence k (equal to $a + {}^-b$) is *uniquely determined* as the solution of $a = b + k$, and by the definition of subtraction, $a - b = k = a + {}^-b$.

We have shown that $a - b = a + {}^-b$, or that subtracting one integer from another is equivalent to adding the inverse of the subtrahend to the minuend. Finding the sum $a + {}^-b$ is an easy approach to subtraction since the operation of addition has already been considered. Furthermore, addition is commutative and associative while subtraction is not. For example, $(9 - 5) - 2 \neq 9 - (5 - 2)$, but $(9 + {}^-5) + {}^-2 = 9 + ({}^-5 + {}^-2)$.

Example 2.
(a) $5 - 3 = 5 + {}^-3 = (2 + 3) + {}^-3 = 2 + (3 + {}^-3) = 2 + 0 = 2$.
(b) $6 - 8 = 6 + {}^-8 = {}^-2$ (omitting some intermediate steps).
(c) $3 - {}^-7 = 3 + 7 = 10$.
(d) ${}^-7 - {}^-6 = {}^-7 + 6 = {}^-1$.
(e) ${}^-4 - 7 = {}^-4 + {}^-7 = {}^-11$.

Example 3. Find the value of x for which the following equation is true: $x - 3 = 12 - 7$.

Solution:

$$x - 3 = 12 - 7$$
$$x - 3 = 5$$
$$(x + {}^-3) + 3 = 5 + 3$$
$$x + ({}^-3 + 3) = 8$$
$$x + 0 = 8$$
$$x = 8$$

EXERCISE 8.5

1. Define subtraction in the integers, J.
2. Using the *definition of subtraction*, find the differences indicated below:
   (a) $7 - 12$ (b) $6 - 4$
   (c) ${}^-6 - 9$ (d) $8 - {}^-12$
   (e) ${}^-8 - 2$ (f) $0 - {}^-3$

3. For all a and b in J, we have shown that $a - b = a + {}^-b$. Use this relation to find the differences in problem 2.

4. Using the fact that $a - b = a + {}^-b$, find the following differences:
   (a) $7 - 9$ (b) $3 - {}^-8$
   (c) $5 - {}^-3$ (d) ${}^-12 - 4$
   (e) ${}^-8 - 15$ (f) $0 - 3$
   (g) $0 - {}^-7$ (h) $7 - 0$
   (i) $(8 - 3) - 4$ (j) $(6 - 5) - {}^-3$

5. Prove that subtraction in J is not commutative by showing that $6 - {}^-4 \neq {}^-4 - 6$.

6. Prove that subtraction in J is not associative by showing that $(8 - 4) - {}^-6 \neq 8 - (4 - {}^-6)$.

7. (a) Does $7 - 5 = 5 - 7$? Explain.
   (b) Does $7 - 5 = 7 + {}^-5$? Explain.
   (c) Does $7 + {}^-5 = {}^-5 + 7$? Explain.

8. (a) Does $(8 - 5) - 2 = 8 - (5 - 2)$? Explain.
   (b) Does $(8 - 5) - 2 = (8 + {}^-5) + {}^-2$? Explain.
   (c) Does $(8 + {}^-5) + {}^-2 = 8 + ({}^-5 + {}^-2)$? Explain.

9. Find values of x for which the following equations are true:
   (a) $x - 2 = 7$ (b) $x = 7 - {}^-3$
   (c) $x - {}^-3 = 3$ (d) $x - {}^-4 = 7$
   (e) $x + 7 = 2 - 3$ (f) $x - 3 = 6 - 7$

8.6 Multiplication in the Integers

In considering the product of two integers, there is nothing new to be learned if both factors are non-negative. The multiplication of non-negative integers is the same as the multiplication of whole numbers. However, we must consider the cases where one or both of the factors of a product are negative integers.

First, consider the product of two integers where one is positive and the other negative. If a and b are in N, then a is a positive integer and ${}^-b$ is a negative integer. Below we shall show that $(a)({}^-b) = {}^-(ab)$. For example, $(3)({}^-8) = {}^-(3 \cdot 8) = {}^-24$.

1. $a(b + {}^-b) = a \cdot 0 = 0$ 1. Properties of additive inverse and zero

2. $a(b + {}^-b) = (a)(b) + (a)({}^-b)$ 2. Distributive property

3. $(a)(b) + (a)({}^-b) = 0$ 3. Transitivity of equals applied to steps 1 and 2

4. $(ab) + {}^-(ab) = 0$ 4. Additive inverse

5. $(a)(b) + (a)(^-b) = (ab) + ^-(ab)$ 5. Transitivity of equals applied to steps 3 and 4

6. $(a)(^-b) = ^-(ab)$ 6. Cancellation property of addition

In the above proof we have shown that the product of a positive and a negative integer may be found in terms of the product of two natural numbers. The product, of course, is a negative integer. Since multiplication is commutative, the order of the factors makes no difference and $(a)(^-b) = (^-b)(a) = ^-(ab)$. For example, $(2)(^-7) = (^-7)(2) = ^-14$.

The above proof can be further generalized by letting $(a)(^-b)$ represent the product of an integer and the additive inverse of an integer. The final result, $(a)(^-b) = ^-(ab)$, would then tell us that an ordered pair consisting of an integer and the inverse of an integer is assigned by the binary operation of multiplication the additive inverse of the product of the integers.

Using the general equation $(a)(^-b) = ^-(ab)$, it is easy to find the product of zero and a negative integer by letting $a = 0$ and $b \in N$. Then we see from the following that the product of zero and a negative integer is equal to zero: $(0)(^-b) = ^-(0 \cdot b) = ^-0 = 0$.

Next we shall consider the product of two negative integers. If a and b are in N, then ^-a and ^-b are negative integers. Below we shall show that $(^-a)(^-b) = ab$.

1. $^-a(b + ^-b) = ^-a(0) = 0$ 1. Properties of additive inverse and zero

2. $^-a(b + ^-b) = ^-(ab) + (^-a)(^-b)$ 2. Distributive property

3. $^-(ab) + (^-a)(^-b) = 0$ 3. Transitivity of equals applied to steps 1 and 2

4. $^-(ab) + ab = 0$ 4. Additive inverse

5. $^-(ab) + (^-a)(^-b) = ^-(ab) + ab$ 5. Transitivity of equals applied to steps 3 and 4

6. $(^-a)(^-b) = ab$ 6. Cancellation property of addition

The above proof shows that the product of two negative integers is a positive integer, and it provides a method for finding the product in terms of the product of two natural numbers. For example, $(^-3)(^-6) = 3 \cdot 6 = 18$.

The proof can be further generalized by letting $(^-a)(^-b)$ represent a product in which both factors are the additive inverses of integers. The final result, $(^-a)(^-b) = ab$, would then tell us that an ordered pair consisting of the inverses of two integers is assigned by the binary operation of multiplication the product of the integers.

We are now prepared to find the product of any two integers since all possible cases have been considered.

Example 1. Find the product $(^-a)(b)$ if $a = {}^-2$ and $b = {}^-3$.

Solution: $(^-a)(b) = (^-{}^-2)(^-3) = 2(^-3) = {}^-(2 \cdot 3) = {}^-6$.

Example 2. Find the product $(^-a)(^-b)$ if $a = 7$ and $b = {}^-3$.

Solution: $(^-a)(^-b) = (^-7)(^-{}^-3) = {}^-7(3) = {}^-21$.

EXERCISE 8.6

1. Find the indicated products:
   (a) $2 \cdot {}^-3$ (b) $6(^-4)$
   (c) $(^-3)(5)$ (d) $(^-4)(^-5)$
   (e) $^-(3 \cdot 4)$ (f) $^-(3 \cdot {}^-4)$
   (g) $^-(^-5 \cdot 7)$ (h) $^-(^-9 \cdot {}^-7)$
   (i) $^-7 \cdot 0$ (j) $0(^-17)$

2. Find $(a)(^-b)$ if:
   (a) $a = 2$ and $b = 4$ (b) $a = {}^-5$ and $b = 7$
   (c) $a = 12$ and $b = {}^-1$ (d) $a = 0$ and $b = {}^-7$
   (e) $a = 4$ and $b = 0$ (f) $a = {}^-5$ and $b = {}^-9$

3. Find $(^-a)(^-b)$ if:
   (a) $a = {}^-2$ and $b = 5$ (b) $a = {}^-7$ and $b = 8$
   (c) $a = {}^-4$ and $b = {}^-9$ (d) $a = 0$ and $b = {}^-12$

4. Find the following products in two ways: (i) without using the distributive property and (ii) using the distributive property.
   (a) $6(7 - 4)$ (b) $5(^-4 + 9)$
   (c) $^-9(^-7 + 3)$ (d) $5(^-4 - 7)$
   (e) $^-3(^-4 + {}^-5)$ (f) $^-5(^-2 - {}^-8)$

5. Find the values of x for which the following equations are true:
   (a) $x = 2 + {}^-4(3)$ (b) $x = 3(^-4) + 5$
   (c) $2x = 2(^-4)$ (d) $3x + {}^-7 = 6 + {}^-7$
   (e) $3 + 3x = {}^-4(2 + {}^-5)$ (f) $7 = x - (3)(4)$

8.7

Division in the Integers

In Section 6.17, division was defined for the whole numbers. A similar definition will be given for division in the integers. Again, division is defined in terms of multiplication and, from this point of view, is not considered a fundamental operation.

DEFINITION 8.7.1

If a, b, and q are in J and $b \neq 0$, then $a \div b = q$ if and only if $a = bq$.

As mentioned in Section 6.17, either $a \div b$, $\dfrac{a}{b}$, or a/b may be used to mean "a divided by b."

Example 1.

(a) $\dfrac{-8}{-2} = 4$ since $-8 = (-2)(4)$.

(b) $\dfrac{72}{-8} = -9$ since $72 = (-8)(-9)$.

(c) $-35 \div 7 = -5$ since $-35 = (7)(-5)$.

(d) $\dfrac{0}{-4} = 0$ since $0 = (-4)(0)$.

(e) $8 \div -4 = -2$ since $8 = (-4)(-2)$.

In the set of integers, division by zero is not permitted for essentially the same reasons that this restriction was applied to division in the whole numbers. (See Section 6.17.)

In studying the definition of division in J, it is seen that q exists for the equation $a = bq$ if and only if a is a multiple of b. Since a may not be a multiple of b in some cases, the operation of division does not assign an integer to *all* ordered pairs (a, b) in J, and closure does not hold for division in J.

Two counterexamples are sufficient to show that the commutative and associative properties do not hold for division in J. To illustrate that division is not commutative in J, it is easy to see that $8 \div -4 \neq -4 \div 8$. In testing for associativity, we see that $(-16 \div 4) \div 2 = -4 \div 2 = -2$, while $-16 \div (4 \div 2) = -16 \div 2 = -8$; hence, division is not associative in J.

In summary, none of the properties of closure, commutativity, or associativity hold for division in the integers.

EXERCISE 8.7

1. Find the following quotients:

(a) $\dfrac{8}{-2}$ (b) $\dfrac{^-10}{^-5}$ (c) $\dfrac{0}{^-5}$

(d) $10 \div (^-2)$ (e) $^-48 \div (^-6)$ (f) $^-72 \div 9$

(g) $0 \div 10$ (h) $\dfrac{^-7}{^-1}$ (i) $^-1 \div (^-1)$

2. For what values of a and b does $a \div b = b \div a$?

3. (a) What is the value of $(^-32 \div 8) \div 2$?
   (b) What is the value of $^-32 \div (8 \div 2)$?
   (c) From (a) and (b) what can you conclude concerning the associativity of division in J?

4. Show by example that J is not closed with respect to division.

5. Show by example that division is not commutative in J.

6. (a) Does $\dfrac{8 + {}^-4}{2} = \dfrac{8}{2} + \dfrac{^-4}{2}$?

   (b) Does $\dfrac{^-16 - 4}{2} = \dfrac{^-16}{2} - \dfrac{4}{2}$?

   (c) Does $\dfrac{16}{^-4 + {}^-4} = \dfrac{16}{^-4} + \dfrac{16}{^-4}$?

   (d) Is division distributive over addition? Explain. (See Section 6.17.)

7. Find the integer equivalent to each of the following:

   (a) $\dfrac{^-16}{2} + 7 - 4$

   (b) $\dfrac{6(^-5)}{^-2} + (^-7)(^-1)$

8.8
The Cancellation Properties

In Theorem 6.15.4 the cancellation property of addition was stated for the whole numbers. However, no proof was given for the theorem. We shall now restate and prove the theorem for the integers. Since the whole numbers may be considered a proper subset of the integers, the proof will also apply to the whole numbers.

THEOREM 8.8.1

If a, b, and c are in J and $a + c = b + c$, then $a = b$.

Proof:

$a + c = b + c$	Given
$(a + c) + {}^-c = (b + c) + {}^-c$	Substitution
$a + (c + {}^-c) - b + (c + {}^-c)$	Associative property of addition
$a + 0 = b + 0$	Additive inverse
$a = b$	Additive identity

The cancellation property of multiplication as stated in Theorem 6.15.5 also holds for the integers. If a, b, and c are in J, $c \neq 0$, and $ca = cb$, then $a = b$. Just as the existence of an additive inverse made it easy to prove the cancellation property of addition, the existence of a multiplicative inverse will make it easy to prove the cancellation property of multiplication. Since, in general, we do not have multiplicative inverses in the integers, the cancellation property of multiplication will be proved when we study the rational numbers.

8.9
Ordering the Integers

The "less than" relation was defined on the whole numbers and proved to be an order relation. In a similar way the order relation "less than" will be defined on the integers.

DEFINITION 8.9.1

If a and b are in J, a is less than b (denoted by $a < b$) if and only if there exists a positive integer c such that $a + c = b$.

DEFINITION 8.9.2

If a and b are in J, a is greater than b (denoted by $a > b$) if and only if b is less than a.

Example 1.
(a) $8 < 10$ since $8 + 2 = 10$ and 2 is a positive integer.
(b) ${}^-4 < 2$ since ${}^-4 + 6 = 2$ and 6 is a positive integer.
(c) ${}^-10 < {}^-7$ since ${}^-10 + 3 = {}^-7$ and 3 is a positive integer.
(d) ${}^-7 > {}^-10$ since ${}^-10 < {}^-7$.

Example 2. Since Definition 8.9.2 is an "if and only if" statement, we may also reason as follows:
(a) $6 + 2 = 8$; therefore, $6 < 8$.
(b) $^-7 + 10 = 3$; therefore, $^-7 < 3$.
(c) $^-14 + 2 = ^-12$; therefore, $^-14 < ^-12$.

Example 3. Using the $<$ relation, order the following subset of W: $\{7, ^-3, 4, ^-4, ^-10\}$.

Solution: $(^-10, ^-4, ^-3, 4, 7)$

In examining the number line shown below, we see that $\ldots ^-3 < ^-2 < ^-1 < 0 < 1 < 2 < 3 \ldots$.

The ordering relation "less than" orders the integers on the number line in such a way that any integer is less than the one to its right. For example, $^-3$ is to the left of $^-1$, and $^-3 < ^-1$. Note that every negative integer is to the left of every whole number, and that every negative integer is less than every whole number.

In Section 6.21 we noted that the definitions of "less than," "equals," and "greater than" led to the important property for the whole numbers called the *trichotomy law*. A similar situation arises with the integers, and each ordered pair (a, b) in the product set $J \times J$ may be placed in exactly one of three disjoint subsets of $J \times J$, depending on which of the three relations $a < b$, $a = b$, or $a > b$ is true. A formal statement of the trichotomy law for the integers follows.

The Trichotomy Law for the Integers. For every a and b in J, exactly one of the following is true:

1. $a < b$
2. $a = b$
3. $a > b$

In studying the "less than" relation for the integers, it will be seen that it has the properties of an order relation; the "less than" relation is *irreflexive, asymmetric, transitive,* and *connected.* (See Section 6.21.)

A few basic theorems concerning inequalities in the integers are stated below. Since some proofs were given for similar theorems in the whole numbers, we shall omit proofs here.

THEOREM 8.9.1

If a, b, and c are in J and $a < b$, then $a + c < b + c$.

THEOREM 8.9.2

If a, b, and c are in J and $a + c < b + c$, then $a < b$.

THEOREM 8.9.3

If a and b are in J, c is a positive integer, and $a < b$, then $ca < cb$.

THEOREM 8.9.4

If a and b are in J, c is a positive integer, and $ca < cb$, then $a < b$.

Example 4 illustrates how some of the theorems concerning inequalities may be used.

Example 4. Identify by the roster method

$$\{n \mid (n \in J) \land (3n + 8 < 2)\}.$$

Solution:

1. $3n + 8 < 2$	1. Given
2. $(3n + 8) + ^-8 < 2 + ^-8$	2. Theorem 8.9.1
3. $3n + (8 + ^-8) < 2 + ^-8$	3. Why?
4. $3n + 0 < ^-6$	4. Why?
5. $3n < ^-6$	5. Why?
6. $3n < 3(^-2)$	6. Why?
7. $n < ^-2$	7. Theorem 8.9.4

We see from the solution that if $3n + 8 < 2$, then $n < ^-2$. Since, in this case, the order of steps 1 through 7 may be reversed, it is also true that if $n < ^-2$, then $3n + 8 < 2$. Hence we may state that $3n + 8 < 2$ if and only if $n < ^-2$, and thus the two inequalities have the same solutions. But we know from the definition of the $<$ relation that if $n < ^-2$, then $n \in \{\ldots, ^-5, ^-4, ^-3\}$. Therefore, $\{n \mid (n \in J) \land (3n + 8 < 2)\} = \{\ldots, ^-5, ^-4, ^-3\}$.

EXERCISE 8.9

1. State the cancellation properties of addition and multiplication as they apply to the integers.

2. (a) Prove by the use of additive inverses that if $a + 2 = {}^-7$, then $a = {}^-9$.
   (b) Use the cancellation property of addition to show that if $a + 2 = {}^-7$, then $a = {}^-9$.

3. Use the cancellation property of multiplication to show that if $7x = {}^-28$, then $x = {}^-4$.

4. Define the relation "less than" for the integers.

5. (a) Use the definition of the "less than" relation to show that if $a < b$, then $b - a = c$ where $c \in N$.
   (b) Is it also true that if $b - a = c$ where $c \in N$, then $a < b$? Explain.

6. Is zero the smallest integer? Explain.

7. (a) Prove Theorem 8.9.1.
   (b) Prove Theorem 8.9.2.

8. Prove that $^-4 < {}^-3$.

9. If $^-10 + 2 = {}^-8$, how does $^-10$ compare with $^-8$? Explain.

10. (a) If $x + y = z$ and $y \in N$, how does x compare with z?
    (b) If $x + y = z$ and $y \in W$, how does x compare with z?
    (c) If $x + y = z$ and $y \in J$, how does x compare with z?

11. Identify by the roster method $\{x \mid (x \in J) \wedge ({}^-3 \leq x < 2)\}$.

12. Using Theorems 8.9.1, 8.9.2, 8.9.3, and 8.9.4 whenever appropriate, identify by the roster method the set whose elements are all integral values of n such that:
    (a) $n + 7 < 9$ (b) $2n - 3 < 5$
    (c) $n - 7 > 5$ (d) $2 + 5n > {}^-8$

13. Theorem 8.9.3 states that if a and b are in J, c is a positive integer, and $a < b$, then $ca < cb$. By trying a few samples and reasoning inductively, how do you believe the theorem should read if c is a negative integer rather than a positive integer?

8.10
Absolute Value

One way of introducing the concept of absolute value is to refer to the number line:

We shall begin by defining the *distance* between any two points on the number line to be the *number* of intervals between the points. The distance between two points, such as those associated with the numbers 2 and 5, can be found simply by counting the intervals between the points. (Recall that we agreed to name points on the number line by the numbers associated with the points; hence we may speak of point 2, point 5, and so on.) In this case there are 3 intervals between point 2 and point 5. An alternative method for finding the distance between points 2 and 5 is to subtract the number 2 from the number 5 and obtain $5 - 2 = 3$. As another example, the distance between point 4 and point $^-3$ is $4 - {}^-3 = 4 + 3 = 7$.

Suppose we wish to write a general expression for the distance between some point a and some other point b on the number line. If we use for the distance the expression $a - b$, and a happens to equal 7 while b equals 2, everything works out very well. The result is $a - b = 7 - 2 = 5$. However, if we let $a = 2$ and $b = 7$, then the difference is $a - b = 2 - 7 = {}^-5$. By counting the intervals between the points we know that the result should be the natural (counting) number 5 rather than its inverse $^-5$. It appears that if the expression $a - b$ is used to find the distance between two points on the number line, we shall either obtain the natural number we desire or its inverse, depending on whether $a > b$ or $b > a$. (If $a = b$, of course, the distance is zero.) This is indeed the case since $a - b$ and $b - a$ are additive inverses, as can be proved by showing that their sum is zero:

$$
\begin{aligned}
(a - b) + (b - a) &= (a + {}^-b) + (b + {}^-a) \\
&= a + ({}^-b + b) + {}^-a \\
&= a + 0 + {}^-a \\
&= a + {}^-a \\
&= 0
\end{aligned}
$$

It is seen, therefore, that the expression $a - b$ may be used to represent the distance between a and b if $a - b \geq 0$, or the inverse $^-(a - b)$ may be used if $a - b < 0$. To assist in this and other situations, we use the concept known as the *absolute value* of a number.

DEFINITION 8.10.1

If n is an integer, the **absolute value** of n, denoted by $|n|$, is as follows:

If $n \geq 0$, then $|n| = n$.
If $n < 0$, then $|n| = {}^-n$.

Example 1.
(a) $|17| = 17$.
(b) $|0| = 0$.
(c) $|{}^-8| = {}^-({}^-8) = 8$.
(d) $|7 - 2| = |5| = 5$.
(e) $|2 - 7| = |2 + {}^-7| = |{}^-5| = {}^-({}^-5) = 5$.
(f) $|{}^-4 - 7| = |{}^-4 + {}^-7| = |{}^-11| = {}^-({}^-11) = 11$.

DEFINITION 8.10.2

The **distance** between any two points a and b on the number line is the absolute value of the difference between the numbers associated with the points, that is, $|a - b|$.

Example 2. Using Definition 8.10.2, find the distance between points a and b if:
(a) $a = 20$ and $b = 8$.

  Solution: $|a - b| = |20 - 8| = |12| = 12$.

(b) $a = 8$ and $b = 20$.

  Solution: $|a - b| = |8 - 20| = |{}^-12| = {}^-({}^-12) = 12$.

(c) $a = 32$ and $b = 32$.

  Solution: $|a - b| = |32 - 32| = |0| = 0$.

Example 3. Identify members of the following set by the roster method and plot the points on the number line: $\{x \mid (x \in J) \wedge (|x| < 5)\}$.

Solution: We see that $|x| < 5$ if and only if x is between $^-5$ and 5 or $^-5 < x < 5$. Therefore, the solution set is

$$\{^-4, {}^-3, {}^-2, {}^-1, 0, 1, 2, 3, 4\}.$$

Properties of Absolute Value. Some useful properties of absolute value are as follows:

1. $|a - b| = |b - a|$.
2. $|a \cdot b| = |a| \cdot |b|$.
3. $|a + b| \leq |a| + |b|$.

Although no formal proofs will be given for these statements, the reader may easily verify them by using various values for a and b.

EXERCISE 8.10

1. Define the *absolute value* of a number.

2. Define the distance between two points a and b on the number line.

3. Find the distance between each of the following pairs of points on the number line:
   (a) 2 and 9   (b) 14 and 8
   (c) x and y (d) 23 and ⁻23
   (e) ⁻4 and 7   (f) ⁻8 and ⁻2
   (g) 14 and 14   (h) 0 and ⁻9

4. Identify the following sets by the roster method and, when possible, plot all the points on the number line:
   (a) $\{x \mid (x \in J) \wedge (|x| < 3)\}$
   (b) $\{x \mid (x \in J) \wedge (|x| \leq 3)\}$
   (c) $\{x \mid (x \in J) \wedge (|x| > 2)\}$
   (d) $\{x \mid (x \in J) \wedge (|x - 2| \leq 4)\}$

5. Identify the *complements* of the following sets by the roster method and, when possible, plot all the points on the number line. Assume the universe to be J.
   (a) $\{x \mid (x \in J) \wedge (|x| > 5)\}$
   (b) $\{x \mid (x \in J) \wedge (|x| < 2)\}$
   (c) $\{x \mid (x \in J) \wedge (|x| \geq 4)\}$
   (d) $\{x \mid (x \in J) \wedge (|x - 2| > 3)\}$

6. (a) Write an expression for the distance from point 4 to point n on the number line.
   (b) Using this expression, what is the distance from point 4 to point n if: $n = 3$? $n = 0$? $n = $ ⁻7?

7. Verify that $|a - b| = |b - a|$ by letting:
   (a) $a = 3$ and $b = 5$
   (b) $a = $ ⁻4 and $b = 7$
   (c) $a = $ ⁻8 and $b = $ ⁻3

8. Verify that $|a \cdot b| = |a| \cdot |b|$ by letting:
   (a) $a = 5$ and $b = 2$
   (b) $a = 3$ and $b = {}^-4$
   (c) $a = {}^-9$ and $b = {}^-3$

9. Verify that $|a + b| \leq |a| + |b|$ by letting:
   (a) $a = 7$ and $b = 3$
   (b) $a = {}^-4$ and $b = 12$
   (c) $a = {}^-5$ and $b = {}^-8$

REVIEW EXERCISES

1. Name the additive inverses of each of the following:
   (a) ${}^-27$ (b) 0 (c) ${}^-(b + c)$ (d) ${}^{--}(b + c)$

2. (a) Neglecting order, how many different pairs of whole numbers have a sum of 7? Name them.
   (b) How many different pairs of integers have a sum of 7? Name ten such pairs.

3. If a, b, and c are integers, which of the following statements are true?
   (a) $a + b = b + a$ (b) $a - b = b - a$
   (c) $(a + b) + c = a + (b + c)$ (d) $(a - b) - c = a - (b - c)$
   (e) $a + 0 = 0 + a$ (f) $a - 0 = 0 - a$

4. Find the following products in two ways: (i) without using the distributive property, and (ii) using the distributive property.
   (a) $4({}^-7 + 3)$ (b) $9(4 - 8)$
   (c) ${}^-5(11 + 4)$ (d) ${}^-7(7 + {}^-5)$
   (e) $3(9 - 3 - 2)$ (f) ${}^-5(7 - 9 + {}^-3)$

5. If a, b, and c are integers, which of the following statements are true?
   (a) $a \div b = b \div a$
   (b) $(a \div b) \div c = a \div (b \div c)$
   (c) $a \div (b + c) = (a \div b) + (a \div c)$
   (d) $(a + b) \div c = (a \div c) + (b \div c)$

6. Is zero a positive integer or a negative integer?

7. (a) Prove the cancellation property of addition for the integers.
   (b) Why is it unnecessary to prove the cancellation property of addition for the whole numbers if it has been proved for the integers?

8. (a) What is the smallest whole number?
   (b) What is the largest whole number?
   (c) What is the smallest positive integer?
   (d) What is the largest positive integer?
   (e) What is the smallest negative integer?
   (f) What is the largest negative integer?

9. (a) What integer has the smallest absolute value?
   (b) What positive integer has the smallest absolute value?
   (c) What negative integer has the smallest absolute value?

10. (a) Identify by the roster method $\{x \mid (x \in J) \wedge (|x| < 7)\}$.
    (b) Identify by the roster method $\{x \mid (x \in J) \wedge (|x - 2| < 7)\}$.

Chapter Nine
Number Theory and Mathematical Systems

The study of the properties of the integers and their relationships with each other has fascinated man for centuries. Such studies resulted in the belief that some numbers had great mystical significance. Even today many public buildings do not have a floor numbered 13! Do you know people who consider 7 a lucky number? Each year without exception, the author's wife receives a check for $7 from her father upon celebrating her birthday.

The study of the integers and their properties is known as *number theory*. Number theory is one of the few branches of mathematics in which the layman has been able to make unique contributions without considerable specialized training. Even though it is becoming more difficult to make original contributions to the theory of numbers, it is a field in which the mathematician and layman alike may have the satisfaction of rediscovering certain properties and relationships. In this chapter we shall introduce very briefly a few of the many topics in the theory of numbers.

Although modern mathematicians do not spend their time considering whether or not a number may have mystical properties, they are still attempting to discover new relationships among the numbers and to solve some classical problems that have been attempted for hundreds of years. For example, the equation $x^2 + y^2 = z^2$ has many positive integral solutions, such as $3^2 + 4^2 = 5^2$, $5^2 + 12^2 = 13^2$, and $6^2 + 8^2 = 10^2$. However, $x^n + y^n = z^n$ has no known positive integral solutions for $n > 2$. Pierre Fermat (1601–1665), a great French mathematician, claimed in 1637 to have proved that the equation $x^n + y^n = z^n$ has no positive integral solutions for $n > 2$. However, he did not show his proof and his statement has become known as "Fermat's Last Theorem." Fermat wrote, "I have discovered a truly remarkable proof but the margin is too small to contain it." To this day, except for special cases, the problem remains unsolved.

There are many other unsolved classical problems in number theory; there are also many new problems that are being formulated and solved by today's mathematicians. This field of mathematics seems almost unlimited.

In studying the whole numbers it was mentioned that a and b are called *factors* of the *product* $a \cdot b$; the product $a \cdot b$ is also said to be a *multiple* of both a and b. Some whole numbers have many distinct factors while others have few. For example, the factors of 20 comprise the set $F_{20} = \{1, 2, 4, 5, 10, 20\}$, while the factors of 47 are the members of the set $F_{47} = \{1, 47\}$. A number such as 47 which has *only* itself and one as factors is said to be *prime*. Every whole number, of course, has itself and one as factors since one is the multiplicative identity and $n = n \cdot 1$.

DEFINITION 9.2.1

A number n in W is said to be **prime** if and only if $n > 1$ and its only factors are n and 1.

DEFINITION 9.2.2

A number n in W is said to be **composite** if and only if $n > 1$ and n is not prime.

From the above definitions it is seen that the first five prime numbers in W are 2, 3, 5, 7, and 11, while the first five composite numbers in W are 4, 6, 8, 9, and 10. Noticeably absent from the sets of prime and composite numbers are the whole numbers 0 and 1. The numbers 0 and 1 are neither prime nor composite. An alternative way of defining a prime number is to say that it is a whole number with exactly two *distinct* factors. Zero, of course, has every whole number as a factor: $0 = 0 \cdot 0 = 0 \cdot 1 = 0 \cdot 2 = 0 \cdot 3$, and so on. The number 1 has only itself as a distinct factor: $1 = 1 \cdot 1$.

Many students wonder why prime numbers are defined in such a way as to exclude the number 1. If we were to remove the restriction $n > 1$ from Definition 9.2.1, the number 1 would qualify as a prime since its only factors are itself (1) and 1. One reason for excluding 1 as a prime is that many theorems can be proved which hold for the primes but not for the composite numbers or for 0 and 1; the Fundamental Theorem of Arithmetic discussed in the next section is an example. If 1 were included as a prime, it would be necessary to say that such theorems are true for all primes p, $p \neq 1$.

Incidentally, we could define prime and composite numbers to include the negative integers by saying that a negative integer is prime if its additive inverse is prime, and that a negative integer is composite if it is not prime.

It would be very convenient to have a mathematical formula that could be used to generate in succession all the primes. However, no one has yet produced such a formula although many have tried. Some expressions, such as $n^2 - n + 41$, may be used to generate a large number of primes. The expression $n^2 - n + 41$ will yield a prime number for every positive integer n such that $1 \leq n \leq 40$. We get the numbers 41, 43, 47, 53, 61, 71, 83, and so on—all of which are prime. However, if $n = 41$, the result is $41^2 - 41 + 41 = 41^2 = 41 \cdot 41$, and $41 \cdot 41$ is obviously not prime. The student who invents a formula for generating all the primes will live in history.

One rather crude but effective method for determining all the primes less than or equal to a given number n is to use the "Sieve of Eratosthenes." Eratosthenes (about 230 B.C.) was a Greek mathematician. The reason for calling his method of finding primes a sieve will be obvious as soon as the procedure is explained. Suppose, for example, we wish to find all the primes less than or equal to 50. Write down the numbers from 1 to 50 and immediately strike out 1, which is not prime. Then circle 2 (the first prime) and strike out all multiples of 2 greater than 2: 4, 6, 8, and so on. We then have:

$$
\begin{array}{cccccccccc}
\not{1} & ② & 3 & \not{4} & 5 & \not{6} & 7 & \not{8} & 9 & \not{10} \\
11 & \not{12} & 13 & \not{14} & 15 & \not{16} & 17 & \not{18} & 19 & \not{20} \\
21 & \not{22} & 23 & \not{24} & 25 & \not{26} & 27 & \not{28} & 29 & \not{30} \\
31 & \not{32} & 33 & \not{34} & 35 & \not{36} & 37 & \not{38} & 39 & \not{40} \\
41 & \not{42} & 43 & \not{44} & 45 & \not{46} & 47 & \not{48} & 49 & \not{50}
\end{array}
$$

Next circle 3 and strike out all of its multiples greater than 3. (Some multiples of 3 will have already been eliminated as multiples of 2.) Next circle 5 and continue this process. When finished, all the prime numbers less than or equal to 50 will be circled as follows:

$$
\begin{array}{cccccccccc}
\not{1} & ② & ③ & \not{4} & ⑤ & \not{6} & ⑦ & \not{8} & \not{9} & \not{10} \\
⑪ & \not{12} & ⑬ & \not{14} & \not{15} & \not{16} & ⑰ & \not{18} & ⑲ & \not{20} \\
\not{21} & \not{22} & ㉓ & \not{24} & \not{25} & \not{26} & \not{27} & \not{28} & ㉙ & \not{30} \\
㉛ & \not{32} & \not{33} & \not{34} & \not{35} & \not{36} & ㊲ & \not{38} & \not{39} & \not{40} \\
㊶ & \not{42} & ㊸ & \not{44} & \not{45} & \not{46} & ㊼ & \not{48} & \not{49} & \not{50}
\end{array}
$$

There are many interesting and easily stated problems concerning prime numbers that have not been solved. We do not know, for example, whether there is a greatest pair of *twin primes*. Twin primes are pairs of primes whose difference is 2; some twin primes are (3, 5), (5, 7), (11, 13), (41, 43), and (59, 61).

In 1742 the mathematician Christian Goldbach conjectured that every even integer greater than 4 may be expressed as the sum of two odd primes, and that every odd number greater than 7 may be expressed as the sum of three odd primes. No one has been able to either prove or disprove Goldbach's conjectures. It seems that some of the questions that can be stated most simply are among the most difficult to prove.

An interesting fact, proved by Euclid (about 300 B.C.), is that no greatest prime exists and hence there are infinitely many primes. His type of proof is slightly different from those previously presented in this text. Euclid reasoned as follows: Suppose there is a finite set of primes $\{p_1, p_2, p_3, p_4, \ldots, p_n\}$, where p_n is the greatest prime. Consider the number $M = p_1 \cdot p_2 \cdot p_3 \cdot p_4 \cdot \cdots \cdot p_n + 1$. Note that M is the sum of two addends; the first addend is the product of all the primes and the second addend is 1. M must be either prime or composite. If M is prime, then there is a larger prime than p_n since $M > p_n$. This contradicts the supposition that p_n is the greatest prime. If, however, M is composite, then it must be divisible by some prime (as we shall see in Section 9.3). But M is not divisible by any of the primes p_1, p_2, p_3, $\ldots$, p_n since there will be a remainder of 1 in each case, and hence M must be divisible by some prime greater than p_n. This also contradicts the supposition that p_n is the greatest prime. In either case, there is no greatest prime and hence there are infinitely many primes. A large number known to be prime is $2^{3217} - 1$ (approximately equal to 10^{968}). A still larger prime is $2^{11213} - 1$. Euclid's proof, however, assures us that even this very large number is not the greatest prime!

9.3 The Fundamental Theorem of Arithmetic

Composite numbers may be expressed or named as the product of factors. For example: $12 = 1 \cdot 12$, $12 = 2 \cdot 6$, $12 = 3 \cdot 4$, and $12 = 2 \cdot 2 \cdot 3$. Each of these indicated products is called a factorization of the number 12. Every composite number may be expressed as the product of prime numbers by selecting any factorization of the number that does not include 1 and continuing to factor those factors that are not already prime. Consider 24 as an example: $24 = 3 \cdot 8$; 3 is prime but 8 is not and can therefore be factored. So we write $24 = 3 \cdot 8 = 3 \cdot 2 \cdot 4$. Now we see that all factors are prime except 4. Continuing, we finally have $24 = 3 \cdot 8 = 3 \cdot 2 \cdot 4 = 3 \cdot 2 \cdot 2 \cdot 2$. The last expression, $3 \cdot 2 \cdot 2 \cdot 2$, is called the prime factorization or the complete factorization of the number 24 since all the factors are prime. It is common practice to arrange the prime factors in order from least to greatest and to write $24 = 2 \cdot 2 \cdot 2 \cdot 3 = 2^3 \cdot 3$.

Another method for factoring a composite number into prime factors is to test the primes as divisors in succession beginning with the least prime: 2, 3, 5, 7, 11, 13, and so on. Continue dividing by each prime as many times as possible before going to the next. Several illustrations follow.

Example 1.   Factor 48 into prime factors.

Solution:

$$48 = 2 \cdot 24$$
$$= 2 \cdot 2 \cdot 12$$
$$= 2 \cdot 2 \cdot 2 \cdot 6$$
$$= 2 \cdot 2 \cdot 2 \cdot 2 \cdot 3$$
$$= 2^4 \cdot 3$$

$$2)\overline{48}$$
$$2)\overline{24}$$
$$2)\overline{12}$$
$$2)\underline{6}$$
$$3$$

Example 2.   Find the prime factorization of 700.

Solution:

$$700 = 2 \cdot 350$$
$$= 2 \cdot 2 \cdot 175$$
$$= 2 \cdot 2 \cdot 5 \cdot 35$$
$$= 2 \cdot 2 \cdot 5 \cdot 5 \cdot 7$$
$$= 2^2 \cdot 5^2 \cdot 7$$

$$2)\overline{700}$$
$$2)\overline{350}$$
$$5)\overline{175}$$
$$5)\underline{35}$$
$$7$$

Example 3.   Find the complete factorization of 1547.

Solution:

$$1547 = 7 \cdot 221$$
$$= 7 \cdot 13 \cdot 17$$

$$7)\overline{1547}$$
$$13)\underline{221}$$
$$17$$

Factoring very large numbers into primes can become tedious and is best accomplished by using modern high-speed computers. Finding the prime factors of 2,839,003 (which are 743 and 3821) might prove to be less than exciting. Of course, if we test for prime divisors of 743 and 3821, there will be none except the numbers themselves since 743 and 3821 are prime.

In searching for the prime factors of a given number, it is useful to know that we need try no primes larger than the square root of the number. To see why this is true, let us examine, for example, all the pairs of factors of 100.

$$
\begin{aligned}
1 &\times 100 \\
2 &\times 50 \\
4 &\times 25 \\
5 &\times 20 \\
10 &\times 10 \quad \longleftarrow \\
20 &\times 5 \\
25 &\times 4 \\
50 &\times 2 \\
100 &\times 1
\end{aligned}
$$

Note that as larger numbers are used for the first factor of 100, smaller numbers must be used for the second factor. Upon reaching 10 (the square root of 100), the two factors are equal. From the list of factors it is apparent that all pairs of factors following 10×10 may be found simply by commuting previous pairs of factors. Hence there is no need to test numbers larger than 10 as factors of 100 since they were found by testing smaller numbers.

Example 4.   Find the prime factorization of 143.

Solution: Since $11^2 = 121$ and $12^2 = 144$, we see that $11 < \sqrt{143} < 12$. Therefore, we need to test as divisors only prime numbers less than 12. In succession we test 2, 3, 5, 7, and 11. Upon dividing by 11 we find that $143 = 11 \cdot 13$; and since 13 is also prime, the factorization is complete.

Example 5.   Factor 819 into prime factors.

Solution: Since $28^2 = 784$ and $29^2 = 841$, primes to be tested are those less than 29: 2, 3, 5, 7, 11, 13, 17, 19, and 23. Upon dividing by 3 we find that $819 = 3 \cdot 273$. Now, since $16 < \sqrt{273} < 17$, it is necessary to consider only those primes less than 17: 2, 3, 5, 7, 11, and 13. However, 3 is again a divisor and $819 = 3 \cdot 3 \cdot 91$. Now it is necessary to test only primes less than 10, and the result is $819 = 3 \cdot 3 \cdot 7 \cdot 13$. All these factors are prime and the factorization is complete.

Example 6. Find the complete factorization of 743.

Solution: Since $27^2 = 729$ and $28^2 = 784$, only primes less than 28 need to be considered: 2, 3, 5, 7, 11, 13, 17, 19, and 23. Since none of these divides 743, we conclude that 743 is prime.

Not only is there a prime factorization for every composite number, but the prime factorization is *unique*. Although no formal proof will be given, we shall state this concept as a theorem. The theorem is known as the *Fundamental Theorem of Arithmetic* and also by the more descriptive title, the *Unique Prime Factorization Theorem*.

THEOREM 9.3.1

The Fundamental Theorem of Arithmetic (Unique Prime Factorization Theorem). Every composite number can be expressed uniquely as the product of prime factors, if the order of the factors is disregarded.

The proof of the Fundamental Theorem of Arithmetic may be found in almost any text on the theory of numbers.

EXERCISE 9.3

1. Define a *prime* number.

2. Define a *composite* number.

3. Using the Sieve of Eratosthenes:
   (a) Find all primes less than 100.
   (b) Identify all twin primes less than 100.

4. Show that each of the following even numbers may be written as the sum of two (not necessarily distinct) odd primes: 6, 8, 10, 12, 72, 84.

5. Write 22 as the sum of two primes in as many ways as possible.

6. Show that each of the following odd numbers may be written as the sum of three (not necessarily distinct) odd primes: 9, 11, 13, 15, 35.

7. Find the prime factorization of the following numbers:
   (a) 60   (b) 108   (c) 51
   (d) 156   (e) 510   (f) 362

8. (a) Try to find two different prime factorizations of 24 by starting first with $24 = 8 \times 3$ and then with $24 = 6 \times 4$.
   (b) State the Fundamental Theorem of Arithmetic.

9. Factor $^-18$ uniquely as the product of $^-1$ and prime factors.

10. A perfect number P is a number which equals the sum of its distinct factors, excluding P itself. For example: $F_6 = \{1, 2, 3, 6\}$ and $6 = 1 + 2 + 3$. Two other perfect numbers are 496 and 8128. There is only one two-digit perfect number. See if you can find it. *Hint:* It is less than 40.

11. A number is said to be a cubic number if it is equal to x^3 where $x \in N$. The first four cubic numbers are $1 = 1^3$, $8 = 2^3$, $27 = 3^3$, and $64 = 4^3$. The smallest number which may be written as the sum of two cubic numbers in two different ways is 1729. It is the sum of 12^3 and 1^3. See if you can find the other two cubic numbers whose sum is 1729.

9.4
Odd and Even Numbers

Odd and even numbers have already been referred to in the text since it was assumed that most students have some knowledge of them. However, a formal definition of odd and even numbers will now be given.

DEFINITION 9.4.1

A number n in W is said to be an even number if and only if it has a factor of 2.

The even numbers, then, are the members of $E = \{0, 2, 4, 6, 8, \ldots\}$. A similar definition can be given for the integers. The even integers are the members of $\{\ldots, ^-6, ^-4, ^-2, 0, 2, 4, 6, \ldots\}$.

DEFINITION 9.4.2

A number n in W is said to be an odd number if it is not an even number.

The definition of an odd number implies that it is a member of the set $F = \{1, 3, 5, 7, \ldots\}$. Extending the definition to the integers, the odd integers are the members of $\{\ldots, ^-5, ^-3, ^-1, 1, 3, 5, \ldots\}$.

The even whole numbers may be identified as the set $E = \{x \mid x = 2n, n \in W\}$. Similarly, the set of odd whole numbers may be indicated by $F = \{x \mid x = 2n + 1, n \in W\}$. As will be seen in the examples below, it is frequently convenient to represent an even number in the form $2n$ and an odd number in the form $2n + 1$. Unless otherwise stated, the terms odd and even numbers will refer to the odd and even whole numbers rather than to the integers.

Example 1. Does the closure property hold for addition in the set of even numbers?

Solution: Let $2a$ and $2b$ represent any two even numbers. Then their sum $2a + 2b = 2(a + b)$ by the distributive property. Since a and b are in W and since the closure property holds for addition in W, we can write $a + b = c$ where $c \in W$. Then $2(a + b) = 2c$, but $2c$ is by definition an even number. Therefore, the sum of any two even numbers is an even number and the closure property holds for addition in the even numbers.

Example 2.   Does the closure property hold for addition in the set of odd numbers?

Solution: One counterexample is sufficient to show that the closure property does not hold for addition in the odd numbers. Since $7 = 2(3) + 1$ and $9 = 2(4) + 1$, 7 and 9 are by definition odd numbers. However, their sum $7 + 9 = 16 = 2(8)$, which we recognize as an even number. Therefore, the set of odd numbers is not closed under addition.

EXERCISE 9.4

1. Prove that the sum of any two odd numbers is an even number.

2. Prove that the sum of any even number and any odd number is an odd number.

3. Prove that the set of odd numbers is closed with respect to the operation of multiplication.

4. Prove that the product of any even number and any odd number is an even number.

5. Note that:

$$1 = 1^2$$
$$1 + 3 = 4 = 2^2$$
$$1 + 3 + 5 = 9 = 3^2$$
$$1 + 3 + 5 + 7 = 16 = 4^2$$

   (a) By inductive reasoning, what would you expect to be the sum of $1 + 3 + 5 + 7 + 9$?
   (b) Can you suggest a general mathematical expression for the sum of the first n odd numbers? Test your expression by using a few examples.

6. Why must a number be a perfect square if it has an odd number of distinct factors?

9.5
Greatest
Common
Divisor

In studying the common divisors of two or more given integers, we shall consider only positive divisors. If a and b are integers and if a positive integer d divides both a and b, then d is called a common divisor of a and b. For example, $3 \mid 12$ (3 divides 12) and $3 \mid {}^-18$; therefore, 3 is a common divisor of 12 and $^-18$. If a number d divides both a and b, it is, of course, a factor of both a and b and may also be called a common factor of a and b. In the example above, 3 is a common factor of 12 and $^-18$. However, it is not the only common factor.

The positive divisors (or factors) of 12 are the members of the set $A = \{1, 2, 3, 4, 6, 12\}$, and the positive divisors of $^-18$ are the elements of $B = \{1, 2, 3, 6, 9, 18\}$. The common divisors (or factors) of 12 and $^-18$ are found in the intersection of the two sets, $A \cap B = \{1, 3, 6\}$. From the set notation it is easy to see that the *greatest common divisor* (g.c.d.) of 12 and $^-18$ is 6.

DEFINITION 9.5.1

The greatest common divisor of the integers a and b, denoted by g.c.d.(a, b), is the largest natural number d such that $d \mid a$ and $d \mid b$.

Example 1. Find the common divisors of 48 and 60 and identify g.c.d.$(48, 60)$.

Solution: The divisors of 48 are the members of $A = \{1, 2, 3, 4, 6, 8, 12, 16, 24, 48\}$. The divisors of 60 are the members of $B = \{1, 2, 3, 4, 5, 6, 10, 12, 15, 20, 30, 60\}$. The common divisors of 48 and 60 are the members of $A \cap B = \{1, 2, 3, 4, 6, 12\}$ and g.c.d.$(48, 60) = 12$.

Another method for finding the greatest common divisor of two numbers utilizes the prime factorization of each number. Using, once again, the numbers 48 and 60, we see that $48 = 2^4 \cdot 3$ and $60 = 2^2 \cdot 3 \cdot 5$. The greatest power of 2 common to 48 and 60 is 2^2, and the greatest power of 3 common to the numbers is 3^1. Since no other prime factors are common to 48 and 60, the greatest common divisor must be $(2^2 \cdot 3) = 12$. Note that $48 = (2^2 \cdot 3)(2^2)$ and $60 = (2^2 \cdot 3)(5)$ which shows that $(2^2 \cdot 3)$ is indeed a divisor of both numbers.

The concept of the greatest common divisor may be extended to include more than two numbers as shown below. Negative integers may also be considered.

Example 2.   What is the greatest common divisor of $^-120$, 180, and 780?

Solution:

$$^-120 = {}^-1 \cdot 2 \cdot 2 \cdot 2 \cdot 3 \cdot 5 = {}^-1 \cdot 2^3 \cdot 3 \cdot 5.$$
$$180 = 2 \cdot 2 \cdot 3 \cdot 3 \cdot 5 = 2^2 \cdot 3^2 \cdot 5.$$
$$780 = 2 \cdot 2 \cdot 3 \cdot 5 \cdot 13 = 2^2 \cdot 3 \cdot 5 \cdot 13.$$

The product of the highest powers of the prime factors common to the three numbers is the greatest common divisor. This number is $2^2 \cdot 3 \cdot 5 = 60$. Note that $^-120 = (2^2 \cdot 3 \cdot 5)(^-2)$, $180 = (2^2 \cdot 3 \cdot 5)(3)$, and $780 = (2^2 \cdot 3 \cdot 5)(13)$.

DEFINITION 9.5.2

If the greatest common divisor of the integers a and b is 1, then a and b are said to be relatively prime.

The numbers 4 and 9 are relatively prime since g.c.d.$(4, 9) = 1$. Note that although 4 and 9 are relatively prime, neither 4 nor 9 is prime. Other examples of relatively prime numbers are $(12, 17)$, $(15, 14)$, $(7, 9)$, and $(35, 24)$. Although fractions will not be discussed until the next chapter, it is of interest to note that a fraction such as $\frac{48}{60}$ may be named more simply as $\frac{4}{5}$ by dividing both the numerator and denominator by their greatest common divisor 12. The fraction $\frac{4}{9}$, however, may not be renamed in this way since 4 and 9 are relatively prime.

It is tedious to find the g.c.d. of large numbers by expressing them as the product of their prime factors. If the numbers are large, the g.c.d. may be found more easily by the repeated use of the division algorithm: $a = bq + r$ where $0 \leq r < b$ (see Theorem 7.5.1).

Suppose we wish to find g.c.d.$(164, 48)$. By applying the division algorithm to 164 and 48, we can write:

$$164 = 48(3) + 20$$

From the above we see that $164 - 48(3) = 20$, and by the distributive property a common divisor of 164 and 48 will be a factor of the left member of this equation and hence must also be a factor of 20. Therefore, any number that divides 164 and 48 must also divide 20, so we shall look for g.c.d.$(48, 20)$ instead of g.c.d.$(164, 48)$. Again applying the division algorithm, we divide 48 by 20 and write:

$$48 = 20(2) + 8$$

But, by the method of reasoning that was used above, g.c.d.$(48, 20) =$

g.c.d.(20, 8). Since $20 = 8(2) + 4$, g.c.d.(20, 8) = g.c.d.(8, 4). However, $8 = 4(2) + 0$ and we see that $4 \mid 8$ since the remainder is zero. Therefore, g.c.d.(8, 4) is 4 since $4 \mid 8$ and $4 \mid 4$. Finally, by applying the transitive property of equals, we see that g.c.d.(164, 48) = g.c.d.(8, 4) = 4.

Example 3. Find g.c.d.(102, 44).

Solution:

$$102 = 44(2) + 14; \qquad \text{g.c.d.}(102, 44) = \text{g.c.d.}(44, 14)$$
$$44 = 14(3) + 2; \qquad \text{g.c.d.}(44, 14) = \text{g.c.d.}(14, 2)$$
$$14 = 2(7) + 0; \qquad \text{g.c.d.}(14, 2) = 2 \text{ since } 2 \mid 14 \text{ and } 2 \mid 2$$

Therefore, by the transitive property of equals, g.c.d.(102, 44) = 2.

Example 4. Find g.c.d.(63, 52).

Solution:

$$63 = 52(1) + 11; \qquad \text{g.c.d.}(63, 52) = \text{g.c.d.}(52, 11)$$
$$52 = 11(4) + 8; \qquad \text{g.c.d.}(52, 11) = \text{g.c.d.}(11, 8)$$
$$11 = 8(1) + 3; \qquad \text{g.c.d.}(11, 8) = \text{g.c.d.}(8, 3)$$
$$8 = 3(2) + 2; \qquad \text{g.c.d.}(8, 3) = \text{g.c.d.}(3, 2)$$
$$3 = 2(1) + 1; \qquad \text{g.c.d.}(3, 2) = \text{g.c.d.}(2, 1)$$
$$2 = 1(2) + 0; \qquad \text{g.c.d.}(2, 1) = 1 \text{ since } 1 \mid 2 \text{ and } 1 \mid 1$$

Therefore, by the transitive property of equals, g.c.d.(63, 52) = 1 and we note that 63 and 52 are relatively prime.

The set of equations (such as those in Examples 3 and 4 above) that is obtained by the repeated use of the division algorithm in finding the greatest common divisor of two numbers is called *Euclid's Algorithm.*

EXERCISE 9.5

1. Define the *greatest common divisor* of the integers a and b.
2. Given integers 54 and 60:
   (a) Identify the set D_{54} whose members are the divisors of 54.
   (b) Identify the set D_{60} whose members are the divisors of 60.
   (c) Identify the set $D_{54} \cap D_{60}$ whose members are the common divisors of 54 and 60.
   (d) What is g.c.d.(54, 60)?
3. By the method of problem 2, find g.c.d.(140, 150).

4. Utilize the prime factorization of each number to find the g.c.d. of the following:
   (a) 24, 36 (b) 54, 60
   (c) ⁻60, 48 (d) 140, ⁻150
   (e) 54, 60, 72 (f) 90, 84, 72

5. What is g.c.d.$(0, a)$ if $a \in J$ and $a \neq 0$?

6. What is g.c.d.(a, b) if a and b are both prime?

7. Define the term *relatively prime* for integers a and b.

8. Which of the following pairs of integers are relatively prime?
   (a) 12, 15 (b) 14, 15
   (c) ⁻34, 51 (d) 26, 39
   (e) ⁻8, 27 (f) 24, 81

9. Using Euclid's Algorithm find the g.c.d. of the following pairs of integers.
   (a) 220 and 315 (b) 140 and 64
   (c) 2695 and 1344 (d) 78 and 715
   (e) 385 and 192 (f) 3612 and 13,760

10. Must two distinct prime numbers be relatively prime? Explain.

11. Must two relatively prime numbers be distinct prime numbers? Explain.

12. (a) Give an example of two composite numbers that are relatively prime.
    (b) Give an example of a composite number and a prime number that are relatively prime.

13. What is the smallest integer n, $n > 1$, that is relatively prime to:
    (a) 6 (b) 30
    (c) 15 (d) 42

14. If we define a prime number to be a whole number with exactly two distinct factors:
    (a) Does this definition preclude 0 and 1 as prime numbers? Explain.
    (b) Write a companion definition for composite numbers.
    (c) Does your definition in part (b) preclude 0 and 1 as composite numbers? Explain.

9.6 Least Common Multiple

Our study of common multiples will be limited to the natural numbers or positive integers. If $a \mid m$, then m is said to be a *multiple* of a. For example, $3 \mid 12$ and 12 is a multiple of 3. The multiples of 3 may be written as $3k$ where $k \in N$. The multiples of 3 are the elements of $\{3, 6, 9, 12, 15, \ldots, 3k, \ldots\}$ or $\{x \mid (x = 3k) \wedge (k \in N)\}$. In general, the multiples of any natural number a may be written in the form $a \cdot k$, where $k \in N$.

If $a \mid m$ and $b \mid m$, then m is a common multiple of a and b. For example, $4 \mid 36$ and $6 \mid 36$; therefore, 36 is a common multiple of 4 and 6. The multiples of 4 are the members of $A = \{4, 8, 12, 16, 20, 24, 28, 32, 36, 40, 44, 48, 52, \ldots, 4k, \ldots\}$, and the multiples of 6 are the members of $B = \{6, 12, 18, 24, 30, 36, 42, 48, 54, \ldots, 6k, \ldots\}$. The common multiples of 4 and 6 are the elements of $A \cap B = \{12, 24, 36, 48, \ldots, 12k, \ldots\}$. From the set notation it is apparent that there are infinitely many common multiples of 4 and 6 and that their *least common multiple* (l.c.m.) is 12. Note that the least common multiple 12 divides all other common multiples.

DEFINITION 9.6.1

The least common multiple of the integers a and b, denoted by l.c.m.(a, b), is the smallest natural number m such that $a \mid m$ and $b \mid m$.

In finding the least common multiple of two numbers, it is helpful to begin by factoring each into its prime factors. For example, in finding the l.c.m. of 4 and 6, we see that $4 = 2^2$ and $6 = 2 \cdot 3$. If a number is a multiple of 4, it must contain the factors of 4; and if it is a multiple of 6, it must contain the factors of 6. We conclude, then, that the least common multiple of two numbers must contain the highest power of each of the different prime factors that occur in the given numbers, but no other prime factors. In the case of 4 and 6, the least common multiple is $2^2 \cdot 3 = 12$.

Example 1.   Find l.c.m.$(126, 1200)$.

Solution:

$$126 = 2 \cdot 3^2 \cdot 7$$
$$1200 = 2^4 \cdot 3 \cdot 5^2$$

The l.c.m. will contain the highest power of each of the different prime factors of 126 and 1200. It is, therefore, $2^4 \cdot 3^2 \cdot 5^2 \cdot 7 = 25{,}200$.

The concept of the least common multiple may be extended to include more than two numbers as illustrated in the example below.

Example 2.   Find the l.c.m. of 28, 32, 54, and 85.

Solution:

$$28 = 2^2 \cdot 7$$
$$32 = 2^5$$
$$54 = 2 \cdot 3^3$$
$$85 = 5 \cdot 17$$

The l.c.m. is $2^5 \cdot 3^3 \cdot 5 \cdot 7 \cdot 17 = 514{,}080$.

The least common multiple of relatively small numbers can be quite large if the numbers have few common factors. This was the case in Example 2 above.

As will be seen in Chapter 10, the concept of the least common multiple can be advantageously applied to finding common denominators when adding or subtracting fractions.

EXERCISE 9.6

1. Define the *least common multiple* of the integers a and b.

2. What are the common multiples of 6 and 9?

3. Find the l.c.m. of each of the following pairs of numbers using the prime factorization method:
   (a) 24, 36   (b) 15, 27
   (c) 13, 11   (d) 14, 42
   (e) 66, 35   (f) 84, 96

4. Find the g.c.d. of the numbers in problem 3.

5. Find the l.c.m. of the following:
   (a) 14, 6, 9   (b) 18, 26, 39
   (c) 30, 39, 70   (d) 15, 21, 28
   (e) 24, 30, 48, 50   (f) 20, 24, 35, 54

6. If a and b are prime, what is l.c.m.(a, b)?

7. If a, b, and c represent prime numbers, find the l.c.m. of the following:
   (a) ab, a (b) ab, ac
   (c) a^2b, ac (d) ab^2c, a^3b^2
   (e) ab^2, ac^2, b^2c^5 (f) $ab^2, ac^2, b^2c^3, a^2c^3$

8. If a and b are composite, under what conditions will l.c.m.$(a, b) = ab$?

9.7
Finite Mathematical Systems

We have already defined and discussed two number systems—the system of whole numbers and the system of integers. Each of these systems has infinitely many elements. Mathematical systems may also be constructed using a finite number of elements; such systems are called finite systems. It is rather easy to create a system with only a few elements. We shall construct a mathematical system with four elements by referring to a "four-hour clock" as a model; see Figure 9.7.1. Once the system has been established, however, it will no longer be necessary to refer to the model from which it was abstracted.

From the figure we see that in one hour the hand on the clock

FIGURE 9.7.1

will move from 0 to 1, in two hours from 0 to 2, and so on. In four hours the hand will have made one complete revolution and will be back to 0 again. Note that the origin, or starting point, on the clock could have been named either 0 or 4. On a conventional twelve-hour clock, the origin is designated as 12; it could equally well be called 0.

We have identified the set of elements in our finite system as $\{0, 1, 2, 3\}$. Next we shall define a binary operation on the set—addition $(+)$. Suppose we wish to find the sum $1 + 2$. We place the hand on 1 and move it in a clockwise direction 2 units; it will then be at 3 and we see that $1 + 2 = 3$. Similarly, if we wish to find the sum $2 + 3$, we place the hand on 2 and move it 3 units in a clockwise direction and find that $2 + 3 = 1$. In general, then, if we wish to find the sum $a + b$, we place the hand on a and move it clockwise b units. The reading taken at this position is the sum $a + b$. The fact that $2 + 3 = 1$ should not seem particularly strange to those who are accustomed to twelve-hour clocks. If it is 11 o'clock, using a twelve-hour clock, four hours later it will be 3 o'clock. In this case $11 + 4 = 3$.

In constructing an addition table for a four-hour clock arithmetic, it is necessary to consider only the elements 0, 1, 2, and 3. Using the method for finding sums which has been described, an addition table can be constructed as in Figure 9.7.2. Check the results and see if you agree that they are correct.

FIGURE 9.7.2

+	0	1	2	3
0	0	1	2	3
1	1	2	3	0
2	2	3	0	1
3	3	0	1	2

We now have a set of elements for our mathematical system and an operation, addition $(+)$, defined on the set. What are some of the properties of this mathematical system?

In examining the addition table in Figure 9.7.2, it is obvious that the closure property for addition is satisfied since for each ordered pair of elements (a, b) in the set, there exists a unique element $a + b$ in the set.

The commutative property also holds since for all (a, b) in the set, $a + b = b + a$. This can be determined without testing all possible sums in the table. The table is symmetric about the diagonal extending from the upper left corner to the lower right corner; and since each sum $a + b$ is reflected across this diagonal to $b + a$, symmetry indicates that $a + b = b + a$.

The associative property will be found to hold for addition, although quite a few tests must be made to exhaust all possibilities. The truth of the associative property may be verified (but not proved) by testing several cases at random to see if $(a + b) + c = a + (b + c)$.

An identity element for addition exists and is the number 0 (zero). For every element a contained in the set, $a + 0 = 0 + a = a$.

Each element in the set has an additive inverse since for each element a there exists an element ^-a such that $a + {}^-a = 0$. By examining the addition table, it is easy to see that every element has an additive inverse since the identity element 0 appears in every row and column. The inverse of 0 is 0 since $0 + 0 = 0$. The inverse of 1 is 3 — ? since $1 + 3 = 0$. Similarly, the additive inverse of 2 is 2, and the inverse of 3 is 1. It is interesting to note that both 0 and 2 are their own additive inverses, while 1 and 3 are inverses of each other.

Mathematical systems having certain specific properties are sufficiently important and occur frequently enough to be given special names such as *group, ring,* and *field.* A mathematical system such as the one we abstracted by using a four-hour clock is called a *commutative group* (or an *Abelian group* in honor of the Norwegian mathematician Niels Henrik Abel, 1802–1829). Without the commutative property, the mathematical system would simply be called a *group.* The properties of groups and some other types of mathematical systems will be discussed in Section 9.8.

EXERCISE 9.7

1. (a) Construct an addition table for a three-hour clock arithmetic using elements of $\{0, 1, 2\}$.
   (b) Is addition commutative?

(c) Check several cases such as $(2 + 1) + 2$ and $2 + (1 + 2)$ and indicate if addition seems to be associative.

2. (a) Construct an addition table for a finite mathematical system using a five-hour clock as a model.
   (b) What is the additive inverse of each element of the system?
   (c) What is the identity element for addition?
   (d) Designate the origin on the clock by 5 instead of 0. What is the identity element for addition now?
   (e) What is the identity element for addition using a conventional twelve-hour clock?

3. Why is 3 P.M. sometimes expressed as 1500 hours (particularly by members of the military)? What would 0300 hours mean? 1620 hours?

4. Using a conventional twelve-hour clock, what time will it be in 64 hours if it is now 5 P.M.?

5. Using a five-hour clock, what time will it be in 24 hours if it is now 2 o'clock?

9.8
Commutative Groups, Rings, and Fields

Since a commutative (Abelian) group was identified in the previous section by using a four-hour clock as a model, we shall now give a formal definition of a commutative group.

DEFINITION 9.8.1

A commutative group is a mathematical system consisting of a set of elements, one binary operation $+$ defined on the set, and the following properties for all a, b, and c in the set:

1. *Closure.* $a + b$ is a unique element of the set.
2. *Commutativity.* $a + b = b + a$.
3. *Associativity.* $(a + b) + c = a + (b + c)$.
4. *Identity Element.* There exists an element i in the set such that $a + i = i + a = a$.
5. *Inverse Elements.* For every a there exists an element ^-a such that $a + {}^-a = i$.

If the commutative property does not hold, the system is simply called a group rather than a *commutative group*.

A mathematical system having the minimum properties necessary to qualify as a commutative group may have other properties as well. The system we abstracted by using a four-hour clock in Section 9.7 is a good example. In the four-hour clock arithmetic, a second operation, multiplication ($\cdot$), may be defined on $\{0, 1, 2, 3\}$. This can be done quite easily by using the repeated addend approach to multiplication (Definition 6.9.1). With this approach and with reference to the addition table in Figure 9.7.2, we find, for example, that $3 \cdot 2 = 2 + 2 + 2 = (2 + 2) + 2 = 0 + 2 = 2$. Using this method to compute all possible products, we can construct a multiplication table as shown in Figure 9.8.1.

$\cdot$	0	1	2	3
0	0	0	0	0
1	0	1	2	3
2	0	2	0	2
3	0	3	2	1

FIGURE 9.8.1

In studying the multiplication table, it is obvious that closure holds since there exists a unique product for every ordered pair (a, b). Since the table is symmetric about a diagonal from the upper left corner to the lower right corner, multiplication is commutative and $a \cdot b = b \cdot a$. The associative property also holds and $(a \cdot b) \cdot c = a \cdot (b \cdot c)$; the reader may wish to verify this by testing several cases. Finally, by inspecting the table, the number 1 is readily seen to be the multiplicative identity for the set.

If a multiplicative inverse existed for each element of the set, then the identity element 1 would appear in every row and column of the multiplication table. In this event, the four-hour clock system would be a commutative group not only under addition but also under the operation of multiplication. However, in examining the multiplication table, we see that neither 0 nor 2 has a multiplicative inverse. The numbers 1 and 3 are multiplicative inverses of themselves since $1 \cdot 1 = 1$ and $3 \cdot 3 = 1$.

Even though the four-hour clock arithmetic does not qualify as a commutative group under multiplication, it more than satisfies the qualifications for being a *ring*. A ring is defined in Definition 9.8.2.

DEFINITION 9.8.2

A **ring** is a mathematical system consisting of a set of elements, two binary operations $+$ and $\cdot$ defined on the set, and the following properties for all a, b, and c in the set:

1. The set is a commutative group under the operation $+$ and therefore has all the properties of a commutative group (Definition 9.8.1).
2. The second operation $\cdot$ has the properties of:
   Closure. $a \cdot b$ is a unique element of the set.
   Associativity. $(a \cdot b) \cdot c = a \cdot (b \cdot c)$.
3. Multiplication $(\cdot)$ is distributive over addition $(+)$.
   Distributive Properties. $a \cdot (b + c) = (a \cdot b) + (a \cdot c)$ and $(b + c) \cdot a = (b \cdot a) + (c \cdot a)$.

In the definition of a ring, both the left and right distributive properties must be mentioned since the operation $\cdot$ is not necessarily commutative. It is interesting to note that the set of integers J is a ring. Although J is a commutative group under addition, it is not a group under multiplication, since not every element has a multiplicative inverse.

Referring again to Section 9.7, it was not by chance that a four-hour clock was used as a model for a mathematical system; the number 4 was selected because it is a composite number. If a prime number such as 5 had been used in our model, each element except 0 would have had a multiplicative inverse. The addition and multiplication tables for a five-hour clock mathematical system are presented in Figure 9.8.2.

$+$	0	1	2	3	4
0	0	1	2	3	4
1	1	2	3	4	0
2	2	3	4	0	1
3	3	4	0	1	2
4	4	0	1	2	3

$\cdot$	0	1	2	3	4
0	0	0	0	0	0
1	0	1	2	3	4
2	0	2	4	1	3
3	0	3	1	4	2
4	0	4	3	2	1

FIGURE 9.8.2

In studying the multiplication table in Figure 9.8.2, it will be seen that every element except 0 (the additive identity) has a multiplicative inverse. Note that the number 1 appears in every row and column except those headed by 0.

The five-hour clock arithmetic has properties that qualify it as a commutative group under addition; and if the additive identity element 0 is removed from the set, it is also a commutative group under multiplication. Furthermore, multiplication is distributive over addition. A system with these properties is called a *field*.

DEFINITION 9.8.3

A field is a mathematical system consisting of a set containing at least two distinct elements, two binary operations + and · defined on the set, and the following properties:

1. The set of elements is a commutative group under addition.
2. The set of elements, with the identity element for addition (0) removed, is a commutative group under multiplication.
3. Multiplication is distributive over addition.

Any finite clock system with a prime number of elements is a field. The system of rational numbers with infinitely many elements is also a field, and will be considered in the next chapter.

EXERCISE 9.8

1. Define the word *group* as it is used to identify a mathematical system.
2. What is the difference between a *group* and a *commutative group?*
3. What is a *ring?*
4. What is a *field?*
5. Does a four-hour clock number system constitute:
    (a) a group under addition? under multiplication?
    (b) a commutative group under addition? under multiplication?
    (c) a ring under addition and multiplication?
    (d) a field under addition and multiplication?
6. Does a five-hour clock number system constitute:
    (a) a group under addition? under multiplication?
    (b) a commutative group under addition? under multiplication?
    (c) a ring under addition and multiplication?
    (d) a field under addition and multiplication?
7. (a) What modification in a five-hour clock arithmetic will enable it to then qualify as a commutative group under multiplication?
    (b) Is a similar restriction necessary for addition? Explain.
8. (a) Are all groups rings?
    (b) Are all rings groups?
    (c) Are all groups fields?
    (d) Are all fields groups?
9. Is the system of integers a ring? a field? Explain.

With reference to a clock arithmetic based on a five-hour clock, it is easy to answer the question, "If it is 4 o'clock, what time will it be 3 hours later?" The answer is $4 + 3 = 2$, as shown in Figure 9.8.2. However, suppose we ask, "If it is 4 o'clock, what time will it be 17 hours from now?" Since the number 17 is not "on the clock," we cannot add 4 and 17 within the system. However, we know that in 5 hours the hand on the clock will be back where it started. Since $17 = 5 + 5 + 5 + 2 = 3(5) + 2$, the hand on the clock will make three complete revolutions and then move two units farther. Therefore, if it is 4 o'clock, 17 hours later the hand will point to $4 + 2 = 1$. Figure 9.9.1 illustrates

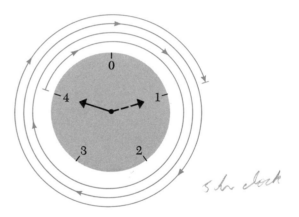

FIGURE 9.9.1

this situation. We see that 17 "behaves like" 2 in a five-hour clock arithmetic. The number 2 can be determined by dividing 17 by 5 and finding the remainder. We also note that the difference between 17 and 2 is a multiple of 5; since $17 = 3(5) + 2$, then $17 - 2 = 3(5)$.

A finite mathematical system, such as a five-hour clock arithmetic, is known as a modular system or congruence if it is extended in such a way that each integer may be considered equivalent to some element within the finite system. Modular systems have important applications in the realm of rotating objects, which includes wheels, dials, axles, and so on.

In the extension of the five-hour clock arithmetic, 5 is called the modulus of the system; the operations and relations on the system are said to be defined *modulo* 5, written (mod 5).

We showed above that 17 is equivalent to 2 in a modulo 5 system.

To express this equivalence relation between two integers, we say that they are *congruent* and use the symbol $\equiv$. We read "$17 \equiv 2$ (mod 5)" as "17 is congruent to 2 modulo 5." We shall now give a formal definition for the congruence relation.

DEFINITION 9.9.1

The integer a is **congruent** to the integer b modulo m $(m \in N)$ if and only if $a - b$ is a multiple of m. Symbolically, $a \equiv b$ (mod m) iff $a - b = km$ $(k \in J)$.

The above definition could have stated that $m \mid (a - b)$ since this is true if $a - b$ is a multiple of m. It can also be seen that a and b have the same remainder when divided by m. This fact is used by some authors in defining congruence.

Example 1.   Show that $12 \equiv 27$ (mod 5).

Solution: We must show that $12 - 27$ is a multiple of 5. $12 - 27 = {}^-15 = {}^-3(5)$. Therefore, by definition, $12 \equiv 27$ (mod 5).

Example 2.   Given $12 \equiv 27$ (mod 5), show that 12 and 27 have the same remainder when divided by 5.

Solution: $12 = 2(5) + 2$ and $27 = 5(5) + 2$. In both cases, 2 is the remainder.

Example 3.

$19 \equiv 7$ (mod 3) since $19 - 7 = 12 = 4(3)$.
$13 \equiv 37$ (mod 6) since $13 - 37 = {}^-24 = {}^-4(6)$.
$45 \equiv 10$ (mod 7) since $45 - 10 = 35 = 5(7)$.
$13 \not\equiv 8$ (mod 4) since $13 - 8 = 5 \neq k(4)$ where $k \in J$.
${}^-4 \equiv 14$ (mod 3) since ${}^-4 - 14 = {}^-18 = {}^-6(3)$.
${}^-19 \equiv {}^-9$ (mod 5) since ${}^-19 - {}^-9 = {}^-19 + 9 = {}^-10 = {}^-2(5)$.

Example 4.   Show that if two numbers, a and b, have the same remainder when divided by 5, then $a - b$ is a multiple of 5 and therefore $a \equiv b$ (mod 5).

Solution:

Assertions	Reasons
1. $a = 5q_1 + r_1$ and $b = 5q_2 + r_1$	1. a and b have the same remainder when divided by 5.

Assertions	*Reasons*
2. $a - b = (5q_1 + r_1)$ $- (5q_2 + r_1)$	2. Substitution
3. $a - b = 5q_1 + r_1$ $+ {}^-5q_2 + {}^-r_1$	3. Definition of subtraction
4. $a - b = 5q_1 + {}^-5q_2$ $+ (r_1 + {}^-r_1)$	4. Commutative and associative properties of addition
5. $a - b = 5(q_1 + {}^-q_2) + 0$	5. Distributive property and additive inverse
6. $a - b = 5q_3$	6. Closure for addition and additive identity
7. $(a - b)$ is a multiple of 5	7. Definition of multiple
8. $a \equiv b \pmod 5$	8. Definition of congruence

In general, it may be shown that $a \equiv b \pmod m$ if and only if a and b have the same remainder when divided by m. Furthermore, if a divided by m has a remainder r, then $a \equiv r \pmod m$. This is true since $a = km + r$ implies that $a - r = km$, and hence by the definition of congruence, $a \equiv r \pmod m$. For example, if we divide 22 by 5, we have $22 = 4(5) + 2$ and $22 \equiv 2 \pmod 5$.

Example 5. Find the smallest positive integer congruent to 44 (mod 6) by using the division algorithm.

Solution: $44 = 7(6) + 2$; therefore, $44 \equiv 2 \pmod 6$.

Example 6. Show that $^-14 \equiv 2 \pmod 4$ by using the division algorithm. (Recall that in the division algorithm $a = bq + r$, the remainder r is such that $0 \le r < b$.)

Solution: $^-14 = {}^-4(4) + 2$; therefore, $^-14 \equiv 2 \pmod 4$.

The congruence relation defined on J is an equivalence relation. To show this, it must be proved that the relation is reflexive, symmetric, and transitive.

1. *The Reflexive Property*
$a \equiv a \pmod m$ since $a - a = 0 = 0 \cdot m \ (0 \in J)$.

2. *The Symmetric Property*
If $a \equiv b \pmod m$, then by definition of the congruence relation, $a - b = km \ (k \in J)$. However, $^-(a - b) = b - a = {}^-km \ (^-k \in J)$,

which implies that $b \equiv a \pmod{m}$. Hence, if $a \equiv b \pmod{m}$, then $b \equiv a \pmod{m}$ and the symmetric property holds for the congruence relation.

3. *The Transitive Property*

We must show that if $a \equiv b \pmod{m}$ and $b \equiv c \pmod{m}$, then $a \equiv c \pmod{m}$. If $a \equiv b \pmod{m}$ and $b \equiv c \pmod{m}$, we know that $a - b = k_1 m$ and $b - c = k_2 m$. By substitution we have $(a - b) + (b - c) = k_1 m + k_2 m$, or $a - c = (k_1 + k_2)m$, and by the closure property for addition, $a - c = k_3 m$. Hence, $a \equiv c \pmod{m}$ by the definition of congruence.

Since the congruence relation is an equivalence relation, it will partition a set on which it is defined into disjoint subsets or equivalence classes (see Section 3.8). For example, the congruence relation modulo 5 partitions the integers into five equivalence classes which we shall identify as [0], [1], [2], [3], and [4].

$$[0] = \{\ldots, {}^-10, {}^-5, 0, 5, 10, 15, \ldots\}$$
$$[1] = \{\ldots, {}^-9, {}^-4, 1, 6, 11, 16, \ldots\}$$
$$[2] = \{\ldots, {}^-8, {}^-3, 2, 7, 12, 17, \ldots\}$$
$$[3] = \{\ldots, {}^-7, {}^-2, 3, 8, 13, 18, \ldots\}$$
$$[4] = \{\ldots, {}^-6, {}^-1, 4, 9, 14, 19, \ldots\}$$

Note that the difference between any two elements in each equivalence class above is a multiple of 5. Observe also that the members of any particular equivalence class have the same remainder when divided by 5. For example, $^-6$ and 9 are both members of [4], and both have remainders of 4 when divided by 5 since, by the division algorithm, $^-6 = {}^-2(5) + 4$ and $9 = 1(5) + 4$. Similarly, members of [0] have remainders of 0, members of [1] have remainders of 1, and so on.

Since in a modulo 5 system each integer may be considered equivalent to some element of the finite set $\{0, 1, 2, 3, 4\}$, the addition and multiplication tables of the five-hour clock system may also be used for the modulo 5 system. In constructing the tables, however, our work is facilitated by using the congruence relation. For example, to find the sum $3 + 4$, we have $3 + 4 = 7 = 1(5) + 2$; therefore, $3 + 4 \equiv 2 \pmod 5$. To find a product such as $3 \cdot 2$, we have $3 \cdot 2 = 6 = 1(5) + 1$; therefore, $3 \cdot 2 \equiv 1 \pmod 5$.

It is interesting to learn that in constructing addition and multiplication tables for a modular system, we may use any representative from each of the equivalence classes. For example, in the modulo 5 system we used as representatives the members of $\{0, 1, 2, 3, 4\}$, but we could have used the members of $\{1, 2, 3, 4, 5\}$ or $\{12, 13, 14, 15, 16\}$ or even

$\{^-10, 6, ^-3, ^-7, 19\}$. The only requirement is that we use exactly one representative element from each equivalence class.

Since both the equals relation and the congruence relation are equivalence relations, they have many properties in common, as illustrated by Theorem 9.9.1.

THEOREM 9.9.1

If $a \equiv b \pmod{m}$ and $c \equiv d \pmod{m}$, then:

(a) $a + c \equiv b + d \pmod{m}$ and
(b) $ac \equiv bd \pmod{m}$.

Proof of part (a):

1. $a - b = k_1 m$ and $c - d = k_2 m$ by the definition of congruence.
2. By substitution we have:
   $(a - b) + (c - d) = k_1 m + k_2 m$ or
   $(a + c) - (b + d) = (k_1 + k_2)m = k_3 m$.
3. Therefore, $a + c \equiv b + d \pmod{m}$ since their difference is a multiple of m.

Proof of part (b):

1. $a - b = k_1 m$ and $c - d = k_2 m$ by the definition of congruence.
2. Then $a = k_1 m + b$ and $c = k_2 m + d$.
3. By substitution we have:
   $ac = k_1 m k_2 m + k_1 m d + b k_2 m + bd$ or
   $ac - bd = (k_1 k_2 m + k_1 d + b k_2)m = k_3 m$.
4. Therefore, $ac \equiv bd \pmod{m}$ since their difference is a multiple of m.

Example 7. Given $18 \equiv 3 \pmod 5$ and $23 \equiv 8 \pmod 5$, show that $18 + 23 \equiv 3 + 8 \pmod 5$.

Solution: $18 + 23 = 41$ and $3 + 8 = 11$. Since $41 - 11 = 30 = 6(5)$, we see, by the definition of congruence, that $41 \equiv 11 \pmod 5$. It follows, then, that $18 + 23 \equiv 3 + 8 \pmod 5$.

Alternative Solution:

$18 + 23 = 41 = 8(5) + 1$; therefore, $41 \equiv 1 \pmod 5$.
$3 + 8 = 11 = 2(5) + 1$; therefore, $11 \equiv 1 \pmod 5$.

Hence, by the transitive property of congruence, $18 + 23 \equiv 3 + 8 \pmod 5$.

Example 8. Express the product $7 \cdot 42$ (mod 4) as a whole number less than the modulus.

Solution: $7 \cdot 42 = 294 = 73(4) + 2$; therefore, $7 \cdot 42 \equiv 2$ (mod 4).

Alternative Solution: $7 \cdot 42 \equiv 7 \cdot 2 \equiv 14 \equiv 2$ (mod 4).

EXERCISE 9.9

1. Define $a \equiv b$ (mod m).

2. Use the definition of problem 1 to show that $46 \equiv 22$ (mod 6).

3. Apply the division algorithm to the integers and find the remainder when each of the following numbers is divided by 4.
   - (a) 13
   - (b) 15
   - (c) 2
   - (d) ⁻5
   - (e) ⁻18
   - (f) 0
   - (g) ⁻14
   - (h) ⁻20
   - (i) ⁻23

4. (a) Find the smallest positive integer congruent to 20 modulo 3 by using the division algorithm.
   (b) Check your result in part (a) by using the definition of the congruence relation.

5. Perform each of the following operations and express the result as a whole number less than the given modulus:
   - (a) $6 \cdot 8$ (mod 5)
   - (b) $4 + 7$ (mod 3)
   - (c) $22 + 33$ (mod 6)
   - (d) $7 + (9 + 22)$ (mod 7)
   - (e) 5^3 (mod 9)
   - (f) $2 - 7$ (mod 4)
   - (g) $16 - 24$ (mod 7)
   - (h) $^-2(^-4 + 22)$ (mod 5)
   - (i) $62 \cdot 35$ (mod 9)
   - (j) $35 \cdot 24$ (mod 10)

6. Using the elements in $\{0, 1, 2, 3, 4, 5, 6\}$:
   (a) Construct an addition table modulo 7.
   (b) Construct a multiplication table modulo 7.
   (c) Is the mathematical system a commutative group under addition? Explain.
   (d) Is the mathematical system a commutative group under multiplication? Explain.
   (e) Is the mathematical system a commutative group under multiplication with zero removed?

9.10
Congruence and Casting Out Nines

For many years "casting out nines" has been used as a partial check for arithmetic computations. With experience it can be applied rapidly and is especially helpful as applied to multiplication and division where large numbers are involved. Although its application is limited, particularly with the widespread use of calculating machines, the theory is interesting.

The casting out of nines check is actually an application of Theorem 9.9.1 in a modulo 9 system. The key to the check by nines is to be able to rapidly find congruences using modulo 9. First note that $1000 - 1 = 999 = k_1(9)$, $100 - 1 = 99 = k_2(9)$, and $10 - 1 = 9 = k_3(9)$. By definition, then, $1000 \equiv 1 \pmod 9$, $100 \equiv 1 \pmod 9$, and $10 \equiv 1 \pmod 9$. It can be shown that, in general, any power of 10 is congruent to 1 modulo 9. Furthermore, it can be shown that any number is congruent to the sum of its digits modulo 9. For example, $8234 \equiv 8(1000) + 2(100) + 3(10) + 4 \equiv 8(1) + 2(1) + 3(1) + 4 \equiv 8 + 2 + 3 + 4 \equiv 17 \pmod 9$. Similarly, $17 \equiv 1(10) + 7 \equiv 1(1) + 7 \equiv 1 + 7 \equiv 8 \pmod 9$. Therefore, $8234 \equiv 8 \pmod 9$. The algorithm may be shortened to $8234 \equiv 8 + 2 + 3 + 4 \equiv 17 \equiv 1 + 7 \equiv 8 \pmod 9$.

Using the concepts of the previous paragraph along with Theorem 9.9.1, we can partially check addition, multiplication, and division, as shown in the following examples. We have only a *partial check* by "casting out nines" because any number congruent to the correct result modulo 9 would "check," even though it were not a correct result. The chance of having an incorrect result that "checks" is remote but certainly possible.

Example 1. Find the sum $248 + 324 + 672$ and check by casting out nines.

Solution:

$$248 \equiv 2 + 4 + 8 \equiv 14 \equiv 5 \pmod 9$$
$$324 \equiv 3 + 2 + 4 \equiv 9 \equiv 0 \pmod 9$$
$$672 \equiv 6 + 7 + 2 \equiv 15 \equiv 6 \pmod 9$$
$$11 \equiv \boxed{2} \pmod 9$$

↑ check number

$$1244 \equiv 1 + 2 + 4 + 4 \equiv 11 \equiv \boxed{2} \pmod 9$$

The above work can be shortened in several ways. For example, in finding $672 \equiv 6 \pmod 9$, we may add 6 and 7 and obtain 13; then add the digits of 13 and obtain 4; and finally add 4 to the remaining digit 2 and obtain 6. By this process we may simply write $672 \equiv 6 \pmod 9$. All the manipulations may be performed mentally in rapid succession so that nothing is written except the final result.

Example 2. Find the product 84×428 and check by casting out nines.

Solution:

$$428 \equiv 14 \equiv 5 \pmod 9$$
$$\cancel{\times}84 \equiv 12 \equiv \cancel{\times}3 \pmod 9$$
$$\overline{1712} \qquad\qquad \overline{15} \equiv \boxed{6} \pmod 9$$

$$3424$$

check number

$$\overline{35952} \equiv 24 \equiv \boxed{6} \pmod 9$$

Example 3. Find the quotient and remainder for $24{,}532 \div 824$ and check by casting out nines.

Solution:

$$
\begin{array}{r}
29 \\
824\overline{)24532} \\
1648 \\
\hline
8052 \\
7416 \\
\hline
636 \quad \text{(remainder)}
\end{array}
$$

In checking, we must show that $24{,}532 \equiv 824(29) + 636 \pmod 9$.

$$24{,}532 \equiv 2 + 4 + 5 + 3 + 2 \equiv 16 \equiv \boxed{7} \pmod 9$$

check number

$$824(29) + 636 \equiv 5(2) + 6 \equiv 10 + 6 \equiv 16 \equiv \boxed{7} \pmod 9$$

EXERCISE 9.10

1. Cast out nines from the following numbers:
   - (a) 23
   - (b) 264
   - (c) 23,425
   - (d) 62,397
   - (e) 823,429
   - (f) 6,234,425

2. Add the following and check by casting out nines:
   - (a) $534 + 928$
   - (b) $325 + 6243$
   - (c) $62 + 34 + 125$
   - (d) $2432 + 72{,}395$
   - (e) $62{,}345 + 82{,}347$
   - (f) $234 + 9235 + 17{,}238$

3. Multiply the following and check by casting out nines:
   - (a) $34 \cdot 523$
   - (b) $22 \cdot 492$
   - (c) $33 \cdot 485$
   - (d) $242 \cdot 359$
   - (e) $27 \cdot 32{,}446$
   - (f) $444 \cdot 6724$

4. Divide the following and check by casting out nines:
   (a) $624 \div 34$ (b) $8429 \div 67$
   (c) $244 \div 23$ (d) $89{,}276 \div 3$
   (e) $26{,}000 \div 14$ (f) $82{,}925 \div 643$

5. Explain how casting out nines can be used to check subtraction.

9.11
Tests for Divisibility

In this section we shall discuss tests for divisibility by each of the whole numbers from 2 to 11. Let us begin by discussing divisibility by 9. A whole number is, of course, divisible by 9 if and only if it has a remainder of 0 when divided by 9. However, as we learned in Section 9.9, a number n is congruent to b (mod 9) if and only if n and b have the same remainder when divided by 9. Hence if $n \equiv b$ (mod 9), then n is divisible by 9 if and only if b is divisible by 9. This means that if we wish to test a given number n for divisibility by 9, we may instead test any other number b that is congruent to it (mod 9); but we know that any number n is congruent to the sum of its digits (mod 9). Therefore, a number is divisible by 9 if and only if the sum of its digits is divisible by 9.

Example 1.

(a) $8352 \equiv 8 + 3 + 5 + 2 \equiv 18$ (mod 9).
     Since $9 \mid 18,\ 9 \mid 8352$.
(b) $7587 \equiv 7 + 5 + 8 + 7 \equiv 27 \equiv 9$ (mod 9).
     Since $9 \mid 9,\ 9 \mid 7587$.
(c) $47{,}623 \equiv 4 + 7 + 6 + 2 + 3 \equiv 22 \equiv 4$ (mod 9).
     Since $9 \nmid 4,\ 9 \nmid 47{,}623$.

A test for divisibility by 3 which is similar to that for 9 will be considered next. First note that $1000 - 1 = 999 = k_1(3)$, $100 - 1 = 99 = k_2(3)$, and $10 - 1 = 9 = k_3(3)$. Then, by definition, $1000 \equiv 1$ (mod 3), $100 \equiv 1$ (mod 3), and $10 \equiv 1$ (mod 3). In a similar way it may be shown that any power of 10 is congruent to 1 modulo 3. Hence it may also be shown that any number is congruent to the sum of its digits modulo 3. For example, $7456 \equiv 7(1000) + 4(100) + 5(10) + 6 \equiv 7(1) + 4(1) + 5(1) + 6(1) \equiv 7 + 4 + 5 + 6 \equiv 22$ (mod 3). Similarly, $22 \equiv 2 + 2 \equiv 4$ (mod 3); therefore, $7456 \equiv 4$ (mod 3). The algorithm may be shortened to $7456 \equiv 7 + 4 + 5 + 6 \equiv 22 \equiv 2 + 2 \equiv 4$ (mod 3). (Note that 7456 and 22 and 4 all have the same remainder, 1, when divided by 3.)

If a number n is divisible by 3, it will, of course, have a remainder of 0 when divided by 3. However, a number n is congruent to b (mod 3) if and only if n and b have the same remainder when divided by 3. Hence if $n \equiv b$ (mod 3), then n is divisible by 3 if and only if b is divisible by 3; but, since any number n is congruent to the sum of its digits (mod 3), a number is divisible by 3 if and only if the sum of its digits is divisible by 3.

Example 2.

(a) $138 \equiv 1 + 3 + 8 \equiv 12$ (mod 3).
     Since $3 \mid 12$, $3 \mid 138$.

(b) $12{,}456 \equiv 1 + 2 + 4 + 5 + 0 = 18 = 1 + 8 = 9$ (mod 3).
     Since $3 \mid 9$, $3 \mid 12{,}456$.

(c) $4264 \equiv 4 + 2 + 6 + 4 \equiv 16 \equiv 1 + 6 \equiv 7$ (mod 3).
     Since $3 \nmid 7$, $3 \nmid 4264$.

Tests for divisibility by 2, 4, and 8 are similar and will be considered next. First, recall that any whole number may be written in the form $n = a_k 10^k + \cdots + a_2 10^2 + a_1 10^1 + a_0$. It is obvious that each addend in this expression, with the exception of a_0, has at least one factor of 10 and, therefore, has at least one factor of 2 since $10 = 2 \cdot 5$. If a_0 has a factor of 2, then by the distributive property, 2 is a factor of the whole number n, and therefore 2 divides n. The converse statement is also true; that is, if the whole number n is divisible by 2, then its last digit is divisible by 2. If n is divisible by 2, we may write $n = 2b = 2(a_k 10^{k-1} \cdot 5 + \cdots + a_2 10 \cdot 5 + a_1 5) + a_0$. Then $a_0 = 2(b - a_k 10^{k-1} \cdot 5 - \cdots - a_2 10 \cdot 5 - a_1 5)$ and a_0 is, therefore, divisible by 2. Hence we may make the following "if and only if" statement: A number is divisible by 2 if and only if the number represented by the last digit of its numeral is divisible by 2.

In a similar way, if we examine a whole number $n = a_k 10^k + \cdots + a_2 10^2 + a_1 10^1 + a_0$, we see that each of the addends except the last two has at least two factors of 10 and, therefore, at least two factors of 2 or one factor of 4. Hence, if 4 divides $(a_1 10^1 + a_0)$, then 4 divides the number n. We can also show that the converse is true and conclude that a number is divisible by 4 if and only if the number represented by its last two digits is divisible by 4.

It should now be easy to see that a number is divisible by 2^3 or 8 if and only if the number represented by its last three digits is divisible by 8. What statement could be made for divisibility by 2^4 or 16?

Example 3.

(a) 17,256 is divisible by 2 since $2 \mid 6$; it is divisible by 4 since $4 \mid 56$; and it is divisible by 8 since $8 \mid 256$.

(b) 879,324 is divisible by 2 since $2 \mid 4$; it is divisible by 4 since $4 \mid 24$; but it is not divisible by 8 since $8 \nmid 324$.

A number has a factor of 6 if and only if it has factors of 2 and 3 since $6 = 2 \cdot 3$. Hence, a number is divisible by 6 if and only if it is divisible by 2 and by 3.

Considering once again a whole number $n = a_k 10^k + \cdots + a_2 10^2 + a_1 10^1 + a_0$, we see that each addend except a_0 has at least one factor of 10. Therefore, since 10 is divisible by 5, the number n will be divisible by 5 if the digit a_0 is divisible by 5. Since the only digits divisible by 5 are 0 and 5, we conclude that a number is divisible by 5 if its terminal digit is 0 or 5. Also, if a number has a factor of 5, then its terminal digit must be either 0 or 5. Hence, a number is divisible by 5 if and only if its terminal digit is 0 or 5.

A number is divisible by 10 if and only if it is divisible by 2 and 5 since $10 = 2 \cdot 5$. However, a number is divisible by 2 and by 5 if and only if its terminal digit is divisible by 2 and by 5. Since the only digit divisible by both 2 and 5 is 0, we conclude that a number is divisible by 10 if and only if its terminal digit is 0.

A test for divisibility by 11 can be found by using the congruence relation in a way similar to that which was used for divisibility by 9. First note that $10 \equiv {}^-1 \pmod{11}$, $10^2 \equiv 10 \cdot 10 \equiv ({}^-1)({}^-1) \equiv 1 \pmod{11}$, $10^3 \equiv 10 \cdot 10 \cdot 10 \equiv ({}^-1)({}^-1)({}^-1) \equiv {}^-1 \pmod{11}$, and so on. In general, we see that $10^n \equiv ({}^-1)^n \pmod{11}$; furthermore, $({}^-1)^n = 1$ if n is an even number and $({}^-1)^n = {}^-1$ if n is an odd number. Therefore, a whole number $n = a_0 + a_1 10^1 + a_2 10^2 + a_3 10^3 + \cdots + a_k 10^k \equiv a_0 + a_1({}^-1) + a_2(1) + a_3({}^-1) + \cdots + a_k({}^-1)^k \equiv a_0 - a_1 + a_2 - a_3 + \cdots \equiv [(a_0 + a_2 + a_4 + \cdots) - (a_1 + a_3 + a_5 + \cdots)] \pmod{11}$. However, if a number is divisible by 11, it will, of course, have a remainder of 0 when divided by 11. Since numbers are congruent modulo 11 if and only if they have the same remainder when divided by 11, we conclude that a number $n = a_k \ldots a_3 a_2 a_1 a_0$ is divisible by 11 if and only if $[(a_0 + a_2 + a_4 + \cdots) - (a_1 + a_3 + a_5 + \cdots)]$ is divisible by 11.

Example 4.

(a) 180,829 is divisible by 11 since $(9 + 8 + 8) - (2 + 0 + 1) = 25 - 3 = 22$ and 11 divides 22.

(b) 29,183 is divisible by 11 since $(3 + 1 + 2) - (8 + 9) = 6 - 17 = {}^-11$ and 11 divides ${}^-11$.

(c) 435,628 is not divisible by 11 since $(8 + 6 + 3) - (2 + 5 + 4) = 17 - 11 = 6$ and 11 does not divide 6.

An interesting test for divisibility by 7 is as follows: (1) Multiply the terminal digit of the given number by 2. (2) Subtract this product from the number determined by omitting the terminal digit from the original number. (3) The original number is divisible by 7 if and only if the difference is divisible by 7. The method is illustrated below:

Example 5.   Is 273 divisible by 7?

Solution:

$$
\begin{array}{c c | c}
2 & 7 & 3 \\
 & 6 & \\
\hline
2 & 1 &
\end{array}
$$

Since $7 \mid 21$, $7 \mid 273$.

If the above example is examined closely, it will be seen that 3 is multiplied by 2, but since its product is placed below the 7, which is in the tens place, this is equivalent to multiplying 3 by 20. Furthermore, since the units place digit is dropped, we have in effect subtracted $21 \cdot 3$ from 273 since $20 \cdot 3 + 1 \cdot 3 = (20 + 1)3 = 21 \cdot 3$. Finally, as will be shown below by applying the distributive property, if the difference 21 is divisible by 7, then the original number is divisible by 7. Note that the difference is actually $273 - 63 = 210$. But $210 = 21 \cdot 10$, and if $7 \mid 21$, then $7 \mid 210$. The use of the distributive property is readily seen if we write $273 = 63 + 210 = (7 \cdot 9 + 7 \cdot 30) = 7(9 + 30) = 7(39)$.

The process for testing for divisibility by 7 may be repeated as shown in Example 6.

Example 6.

(a) Does $7 \mid 2093$?

Solution:

$$
\begin{array}{c c c | c}
2 & 0 & 9 & 3 \\
 & & 6 & \\
\hline
2 & 0 & 3 & \\
 & 6 & & \\
\hline
1 & 4 & &
\end{array}
$$

Therefore, since $7 \mid 14$, $7 \mid 203$ and hence $7 \mid 2093$.

(b) Does $7 \mid 3492$?

Solution:

$$
\begin{array}{r}
3\ 4\ 9\,|\,2 \\
4 \\
\hline
3\ 4\,|\,5 \\
1\ 0 \\
\hline
2\ 4
\end{array}
$$

Since $7 \nmid 24$, $7 \nmid 3492$.

Various divisibility tests may be devised for any whole number, but sometimes the tests are more complicated to use than the usual division algorithm. This seems to be the case with the above test for divisibility by 7, even though you may find it interesting.

EXERCISE 9.11

1. Test each of the following numbers for divisibility by 3 and 9:
   (a) 1470   (b) 8316   (c) 235,425
   (d) 172,493   (e) 23,423,535   (f) 92,745,627

2. Test each of the following numbers for divisibility by 2, 4, and 8:
   (a) 2372   (b) 1864   (c) 26,428
   (d) 62,372   (e) 1,926,238   (f) 2,364,936

3. Which of the following numbers are divisible by 11?
   (a) 22,814   (b) 81,928   (c) 623,469
   (d) 214,192   (e) 745,396   (f) 269,789

4. Which of the following numbers are divisible by 7?
   (a) 336   (b) 686   (c) 1848
   (d) 1912   (e) 452,753   (f) 150,024

5. Test each of the following for divisibility by 2, 3, 4, 5, 6, 7, 8, 9, 10, and 11:
   (a) 440   (b) 1848   (c) 55,440

6. If a number is divisible by 8, what can you conclude concerning its divisibility by 2, 4, and 16?

7. How could a number be tested for divisibility by 16? By 2^n?

8. Devise a test for divisibility by 15.

9. Devise a test for divisibility by 25.

10. Does the test for divisibility by 2 in a base ten numeral system work in base four? In base three? Explain.

11. A number is divisible by 6 if it is divisible by 2 and by 3. Is a number divisible by 18 if it is divisible by 3 and by 6? Explain.

12. If a number is divisible by 4 and by 3, is it divisible by 12? Explain.

REVIEW EXERCISES

1. Find the greatest common divisor of 912 and 19,656:
   (a) by using prime factors.
   (b) by using Euclid's Algorithm.

2. Which of the following pairs of integers are relatively prime?
   (a) 4, 9   (b) 15, 56
   (c) 26, 91   (d) ⁻24, 81
   (e) 34, 85   (f) 78, 715

3. Find the least common multiple of each of the following pairs of numbers:
   (a) 14, 22   (b) 15, 35
   (c) 18, 37   (d) 48, 52
   (e) 88, 98   (f) 92, 58

4. What is the least common multiple of 27, 28, 29, and 30?

5. Using the elements of $\{0, 1, 2, 3, 4\}$, construct an addition table modulo 5.

6. Using the elements of $\{0, 1, 2, 3, 4\}$, construct a multiplication table modulo 5.

7. Find the following products and check by casting out nines:
   (a) (78)(346)
   (b) (243)(6249)
   (c) (2734)(62,303)

8. Find the following quotients and check by casting out nines:
   (a) 625 ÷ 32
   (b) 16,435 ÷ 27
   (c) 83,495 ÷ 724

9. Test each of the following numbers for divisibility by 3, 9, and 11 and state your results.
   (a) 792   (b) 7073
   (c) 291   (d) 23,475
   (e) 62,348   (f) 158,400

10. Test each of the following for divisibility by 2, 4, 6, 7, and 8 and state your results.
    (a) 504   (b) 3528
    (c) 18,424   (d) 26,648
    (e) 128,968   (f) 294,144

Chapter Ten
The System
of Rational Numbers

10.1
Introduction

In Chapter 8 the system of whole numbers was extended to include negative integers. By extending the system in this way, we obtained closure for subtraction. In a similar way, the system of integers can be extended so that, with zero removed from the set, we have closure for division. This enlarged number system is called the *system of rational numbers*. In addition to making division possible for all divisors (except zero), the rational numbers offer many other advantages. For example, the rational numbers can be associated not only with those points on the number line previously associated with the integers, but also with many other points. As a result, we shall be able to make many more physical measurements of length, area, volume, and so on.

In considering the system of rational numbers, we shall first identify the elements of the set. Relations and operations on the set will be defined, and the various properties of the system will be discussed. In summarizing the essential features of the system, it will be seen that the rational number system has all the qualifications necessary to be classified as a *field*.

10.2
An Equivalence Relation for Ordered Pairs

You are probably already familiar with the fact that an ordered pair of integers such as (2, 3) may be written as $\frac{2}{3}$ or 2/3 and may be thought of as "$2 \div 3$," or as a "ratio," or as a "fraction." Ordered pairs of integers may also be thought of simply as elements of a mathematical system. The fact that ordered pairs of integers may be considered from several points of view in no way implies an inconsistency. In fact, the various interpretations of ordered pairs complement each other and give us greater insight into the nature of the rational number system. The fact that, depending upon conditions, the ordered pair $\frac{2}{3}$ may be referred to as $2 \div 3$, as the ratio of 2 to 3, as the fraction two-thirds, or as an element of a mathematical system, should disturb us no more than hearing the same man referred to as father, brother, husband, or son under different circumstances. Various interpretations of a concept should enrich rather than hinder our understanding.

Regardless of the particular interpretation given an ordered pair of integers such as $\frac{2}{3}$, there are infinitely many other ordered pairs that are *equivalent* to $\frac{2}{3}$. Examples are $\frac{4}{6}$, $\frac{6}{9}$, $\frac{20}{30}$, and $\frac{-2}{-3}$. Since rational numbers will be defined in terms of equivalence classes of ordered pairs of integers, we shall first define equivalent ordered pairs.

213

DEFINITION 10.2.1

If a, b, c, and d are integers with $c \neq 0$ and $d \neq 0$, the ordered pair $\frac{a}{b}$ is equivalent to the ordered pair $\frac{c}{d}$ if and only if $ad = bc$. Symbolically, $\frac{a}{b} \cong \frac{c}{d}$ iff $ad = bc$.

Example 1.

(a) $\frac{2}{3} \cong \frac{6}{9}$ since $2 \cdot 9 = 3 \cdot 6 = 18$.

(b) $\frac{-3}{5} \cong \frac{-6}{10}$ since $^-3(10) = 5(^-6) = ^-30$.

(c) $\frac{5}{2} \cong \frac{-20}{-8}$ since $5(^-8) = 2(^-20) = ^-40$.

(d) $\dfrac{a}{b} \cong \dfrac{5a}{5b}$ since $a(5b) = b(5a) = 5ab$.

The relation indicated by $\cong$ and defined on the set of ordered pairs of integers (a, b) or $\frac{a}{b}$ $(b \neq 0)$ is an *equivalence relation*. It is for this reason that we make statements such as "$\frac{1}{2}$ is equivalent to $\frac{2}{4}$," or "$\frac{-2}{5}$ is equivalent to $\frac{2}{-5}$." We can prove that the relation indicated by $\cong$ is an equivalence relation by showing that it has the reflexive, symmetric, and transitive properties.

Proof that $\cong$ is reflexive: We must show that $\frac{a}{b} \cong \frac{a}{b}$ for the ordered pair of integers $\frac{a}{b}$ $(b \neq 0)$. By definition, $\frac{a}{b} \cong \frac{a}{b}$ if and only if $ab = ba$. However, $ab = ba$ by the commutative property of multiplication in J; therefore, $\frac{a}{b} \cong \frac{a}{b}$.

Proof that $\cong$ is symmetric: This is left as an exercise for the student.

Proof that $\cong$ is transitive: We must show that if $\frac{a}{b} \cong \frac{c}{d}$ and $\frac{c}{d} \cong \frac{e}{f}$, then $\frac{a}{b} \cong \frac{e}{f}$, where $\frac{a}{b}$, $\frac{c}{d}$, and $\frac{e}{f}$ are ordered pairs of integers with b, d, and $f \neq 0$.

1. $ad = bc$ since $\frac{a}{b} \cong \frac{c}{d}$.
2. $cf = de$ since $\frac{c}{d} \cong \frac{e}{f}$.
3. $(ad)(cf) = (bc)(de)$ by substitution.
4. $(af)(cd) = (be)(cd)$ by the commutative and associative properties of multiplication in J.
5. $af = be$ by the cancellation property of multiplication in J.
6. $\frac{a}{b} \cong \frac{e}{f}$ by definition of the relation $\cong$.

EXERCISE 10.2

1. Define the equivalence relation $\cong$ for ordered pairs of integers.

2. Show that the following ordered pairs of integers are equivalent:

   (a) $\frac{4}{3}$ and $\frac{8}{6}$ 　　　　　(b) $\frac{2}{-7}$ and $\frac{-2}{7}$

   (c) $\frac{4}{9}$ and $\frac{-4}{-9}$ 　　　　(d) $\frac{-6}{4}$ and $\frac{9}{-6}$

   (e) $\frac{-7}{2}$ and $\frac{21}{6}$ 　　　(f) $\frac{a(b+c)}{a}$ and $\frac{b+c}{1}$

3. Find the values of x such that:

   (a) $\frac{2}{5} \cong \frac{x}{15}$ 　　　　(b) $\frac{8}{4} \cong \frac{2}{x}$

   (c) $\frac{1}{3} \cong \frac{2x}{12}$ 　　　　(d) $\frac{7x}{5} \cong \frac{42}{10}$

   (e) $\frac{0}{5} \cong \frac{x}{9}$ 　　　　(f) $\frac{x+3}{2} \cong \frac{10}{4}$

   (g) $\frac{x-4}{3} \cong \frac{6}{9}$ 　　　(h) $\frac{3}{5} \cong \frac{11-x}{17-x}$

4. Prove that the relation $\cong$ for ordered pairs of integers is symmetric.

5. (a) Is $\frac{0}{5} \cong \frac{0}{25}$? Explain.
   (b) Is $\frac{7}{6} \cong \frac{14}{0}$? Explain.

6. Is $\dfrac{2}{3} \cong \dfrac{2k}{3k}$:

   (a) If $k = 1$? Explain.
   (b) If $k = 2$? Explain.
   (c) If $k = {}^-3$? Explain.
   (d) If $k = 0$? Explain.

7. Find four members of the defined set if a and b are in J with $b \neq 0$:

   (a) $\{x \mid (x = \frac{a}{b}) \wedge (ab = 4)\}$
   (b) $\{x \mid (x = \frac{a}{b}) \wedge (a + b = 4)\}$
   (c) $\{x \mid (x = \frac{a}{b}) \wedge (a + b = {}^-3)\}$

8. Give an example that illustrates that the equivalence relation $\cong$ is transitive.

9. Prove by a counterexample that the following general statement is false:

$$\text{If } \frac{a}{b} \neq \frac{c}{d} \text{ and } \frac{c}{d} \neq \frac{e}{f}, \text{ then } \frac{a}{b} \neq \frac{e}{f}.$$

You will recall that an equivalence relation will partition the set on which it is defined into disjoint subsets called *equivalence classes* (Section 3.8). In the preceding chapter, an interesting example of an equivalence relation was the congruence relation, which partitions the set of integers into equivalence classes (Section 9.9). Similarly, the relation $\cong$ is an equivalence relation that partitions the set of ordered pairs of integers $\frac{a}{b}\,(b \neq 0)$ into equivalence classes. In this case, however, there are infinitely many equivalence classes, and each equivalence class has infinitely many elements.

Examples of equivalence classes of ordered pairs of integers determined by the relation $\cong$ are $\{\ldots, \frac{-3}{-6}, \frac{-2}{-4}, \frac{-1}{-2}, \frac{1}{2}, \frac{2}{4}, \frac{3}{6}, \ldots\}$, $\{\ldots, \frac{-6}{-9}, \frac{-4}{-6}, \frac{-2}{-3}, \frac{2}{3}, \frac{4}{6}, \frac{6}{9}, \ldots\}$, and $\{\ldots, \frac{-15}{-6}, \frac{-10}{-4}, \frac{-5}{-2}, \frac{5}{2}, \frac{10}{4}, \frac{15}{6}, \ldots\}$. Each of these equivalence classes is a rational number. It may at first seem strange and somewhat awkward to think of a single rational number as a set consisting of an infinite number of elements, each of which is an ordered pair of integers. However, since equivalence classes are disjoint sets, any rational number may be named without ambiguity simply by placing any one of its elements in brackets. For example, we may name the rational number $\{\ldots, \frac{-3}{-6}, \frac{-2}{-4}, \frac{-1}{-2}, \frac{1}{2}, \frac{2}{4}, \frac{3}{6}, \ldots\}$ as $[\frac{-1}{-2}]$, or $[\frac{1}{2}]$, or $[\frac{2}{4}]$, and so on. In practice, we usually abbreviate our symbolism even more by using any one of the elements $\frac{-1}{-2}$, or $\frac{1}{2}$, or $\frac{2}{4}$, and so on, without brackets. Furthermore, if we use a representative element such as $\frac{1}{2}$ to name the rational number $\{\ldots, \frac{-3}{-6}, \frac{-2}{-4}, \frac{-1}{-2}, \frac{1}{2}, \frac{2}{4}, \frac{3}{6}, \ldots\}$, we may refer to $\frac{1}{2}$ as "the rational number one-half." When we wish to consider ordered pairs such as $\frac{1}{2}$ and $\frac{2}{4}$ as numerals that name the same rational number, we write $\frac{1}{2} = \frac{2}{4}$; however, when we wish to indicate that $\frac{1}{2}$ and $\frac{2}{4}$ are members of the same equivalence class, we shall continue to write $\frac{1}{2} \cong \frac{2}{4}$.

DEFINITION 10.3.1

A rational number is an equivalence class of ordered pairs of integers which may be denoted by $[\frac{a}{b}]$, $b \neq 0$; the *set of rational numbers* is the set of all such equivalence classes.

Since we have agreed to use any element of a given equivalence class to name a rational number, this implies that $\frac{a}{b}$ and $\frac{c}{d}$ name the same rational number if and only if $\frac{a}{b} \cong \frac{c}{d}$ or $ad = bc$. The particular representative element we use in naming any given rational number may be chosen to suit our purposes. For example, in finding the sum $\frac{1}{2} + \frac{11}{16}$, we may wish to replace $\frac{1}{2}$ by $\frac{8}{16}$. At other times we may wish to use the element that is in *simplest form* or *reduced form* as defined below.

DEFINITION 10.3.2

A representative element $\frac{a}{b}$ of a rational number is said to be in simplest form if and only if a and b are relatively prime and b is positive.

You will recall that relatively prime integers have a greatest common divisor of 1 (Definition 9.5.2). If a representative element $\frac{a}{b}$ (b positive) of a rational number is not in simplest form, the simplest form may be found by dividing both a and b by their greatest common divisor. The following representatives of rational numbers are in simplest form: $\frac{1}{2}$, $\frac{3}{17}$, $\frac{-3}{4}$, $\frac{17}{1}$, $\frac{0}{1}$, and $\frac{-15}{2}$. The following representatives of rational numbers are not in simplest form: $\frac{4}{8}$, $\frac{-9}{3}$, $\frac{0}{7}$, and $\frac{-2}{3}$; the simplest forms are: $\frac{1}{2}$, $\frac{-3}{1}$, $\frac{0}{1}$, and $\frac{-2}{3}$.

It is interesting to observe that all other members of any particular equivalence class may be generated by using the *simplest form* $\frac{a}{b}$ and multiplying both a and b by k where $k \in J$ and $k \neq 0$. For example, if we let $\frac{a}{b} = \frac{-2}{3}$, then

$$\left\{ \frac{-2k}{3k} \,\middle|\, (k \in J) \wedge (k \neq 0) \right\} = \left\{ \ldots, \frac{6}{-9}, \frac{4}{-6}, \frac{2}{-3}, \frac{-2}{3}, \frac{-4}{6}, \frac{-6}{9}, \ldots \right\}$$

In general, it may be shown that $\frac{a}{b} \cong \frac{ak}{bk}$, where a, b, and k are in J with $b \neq 0$ and $k \neq 0$. The proof is left as an exercise for the student.

EXERCISE 10.3

1. Define the relation $\cong$ for ordered pairs of integers.
2. Define a *rational number* and tell what is meant by the *set of rational numbers*.
3. (a) Name three representatives of the equivalence class $[\frac{3}{5}]$ using ordered pairs of positive integers.
   (b) Name three representatives of the equivalence class $[\frac{3}{5}]$ using ordered pairs of negative integers.
4. Explain why $[\frac{1}{2}] = [\frac{3}{6}]$.
5. What is meant by "the representative of a rational number in *simplest or reduced form*"?
6. Tell why each of the following is not in simplest form.
   - (a) $\frac{4}{8}$
   - (b) $\frac{-15}{5}$
   - (c) $\frac{-6}{-9}$
   - (d) $\frac{0}{4}$
   - (e) $\frac{-2}{-3}$
   - (f) $\frac{-5}{-2}$
   - (g) $\frac{51}{17}$
   - (h) $\frac{-2}{-3}$
   - (i) $\frac{-0}{-1}$

7. Find the element in simplest form which may be used to represent each rational number indicated in problem 6.

8. Name five elements of the equivalence class $[\frac{0}{1}]$.

9. Is $[\frac{1}{0}]$ a rational number? Explain.

10. Will all the elements of $\left[\dfrac{2}{4}\right]$ be generated by $\left\{\dfrac{2k}{4k}\;\middle|\;(k \in J) \wedge (k \neq 0)\right\}$? Explain.

11. Prove that for any ordered pair of integers $\frac{a}{b}$ where $b \neq 0$, $\frac{a}{b} \cong \frac{ak}{bk}$ where $k \in J$ and $k \neq 0$.

12. From what point of view may we refer to $\frac{3}{4}$ as "the rational number three-fourths"?

13. Find the *simplest form* for each of the following by dividing both numerator and denominator by their greatest common divisor.
  (a) $\frac{18}{42}$ (b) $\frac{60}{114}$ (c) $\frac{-75}{50}$ (d) $\frac{52}{-39}$

14. Use the Euclidean Algorithm (discussed in Section 9.5) to find the *reduced form* of:
  (a) $\frac{84}{320}$ (b) $\frac{220}{315}$ (c) $\frac{727}{1441}$

10.4 The Fraction Concept

The concept of a fraction has for many years been introduced to young children by starting with a region in a plane and dividing it into subregions of the "same size and shape." Regions of the same size and shape are said to be congruent. The subregions of the original region may be congruent rectangles, squares, triangles, and so on. In Figure 10.4.1, four diagrams are shown to illustrate ways in which various regions may be divided into a natural number of congruent subregions.

If we relate the shaded subregions to the total number of congruent subregions in each of the diagrams, (A), (B), (C), and (D) of Figure 10.4.1, we have the following ordered pairs of integers: (1, 6), (3, 5), (0, 4), and (7, 9). These ordered pairs may be written $\frac{1}{6}$, $\frac{3}{5}$, $\frac{0}{4}$, and $\frac{7}{9}$, and are read "one-sixth," "three-fifths," "zero-fourths," and "seven-ninths." Ordered pairs such as these are commonly referred to as fractions; the word fraction is derived from the Latin word *fractio* meaning "to break." In general, the fraction concept involves the association of an ordered pair of integers with zero or more of the total number of equal parts of a whole. Note that in each fraction the first of the ordered pair of integers is placed above the horizontal bar, and the second of the ordered pair of integers is placed below the bar. The integer above the bar indicates the number of shaded congruent subregions and is called the numerator of the fraction. The integer below the bar indicates the total number of congruent subregions in each figure and is called the denominator of the fraction.

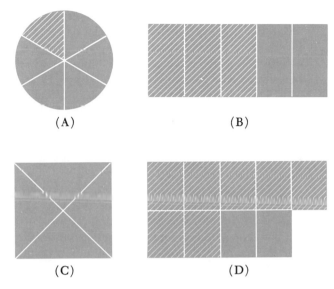

(A)   (B)

(C)   (D)

FIGURE 10.4.1

Each diagram in Figure 10.4.1 is called a unit figure since each region represents the number 1. If all the congruent subregions of each unit figure were shaded, the result could be represented by the fractions $\frac{6}{6}$, $\frac{5}{5}$, $\frac{4}{4}$, and $\frac{8}{8}$. Each of these fractions is equivalent to $\frac{1}{1}$. If none of the subregions was shaded, the fractions $\frac{0}{6}$, $\frac{0}{5}$, $\frac{0}{4}$, and $\frac{0}{8}$ could be used. These fractions are equivalent to $\frac{0}{1}$. Note that 0 may be a numerator but never a denominator since we never consider a *total* of 0 congruent subregions. If we were to consider a total of 0 congruent subregions, we could shade only 0 of them, and this concept appears to have little value.

The concept of a fraction can be extended by using more than one unit figure. In fact, the number of unit figures may be extended indefinitely, as indicated in Figure 10.4.2 by the dots to the right of the third

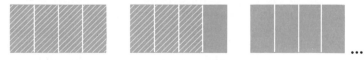

FIGURE 10.4.2

unit figure. In Figure 10.4.2, each unit figure is divided into four congruent subregions. The denominator of the fraction will indicate the number of congruent subregions in *each unit figure,* and the numerator will indicate the total number of shaded subregions. In this case there are seven shaded subregions, and the situation is represented by the fraction $\frac{7}{4}$. By studying Figure 10.4.2, we can see that $\frac{7}{4} = \frac{4}{4} + \frac{3}{4} = 1 + \frac{3}{4}$; sums such as $1 + \frac{3}{4}$ are usually written $1\frac{3}{4}$ and read "one and three-fourths." In a similar way we can write $\frac{8}{3} = 2\frac{2}{3}$, $\frac{9}{5} = 1\frac{4}{5}$, and so on.

The concept of a fraction was introduced by using unit figures divided into subregions of the same size and shape. The number line may also be used to develop the concept of a fraction. You will recall that the concept of unit distances or unit intervals on the number line was introduced in studying the whole numbers and further extended in our study of the integers.

In developing the concept of a fraction by using the number line, we begin by dividing each unit interval into a given natural number of congruent subintervals. For example, if each unit interval on the number line is divided into four congruent subintervals, we may associate each fraction having a denominator of 4 with a point on the number line, as shown in Figure 10.4.3. The numerator of the fraction tells the number of

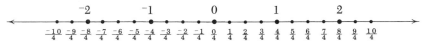

FIGURE 10.4.3

subintervals that must be counted to the right or left of zero in order to find the point associated with the fraction. For example, the fraction $\frac{6}{4}$ will be associated with the point that is six subintervals to the right of zero; $\frac{-6}{4}$ will be associated with the point six subintervals to the left of zero.

In general, any fraction $\frac{a}{b}$ with a *positive denominator* may be associated with a point on the number line by the following method. First, divide each unit interval into b congruent subintervals. The fraction $\frac{a}{b}$ will be associated with the point that is a subintervals to the right or to the left of zero, depending on whether a is positive or negative. If a is zero, $\frac{a}{b}$ is associated with the point zero.

Any given fraction with a negative denominator will be associated with the same point on the number line as those fractions with positive denominators which belong to the equivalence class of the given fraction. For example, $\frac{-3}{-4}$ is associated with the same point on the number line as $\frac{-3}{4}$ or any other member of the equivalence class $[\frac{-3}{4}] = \{\ldots, \frac{-9}{-12}, \frac{6}{-8}, \frac{3}{-4}, \frac{-3}{4}, \frac{-6}{8}, \frac{-9}{12}, \ldots\}$.

Each equivalence class of ordered pairs is a single rational number, and all fractions belonging to the same equivalence class are associated with the same point on the number line. This means that each rational number is associated with exactly one point on the number line. Furthermore, each point on the number line is associated with at most one rational number. (Some points are not associated with any rational number.) Figure 10.4.4 illustrates how all fractions that are members of

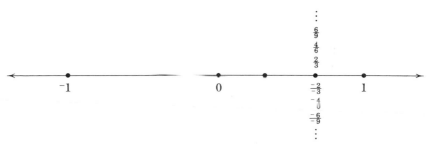

FIGURE 10.4.4

a given equivalence class, such as $[\frac{2}{3}]$, are associated with the same point on the number line. Note, however, that $[\frac{2}{3}]$ is a single rational number and that no other rational number is associated with this same point on the number line.

Since equivalent fractions such as $\frac{2}{3}$ and $\frac{4}{6}$ may be used to name the same rational number $[\frac{2}{3}]$, we may say that $\frac{2}{3} = \frac{4}{6}$. However, from some other point of view the fractions $\frac{2}{3}$ and $\frac{4}{6}$ may not be considered equal. Certainly cutting a cake into three equal parts and taking two is not the same as cutting a cake into six equal parts and taking four. In this situation we may prefer to say that $\frac{2}{3}$ is equivalent, rather than equal, to $\frac{4}{6}$.

EXERCISE 10.4

1. Draw three congruent rectangular unit figures adjacent to each other and divide each into subregions in such a way as to illustrate that $\frac{3}{4}$, $\frac{6}{8}$, and $\frac{9}{12}$ are equivalent fractions.

2. (a) From what point of view may $\frac{1}{2}$ and $\frac{2}{4}$ be considered equivalent rather than equal?
   (b) From what point of view may $\frac{1}{2}$ and $\frac{2}{4}$ be considered equal?

3. Using unit figures, make a drawing to illustrate the fraction $\frac{8}{3}$.

4. What fraction is equal to $2\frac{3}{4}$? Explain.

5. Identify points on the number line that correspond to the fractions:
   (a) $\frac{2}{5}$ (b) $\frac{-3}{2}$ (c) $\frac{0}{5}$ (d) $\frac{-7}{3}$ (e) $\frac{10}{3}$

6. Identify three fractions other than $\frac{5}{3}$ that name the rational number five-thirds.

7. How many distinct points on the number line are identified by the fractions $\frac{3}{4}$, $\frac{2}{3}$, $\frac{3}{8}$, $\frac{6}{8}$, $\frac{6}{9}$, $\frac{8}{12}$, $\frac{10}{18}$, and $\frac{1}{2}$?

8. Identify the point on the number line associated with the rational number:

(a) $[\frac{3}{2}]$ (b) $[\frac{-3}{2}]$ (c) $[\frac{-3}{2}]$ (d) $[\frac{-3}{-2}]$

10.5

Addition of Rational Numbers

In deciding upon a definition for the addition of rational numbers, reference will again be made to unit figures. Suppose it is desired to find the sum $\frac{3}{5} + \frac{4}{5}$. Since the denominators of the fractions are both 5, we partition each of several unit figures into five congruent subregions, as shown in Figure 10.5.1. A model may be made for the fraction $\frac{3}{5}$ by

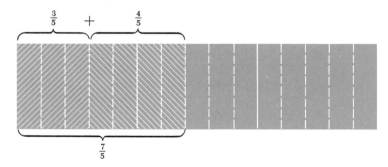

$$\frac{3}{5} \quad + \quad \frac{4}{5}$$

$$\frac{7}{5}$$

FIGURE 10.5.1

shading three subregions and for $\frac{4}{5}$ by shading four more subregions. We then see that the total number of shaded subregions is $3 + 4$, or 7, and conclude that the sum

$$\frac{3}{5} + \frac{4}{5} = \frac{3+4}{5} = \frac{7}{5}.$$

It appears that if two rational numbers are named by fractions having equal denominators, then their sum will be named by a fraction having a numerator equal to the sum of the numerators of the addends and a denominator equal to the common denominator of the addends. If we generalize in this way, we can write

$$\frac{a}{b} + \frac{c}{b} = \frac{a+c}{b}.$$

Of course, the denominators of the fractions naming two rational numbers are not always equal. Suppose, for example, we wish to find the sum $\frac{2}{3} + \frac{4}{5}$. If we multiply both the numerator and denominator of $\frac{2}{3}$ by 5, we obtain an equivalent ordered pair $\dfrac{2 \cdot 5}{3 \cdot 5}$, which is a numeral for the same rational number. Similarly, $\dfrac{4}{5} = \dfrac{3 \cdot 4}{3 \cdot 5}$. We then have

$$\frac{2}{3} + \frac{4}{5} = \frac{2 \cdot 5}{3 \cdot 5} + \frac{3 \cdot 4}{3 \cdot 5} = \frac{10}{15} + \frac{12}{15} = \frac{10 + 12}{15} = \frac{22}{15},$$

or, in general,

$$\frac{a}{b} + \frac{c}{d} = \frac{ad}{bd} + \frac{bc}{bd} = \frac{ad + bc}{bd}.$$

At this point, we have really *proved* nothing concerning the sum of rational numbers. We have, however, done much to decide what might be a useful *definition* for the sum of two rational numbers. On the basis of our explorations, we define the sum of two rational numbers as follows:

DEFINITION 10.5.1

If $\dfrac{a}{b}$ and $\dfrac{c}{d}$ are any two rational numbers, then their sum $\dfrac{a}{b} + \dfrac{c}{d} = \dfrac{ad + bc}{bd}$.

Example 1. Find the sum $\dfrac{3}{4} + \dfrac{9}{11}$.

Solution:

$$\frac{3}{4} + \frac{9}{11} = \frac{3 \cdot 11 + 4 \cdot 9}{4 \cdot 11} = \frac{33 + 36}{44} = \frac{69}{44}.$$

Example 2. Find the sum $\dfrac{2}{3} + \dfrac{^-4}{5}$.

Solution:

$$\frac{2}{3} + \frac{^-4}{5} = \frac{2 \cdot 5 + 3 \cdot {^-4}}{3 \cdot 5} = \frac{10 + {^-12}}{15} = \frac{^-2}{15}.$$

If we apply the definition of addition for rational numbers to the sum $\frac{1}{2} + \frac{3}{5}$, the result is

$$\frac{1}{2} + \frac{3}{5} = \frac{1 \cdot 5 + 2 \cdot 3}{2 \cdot 5} = \frac{5 + 6}{10} = \frac{11}{10}.$$

Since $\frac{1}{2}$ and $\frac{2}{4}$ name the same rational number, we should obtain the same sum by replacing $\frac{1}{2}$ with $\frac{2}{4}$. In so doing we have:

$$\frac{2}{4} + \frac{3}{5} = \frac{2 \cdot 5 + 4 \cdot 3}{4 \cdot 5} = \frac{10 + 12}{20} = \frac{22}{20}.$$

However, $\frac{22}{20} \cong \frac{11}{10}$; hence the two fractions belong to the same equivalence class, and either may be used to name the rational number $[\frac{11}{10}]$. The important thing to realize is that if we use any member of the equivalence class $[\frac{1}{2}]$ and any member of the class $[\frac{3}{5}]$ to find a sum, we shall obtain some member of a unique class, in this case $[\frac{11}{10}]$.

Keeping in mind that rational numbers and their sums are defined in terms of equivalence classes, we shall investigate the system to see if the properties of closure, commutativity, associativity, and so on hold for the operation of addition.

The Properties of Addition

(a) *Closure Property of Addition.* If the set of rational numbers is to be closed under addition, then the sum of any two rational numbers must *exist* and be *unique.* First, we shall show that for any ordered pair of representatives of rational numbers $\left(\frac{a}{b}, \frac{c}{d}\right)$, the sum $\frac{ad + bc}{bd}$ exists in the set of rational numbers.

As a result of the closure properties of multiplication and addition in the integers,

$$\frac{ad + bc}{bd} = \frac{e}{f},$$

where e and f are in J. Since $b \neq 0$ and $d \neq 0$, $f \neq 0$; therefore, $\frac{e}{f}$ represents a rational number.

Next we must show that regardless of the representative elements used for any two rational numbers, their sum is *unique.* If we were to obtain different sums when we used different representative elements for the same two addends, our definition for the addition of rational numbers would indeed leave much to be desired. However, we shall show that our definition for addition is such that sums are unique.

Let $\frac{a}{b}$ and $\frac{c}{d}$ represent the same rational number. Also let $\frac{e}{f}$ and $\frac{g}{h}$

represent a single rational number. Then we must show that

$$\frac{a}{b} + \frac{e}{f} = \frac{c}{d} + \frac{g}{h}$$

or that

$$\frac{af + be}{bf} \cong \frac{ch + dg}{dh}.$$

However, the last two expressions are equivalent if and only if $(af + be)dh = bf(ch + dg)$ or $afdh + bedh = bfch + bfdg$. Since $\frac{a}{b} \simeq \frac{c}{d}$ and $\frac{e}{f} = \frac{g}{h}$, we know that $ad = bc$ and $eh = fg$. By substituting ad for bc and eh for fg, we see that the equation $afdh + bedh = bfch + bfdg$ is true. Hence,

$$\frac{af + be}{bf} \cong \frac{ch + dg}{dh}$$

and the expressions represent the same rational number. Thus, the sum of any two rational numbers is unique.

Since both the existence and uniqueness properties of closure are satisfied, the set of rational numbers is closed under addition.

(b) *Commutative Property of Addition.* We must show that

$$\frac{a}{b} + \frac{c}{d} = \frac{c}{d} + \frac{a}{b}$$

or that

$$\frac{ad + bc}{bd} = \frac{cb + da}{db}.$$

It is easy to see that $ad + bc = cb + da$ by using properties of the integers. Also $bd = db$. Therefore,

$$\frac{ad + bc}{bd} = \frac{cb + da}{db} \qquad \text{and} \qquad \frac{a}{b} + \frac{c}{d} = \frac{c}{d} + \frac{a}{b}.$$

(c) *Associative Property of Addition.* If addition in the integers is associative, it must be true that $(\frac{a}{b} + \frac{c}{d}) + \frac{e}{f} = \frac{a}{b} + (\frac{c}{d} + \frac{e}{f})$. The proof involves using the definition of addition for rational numbers and properties of the integers. It is left as an exercise for the reader.

An example to verify (but not prove) the associative property follows.

Example 3.

$$\left(\frac{2}{3} + \frac{1}{5}\right) + \frac{3}{4} = \frac{10 + 3}{15} + \frac{3}{4} = \frac{13}{15} + \frac{3}{4} = \frac{52 + 45}{60} = \frac{97}{60}.$$

Also,

$$\frac{2}{3} + \left(\frac{1}{5} + \frac{3}{4}\right) = \frac{2}{3} + \frac{4 + 15}{20} = \frac{2}{3} + \frac{19}{20} = \frac{40 + 57}{60} = \frac{97}{60}.$$

Therefore, $\left(\frac{2}{3} + \frac{1}{5}\right) + \frac{3}{4} = \frac{2}{3} + \left(\frac{1}{5} + \frac{3}{4}\right).$

(d) *Identity Element for Addition.* The identity element for addition in the rational numbers is $[\frac{0}{1}]$. We usually use the fraction $\frac{0}{1}$ (which is in simplest form) to represent the identity element. However, any member of the equivalence class $[\frac{0}{1}]$ may be used. The number $\frac{0}{1}$ is unique and for every rational number $\frac{a}{b}$, $\frac{a}{b} + \frac{0}{1} = \frac{0}{1} + \frac{a}{b} = \frac{a}{b}$. The rational number $\frac{0}{1}$ corresponds to the number 0 in the system of integers.

Example 4.

(a) $\dfrac{5}{6} + \dfrac{0}{1} = \dfrac{5 \cdot 1 + 6 \cdot 0}{6 \cdot 1} = \dfrac{5 + 0}{6} = \dfrac{5}{6}.$

(b) $\dfrac{0}{9} + \dfrac{5}{6} = \dfrac{0 \cdot 6 + 9 \cdot 5}{9 \cdot 6} = \dfrac{0 + 45}{54} = \dfrac{45}{54} = \dfrac{5}{6}.$

(e) *Additive Inverse.* As you will recall from studying the integers and certain finite number systems in Chapter 9, the sum of a number and its additive inverse is equal to the identity element for addition. In the system of rational numbers, every element has an additive inverse.

For each rational number $\frac{a}{b}$ there exists a unique element $\frac{^-a}{b}$ such that $\frac{a}{b} + \frac{^-a}{b} = \frac{^-a}{b} + \frac{a}{b} = \frac{0}{1}.$

Example 5.

$$\frac{3}{4} + \frac{^-3}{4} = \frac{3 \cdot 4 + 4 \cdot {^-3}}{4 \cdot 4} = \frac{12 + {^-12}}{16} = \frac{0}{16} = \frac{0}{1},$$

and

$$\frac{^-3}{4} + \frac{3}{4} = \frac{^-3 \cdot 4 + 4 \cdot 3}{16} = \frac{^-12 + 12}{16} = \frac{0}{16} = \frac{0}{1}.$$

In general, we see that

$$\frac{a}{b} + \frac{^-a}{b} = \frac{ab + b \cdot {^-a}}{bb} = \frac{ab + {^-ab}}{b^2} = \frac{0}{b^2} = \frac{0}{1}.$$

Since the addition of rational numbers is commutative, it will also be true that $\frac{-a}{b} + \frac{a}{b} = \frac{0}{1}$.

Example 6. An equation such as $x + \frac{2}{7} = \frac{3}{5}$ may easily be solved by using an additive inverse:

$$x + \tfrac{2}{7} = \tfrac{3}{5}$$
$$(x + \tfrac{2}{7}) + \tfrac{-2}{7} = \tfrac{3}{5} + \tfrac{-2}{7}$$
$$x + (\tfrac{2}{7} + \tfrac{-2}{7}) = \tfrac{3}{5} + \tfrac{-2}{7}$$
$$x + 0 = \frac{21 + {}^-10}{35}$$
$$x = \tfrac{11}{35}.$$

THEOREM 10.5.1

If $\dfrac{a}{c}$ and $\dfrac{b}{c}$ are rational numbers, then $\dfrac{a}{c} + \dfrac{b}{c} = \dfrac{a+b}{c}$.

(The reader should be able to justify each step in the following proof.)

Proof:

$$\frac{a}{c} + \frac{b}{c} = \frac{ac + cb}{cc} = \frac{ca + cb}{cc} = \frac{c(a+b)}{cc} = \frac{a+b}{c}.$$

Therefore,

$$\frac{a}{c} + \frac{b}{c} = \frac{a+b}{c}.$$

Theorem 10.5.1 can be used to justify the "least common denominator" method of adding rational numbers. By this method we first find the least common multiple of the denominators of the numbers to be added. This number is then used as the common denominator of the addends and is called their *least common denominator*. The familiar procedure is illustrated in the examples below. For a review of the method for finding the least common multiple of numbers, see Section 9.6.

Example 7. Find the sum $\frac{5}{6} + \frac{7}{10}$ by finding the least common denominator of the addends.

Solution: The least common multiple of 6 and 10 is 30. Using 30 as the least common denominator and using Theorem 10.5.1, we have:

$$\frac{5}{6} + \frac{7}{10} = \frac{5 \cdot 5}{6 \cdot 5} + \frac{7 \cdot 3}{10 \cdot 3} = \frac{25}{30} + \frac{21}{30} = \frac{25 + 21}{30} = \frac{46}{30} = \frac{23}{15}.$$

Example 8. Find the sum $\frac{5}{8} + \frac{^-3}{10}$ by the least common denominator method.

Solution:

$$\frac{5}{8} + \frac{^-3}{10} = \frac{5 \cdot 5}{8 \cdot 5} + \frac{^-3 \cdot 4}{10 \cdot 4} = \frac{25}{40} + \frac{^-12}{40} = \frac{25 + ^-12}{40} = \frac{13}{40}.$$

THEOREM 10.5.2

If $\dfrac{a}{b}$, $\dfrac{c}{d}$, and $\dfrac{e}{f}$ are rational numbers and $\dfrac{a}{b} + \dfrac{e}{f} = \dfrac{c}{d} + \dfrac{e}{f}$, then $\dfrac{a}{b} = \dfrac{c}{d}$.

The above theorem may be referred to as the cancellation property of addition in the rational numbers. The proof is similar to the proof of the cancellation property of addition in the integers (see Theorem 8.8.1) and is left as an exercise for the reader.

10.6
The Integers as a Subsystem of the Rational Numbers

In Section 8.2 we noted that the natural numbers "behave in exactly the same way" as the positive integers, and no distinction was made between them. In a similar way the set of integers behaves like the set of rational numbers with denominators of 1. For this reason we shall consider any integer a and the rational number $\frac{a}{1}$ to be names for the same number and we may write $a = \frac{a}{1}$. The set of integers and the set of rational numbers with denominators of 1 may be put in a one-to-one correspondence as shown below:

$$
\begin{array}{ccccccccc}
\cdots & ^-3 & ^-2 & ^-1 & 0 & 1 & 2 & 3 & \cdots \\
& \updownarrow & \updownarrow & \updownarrow & \updownarrow & \updownarrow & \updownarrow & \updownarrow & \\
\cdots & \frac{^-3}{1} & \frac{^-2}{1} & \frac{^-1}{1} & \frac{0}{1} & \frac{1}{1} & \frac{2}{1} & \frac{3}{1} & \cdots
\end{array}
$$

To illustrate that these two sets behave alike under the operation of addition, let us compare the sum $2 + 3$ with the sum $\frac{2}{1} + \frac{3}{1}$:

$$2 + 3 = 5.$$

$$\frac{2}{1} + \frac{3}{1} = \frac{2 \cdot 1 + 1 \cdot 3}{1 \cdot 1} = \frac{2 + 3}{1} = \frac{5}{1}.$$

Since 5 corresponds to $\frac{5}{1}$, we see that 5 and $\frac{5}{1}$ are names for the same sum. In general, we have:

$$a + b = \frac{a}{1} + \frac{b}{1} = \frac{a \cdot 1 + 1 \cdot b}{1 \cdot 1} = \frac{a + b}{1}, \quad \text{or} \quad a + b = \frac{a + b}{1}$$

by the transitive property of equals. (It will be shown later, in the section on multiplication, that $a \cdot b = \frac{a}{1} \cdot \frac{b}{1}$.)

Sets that behave in the same way are said to be isomorphic. Since the integers are isomorphic to a subset of the rational numbers, they may be referred to as a subsystem of the rational numbers. Isomorphisms are considered in detail in more advanced texts on number systems or abstract algebra.

We usually write the sum of an integer and a rational number, such as $3 + \frac{2}{5}$, by leaving out the plus sign and closing up the space, as in $3\frac{2}{5}$. An expression such as $3\frac{2}{5}$ is sometimes called a mixed fraction or mixed numeral since it involves both an integer and a fraction. Of course, the mixed fraction $3\frac{2}{5}$ may be written as an ordered pair of integers (a fraction) by adding 3 and $\frac{2}{5}$ as shown in Example 1.

Example 1.   Write $3\frac{2}{5}$ in fraction form.

Solution:

$$3\frac{2}{5} = 3 + \frac{2}{5} = \frac{3}{1} + \frac{2}{5} = \frac{15 + 2}{5} = \frac{17}{5}.$$

Example 2.   Write $\frac{17}{5}$ as a mixed fraction.

Solution:

$$\frac{17}{5} = \frac{15 + 2}{5} = \frac{15}{5} + \frac{2}{5} = 3 + \frac{2}{5} = 3\frac{2}{5}.$$

Example 3.   Find the sum $2\frac{2}{3} + 3\frac{1}{7}$.

Solution:

$$2\frac{2}{3} + 3\frac{1}{7} = (2 + \frac{2}{3}) + (3 + \frac{1}{7}) = (2 + 3) + (\frac{2}{3} + \frac{1}{7})$$

$$= 5 + \frac{14 + 3}{21} = 5 + \frac{17}{21} = 5\frac{17}{21}.$$

Example 4.   Add $2\frac{1}{5}$ and $^-5\frac{2}{7}$.

Solution:

$$2\frac{1}{5} + {^-5\frac{2}{7}} = (2 + \frac{1}{5}) + ({^-5} + \frac{{^-2}}{7}) = (2 + {^-5}) + (\frac{1}{5} + \frac{{^-2}}{7})$$

$$= {^-3} + \frac{7 + {^-10}}{35} = {^-3} + \frac{{^-3}}{35} = {^-3\frac{3}{35}}.$$

Alternative Solution:

$$2\tfrac{1}{5} + {}^-5\tfrac{2}{7} = \frac{11}{5} + \frac{{}^-37}{7} = \frac{77 + {}^-185}{35}$$

$$= \frac{{}^-108}{35} = \frac{{}^-105 + {}^-3}{35} = \frac{{}^-105}{35} + \frac{{}^-3}{35}$$

$$= {}^-3 + \frac{{}^-3}{35} = {}^-3\tfrac{3}{35}.$$

EXERCISE 10.6

1. Define the sum of two rational numbers.

2. Using the definition for the sum of two rational numbers, find the following sums and express the results in simplest form.

(a) $\frac{2}{3} + \frac{3}{4}$ (b) $\frac{2}{5} + \frac{^-1}{2}$ (c) $\frac{7}{3} + \frac{4}{38}$

(d) $\frac{^-3}{2} + \frac{^-4}{15}$ (e) $\frac{^-2}{3} + \frac{^-3}{8}$ (f) $\frac{7}{6} + \frac{5}{10}$

(g) $\frac{^-8}{3} + \frac{^-7}{4}$ (h) $\frac{^-5}{7} + \frac{3}{24}$ (i) $\frac{^-10}{^-3} + \frac{^-4}{^-5}$

(j) $\frac{^-8}{^-3} + \frac{^-7}{34}$ (k) $\frac{^-5}{13} + \frac{4}{^-7}$ (l) $\frac{^-6}{^-7} + \frac{^-3}{14}$

3. Verify that the addition of rational numbers is commutative by showing that $\frac{2}{7} + \frac{4}{5} = \frac{4}{5} + \frac{2}{7}$.

4. Prove that the operation of addition as defined on the rational numbers is commutative.

5. Verify that the addition of rational numbers is associative by showing that $(\frac{2}{3} + \frac{4}{5}) + \frac{3}{7} = \frac{2}{3} + (\frac{4}{5} + \frac{3}{7})$.

6. Prove that the operation of addition as defined on the rational numbers is associative.

7. (a) What is the general meaning of an identity element for the operation of addition in a mathematical system?
   (b) What is the identity element for addition in the integers?
   (c) What is the identity element for addition in the rational numbers?
   (d) What is the sum of $\frac{2}{3}$ and $\frac{0}{^-5}$?

8. (a) Why can we say that $\frac{0}{1}$ is in simplest form?
   (b) Are there any other representative elements of $[\frac{0}{1}]$ that are in simplest form? Explain.

9. What is meant by saying that an element in a mathematical system has an additive inverse?

10. Express in simplest form the additive inverse of each of the following.

(a) $\frac{2}{5}$ (b) $\frac{^-3}{7}$ (c) $\frac{7}{2}$

(d) $\frac{a}{b}$ (e) $\frac{^-2}{^-7}$ (f) $\frac{^-3}{^-2}$

(g) $\frac{^-4}{^-21}$ (h) $\frac{^-a}{b}$ (i) $2\tfrac{1}{3}$

(j) $^-4\tfrac{2}{3}$ (k) $\frac{^--2}{35}$ (l) $\frac{^--a}{b}$

11. Using the concept of an additive inverse, solve for x in each of the following equations.

   (a) $x + \frac{1}{2} = \frac{3}{5}$ (b) $x + \frac{-2}{3} = \frac{1}{2}$

   (c) $\frac{-3}{5} + x = \frac{4}{3}$ (d) $\frac{3}{4} = x + 7$

   (e) $x + \frac{-9}{7} = \frac{2}{3}$ (f) $\frac{2}{3} = \frac{3}{4} + x$

12. Find each sum in problem 2 by finding the least common denominator of the addends.

13. Express each of the following in fraction form.

   (a) $2\frac{1}{3}$ (b) $7\frac{2}{15}$ (c) $^-3\frac{2}{5}$

14. Express each of the following as a mixed fraction.

   (a) $\frac{7}{3}$ (b) $\frac{18}{5}$ (c) $\frac{-17}{7}$

15. Find the following sums and express each result first as a fraction and then as a mixed fraction.

   (a) $\frac{2}{7} + \frac{9}{2}$ (b) $\frac{3}{5} + \frac{-11}{3}$

   (c) $2 + \frac{7}{8}$ (d) $^-3 + \frac{2}{3}$

   (e) $^-7 + \frac{-3}{4}$ (f) $\frac{7}{5} + {}^-14$

16. Add the following:

   (a) $2\frac{2}{3}$ and $3\frac{1}{5}$ (b) $3\frac{5}{7}$ and $\frac{2}{3}$

   (c) $\frac{-5}{7}$ and $2\frac{1}{3}$ (d) $2\frac{3}{4}$ and $^-3\frac{1}{4}$

   (e) $1\frac{2}{35}$ and $^-2\frac{7}{8}$ (f) $^-4\frac{1}{2}$ and $^-3\frac{3}{42}$

17. Prove Theorem 10.5.2 (the cancellation property of addition).

10.7 Subtraction of Rational Numbers

We shall define subtraction of rational numbers in terms of addition. From a logical viewpoint, we could first define subtraction and then define addition in terms of subtraction because, as we shall soon see, the rational numbers (like the integers) are closed under subtraction. However, it seems more convenient and somewhat simpler to do the reverse. It would have been impossible to define the addition of whole numbers in terms of subtraction because the whole numbers are not closed under subtraction.

DEFINITION 10.7.1

If $\frac{a}{b}$, $\frac{c}{d}$, and $\frac{e}{f}$ are rational numbers, then $\frac{a}{b} - \frac{c}{d} = \frac{e}{f}$ if and only if $\frac{a}{b} = \frac{c}{d} + \frac{e}{f}$.

Referring to the above definition, it will be seen that closure for subtraction depends upon the *existence* of a *unique* rational number $\frac{e}{f}$ such that $\frac{a}{b} = \frac{c}{d} + \frac{e}{f}$ for all rational numbers $\frac{a}{b}$ and $\frac{c}{d}$. If this is the case, then, by definition, $\frac{a}{b} - \frac{c}{d} = \frac{e}{f}$.

First, we shall prove that the difference $\frac{e}{f}$ exists in the set of rational numbers by showing that if $\frac{e}{f}$ is equal to $\frac{a}{b} + \frac{-c}{d}$, then the equation $\frac{a}{b} = \frac{c}{d} + \frac{e}{f}$ will be true.

Proof that if $\frac{e}{f} = \frac{a}{b} + \frac{-c}{d}$, *then* $\frac{a}{b} = \frac{c}{d} + \frac{e}{f}$:

Let $\frac{e}{f} = \frac{a}{b} + \frac{-c}{d}$

Then, $\frac{c}{d} + \frac{e}{f} = \frac{c}{d} + \left(\frac{a}{b} + \frac{-c}{d} \right)$

$$= \frac{c}{d} + \left(\frac{-c}{d} + \frac{a}{b} \right)$$

$$= \left(\frac{c}{d} + \frac{-c}{d} \right) + \frac{a}{b}$$

$$= \frac{0}{1} + \frac{a}{b}$$

$$= \frac{a}{b}$$

Hence, $\frac{a}{b} = \frac{c}{d} + \frac{e}{f}$ if $\frac{e}{f} = \frac{a}{b} + \frac{-c}{d}$.

We have proved that the difference $\frac{e}{f}$ (equal to $\frac{a}{b} + \frac{-c}{d}$) *exists* in the set of rational numbers. We shall now show that $\frac{e}{f}$ is *unique*, and in so doing we shall prove that the set of rational numbers is closed with respect to subtraction.

Suppose there is some other rational number $\frac{g}{h}$ such that $\frac{a}{b} = \frac{c}{d} + \frac{g}{h}$. Then $\frac{c}{d} + \frac{g}{h} = \frac{a}{b} = \frac{c}{d} + \frac{e}{f}$, and, by the transitive property of equals, $\frac{c}{d} + \frac{g}{h} = \frac{c}{d} + \frac{e}{f}$. Finally, by the cancellation property of addition, we see that $\frac{g}{h} = \frac{e}{f}$. Hence, $\frac{e}{f}$ (equal to $\frac{a}{b} + \frac{-c}{d}$) is *uniquely determined* as the solution of $\frac{a}{b} = \frac{c}{d} + \frac{e}{f}$, and, by the definition of subtraction, $\frac{a}{b} - \frac{c}{d} = \frac{e}{f} = \frac{a}{b} + \frac{-c}{d}$.

As in the case of the integers, subtracting one rational number from another is equivalent to adding the additive inverse of the subtrahend to the minuend. Using the equation $\frac{a}{b} - \frac{c}{d} = \frac{a}{b} + \frac{-c}{d}$ makes it easy to find the difference of two rational numbers by addition. Furthermore, addition is commutative and associative while subtraction is not. (The proof that subtraction is neither commutative nor associative is left as an exercise for the reader.)

Example 1.

$$\frac{3}{8} - \frac{2}{7} = \frac{3}{8} + \frac{^-2}{7} = \frac{3 \cdot 7 + 8 \cdot {}^-2}{8 \cdot 7} = \frac{21 + {}^-16}{56} = \frac{5}{56}.$$

Example 2.

$$\frac{2}{3} - \frac{^-5}{7} = \frac{2}{3} + \frac{5}{7} = \frac{2 \cdot 7 + 3 \cdot 5}{3 \cdot 7} = \frac{14 + 15}{21} = \frac{29}{21}.$$

Example 3.

$$2\tfrac{2}{5} - 3\tfrac{3}{4} = \frac{12}{5} - \frac{15}{4} = \frac{12}{5} + \frac{^-15}{4} = \frac{48 + {}^-75}{20} = \frac{^-27}{20}.$$

THEOREM 10.7.1

If $\frac{a}{b}$ and $\frac{c}{d}$ are rational numbers, then $\frac{a}{b} - \frac{c}{d} = \frac{ad - bc}{bd}$.

Proof:

$$\frac{a}{b} - \frac{c}{d} = \frac{a}{b} + \frac{^-c}{d}$$

$$= \frac{ad + b(^-c)}{bd} = \frac{ad + {}^-(bc)}{bd} = \frac{ad - bc}{bd}.$$

Therefore, $\frac{a}{b} - \frac{c}{d} = \frac{ad - bc}{bd}$.

Try to justify each step in the above proof by considering the fact that a, b, c, and d are integers with $b \neq 0$ and $d \neq 0$.

THEOREM 10.7.2

If $\frac{a}{c}$ and $\frac{b}{c}$ are rational numbers, then $\frac{a}{c} - \frac{b}{c} = \frac{a - b}{c}$.

Proof: By Theorem 10.7.1,

$$\frac{a}{c} - \frac{b}{c} = \frac{ac - cb}{cc}, \text{ and } \frac{ac - cb}{cc} = \frac{ca - cb}{cc} = \frac{c(a - b)}{cc} = \frac{a - b}{c}.$$

Therefore, $\frac{a}{c} - \frac{b}{c} = \frac{a - b}{c}$.

Theorem 10.7.2 can be used to justify the "least common denominator" method of subtracting rational numbers. The familiar procedure is illustrated in the example below.

Example 4.

$$\frac{5}{8} - \frac{^-7}{10} = \frac{5 \cdot 5}{8 \cdot 5} - \frac{^-7 \cdot 4}{10 \cdot 4} = \frac{25}{40} - \frac{^-28}{40} = \frac{25 - ^-28}{40}$$

$$= \frac{25 + 28}{40} = \frac{53}{40}.$$

EXERCISE 10.7

1. Define subtraction for the rational numbers.

2. Using the equation $\frac{a}{b} - \frac{c}{d} = \frac{a}{b} + \frac{^-c}{d}$, find the following differences.
   (a) $\frac{3}{4} - \frac{2}{3}$ (b) $\frac{7}{8} - \frac{^-3}{5}$
   (c) $\frac{^-9}{2} - \frac{7}{8}$ (d) $\frac{^-4}{9} - \frac{^-3}{8}$
   (e) $\frac{3}{8} - \frac{^-7}{3}$ (f) $\frac{13}{4} - 7$
   (g) $\frac{2}{3} - ^-3$ (h) $8 - \frac{12}{5}$

3. Prove by a counterexample that subtraction in the rational numbers is not commutative.

4. Prove that subtraction in the rational numbers is not associative by showing that $(\frac{3}{4} - \frac{2}{3}) - \frac{1}{5} \neq \frac{3}{4} - (\frac{2}{3} - \frac{1}{5})$.

5. Use the "least common denominator" method to find the following differences:
   (a) $\frac{3}{4} - \frac{2}{3}$ (b) $\frac{7}{8} - \frac{2}{10}$
   (c) $6 - \frac{^-3}{5}$ (d) $\frac{^-11}{12} - \frac{3}{10}$
   (e) $\frac{4}{3} - \frac{3}{7}$ (f) $\frac{^-4}{5} - \frac{^-3}{10}$
   (g) $\frac{22}{7} - 2$ (h) $\frac{25}{4} - 3$

6. Prove Theorem 10.7.1 and justify each step of your proof.

7. Use Theorem 10.7.1 to prove Theorem 10.7.2.

8. Find the value of x that makes each of the following statements true:
   (a) $x - \frac{1}{2} = \frac{2}{7}$ (b) $x + \frac{3}{4} = \frac{7}{12}$
   (c) $\frac{7}{3} + x = \frac{2}{3}$ (d) $\frac{3}{4} = x - 2$

9. Subtract and simplify if possible.
   (a) $\dfrac{7}{bc} - \dfrac{2}{bc}$ (b) $\dfrac{a}{b^2c} - \dfrac{d}{b^2c}$

   (c) $\dfrac{a}{b^3c} - \dfrac{^-3}{bc}$ (d) $\dfrac{x}{y^2z} - \dfrac{t}{yz^2}$

10.8

Multiplication of Rational Numbers

   A definition for multiplication in the rational numbers should be consistent with the models, definitions, and theorems that have already been developed and found useful. We shall examine the fraction concept, the addition of rational numbers, and the multiplication of integers for ideas that may assist us in arriving at such a definition.

First, we shall consider the fraction concept. What, for example, should be the product of $\frac{3}{5}$ and $\frac{3}{4}$? Using a unit region as shown in Figure 10.8.1, we see that the subregion with stripes slanting upward from left to right is a model for the number $\frac{3}{4}$. The subregion striped in two directions represents $\frac{3}{5}$ of $\frac{3}{4}$ and is equal to $\frac{9}{20}$. Since we consider $\frac{3}{5}$ of $\frac{3}{4}$ to mean $\frac{3}{5} \cdot \frac{3}{4}$, it appears that we should have $\frac{3}{5} \cdot \frac{3}{4} = \frac{9}{20}$.

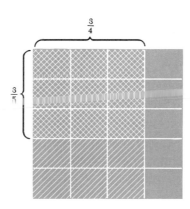

FIGURE 10.8.1

Next considering the equal addends approach to multiplication, it seems that a product such as $3 \cdot \frac{2}{5}$ should equal $\frac{2}{5} + \frac{2}{5} + \frac{2}{5}$ or $\frac{6}{5}$ and that, in general, $a \cdot \dfrac{b}{c}$ should equal $\dfrac{a \cdot b}{c}$ where a, b, and c are in J with $c \neq 0$.

Finally, since the integers correspond to the rational numbers with denominators of 1, a product such as $3 \cdot 5$ should equal $\frac{3}{1} \cdot \frac{5}{1}$ or $\frac{15}{1}$ or 15. In general, we should have

$$a \cdot b = \frac{a}{1} \cdot \frac{b}{1} = \frac{a \cdot b}{1} = a \cdot b.$$

The following definition for multiplication in the rational numbers produces results which are consistent with all the concepts mentioned above; from this point of view it seems reasonable and offers the hope of being extremely useful.

DEFINITION 10.8.1

If $\dfrac{a}{b}$ and $\dfrac{c}{d}$ are any two rational numbers, then their product is

$$\frac{a}{b} \cdot \frac{c}{d} = \frac{a \cdot c}{b \cdot d}.$$

Example 1.

(a) $\dfrac{3}{5} \cdot \dfrac{3}{4} = \dfrac{3 \cdot 3}{5 \cdot 4} = \dfrac{9}{20}.$

(b) $\dfrac{2}{3} \cdot \dfrac{^-5}{11} = \dfrac{2(^-5)}{3(11)} = \dfrac{^-10}{33}.$

(c) $\dfrac{^-3}{7} \cdot \dfrac{0}{1} = \dfrac{^-3 \cdot 0}{7 \cdot 1} = \dfrac{0}{7} = \dfrac{0}{1}.$

(d) $^-7 \cdot \dfrac{2}{3} = \dfrac{^-7}{1} \cdot \dfrac{2}{3} = \dfrac{^-7 \cdot 2}{1 \cdot 3} = \dfrac{^-14}{3}.$

The Properties of Multiplication

(a) *Closure Property of Multiplication.* If the rational numbers are to be closed under multiplication, then for each ordered pair of rational numbers $(\frac{a}{b}, \frac{c}{d})$, the product $\frac{a}{b} \cdot \frac{c}{d} = \frac{ac}{bd}$ must *exist* and be *unique*. By the closure property of multiplication in the integers, ac and bd exist. Also $bd \neq 0$ since $b \neq 0$ and $d \neq 0$. Hence $\frac{ac}{bd}$ exists as a rational number.

To prove that $\frac{ac}{bd}$ is *unique*, we must show that if any other representative elements are used such that $\frac{a}{b} \cong \frac{e}{f}$ and $\frac{c}{d} \cong \frac{g}{h}$, then $\frac{ac}{bd} \cong \frac{eg}{fh}$. If $\frac{a}{b} \cong \frac{e}{f}$, then $af = be$. Similarly, $ch = dg$. Then $(af)(ch) = (be)(dg)$, and by the associative and commutative properties of multiplication in the integers, $(ac)(fh) = (bd)(eg)$. Therefore, $\frac{ac}{bd} \cong \frac{eg}{fh}$.

(b) *Commutative Property of Multiplication.* If multiplication in the rational numbers is commutative, then it must be true that for any two rational numbers $\frac{a}{b}$ and $\frac{c}{d}$, $\frac{a}{b} \cdot \frac{c}{d} = \frac{c}{d} \cdot \frac{a}{b}$. By the definition of multiplication, $\frac{a}{b} \cdot \frac{c}{d} = \frac{ac}{bd}$ and $\frac{c}{d} \cdot \frac{a}{b} = \frac{ca}{db}$. However, $\frac{ac}{bd} = \frac{ca}{db}$ since $ac = ca$ and $bd = db$ by the commutative property of multiplication in J. Therefore, by using properties of the equals relation, $\frac{a}{b} \cdot \frac{c}{d} = \frac{c}{d} \cdot \frac{a}{b}$.

Example 2.

$$\dfrac{2}{5} \cdot \dfrac{3}{4} = \dfrac{2 \cdot 3}{5 \cdot 4} = \dfrac{6}{20} = \dfrac{3}{10},$$

and

$$\dfrac{3}{4} \cdot \dfrac{2}{5} = \dfrac{3 \cdot 2}{4 \cdot 5} = \dfrac{6}{20} = \dfrac{3}{10}.$$

Therefore, $\dfrac{2}{5} \cdot \dfrac{3}{4} = \dfrac{3}{4} \cdot \dfrac{2}{5}.$

(c) *Associative Property of Multiplication.* We must show that

$$\left(\frac{a}{b}\cdot\frac{c}{d}\right)\cdot\frac{e}{f} = \frac{a}{b}\cdot\left(\frac{c}{d}\cdot\frac{e}{f}\right)$$

in order to prove that multiplication is associative. See if you can justify each step in the proof.

$$\left(\frac{a}{b}\cdot\frac{c}{d}\right)\cdot\frac{e}{f} = \left(\frac{ac}{bd}\right)\cdot\frac{e}{f} = \frac{(ac)e}{(bd)f} = \frac{a(ce)}{b(df)},$$

and

$$\frac{a}{b}\cdot\left(\frac{c}{d}\cdot\frac{e}{f}\right) = \frac{a}{b}\cdot\left(\frac{ce}{df}\right) = \frac{a(ce)}{b(df)}.$$

Therefore, $\left(\dfrac{a}{b}\cdot\dfrac{c}{d}\right)\cdot\dfrac{e}{f} = \dfrac{a}{b}\cdot\left(\dfrac{c}{d}\cdot\dfrac{e}{f}\right).$

Example 3.

$$\left(\frac{3}{5}\cdot\frac{4}{7}\right)\cdot\frac{2}{3} = \frac{12}{35}\cdot\frac{2}{3} = \frac{24}{105} = \frac{8}{35},$$

and

$$\frac{3}{5}\cdot\left(\frac{4}{7}\cdot\frac{2}{3}\right) = \frac{3}{5}\cdot\frac{8}{21} = \frac{24}{105} = \frac{8}{35}.$$

Therefore, $\left(\dfrac{3}{5}\cdot\dfrac{4}{7}\right)\cdot\dfrac{2}{3} = \dfrac{3}{5}\cdot\left(\dfrac{4}{7}\cdot\dfrac{2}{3}\right).$

(d) *Distributive Property of Multiplication over Addition.* To prove that multiplication is distributive over addition, we must show that

$$\frac{a}{b}\left(\frac{c}{d}+\frac{e}{f}\right) = \frac{a}{b}\cdot\frac{c}{d}+\frac{a}{b}\cdot\frac{e}{f} \quad \text{and} \quad \left(\frac{c}{d}+\frac{e}{f}\right)\frac{a}{b} = \frac{c}{d}\cdot\frac{a}{b}+\frac{e}{f}\cdot\frac{a}{b}.$$

Of course, since multiplication is commutative, we can easily prove the right distributive property if we first prove the left distributive property, or conversely. A proof for the left distributive property of multiplication over addition follows:

$$\frac{a}{b}\left(\frac{c}{d}+\frac{e}{f}\right) = \frac{a}{b}\left(\frac{cf+de}{df}\right) = \frac{a(cf+de)}{b(df)} = \frac{acf+ade}{bdf},$$

and

$$\frac{a}{b}\cdot\frac{c}{d}+\frac{a}{b}\cdot\frac{e}{f} = \frac{ac}{bd}+\frac{ae}{bf} = \frac{acbf+bdae}{bdbf}$$

$$= \frac{b(acf+ade)}{b(bdf)} = \frac{acf+ade}{bdf}.$$

Therefore, $\dfrac{a}{b}\left(\dfrac{c}{d} + \dfrac{e}{f}\right) = \dfrac{a}{b} \cdot \dfrac{c}{d} + \dfrac{a}{b} \cdot \dfrac{e}{f}$.

Example 4.

$$\frac{2}{3}\left(\frac{3}{5} + \frac{4}{7}\right) = \frac{2}{3}\left(\frac{21 + 20}{35}\right) = \frac{2}{3} \cdot \frac{41}{35} = \frac{82}{105},$$

and

$$\frac{2}{3} \cdot \frac{3}{5} + \frac{2}{3} \cdot \frac{4}{7} = \frac{6}{15} + \frac{8}{21} = \frac{126 + 120}{315} = \frac{246}{315} = \frac{82}{105}.$$

Therefore, $\dfrac{2}{3}\left(\dfrac{3}{5} + \dfrac{4}{7}\right) = \dfrac{2}{3} \cdot \dfrac{3}{5} + \dfrac{2}{3} \cdot \dfrac{4}{7}$.

(e) *Identity Element for Multiplication.* The identity element for multiplication in the rational numbers is $[\frac{1}{1}]$. We usually use the fraction $\frac{1}{1}$ (which is in simplest form) to represent the identity element. However, any member of the equivalence class $[\frac{1}{1}]$ may be used. The number $\frac{1}{1}$ is unique and for every rational number $\frac{a}{b}$, $\frac{a}{b} \cdot \frac{1}{1} = \frac{1}{1} \cdot \frac{a}{b} = \frac{a}{b}$. The rational number $\frac{1}{1}$ corresponds to the number 1 in the system of integers.

Example 5.

(a) $\dfrac{^-7}{3} \cdot \dfrac{1}{1} = \dfrac{^-7 \cdot 1}{3 \cdot 1} = \dfrac{^-7}{3}$.

(b) $\dfrac{3}{5} \cdot \dfrac{6}{6} = \dfrac{3 \cdot 6}{5 \cdot 6} = \dfrac{18}{30} = \dfrac{3}{5}$.

(c) $\dfrac{^-2}{^-2} \cdot \dfrac{^-3}{4} = \dfrac{^-2 \cdot {}^-3}{^-2 \cdot 4} = \dfrac{6}{^-8} = \dfrac{^-3}{4}$.

(f) *Multiplicative Inverses.* For each rational number $\frac{a}{b}$, $\frac{a}{b} \neq \frac{0}{1}$, there exists a unique element $\frac{b}{a}$ such that $\frac{a}{b} \cdot \frac{b}{a} = \frac{b}{a} \cdot \frac{a}{b} = \frac{1}{1}$. The element $\frac{b}{a}$ is called the *multiplicative inverse* or the *reciprocal* of $\frac{a}{b}$. The multiplicative inverse of $\frac{a}{b}$ may also be indicated by writing $(\frac{a}{b})^{-1}$. In considering two rational numbers $\frac{a}{b}$ and $\frac{b}{a}$, it is easy to see that each is the multiplicative inverse of the other.

Recall that the sum of a number and its additive inverse is equal to the identity element for addition. Similarly, the product of a number and its multiplicative inverse is equal to the identity element for multiplication. These properties prove to be useful in many ways, particularly in the solution of equations.

Example 6. The multiplicative inverse of $\frac{4}{7}$ is $\frac{7}{5}$, and $\frac{5}{7} \cdot \frac{7}{5} = \frac{35}{35} = \frac{1}{1}$.

Since every rational number except zero has a multiplicative inverse, the solution of equations such as the one in Example 7 may easily be found.

Example 7. If $\frac{2}{3}x = \frac{3}{5}$, then

$$\frac{3}{2} \cdot \left(\frac{2}{3}x\right) = \frac{3}{2} \cdot \frac{3}{5} \qquad \text{Why?}$$

$$\left(\frac{3}{2} \cdot \frac{2}{3}\right)x = \frac{3}{2} \cdot \frac{3}{5} \qquad \text{Why?}$$

$$\frac{6}{6}x = \frac{9}{10} \qquad \text{Why?}$$

$$x = \frac{9}{10} \qquad \text{Why?}$$

THEOREM 10.8.1

If $\frac{a}{b}, \frac{c}{d}$, and $\frac{e}{f}$ are rational numbers with $\frac{e}{f} \neq \frac{0}{1}$ and $\frac{e}{f} \cdot \frac{a}{b} = \frac{e}{f} \cdot \frac{c}{d}$, then $\frac{a}{b} = \frac{c}{d}$.

The above theorem may be referred to as the cancellation property of multiplication. In Section 8.8 the cancellation property of multiplication was stated for the integers, and it was mentioned that the proof would be given in the chapter on the rational numbers. Of course, if Theorem 10.8.1 holds for the rational numbers, it is also true for the integers, since the integers correspond to (are isomorphic to) a subset of the rationals. The proof of Theorem 10.8.1 follows. Note the use of multiplicative inverses in the proof.

Proof of Theorem 10.8.1:

1. $\frac{e}{f} \cdot \frac{a}{b} = \frac{e}{f} \cdot \frac{c}{d}$ with $\frac{e}{f} \neq \frac{0}{1}$ 1. Given
2. $\frac{f}{e} \cdot \left(\frac{e}{f} \cdot \frac{a}{b}\right) = \frac{f}{e} \cdot \left(\frac{e}{f} \cdot \frac{c}{d}\right)$ 2. Why?
3. $\left(\frac{f}{e} \cdot \frac{e}{f}\right) \cdot \frac{a}{b} = \left(\frac{f}{e} \cdot \frac{e}{f}\right) \cdot \frac{c}{d}$ 3. Why?
4. $\left(\frac{fe}{ef}\right) \cdot \frac{a}{b} = \left(\frac{fe}{ef}\right) \cdot \frac{c}{d}$ 4. Why?
5. $\left(\frac{ef}{ef}\right) \cdot \left(\frac{a}{b}\right) = \left(\frac{ef}{ef}\right) \cdot \left(\frac{c}{d}\right)$ 5. Why?
6. $\frac{1}{1} \cdot \frac{a}{b} = \frac{1}{1} \cdot \frac{c}{d}$ 6. Why?
7. $\frac{a}{b} = \frac{c}{d}$ 7. Why?

EXERCISE 10.8

1. Using a unit region, make a drawing to illustrate the following products.
   (a) $\frac{2}{5} \times \frac{2}{3}$
   (b) $\frac{1}{4} \times \frac{3}{5}$

2. Define multiplication for the rational numbers.

3. (a) Prove that $\frac{3}{4} \cong \frac{9}{12}$ and that $\frac{2}{5} \cong \frac{4}{10}$.
   (b) Show that the product $\frac{3}{4} \cdot \frac{2}{5} = \frac{9}{12} \cdot \frac{4}{10}$.

4. (a) Verify the commutative property of multiplication using the numbers $\frac{3}{7}$ and $\frac{4}{5}$.
   (b) Prove that the multiplication of rational numbers is commutative.

5. (a) Verify the associative property of multiplication by showing that $(\frac{3}{4} \cdot \frac{5}{7}) \cdot \frac{2}{11} = \frac{3}{4} \cdot (\frac{5}{7} \cdot \frac{2}{11})$.
   (b) Prove that the multiplication of rational numbers is associative.

6. Using the definitions of addition and multiplication for the rational numbers, show that:
   (a) $\frac{a}{b} + \frac{0}{c} = \frac{a}{b}$
   (b) $\frac{a}{b} \cdot \frac{c}{c} = \frac{a}{b}$

7. Perform the indicated operations and express the results as fractions in simplest form.
   (a) $\frac{2}{3} \cdot \frac{-4}{7}$ (b) $\frac{-3}{5} \cdot \frac{-7}{9}$
   (c) $\frac{3}{7} \cdot \frac{-4}{9} \cdot \frac{2}{5}$ (d) $\frac{7}{2} \cdot \frac{-1}{3} \cdot \frac{-5}{3}$
   (e) $\frac{13}{7} \cdot \frac{7}{13}$ (f) $\frac{13}{7} \cdot \frac{-7}{13}$
   (g) $\frac{2}{3}(\frac{3}{4} + \frac{1}{2})$ (h) $(\frac{3}{8} + \frac{1}{3}) \cdot \frac{2}{5}$
   (i) $\frac{6}{7} \cdot \frac{1}{2} + \frac{1}{3} \cdot \frac{3}{4}$ (j) $\frac{-2}{3}(\frac{-3}{5} + \frac{1}{-3})$

8. Considering the convention (discussed in Section 6.14) that multiplication and division take precedence over addition and subtraction unless otherwise indicated, perform the following operations.
   (a) $\frac{2}{3} \cdot \frac{3}{4} + \frac{5}{7}$ (b) $\frac{2}{3} \cdot (\frac{3}{4} + \frac{5}{7})$
   (c) $\frac{3}{4}(\frac{2}{3} - \frac{1}{4})$ (d) $\frac{3}{4} \cdot \frac{2}{3} - \frac{1}{4}$

9. Show that $\frac{2}{3} \cdot (\frac{3}{4} + \frac{2}{7}) = (\frac{3}{4} + \frac{2}{7}) \cdot \frac{2}{3}$.

10. Perform the indicated operations.
    (a) $\frac{2}{3} \cdot \frac{4}{7} + \frac{3}{5} \cdot \frac{1}{4}$
    (b) $\frac{2}{3} \cdot (\frac{4}{7} + \frac{3}{5}) \cdot \frac{1}{4}$

11. Simplify the following:
    (a) $\frac{2}{7} \cdot \frac{a}{7}$ (b) $\frac{2}{a^2} \cdot \frac{3}{b}$
    (c) $\frac{a}{x^2 y} \cdot \frac{b}{xy^2}$ (d) $\frac{a}{b}\left(\frac{2}{3} + \frac{1}{5}\right)$
    (e) $\frac{a}{b}\left(\frac{2}{3} - \frac{1}{3}\right)$ (f) $\frac{a}{a^2} \cdot \frac{b}{b^2}$

12. What is the multiplicative inverse or reciprocal of each of the following numbers?

(a) $\dfrac{3}{4}$ (b) $\dfrac{-5}{7}$ (c) $^-\left(\dfrac{2}{3}\right)$

(d) $^-5$ (e) $\dfrac{6}{-5}$ (f) $\dfrac{a}{b}$

(g) $\dfrac{-2}{b}$ (h) $\dfrac{2a}{3b}$ (i) $\dfrac{x}{y}$

13. Solve each of the following equations for x.

(a) $\dfrac{1}{3}x = \dfrac{2}{5}$ (b) $\dfrac{2}{5}x = \dfrac{3}{4}$

(c) $\dfrac{-3}{4}x = \dfrac{2}{5}$ (d) $\dfrac{7}{2}x = \dfrac{3}{5}$

(e) $\dfrac{2}{3} = \dfrac{3}{4}x$ (f) $\dfrac{-4}{5} = \dfrac{3}{2}x$

14. Solve each of the following equations for x.

(a) $2x = \dfrac{3}{4} + \dfrac{1}{5}$ (b) $\dfrac{2}{7}x = ^-5 + \dfrac{2}{3}$

(c) $\dfrac{2}{3}x + \dfrac{1}{5} = \dfrac{4}{7}$ (d) $\dfrac{1}{2} - \dfrac{3}{4}x = 3$

15. If x is the multiplicative inverse of y, what is the multiplicative inverse of x?

16. What is the multiplicative inverse of each of the following numbers?
(a) 6^{-1} (b) $(\frac{2}{3})^{-1}$
(c) 4^{-1} (d) $(\frac{a}{b})^{-1}$

17. Prove that the cancellation property of multiplication (Theorem 10.8.1) holds in the set of rational numbers.

10.9 Division of Rational Numbers

The operation of division was defined on the set of whole numbers and on the set of integers in terms of multiplication. We shall continue to relate the two operations in defining division for the rational numbers.

DEFINITION 10.9.1

If $\dfrac{a}{b}, \dfrac{c}{d}$, and $\dfrac{x}{y}$ are rational numbers and $\dfrac{c}{d} \neq \dfrac{0}{1}$, then $\dfrac{a}{b} \div \dfrac{c}{d} = \dfrac{x}{y}$ if and only if $\dfrac{a}{b} = \dfrac{c}{d} \cdot \dfrac{x}{y}$.

Note that the above definition does not permit division by zero. The reason for this restriction is essentially the same as that given for not allowing division by zero in the whole numbers (see Section 6.17).

It would be somewhat difficult to find quotients by using Definition 10.9.1 directly. However, the definition of division may be used to derive Theorem 10.9.1, which makes it very easy to find quotients in the rational numbers.

THEOREM 10.9.1

If $\dfrac{a}{b}$ and $\dfrac{c}{d}$ are rational numbers with $\dfrac{c}{d} \neq \dfrac{0}{1}$, then $\dfrac{a}{b} \div \dfrac{c}{d} = \dfrac{a}{b} \cdot \dfrac{d}{c}$.

Proof: Let $\dfrac{a}{b} \div \dfrac{c}{d} = \dfrac{x}{y}$. Then, by the definition of division, $\dfrac{a}{b} = \dfrac{c}{d} \cdot \dfrac{x}{y}$. Multiplying each member of this equation by $\dfrac{d}{c}$, we have

$$\frac{d}{c}\left(\frac{a}{b}\right) = \frac{d}{c}\left(\frac{c}{d} \cdot \frac{x}{y}\right) \quad \text{or} \quad \frac{d}{c} \cdot \frac{a}{b} = \left(\frac{d}{c} \cdot \frac{c}{d}\right)\frac{x}{y}.$$

Finally, it is seen that $\dfrac{a}{b} \cdot \dfrac{d}{c} = \dfrac{x}{y}$, and we conclude that $\dfrac{a}{b} \div \dfrac{c}{d} = \dfrac{a}{b} \cdot \dfrac{d}{c}$. The reader should write and *justify* each step in this proof.

Theorem 10.9.1 justifies the rule that if one rational number is divided by another, the quotient is equal to the dividend multiplied by the reciprocal of the divisor. (Hence the expression, "Invert the divisor and multiply.") Since every rational number except $\dfrac{0}{1}$ has a reciprocal, Theorem 10.9.1 shows that division in the rationals is always possible except when the divisor is $\dfrac{0}{1}$.

Example 1.

(a) $\frac{2}{3} \div \frac{3}{4} = \frac{2}{3} \cdot \frac{4}{3} = \frac{8}{9}$.

(b) $\frac{7}{4} \div \frac{-3}{5} = \frac{7}{4} \cdot \frac{5}{-3} = \frac{35}{-12} = \frac{-35}{12}$.

(c) $\frac{0}{1} \div \frac{2}{3} = \frac{0}{1} \cdot \frac{3}{2} = \frac{0}{2} = \frac{0}{1}$.

(d) $\frac{4}{5} \div \frac{0}{1}$ has no solution. Division by zero is undefined.

Consider the quotient $a \div b$ where a and b are integers. Since a and b correspond to the rational numbers $\dfrac{a}{1}$ and $\dfrac{b}{1}$, we have the following:

$$a \div b = \frac{a}{1} \div \frac{b}{1} = \frac{a}{1} \cdot \frac{1}{b} = \frac{a \cdot 1}{1 \cdot b} = \frac{a}{b}, \quad \text{or} \quad a \div b = \frac{a}{b}.$$

Thus we may consider the symbol $\dfrac{a}{b}$ to mean the integer a divided by the integer b, and we may also think of $\dfrac{a}{b}$ as the single rational number that is the quotient of a divided by b. For example, $\frac{2}{3}$ may mean $2 \div 3$, and it may also express the single rational number two-thirds.

We may indicate the division of two rational numbers by $\dfrac{\frac{a}{b}}{\frac{c}{d}}$ as well

as by $\frac{a}{b} \div \frac{c}{d}$. One method of justifying the statement that $\dfrac{\frac{a}{b}}{\frac{c}{d}} = \frac{a}{b} \cdot \frac{d}{c}$ is

based on multiplying both the numerator and denominator of $\dfrac{\frac{a}{b}}{\frac{c}{d}}$ by some

rational number k. This will give an equivalent result since $\frac{k}{k} = \frac{1}{1}$. The
number we select for k is $\frac{d}{c}$, which is the multiplicative inverse or reciprocal of the denominator $\frac{c}{d}$. The reason for selecting k in this way is
apparent from the procedure shown below.

$$\frac{\frac{a}{b}}{\frac{c}{d}} = \frac{\frac{a}{b} \cdot \frac{d}{c}}{\frac{c}{d} \cdot \frac{d}{c}} = \frac{\frac{a}{b} \cdot \frac{d}{c}}{1} = \frac{a}{b} \cdot \frac{d}{c}.$$

Example 2.

(a) $\dfrac{\frac{2}{3}}{\frac{3}{4}} = \dfrac{\frac{2}{3} \cdot \frac{4}{3}}{\frac{3}{4} \cdot \frac{4}{3}} = \dfrac{\frac{8}{9}}{1} = \frac{8}{9}.$

(b) $\dfrac{\frac{7}{4}}{\frac{-3}{5}} = \dfrac{\frac{7}{4} \cdot \frac{5}{-3}}{\frac{-3}{5} \cdot \frac{5}{-3}} = \dfrac{\frac{35}{-12}}{1} = \frac{-35}{12}.$

(c) $\dfrac{\frac{2}{7}}{\frac{x}{3}} = \dfrac{\frac{2}{7} \cdot \frac{3}{x}}{\frac{x}{3} \cdot \frac{3}{x}} = \dfrac{\frac{6}{7x}}{1} = \frac{6}{7x}.$

Fractions, such as those of Example 2, in which the numerators
and denominators themselves contain fractions are called complex
fractions. More complicated complex fractions are shown below; they
may be simplified by using the theory that has already been developed
in this chapter.

Example 3.

(a) $\dfrac{\frac{2}{3} + 5}{\frac{1}{2} + \frac{3}{4}} = \dfrac{\frac{2}{3} + \frac{5}{1}}{\frac{1}{2} + \frac{3}{4}} = \dfrac{\frac{2 + 15}{3}}{\frac{4 + 6}{8}}$

$$= \dfrac{\frac{17}{3}}{\frac{10}{8}} = \frac{17}{3} \cdot \frac{8}{10} = \frac{136}{30} = \frac{68}{15}.$$

$$\text{(b)} \quad \frac{\dfrac{1}{2} - \dfrac{2}{7}}{\dfrac{3}{4}} = \frac{\dfrac{1}{2} + \dfrac{^-2}{7}}{\dfrac{3}{4}} = \frac{\dfrac{7 + {}^-4}{14}}{\dfrac{3}{4}}$$

$$= \frac{\dfrac{3}{14}}{\dfrac{3}{4}} = \frac{3}{14} \cdot \frac{4}{3} = \frac{12}{42} = \frac{2}{7}.$$

In Exercise 10.9 you will be asked to solve some equations. An example is given below. Note that several of the concepts developed in this chapter are used in the solution of the equation. See if you can justify each step.

Example 4. Solve for x: $\dfrac{2}{3}x + \dfrac{3}{5} = 2 - \dfrac{1}{4}$.

Solution:

$$\frac{2}{3}x + \frac{3}{5} = 2 - \frac{1}{4}$$

$$\left(\frac{2}{3}x + \frac{3}{5}\right) + \frac{^-3}{5} = \left(2 - \frac{1}{4}\right) + \frac{^-3}{5}$$

$$\frac{2}{3}x + \left(\frac{3}{5} + \frac{^-3}{5}\right) = \left(\frac{2}{1} + \frac{^-1}{4}\right) + \frac{^-3}{5}$$

$$\frac{2}{3}x + 0 = \frac{8 + {}^-1}{4} + \frac{^-3}{5}$$

$$\frac{2}{3}x = \frac{7}{4} + \frac{^-3}{5} = \frac{35 + {}^-12}{20} = \frac{23}{20}$$

$$\frac{3}{2} \cdot \frac{2}{3}x = \frac{3}{2} \cdot \frac{23}{20}$$

$$x = \frac{69}{40}$$

EXERCISE 10.9

1. Define division for the rational numbers.
2. Prove Theorem 10.9.1. Justify each step in your proof.
3. Using Theorem 10.9.1, find the following quotients.

   (a) $\frac{2}{5} \div \frac{4}{3}$ (b) $\frac{9}{2} \div \frac{^-3}{5}$ (c) $\frac{1}{4} \div \frac{1}{4}$

   (d) $\frac{0}{1} \div \frac{2}{7}$ (e) $\frac{^-2}{5} \div \frac{^-5}{7}$ (f) $\frac{a}{b} \div \frac{2}{3}$

   (g) $\frac{2}{3} \div 5$ (h) $7 \div \frac{3}{4}$ (i) $^-3 \div \frac{2}{5}$

4. Prove that division is not commutative by showing that $\frac{2}{3} \div \frac{5}{7} \neq \frac{5}{7} \div \frac{2}{3}$.

5. Prove that division is not associative by showing that $(\frac{3}{5} \div \frac{2}{3}) \div \frac{7}{2} \neq \frac{3}{5} \div (\frac{2}{3} \div \frac{7}{2})$.

6. Divide 3 by 8 using the corresponding rational numbers $\frac{3}{1}$ and $\frac{8}{1}$.

7. Express each of the following as a fraction in simplest form.

(a) $\dfrac{\frac{2}{3}}{\frac{4}{5}}$

(b) $\dfrac{\frac{3}{4} + \frac{2}{7}}{\frac{-5}{2}}$

(c) $\dfrac{2 + \frac{3}{4}}{\frac{2}{3}}$

(d) $\dfrac{\frac{3}{4} - \frac{1}{2}}{\frac{2}{5}}$

(e) $\dfrac{6 - 5}{\frac{2}{3}}$

(f) $\dfrac{\frac{5}{8}}{2 + 4}$

(g) $\dfrac{\frac{2}{7}}{3 + \frac{1}{5}}$

(h) $\dfrac{\frac{2}{3} - \frac{1}{2}}{3}$

(i) $\dfrac{3 + (\frac{2}{5})^{-1}}{4}$

(j) $\dfrac{\frac{3}{4} \cdot \frac{11}{5}}{\frac{5}{6} - \frac{-3}{5}}$

8. Perform the indicated operations and express the results in simplest form:

(a) $2\frac{2}{3} + \frac{2}{5}$

(b) $3\frac{1}{5} + \frac{2}{7}$

(c) $7 \div 2\frac{1}{3}$

(d) $\dfrac{3\frac{1}{2}}{\frac{2}{5}}$

(e) $\dfrac{-6}{3\frac{1}{2}}$

(f) $\dfrac{-3}{2 + \frac{1}{3}}$

(g) $2\frac{2}{3}(3 + 2)$

(h) $3\frac{1}{5} \div {}^{-}4\frac{1}{2}$

(i) $\frac{2}{3} \div (6 + \frac{1}{5})$

(j) $(3 - \frac{2}{5}) \div (3 + \frac{2}{5})$

9. Solve each of the following equations for x.

(a) $\frac{2}{3}x = \frac{5}{3}$

(b) $\frac{3}{6}x + \frac{1}{2} = \frac{2}{3}$

(c) $2x + \frac{1}{2}x = 15$

(d) $\frac{2}{3} = \frac{3}{5}x$

(e) $\frac{3}{4}x = \frac{2}{3}x - \frac{3}{4}$

(f) $x + 3 = 2x + \frac{1}{2}$

10. If three-fourths of a number divided by five is equal to three, find the number.

10.10

The System of Rational Numbers

The essential features of the system of rational numbers have been discussed and are summarized below. You will find it interesting to compare the definition for the system of rational numbers with Definition 6.19.1 for the system of whole numbers and Definition 8.3.1 for the system of integers. While the system of integers qualifies as a *ring*, the system of rational numbers is a *field* (see Section 9.8).

DEFINITION 10.10.1

The system of rational numbers consists of the set $R = \{x \mid x = [\frac{a}{b}],$ a and b in J, $b \neq 0\}$, and the binary operations of addition $(+)$ and multiplication ($\cdot$). The system has the following properties for any $[\frac{a}{b}]$, $[\frac{c}{d}]$, and $[\frac{e}{f}]$ in R. (For simplicity, brackets are omitted in the expressions below.)

Closure Properties

1. There is a uniquely determined sum $\dfrac{a}{b} + \dfrac{c}{d} = \dfrac{ad + bc}{bd}$ in R.

2. There is a uniquely determined product $\dfrac{a}{b} \cdot \dfrac{c}{d} = \dfrac{ac}{bd}$ in R.

Commutative Properties

3. $\frac{a}{b} + \frac{c}{d} = \frac{c}{d} + \frac{a}{b}$.

4. $\frac{a}{b} \cdot \frac{c}{d} = \frac{c}{d} \cdot \frac{a}{b}$.

Associative Properties

5. $(\frac{a}{b} + \frac{c}{d}) + \frac{e}{f} = \frac{a}{b} + (\frac{c}{d} + \frac{e}{f})$.

6. $(\frac{a}{b} \cdot \frac{c}{d}) \cdot \frac{e}{f} = \frac{a}{b} \cdot (\frac{c}{d} \cdot \frac{e}{f})$.

Distributive Property of Multiplication over Addition

7. $\frac{a}{b} \cdot (\frac{c}{d} + \frac{e}{f}) = \frac{a}{b} \cdot \frac{c}{d} + \frac{a}{b} \cdot \frac{e}{f}$ (left distributive property).

$(\frac{c}{d} + \frac{e}{f}) \cdot \frac{a}{b} = \frac{c}{d} \cdot \frac{a}{b} + \frac{e}{f} \cdot \frac{a}{b}$ (right distributive property).

Identities

8. There exists a unique element $\frac{0}{1}$ such that for any $\frac{a}{b}$ in R, $\frac{a}{b} + \frac{0}{1} = \frac{0}{1} + \frac{a}{b} = \frac{a}{b}$.

9. There exists a unique element $\frac{1}{1}$ such that for any $\frac{a}{b}$ in R, $\frac{a}{b} \cdot \frac{1}{1} = \frac{1}{1} \cdot \frac{a}{b} = \frac{a}{b}$.

Additive Inverses

10. For each $\frac{a}{b}$ in R there exists a unique element $\frac{-a}{b}$ in R such that $\frac{a}{b} + \frac{-a}{b} = \frac{-a}{b} + \frac{a}{b} = \frac{0}{1}$.

Multiplicative Inverses

11. For each $\frac{a}{b}$ in R, $\frac{a}{b} \neq \frac{0}{1}$, there exists a unique element $\frac{b}{a}$ (also written $(\frac{a}{b})^{-1}$) in R such that $\frac{a}{b} \cdot \frac{b}{a} = \frac{b}{a} \cdot \frac{a}{b} = \frac{1}{1}$.

EXERCISE 10.10

1. Using the definition of addition for the rational numbers, prove that
$$\frac{a}{c} + \frac{b}{c} = \frac{a + b}{c}.$$

2. (a) If $\frac{0}{c}$ is a rational number, what numbers are permitted as values of c?
   (b) Using the definition of addition for the rational numbers, show that
   $$\frac{a}{b} + \frac{0}{c} = \frac{a}{b}.$$

3. (a) If $\frac{c}{c}$ is a rational number, what numbers are permitted as values of c?
   (b) Using the definition of multiplication for the rational numbers, show
       that $\frac{a}{b} \cdot \frac{c}{c} = \frac{a}{b}$.

4. In Section 5.6 we define $a^{-p} = \frac{1}{a^p}$ $(a \neq 0)$. Using this definition show
   that:
   (a) $3 \cdot 3^{-1} = 1$ (b) $5 \cdot 5^{-1} = 1$ (c) $7 \cdot 7^{-1} = 1$
   (d) $\frac{2}{3}(\frac{2}{3})^{-1} = 1$ (c) $\frac{-5}{2}(\frac{-5}{2})^{-1} = 1$ (f) $\frac{x}{y}(\frac{x}{y})^{-1} = 1$

5. Using additive and multiplicative inverses, solve each of the following
   equations for x.
   (a) $\frac{3}{4}x + \frac{2}{3} = \frac{1}{2}$
   (b) $\frac{2}{3} = \frac{5}{4}x - \frac{1}{5}$

6. Compare the system of rational numbers (Definition 10.10.1) with the
   system of integers (Definition 8.3.1) and answer the following:
   (a) What important property does the system of rational numbers have
       that the system of integers does not have?
   (b) What are some of the advantages of a number system with this
       property?

10.11
Ordering the Rational Numbers

In studying the integers, we defined a to be less than b if and only if there exists a positive integer c such that $a + c = b$. The *less than* relation for the rational numbers may be defined in an analogous manner; however, such a definition is awkward to apply in determining whether a given rational number is less than another rational number. For this reason, a more convenient definition will be used.

You will recall that in the rational numbers, $\frac{a}{b} = \frac{c}{d}$ if and only if $ad = bc$. Using a similar approach, we shall define $\frac{a}{b} < \frac{c}{d}$.

DEFINITION 10.11.1

If $\frac{a}{b}$ and $\frac{c}{d}$ are rational numbers with b and d positive integers, then $\frac{a}{b} < \frac{c}{d}$ if and only if $ad < bc$.

DEFINITION 10.11.2

If $\frac{a}{b}$ and $\frac{c}{d}$ are rational numbers, then $\frac{a}{b} > \frac{c}{d}$ if and only if $\frac{c}{d} < \frac{a}{b}$.

In applying Definition 10.11.1, it is important to remember that the representative elements chosen for the rational numbers must have positive denominators.

Example 1.

(a) $\frac{2}{3} < \frac{4}{5}$ since $2 \cdot 5 < 3 \cdot 4$ or $10 < 12$.

(b) $2 \cdot 10 < 7 \cdot 3$; therefore, $\frac{2}{7} < \frac{3}{10}$.

Example 2. Show that $\frac{-3}{7} < \frac{4}{9}$.

Solution: First rewrite $\frac{-3}{7}$ as $\frac{-3}{7}$. Then $\frac{-3}{7} < \frac{4}{9}$ since $^-3(9) < 7(4)$ or $^-27 < 28$.

Example 3. Which is smaller, $\frac{5}{7}$ or $\frac{7}{10}$?

Solution: $\frac{7}{10} < \frac{5}{7}$ since $7 \cdot 7 < 10 \cdot 5$ or $49 < 50$.

In Chapter 8 we discussed the trichotomy law for the integers. A similar law holds for the rational numbers as a result of our definitions for "less than," "equals," and "greater than."

The Trichotomy Law for the Rational Numbers. For every $\frac{a}{b}$ and $\frac{c}{d}$ in R, exactly one of the following is true.

1. $\dfrac{a}{b} < \dfrac{c}{d}$

2. $\dfrac{a}{b} = \dfrac{c}{d}$

3. $\dfrac{a}{b} > \dfrac{c}{d}$

It is easy to prove the trichotomy law for the rational numbers. It follows from our definitions that $\frac{a}{b}$ is less than, equal to, or greater than $\frac{c}{d}$, depending on whether ad is less than, equal to, or greater than bc. But ad and bc are integers, and by the trichotomy law for the integers, exactly one of the following must hold: $ad < bc$, $ad = bc$, or $ad > bc$. Hence, exactly one of the following is true: $\frac{a}{b} < \frac{c}{d}$, $\frac{a}{b} = \frac{c}{d}$, or $\frac{a}{b} > \frac{c}{d}$.

The "less than" relation for the rational numbers is irreflexive, asymmetric, transitive, and connected and is, therefore, an order relation. A similar statement may be made for the "greater than" relation. Below we shall prove that the "less than" relation is transitive. (The proofs of the irreflexive, asymmetric, and connected properties will be left for the reader.)

THEOREM 10.11.1

If $\dfrac{a}{b}$, $\dfrac{c}{d}$, and $\dfrac{e}{f}$ are in R with b, d, and f greater than zero, and $\dfrac{a}{b} < \dfrac{c}{d}$

and $\dfrac{c}{d} < \dfrac{e}{f}$, then $\dfrac{a}{b} < \dfrac{e}{f}$.

Proof:

1. $\frac{a}{b} < \frac{c}{d}$ and $\frac{c}{d} < \frac{e}{f}$	1. Given
2. $b > 0$, $d > 0$, and $f > 0$	2. Given
3. $ad < bc$ and $cf < de$	3. Definition of $<$ for R
4. $adf < bcf$ and $bcf < bde$	4. Theorem 8.9.4
5. $adf < bde$	5. Transitive property of $<$ for J
6. $(af)d < (be)d$	6. Associative and commutative properties of multiplication in J
7. $af < be$	7. Theorem 8.9.3
8. $\frac{a}{b} < \frac{e}{f}$	8. Definition of $<$ for R

As with the integers, the "less than" relation orders the rational numbers on the number line in such a way that any rational number is smaller than the one to its right. For example, $\frac{2}{3}$ is to the left of $\frac{3}{4}$ on the number line and $\frac{2}{3} < \frac{3}{4}$.

Theorem 10.11.2 is similar to statements that were made concerning the integers. Although no proofs are given, Theorem 10.11.2 states some important properties of order for the system of rational numbers.

THEOREM 10.11.2

If $\dfrac{a}{b}$, $\dfrac{c}{d}$, and $\dfrac{e}{f}$ are in R and if $\dfrac{a}{b} < \dfrac{c}{d}$, then:

(a) $\dfrac{a}{b} + \dfrac{e}{f} < \dfrac{c}{d} + \dfrac{e}{f}$.

(b) $\dfrac{a}{b} \cdot \dfrac{e}{f} < \dfrac{c}{d} \cdot \dfrac{e}{f}$ if $\dfrac{e}{f} > 0$.

(c) $\dfrac{a}{b} \cdot \dfrac{e}{f} > \dfrac{c}{d} \cdot \dfrac{e}{f}$ if $\dfrac{e}{f} < 0$.

Note in part (c) that multiplying by a negative number reverses the order of the inequality.

Example 4. If $\frac{a}{b} = \frac{2}{3}$ and $\frac{c}{d} = \frac{4}{5}$, then $\frac{2}{3} < \frac{4}{5}$, and the application of Theorem 10.11.2 permits us to make statements such as:

(a) $\frac{2}{3} + \frac{3}{4} < \frac{4}{5} + \frac{3}{4}$, or $\frac{17}{12} < \frac{31}{20}$.

(b) $\frac{2}{3} \cdot \frac{3}{4} < \frac{4}{5} \cdot \frac{3}{4}$, or $\frac{6}{12} < \frac{12}{20}$.

(c) $\frac{2}{3} \cdot \frac{-3}{4} > \frac{4}{5} \cdot \frac{-3}{4}$, or $\frac{-6}{12} > \frac{-12}{20}$.

EXERCISE 10.11

1. Define the "less than" relation for the rational numbers.

2. Use the definition of "less than" to prove each of the following either true or false. Recall that the denominators of the fractions to be tested must be positive.

  (a) $\frac{2}{3} < \frac{3}{4}$ (b) $\frac{5}{7} < \frac{7}{10}$

  (c) $\frac{-9}{8} < \frac{10}{9}$ (d) $\frac{-2}{3} < \frac{1}{2}$

  (e) $\frac{-2}{3} < \frac{-1}{2}$ (f) $\frac{4}{3} < \frac{7}{5}$

  (g) $\frac{-2}{3} < \frac{-1}{2}$ (h) $\frac{-5}{2} < \frac{-2}{3}$

  (i) $\frac{2}{-5} < \frac{-1}{5}$ (j) $^-4 < \frac{-1}{2}$

3. (a) For what integral values of x will $\frac{x}{6}$ be less than $\frac{3}{2}$?

  (b) For what integral values of x will $\frac{x}{6}$ be greater than $\frac{3}{2}$?

  (c) For what integral values of x will $\frac{x}{6}$ be equal to $\frac{3}{2}$?

4. (a) Prove that the "less than" relation for the rational numbers is *irreflexive*.

  (b) Prove that the "less than" relation is *asymmetric*.

5. Insert the correct relation symbol ($<$, $=$, or $>$) between the numbers in each of the following ordered pairs.

  (a) $\frac{3}{4}, \frac{4}{5}$ (b) $\frac{2}{3}, \frac{7}{11}$

  (c) $\frac{-3}{4}, \frac{2}{3}$ (d) $\frac{25}{32}, \frac{83}{100}$

  (e) $\frac{16}{28}, \frac{11}{18}$ (f) $\frac{-3}{2}, \frac{-14}{9}$

6. Identify the set of rational numbers satisfying each of the following inequalities. Express your results using set-builder notation.

  (a) $x + \frac{-1}{3} < \frac{3}{4}$ (b) $x + \frac{2}{5} > \frac{1}{2}$

  (c) $2x < \frac{3}{4}$ (d) $\frac{2}{3} + x > \frac{1}{2}$

  (e) $\frac{x}{5} + 3 < 7$ (f) $5x + (^-4) < 2$

10.12
The Property of Denseness

As you know from studying the integers, it is not always possible to find an integer between two given integers; for example, there is no integer between 4 and 5. In the system of rational numbers, however, it is always possible to find another rational number between any two rational numbers. In other words, if r_1 and r_2 are any two distinct rational numbers with $r_1 < r_2$, then there exists some other rational number k such that $r_1 < k < r_2$, and we say that k is between r_1 and r_2. As an example, let k be equal to M, which corresponds to the point on the number line midway between the points corresponding to r_1 and r_2. See Figure 10.12.1.

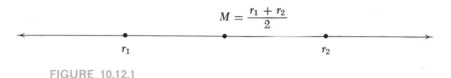

$$M = \frac{r_1 + r_2}{2}$$

FIGURE 10.12.1

If M corresponds to the midpoint between r_1 and r_2, this implies that $M - r_1 = r_2 - M$. Using this equation it can be shown that $M = \frac{r_1 + r_2}{2}$. The number M is called the arithmetic mean or average of r_1 and r_2. See if you can justify each step in the following proof.

Proof that if $M - r_1 = r_2 - M$, then $M = \frac{r_1 + r_2}{2}$:

$$M - r_1 = r_2 - M$$
$$(M + {}^-r_1) + M = (r_2 + {}^-M) + M$$
$$(M + M) + {}^-r_1 = r_2 + ({}^-M + M)$$
$$M(1 + 1) + {}^-r_1 = r_2$$
$$M(2) + {}^-r_1 + r_1 = r_2 + r_1$$
$$2M = r_1 + r_2$$
$$M = \frac{r_1 + r_2}{2}$$

Example 1. Find the number corresponding to the midpoint between $\frac{2}{5}$ and $\frac{4}{7}$.

Solution:

$$M = \frac{r_1 + r_2}{2}$$

$$M = \frac{\frac{2}{5} + \frac{4}{7}}{2} = \frac{\frac{14 + 20}{35}}{\frac{2}{1}} = \frac{34}{35} \cdot \frac{1}{2} = \frac{34}{70} = \frac{17}{35}$$

$$M = \frac{17}{35}$$

Example 2. Find a rational number between $\frac{-2}{3}$ and 7.

Solution:

$$M = \frac{r_1 + r_2}{2}$$

$$M = \frac{\dfrac{-2}{3} + \dfrac{7}{1}}{2} = \frac{\dfrac{-2 + 21}{3}}{\dfrac{2}{1}} = \frac{19}{3} \cdot \frac{1}{2} = \frac{19}{6} = 3\tfrac{1}{6}$$

$$M = 3\tfrac{1}{6}$$

From the examples above, we can see that a rational number k may always be found between any two distinct rational numbers r_1 and r_2 simply by applying the formula $M = \dfrac{r_1 + r_2}{2}$. Similarly, a rational number may also be found between r_1 and k, and between k and r_2, and so on. By this method of reasoning, we conclude that there are infinitely many rational numbers between any two distinct rational numbers r_1 and r_2.

Since we can always find another rational number between any two distinct rational numbers, we say that the rational numbers have the property of denseness or that the rational numbers are dense. By way of contrast, neither the whole numbers nor the integers are dense sets of numbers. It is interesting to realize that no matter how "close together" two rational numbers may be, there are infinitely many rational numbers between them. The advantages of such a number system in making physical measurements of distance, area, volume, weight, and so on are tremendous.

10.13 Absolute Value

Absolute value for the rational numbers will be defined in the same way as it was for the integers in Definition 8.10.1.

DEFINITION 10.13.1

If r is a rational number, the absolute value of r, denoted by $|r|$, is as follows:

If $r \geq 0$, then $|r| = r$.
If $r < 0$, then $|r| = {}^-r$.

The properties of absolute value that were stated for the integers also hold for the rational numbers and are restated below:

1. $|a - b| = |b - a|$.
2. $|a \cdot b| = |a| \cdot |b|$.
3. $|a + b| \leq |a| + |b|$.

Example 1. Find the values of x such that $|2x + 3| = 8$.

Solution: If $|2x + 3| = 8$, either $2x + 3 = 8$ or $2x + 3 = {}^{-}8$. If $2x + 3 = 8$, then $2x = 5$ and $x = \frac{5}{2}$. If $2x + 3 = {}^{-}8$, then $2x = {}^{-}11$ and $x = \frac{-11}{2}$. Therefore, the values of x that satisfy the equation are $\frac{5}{2}$ and $\frac{-11}{2}$.

Example 2. Using set-builder notation, indicate the set of rational numbers satisfying the inequality $|x - 3| < 7$.

Solution: If $|x - 3| < 7$, then two conditions must hold: (a) ${}^{-}7 < x - 3$ and (b) $x - 3 < 7$. If ${}^{-}7 < x - 3$, then ${}^{-}7 + 3 < (x - 3) + 3$ and ${}^{-}4 < x$; and if $x - 3 < 7$, then $(x - 3) + 3 < 7 + 3$ and $x < 10$. Considering conditions (a) and (b) above, we conclude that $|x - 3| < 7$ is true for $\{x \mid x \in R \text{ and } {}^{-}4 < x < 10\}$.

EXERCISE 10.13

1. What is meant when we say that the rational numbers are *dense*?
2. (a) How many integers are between 7 and 12? Name them.
   (b) How many integers are between 1 and 1,000,000? Use set notation to identify them.
   (c) How many integers are between 13 and 14?
3. (a) How many rational numbers are between 3 and 4? Use set notation to identify them. Name two of them.
   (b) How many rational numbers are between $\frac{-1}{2}$ and $\frac{3}{4}$? Use set notation to identify them. Name two of them.
   (c) How many rational numbers are between $\frac{3}{200}$ and $\frac{4}{200}$? Use set notation to identify them. Name two of them.
4. Find the number corresponding to the midpoint between:
   (a) $\frac{1}{2}$ and $\frac{5}{8}$ (b) $\frac{-3}{4}$ and $\frac{2}{5}$ (c) $\frac{2}{5}$ and 7
5. Find the point k on the number line between $\frac{1}{4}$ and $\frac{3}{4}$ such that the distance from $\frac{1}{4}$ to k is $\frac{1}{3}$ of the distance from $\frac{1}{4}$ to $\frac{3}{4}$.
6. (a) What is the smallest positive integer?
   (b) What is the smallest positive rational number?

7. (a) What is the largest negative integer?
   (b) What is the largest negative rational number?

8. (a) Find a rational number less than $\frac{1}{70}$.
   (b) Using the definition of "less than," prove that your result for part (a) is correct.

9. (a) Find a rational number greater than $\frac{-1}{50}$.
   (b) Using the definition of "greater than," prove that your result for part (a) is correct.

10. Find rational solutions for the following equations.
    (a) $|4x - 1| = 2$
    (b) $|8x + 3| = 8$

11. Using set notation, indicate the set of rational numbers satisfying each of the following inequalities.
    (a) $|x| < 3$ (b) $4 > |x - 2|$
    (c) $|x - 2| \leq 4$ (d) $5 \geq |x - 1|$

REVIEW EXERCISES

1. Prove that the equivalence relation $\cong$ for ordered pairs of integers is transitive.

2. Find the element in *simplest form* that may be used to represent each rational number indicated below.
   (a) $\frac{36}{42}$ (b) $\frac{60}{342}$ (c) $\frac{-84}{320}$ (d) $\frac{-52}{-273}$

3. Find a fraction that has a denominator of 14 and is equivalent to $\frac{15}{35}$.

4. Use the least common denominator method to find the sum $\frac{1}{6} + \frac{3}{8} + \frac{7}{18} + \frac{5}{24}$.

5. State in simplest form the multiplicative inverse of each of the following.
   (a) $\frac{2}{7}$ (b) $\frac{-5}{3}$ (c) 17 (d) $\frac{2}{3} + \frac{-5}{7}$ (e) 0

6. (a) Define the relation $<$ for the rational numbers.
   (b) In the definition of the relation $<$ for the rational numbers, there is a restriction concerning the denominators. Illustrate by an example the necessity of such a restriction.
   (c) Using set notation, indicate the set of rational numbers satisfying the inequality $|4x - 7| < 3$.

7. Prove that the order relation $<$ is transitive.

8. Which of the following represents the smallest rational number: $\frac{8}{10}$, $\frac{5}{6}$, $\frac{7}{8}$, or $\frac{6}{7}$?

9. Name the number midway between each of the following pairs.
   (a) $\frac{3}{5}$ and $\frac{6}{7}$
   (b) $\frac{-2}{5}$ and $\frac{19}{6}$

10. If John takes 5 hours to do a job and Mary takes 7 hours for the same job, how long should it take them working together? Assume that neither interferes with the work of the other!

Chapter Eleven
Decimals and Real Numbers

Although the system of rational numbers is definitely more useful to us than the system of integers, it does have some inadequacies. For example, if a square has an area of 3 square units, then the length of each side is $\sqrt{3}$. However, every rational number is either smaller or greater than $\sqrt{3}$; there is no rational number that is exactly equal to $\sqrt{3}$. An equivalent statement would be that the equation $x^2 = 3$ has no solution in the set of rational numbers.

Another disadvantage of the system of rational numbers is the awkward manipulative procedures which often occur. These and other difficulties can be overcome by extending the rational numbers to a new set of numbers called the *real numbers*. The real numbers, which include the rational numbers as a subset, may be represented by numerals called *decimals* and will be introduced through the use of decimals.

Decimals may be classified into three subsets:

(a) The decimal fractions or terminating decimals such as 2.35.

(b) The repeating infinite decimals such as $0.333.\ldots$

(c) The nonrepeating infinite decimals such as $3.141592.\ldots$

It will be seen that every rational number may be represented by either a terminating decimal (decimal fraction) or a repeating infinite decimal. Numbers of a new set, the irrational numbers, are named by the nonrepeating infinite decimals. The union of the rational numbers and the irrational numbers is the set of real numbers.

The decimal fractions identify a subset of the rational numbers and hence do not constitute an extension of our number system. However, the notation for the decimal fractions is similar to the convenient notation used for the integers and is, therefore, extremely useful in making mathematical computations. In fact, it is for this reason that the topics of ratio, proportion, and percent are included in this chapter rather than in the previous chapter.

This chapter concludes with a very brief introduction to the system of real numbers. The real numbers are particularly important in their application to geometric problems. Since the set of points on the number line and the set of real numbers may be put in a one-to-one correspondence, the length of any line segment may be represented by a real number. Furthermore, by using the Cartesian product of the set of real numbers with itself, every point in a plane can be designated by an ordered pair of real numbers. In a similar way, every point in space can be designated by an ordered triplet of real numbers. Using these and other ideas, we have the birth of that part of mathematics known as *analytic geometry*.

Although the set of rational numbers has the distinct asset of being a dense set, computing with fractions can become tedious. Consider, for example, the problems encountered in finding the sum $\frac{2349}{7235} + \frac{239}{4664}$. By contrast, the integers are not a dense set and no integers exist between 1 and 2, 2 and 3, and so on. Computing with integers, however, is relatively easy if the integers are represented by decimal numerals. Fortunately, we can extend the decimal numeration system for the integers to include the decimal fractions, thus making it possible to express all fractions whose denominators are integral powers of ten as decimal fractions. In this way we form a dense set in which computations are easily performed.

Simon Stevin (1548–1620), a quartermaster in the Dutch army, is credited with developing the concept of decimal fractions. The method of extending the decimal numeration system to include the decimal fractions is accomplished by placing a dot, called a decimal point, after the units digit of a numeral and letting the digits to the right of the decimal point represent an integral number of tenths, hundredths, thousandths, and so on. If there is no units digit in a given numeral, a zero is sometimes placed to the left of the decimal point to make the decimal point conspicuous. Examples are 0.24 and 0.0039.

The examples that follow illustrate in detail some important relationships between fractions and decimal fractions.

Example 1.

(a) $0.25 = \dfrac{2}{10} + \dfrac{5}{100} = \dfrac{20}{100} + \dfrac{5}{100} = \dfrac{25}{100} = \dfrac{25}{10^2}$.

(b) $7.3 = 7 + \dfrac{3}{10} = \dfrac{70}{10} + \dfrac{3}{10} = \dfrac{73}{10} = \dfrac{73}{10^1}$.

(c) $29.324 = \dfrac{29{,}324}{1000} = \dfrac{29{,}324}{10^3}$.

(d) $32 = \dfrac{32}{1} = \dfrac{32}{10^0}$.

Example 2.

(a) $\frac{35}{100} = 0.35 = 3 \cdot 10^{-1} + 5 \cdot 10^{-2}$.
(b) $\frac{345}{10} = 34.5 = 3 \cdot 10^1 + 4 \cdot 10^0 + 5 \cdot 10^{-1}$.
(c) $\frac{6345}{100} = 63.45 = 6 \cdot 10^1 + 3 \cdot 10^0 + 4 \cdot 10^{-1} + 5 \cdot 10^{-2}$.

A fraction may be expressed as a decimal fraction or terminating decimal only if it is possible to write the fraction with a denominator that is an integral power of 10. Since $10 = 2 \cdot 5$, $10^2 = 2^2 \cdot 5^2$, $10^3 = 2^3 \cdot 5^3$, or in general, $10^n = 2^n \cdot 5^n$, where n is an integer, we see that the prime factorization of the denominator may contain only integral powers of 2 and 5. For example, $\frac{3}{40}$ may be expressed as a decimal fraction since its denominator $40 = 2 \cdot 2 \cdot 2 \cdot 5$ and we have:

$$\frac{3}{40} = \frac{3}{2 \cdot 2 \cdot 2 \cdot 5} = \frac{3}{2^3 \cdot 5} = \frac{3(5^2)}{2^3 \cdot 5(5^2)} = \frac{3 \cdot 25}{2^3 \cdot 5^3} = \frac{3 \cdot 25}{(2 \cdot 5)^3}$$
$$= \frac{75}{10^3} = \frac{75}{1000} = 0.075.$$

It is easy to see from the above example that if the denominator of a fraction has more factors of 2 than factors of 5, or more factors of 5 than factors of 2, we can write an equivalent fraction so that the denominator will have an equal number of factors of 2 and 5 and thus will equal an integral power of 10.

It may at first appear that a fraction such as $\frac{3}{6}$ cannot be written with a denominator that is an integral power of 10, since $6 = 2 \cdot 3$ and 3 is not a prime factor of 10. However, since the fraction $\frac{3}{6}$ is not in simplest form, 3 and 6 are not relatively prime and we see that $\frac{3}{6} = \frac{1}{2} = \frac{1}{2} \cdot \frac{5}{5} = \frac{5}{10} = 0.5$. It is easier to determine whether a fraction may be written as a decimal fraction if the fraction is first written in simplest form. In fact, we may summarize by saying that if a fraction is written in simplest form and if its denominator contains prime factors of only 2's and 5's, then it may be expressed as a terminating decimal. Fractions such as $\frac{5}{6}$, $\frac{1}{7}$, and $\frac{4}{21}$ cannot be expressed as terminating decimals. Note that these fractions are in simplest form and have denominators with prime factors other than 2 and 5.

It is interesting to observe that if a numeration system with a base other than ten is used, a different set of place value fractions will result. For example, $\frac{1}{3}$ is not a terminating decimal in base ten, but it does terminate in bases 3, 6, 9, 12, and so on.

Example 3.

(a) $(\frac{1}{3})_{\text{ten}} = (\frac{1}{10})_{\text{three}} = 0.1_{\text{three}}$.
(b) $(\frac{1}{3})_{\text{ten}} = (\frac{1}{3} \cdot \frac{2}{2})_{\text{six}} = (\frac{2}{10})_{\text{six}} = 0.2_{\text{six}}$.
(c) $(\frac{1}{3})_{\text{ten}} = (\frac{1}{3})_{\text{nine}} = (\frac{1}{3} \cdot \frac{3}{3})_{\text{nine}} = (\frac{3}{10})_{\text{nine}} = 0.3_{\text{nine}}$.

Example 4.   Change the following to base ten fractions:

(a) 0.3_{nine}
(b) 0.42_{six}

Solution:

(a) $0.3_{\text{nine}} = 3(\frac{1}{9}) = \frac{3}{9} = \frac{1}{3}$.

(b) $0.42_{\text{six}} = 4(\frac{1}{6}) + 2(\frac{1}{6})^2 = \frac{4}{6} + \frac{2}{36} = \frac{26}{36} = \frac{13}{18}$.

EXERCISE 11.2

1. Express each of the following decimal fractions as a fraction in the form $\frac{a}{b}$.
   (a) 2.3   (b) 0.007   (c) 0.067
   (d) 0.183   (e) 27.4   (f) 28
   (g) 289.3   (h) 29.73   (i) 600.001

2. Express each of the following decimal fractions in *expanded form* using denominators of 1, 10, 100, and so on. (For example, $0.96 = \frac{9}{10} + \frac{6}{100}$.)
   (a) 0.31   (b) 3.74   (c) 42.006
   (d) 0.0064   (e) 0.732   (f) 0.6429

3. Express each decimal fraction of problem 1 in expanded form using *exponential notation*. (For example, $63.48 = 6 \cdot 10^1 + 3 \cdot 10^0 + 4 \cdot 10^{-1} + 8 \cdot 10^{-2}$.)

4. How is it possible to tell if a given rational number may be expressed as a terminating decimal?

5. Tell which of the following will result in a terminating decimal and find the terminating decimals.
   (a) $\frac{1}{2}$ (b) $\frac{2}{3}$ (c) $\frac{7}{21}$
   (d) $\frac{7}{35}$ (e) $\frac{15}{20}$ (f) $\frac{12}{15}$
   (g) $\frac{21}{70}$ (h) $\frac{105}{40}$ (i) $\frac{128}{80}$

6. The decimal fractions have the property of denseness since it is always possible to find another decimal fraction between any two given decimal fractions. Name three decimal fractions between each of the following.
   (a) 0.27 and 0.39   (b) 0.31 and 0.33   (c) 0.4 and 0.5

7. Express the following as fractions using base ten numerals.
   (a) $(0.7)_{\text{nine}}$ (b) $(0.31)_{\text{four}}$ (c) $(7.3)_{\text{eight}}$
   (d) $(21.11)_{\text{three}}$ (e) $(E.TE)_{\text{twelve}}$ (f) $(0.34)_{\text{six}}$
   (g) $(1.01)_{\text{two}}$ (h) $(101.1)_{\text{two}}$ (i) $(12.2)_{\text{twenty}}$

8. Insert the correct relation symbol, $<$, $=$, or $>$, between the decimal fractions in each of the following pairs.
   (a) 0.4, 0.5   (b) 0.6, 0.6000
   (c) 0.007, 0.070   (d) 0.093, 0.93
   (e) 1.999, 1.99   (f) 2, 1.99
   (g) 34.099, 34.19   (h) 7, 6.9999

11.3
Addition
and
Subtraction
of Decimal
Fractions

Since the decimal fractions identify a subset of the rational numbers, the definitions for operations in the rationals may be applied in developing algorithms for computations with decimal fractions. For example, suppose we wish to find the sum 12.6 + 3.49. We can write:

$$12.6 + 3.49 = \frac{126}{10} + \frac{349}{100} = \frac{1260}{100} + \frac{349}{100} = \frac{1609}{100} = 16.09.$$

The same result, however, may be obtained by "lining up" the decimal points and using the algorithm shown below.

Example 1. Addition:

$$\begin{array}{r} 12.6 \;=\; \frac{126}{10} \;=\; \frac{1260}{100} \\ 3.49 \;=\; \frac{349}{100} \;=\; \frac{349}{100} \\ \hline 16.09 \qquad\quad \frac{1609}{100} = 16.09 \end{array}$$

We may use algorithms similar to the one illustrated in Example 1 for the addition of more than two addends and for subtraction.

Example 2. Addition:

$$\begin{array}{r} 7.34 \\ 621.70103 \\ 40.02 \\ 317.765 \\ \hline 986.82603 \end{array}$$

Example 3. Subtraction:

(a) $\begin{array}{r} 32.43 \\ 14.7 \\ \hline 17.73 \end{array}$ (b) $\begin{array}{r} 17.904 \\ 6.23 \\ \hline 11.674 \end{array}$ (c) $\begin{array}{r} 16.4 \\ 7.237 \\ \hline 9.163 \end{array}$

In a subtraction problem such as Example 3(c), it may be convenient to write 16.4 as 16.400. A similar statement may be made with reference to the addition of decimal fractions.

Algorithms for the addition and subtraction of decimal fractions in base ten may also be used for other bases.

Example 4. Addition in various bases:

(a) Base three	(b) Base five	(c) Base twelve
2.12	2.34	E.84
2.2	3.2	1.T3
12.02	11.04	11.67

Example 5. Subtraction in various bases:

(a) Base four	(b) Base six	(c) Base eight
3.21	5.42	6.47
1.3	2.34	2.52
1.31	3.04	3.75

11.4
Multiplication of Decimal Fractions

The algorithms developed in Section 11.3 make it possible to add and subtract decimal fractions in the same way that we add and subtract integers. As we would expect, the algorithms used in multiplying and dividing decimal fractions also result in manipulations similar to those used with the integers.

In finding a product such as 2.7×6.23, a possible procedure would be as follows:

$$(2.7)(6.23) = \left(\frac{27}{10^1}\right)\left(\frac{623}{10^2}\right) = \frac{16,821}{10^3} = 16.821.$$

From the example we see that the same result could be obtained by treating 2.7 and 6.23 as though they were the whole numbers 27 and 623. Then, after finding the product $27 \times 623 = 16,821$, all we need do is place the decimal point appropriately, between the digits 6 and 8. The number of digits to the right of the decimal point in the product is equal to the sum of the digits to the right of the decimal points in the two factors (in this case $1 + 2$, or 3). The reason for this rule is easily seen by studying the above example and noting the relationship between $1 + 2 = 3$ and $10^1 \cdot 10^2 = 10^{1+2} = 10^3$.

The common algorithm for finding the product 2.7×6.23 is shown below.

$$
\begin{array}{r}
6.2\,3 \\
2.7 \\
\hline
4\,3\,6\,1 \\
1\,2\,4\,6 \\
\hline
1\,6.8\,2\,1 \\
\end{array}
$$

11.5
Division
of Decimal
Fractions

In developing a convenient algorithm for finding the quotient of two decimal fractions, the object, of course, is to relate the division of the decimal fractions to the division of integers. Let us consider, for example, $14.952 \div 0.24$. We know from previous study that:

$$\frac{14.952}{0.24} = \frac{\frac{14952}{1000}}{\frac{24}{100}} = \frac{14952}{1000} \cdot \frac{100}{24} = \frac{14952}{24} \cdot \frac{100}{1000} = \frac{14952}{24} \cdot \frac{1}{10}$$

$$= 623 \cdot \frac{1}{10} = \frac{623}{10} = 62.3.$$

The same result, however, may be obtained more easily if the divisor is made a whole number by multiplying both it and the dividend by the necessary power of 10—in this case 10^2. We then have:

$$\frac{14.952}{0.24} = \frac{1495.2}{24}.$$

Finally, we apply the long division algorithm as though both 24 and 1495.2 were whole numbers and simply place the decimal point in the quotient directly above the decimal point in the dividend. The usual algorithm for finding the quotient $14.952 \div 0.24$ is shown below. Note that it is not necessary to make the dividend a whole number—only the divisor.

$$
\begin{array}{r}
6\,2.3 \\
.2\,4_\wedge\overline{)1\,4.\,9\,5_\wedge2} \\
1\,4\,4 \\
\hline
5\,5 \\
4\,8 \\
\hline
7\,2 \\
7\,2 \\
\hline
\end{array}
$$

Sometimes it is necessary to annex zeros to the dividend in order to obtain a quotient. The following example illustrates this idea.

Example 1. Rename $\frac{7}{8}$ as a decimal fraction by dividing.

Solution:

$$
\begin{array}{r}
.875 \\
8\overline{)7.000} \\
6\,4 \\
\hline
60 \\
56 \\
\hline
40 \\
40 \\
\hline
\end{array}
$$

Therefore, $\frac{7}{8} = 0.875$.

EXERCISE 11.5

1. Perform the indicated operations.
   (a) $7.2 + 0.31 + 0.342$ (b) $98.23 - 7.4$
   (c) $2.34 + 0.2 - 7.4265$ (d) $0.007 - 7.34 + 20.2$
   (e) $6.24 - (3.1 + 1.005)$ (f) $6.41 - (^-3.2)$
   (g) $2.4 - 3.9$

2. Find the following products.
   (a) $(0.34)(2.73)$ (b) $(7.4)(6.39)$
   (c) $(0.007)(97.04)$ (d) $(6.002)(9.0051)$
   (e) $(6)(0.4)(69.3)$ (f) $2(4.7)(0.005)$

3. Find the products in 2(a) and 2(b) by using fractions with integral numerators and denominators.

4. Find the following quotients.

   (a) $3.2\overline{)20.48}$ (b) $4.3\overline{)26.66}$

   (c) $0.0005\overline{)1042.5}$ (d) $6.04\overline{)28.992}$

   (e) $0.24\overline{)19.2072}$ (f) $0.017\overline{)581.4}$

5. By dividing, rename each of the following fractions as a decimal fraction.
   (a) $\frac{3}{4}$ (b) $\frac{3}{8}$ (c) $\frac{7}{16}$
   (d) $\frac{13}{20}$ (e) $\frac{7}{50}$ (f) $\frac{21}{28}$

6. Find the arithmetic mean of the numbers in each of the following pairs.
   (a) 2.4 and 6.8   (b) 2.03 and 4.9
   (c) 12.008 and 6.5   (d) $^-2.04$ and 6.2

7. Find each of the following sums in the indicated base.
   (a) 2.32_{four} (b) $6.T7_{\text{twelve}}$
      3.12_{four} 2.3_{twelve}

   (c) 11.01_{two} (d) 6.04_{seven}
      101.11_{two} 0.55_{seven}

8. Find each of the following differences in the indicated base.

(a) 4.21_{five} (b) 11.011_{two}
     $\underline{3.31_{\text{five}}}$ $\underline{1.101_{\text{two}}}$

(c) 4.3_{five} (d) $7.\text{ET}_{\text{twelve}}$
     $\underline{2.12_{\text{five}}}$ $\underline{3.\text{T}3_{\text{twelve}}}$

(e) 5.03_{seven} (f) 2.3_{seven}
     $\underline{.66_{\text{seven}}}$ $\underline{1.462_{\text{seven}}}$

11.6
Repeating Decimals

We showed in Section 11.2 that if a rational number can be represented by a fraction in simplest form whose denominator contains prime factors of only 2's and 5's, then the rational number may be expressed as a *terminating decimal*. The decimal fraction for the rational number may, of course, be found by dividing the numerator of the fraction by the denominator. If, however, a fraction in simplest form has a denominator with prime factors other than 2's and 5's, then the result of dividing the numerator by the denominator is a *repeating nonterminating decimal*. By a repeating decimal we mean a numeral in which a particular block of consecutive digits is repeated again and again in a nonterminating sequence.

Shown below are a few examples of rational numbers expressed first as fractions and then as repeating decimals. In each case the repeating decimal is found by dividing the numerator of the fraction by the denominator. Note that the notation can be simplified by placing a bar over the consecutive repeating digits.

Example 1.

(a) $\frac{13}{30} = 0.4333\ldots = 0.4\overline{3}$.
(b) $\frac{2}{3} = 0.666\ldots = 0.\overline{6}$.
(c) $\frac{4}{11} = 0.363636\ldots = 0.\overline{36}$.
(d) $\frac{5}{7} = 0.714285714285\ldots = 0.\overline{714285}$.

It should be noted that not all the digits in a repeating decimal need repeat. In Example 1(a), for instance, the bar is placed only over the digit 3, indicating that only this digit repeats; the digit 4 does not repeat.

What is the maximum number of digits possible in the repeating block of consecutive digits of a repeating decimal? As an aid in answering this question, let us consider the number $\frac{5}{7}$ and examine the division algorithm used in finding its repeating decimal.

Example 2.

$$
\begin{array}{r}
0.7\;1\;4\;2\;8\;5 \\
7\overline{)5.0\;0\;0\;0\;0\;0} \\
4\;9 \\
\hline
①\,0 \\
7 \\
\hline
③\,0 \\
2\;8 \\
\hline
②\,0 \\
1\;4 \\
\hline
⑥\,0 \\
5\;6 \\
\hline
④\,0 \\
3\;5 \\
\hline
⑤
\end{array}
$$

In the division algorithm of Example 2, the remainders have been circled. Since any remainder must be less than the divisor 7, the only possible remainders are 0, 1, 2, 3, 4, 5, and 6. However, if a remainder of 0 is obtained, the decimal terminates. Therefore, if dividing by 7 produces a repeating decimal, there are only six possible remainders: 1, 2, 3, 4, 5, and 6. This means that there will be a maximum of six digits in the repeating portion of the decimal representation of a fraction with a denominator of 7. In the case of $\frac{5}{7}$, the maximum is reached since all possible nonzero remainders are obtained in the division algorithm.

In determining the maximum number of digits possible in the repeating portion of a repeating decimal, it is important to examine the simplest fraction form of the rational number that it represents. Since $\frac{10}{14} = \frac{5}{7}$, for example, $\frac{10}{14}$ can have no more digits in the repeating portion of its decimal representation than $\frac{5}{7}$ has.

In general, if the *simplest* fraction form $\frac{a}{b}$ of a rational number is written as a repeating decimal, there will be a *maximum* of $b - 1$ digits in the repeating portion of the decimal. Of course, many decimals repeat before the maximum possible number of digits is reached. As an example, although the decimal representation of $\frac{4}{11}$ has a possible maximum of $11 - 1$, or 10, repeating digits, $\frac{4}{11}$ is equal to $0.\overline{36}$, which has only 2 repeating digits. Some other number with a denominator such as 3821 may actually have 3820 digits in the repeating portion of its decimal representation; however, we can be assured that it will have no more than that number.

We have seen that it is possible to write every rational number either as a terminating or as a repeating decimal by using the division process of Example 2. It is also possible to express every terminating or repeating decimal as a fraction of the form $\frac{a}{b}$. The procedure for finding the fraction form of a rational number when it is expressed as a repeating infinite decimal is shown by Example 3.

Example 3.   Find the fraction form of the rational number represented by $0.\overline{36}$.

Solution: Let $x - 0.\overline{36}$.

Then $100x = 36.3636\ldots$
Subtract $x = 0.3636\ldots$
$$99x = 36$$
$$x = \tfrac{36}{99} = \tfrac{4}{11}$$

Therefore, $0.\overline{36} = \tfrac{4}{11}$.

Note that in Example 3 we multiply each member of the equation $x = 0.\overline{36}$ by 10^2 or 100 because there are 2 digits in the repeating sequence. If there were n repeating digits, we would multiply each member of the equation by 10^n. The reason for this is apparent as soon as we get to the step where the operation of subtraction is performed. Another example should be sufficient to illustrate the process.

Example 4.   Find the fraction form of the rational number represented by $3.4\overline{263}$.

Solution: Let $x = 3.4\overline{263}$. We now multiply each member of this equation by 10^3 or 1000 because there are 3 digits in the repeating sequence.

$$1000x = 3426.3\overline{263}$$
$$x = 3.4\overline{263}$$
$$999x = 3422.9$$
$$x = \frac{3422.9}{999} = \frac{34,229}{9,990}$$

Therefore, $3.4\overline{263} = \dfrac{34,229}{9,990}$.

Before leaving the topic of repeating decimals, we find it interesting to note that every terminating decimal can be written as an infinite repeating decimal by subtracting 1 from its last digit and annexing an infinite number of 9's. For example, $0.27 = 0.26\overline{9}$, $0.4 = 0.3\overline{9}$, $19.32 = 19.31\overline{9}$, and $4 = 3.\overline{9}$.

$\frac{1}{x} = .044$

Example 5. Prove $0.26\bar{9} = 0.27$.

Solution: Let $x = 0.26\bar{9}$.

Then	$10x = 2.69\bar{9}$
Subtract	$x = 0.26\bar{9}$

$$9x = 2.43$$

$$x = \frac{2.43}{9} = 0.27.$$

Therefore, $0.26\bar{9} = 0.27$.

In order to have a unique decimal representation for each rational number, we do not ordinarily represent terminating decimals as repeating infinite decimals. It is nevertheless somewhat intriguing to find that this can be done.

EXERCISE 11.6

1. Find the terminating or repeating decimal for each of the following and indicate repeating digits by placing a bar over them.
   (a) $\frac{7}{33}$ (b) $\frac{2}{3}$ (c) $\frac{1}{8}$
   (d) $\frac{7}{8}$ (e) $\frac{10}{33}$ (f) $\frac{3}{11}$
   (g) $\frac{5}{7}$ (h) $\frac{9}{11}$ (i) $\frac{28}{111}$

2. Find a fraction numeral for the rational number represented by each of the following repeating decimals.
   (a) $0.\bar{4}$ (b) $0.6\bar{3}$ (c) 0.54
   (d) $0.9\bar{0}$ (e) $0.\overline{393}$ (f) $0.4\overline{23}$
   (g) $98.\bar{7}$ (h) $42.3\overline{54}$ (i) $0.\overline{101}$

3. (a) How many nonzero remainders are possible when a whole number is divided by 13?
   (b) If a whole number is divided by 13, what is the maximum possible number of digits in the repeating block of digits in the quotient?
   (c) If $\frac{5}{13}$ is expressed as a repeating decimal, what is the maximum number of digits in the repeating portion of the sequence?
   (d) Find the repeating decimal for $\frac{5}{13}$.

4. The maximum number of digits in the repeating portion of the quotient $20 \div 52$ is 12. Why is this true?

5. Show that:
   (a) $0.44\bar{9} = 0.45$ (b) $1.\bar{9} = 2$
   (c) $0.\bar{9} = 1$ (d) $7.23\bar{9} = 7.24$

6. If a, b, c, and d are the digits of the repeating decimal $0.\overline{abcd}$, find a fraction to represent this number.

11.7

Mathematical Sentences and Problem Solving

Mathematical sentences have been used previously in the text and will be used rather extensively in the next two sections, so attention to them at this time seems appropriate. Since no attempt will be made in this text to discuss symbolic logic in a rigorous manner, the treatment of mathematical sentences will be informal.

The word "sentence" may be used in mathematics in much the same way that it is used in everyday language. A sentence that relates numbers is called a mathematical sentence. Examples of mathematical sentences are $7 + 5 = 12; 2 + 3 \leq 19; 7 \neq 3; x + y = 5; x + 2 > 24$ and $x + y = z$. Some mathematical sentences such as $2 + 3 > 25$ and $2 + 7 = 9$ can be tested and determined to be either true or false; $2 + 3 > 25$, of course, is false, whereas $2 + 7 = 9$ is true. Sentences such as these are called *statements*.

DEFINITION 11.7.1

A statement is a mathematical sentence that is true or false but not both.

Examples of statements are:

(a) $2 + 4 = 6$.
(b) $7 - 3 > 0$.
(c) $9 - 5 = 2$.
(d) $6 + 4 < 5$.

Statements (a) and (b) are true, while statements (c) and (d) are false.

Mathematical sentences such as the following are called *open sentences*.

(a) $n + 5 = 7$.
(b) $2n < 8 + q$.
(c) $3n - 5 = 16$.
(d) $2x + y \geq 7$.

In the above open sentences the letters n, q, x, and y are used to represent any of various but unspecified numbers and are called variables; numbers such as 5 and 7 are not variable and are called constants. Open sentences are neither true nor false. However, an open sentence becomes a statement, and hence true or false, when each of its variables is replaced by any member of an agreed-upon set of numbers. The agreed-upon set whose members may replace a variable is called the domain of the variable or the replacement set. The domain of the variable may be arbitrary or it may be determined by the nature of the problem. For example, if a variable represents the number of people in a mathematics class, it would necessarily be a whole number. (It would be unusual to have a class with 26.4 people in it!)

DEFINITION 11.7.2

An open sentence is a mathematical sentence which contains one or more variables and which is neither true nor false.

All the replacements for the variable in an open sentence that make the sentence true constitute what is called the solution set of the sentence. The solution set will always be a subset of the replacement set. Consider, for example, the open sentence $n + 5 = 7$. If the replacement set is the set of whole numbers, the solution set in this case contains a single element and is seen to be $\{2\}$. An open sentence is said to be solved when the solution set has been determined, and each member of the solution set is called a solution for the open sentence.

Example 1. In the open sentence $n - 3 = 2$, n is the variable and 3 and 2 are constants. If we arbitrarily define the replacement set, or domain of the variable, to be the whole numbers, the solution set is $\{5\}$. Other members of the domain W are not solutions. For example, if we replace n with 7, we obtain the false statement $7 - 3 = 2$; therefore, 7 is not a member of the solution set.

Example 2. Consider the open sentence $3x < 7$ and let the domain of the variable x be the whole numbers. The solution set is $\{0, 1, 2\}$ since this set contains every whole number that makes $3x < 7$ a true statement and no number that makes $3x < 7$ a false statement.

As mentioned, some open sentences have more than one variable. For example, suppose we wish to find all the possible numbers of girls and boys in a family of four children. If g represents the number of children who are girls and b represents the number of children who are boys, the equation $g + b = 4$ is an open sentence with two variables which mathematically represents the sum of all possible number of girls and boys in the family. The domain of each variable is, of course, the set of whole numbers, and the solution set for the equation is $\{(g, b) \mid g + b = 4\} = \{(0, 4), (1, 3), (2, 2), (3, 1), (4, 0)\}$. The solution set could also be represented in table form as follows.

g	0	1	2	3	4
b	4	3	2	1	0

Mathematical sentences are particularly useful in solving problems stated in ordinary language; such problems are usually referred to as verbal problems. In the solution of a verbal problem, the statement of the problem must be translated into some type of mathematical language such as an equation or inequality. If the solution set can then be found for the equation or inequality, the problem is solved. Of course, it is not always easy to translate a verbal problem into mathematical language, and one should not admit defeat too quickly. It seems to take a fair amount of experience for most individuals to learn to solve verbal problems. Lots of practice in translating verbal problems into mathematical language seems to help much more than attempting to follow an explicit list of procedures. Some complex problems may involve many equations, inequalities, or other types of mathematical sentences, while elementary problems can be quite simply expressed.

Example 3. If 14 is subtracted from 8 times a certain number, the result is 242. Find the number.

Solution: First we translate the problem into an open sentence. Then, applying various properties of the number system, we write a series of equivalent sentences, which eventually enable us to state explicitly the solution set for the original open sentence.

Let n represent the number.

$$\text{Then, } 8n - 14 = 242$$
$$8n - 14 + 14 = 242 + 14$$
$$8n = 256$$
$$\tfrac{1}{8}(8n) = \tfrac{1}{8}(256)$$
$$n = 32.$$

Therefore, the solution set contains only one element and is $\{32\}$. The result can be verified by substituting 32 for n in the *original* open sentence $8n - 14 = 242$. We then have:

$$8(32) - 14 = 242$$
$$256 - 14 = 242$$
$$242 = 242.$$

Example 4. When 3 is added to a certain integer, the sum is less than 7. What numbers satisfy the given conditions?

Solution: Let *x* represent the number.

$$\text{Then, } x + 3 < 7$$
$$x + 3 + {}^-3 < 7 + {}^-3$$
$$x + 0 < 4$$
$$x < 4.$$

Therefore the solution set is $\{\ldots, {}^-2, {}^-1, 0, 1, 2, 3\}$. Any member of this set may be verified as a solution by substituting it for *x* in the open sentence $x + 3 < 7$.

EXERCISE 11.7

1. Find the solution set for each of the following sentences if the domain of the variable in each case is the set of whole numbers.
   (a) $2x = 16$ (b) $5x - 12 = 2x$
   (c) $3x < 9$ (d) $7x > 20$
   (e) $20 \geq 5x$ (f) $3 = 7x - 18$
   (g) $10 = 2 + 3x$ (h) $12 + x > 23$

2. (a) Express in mathematical language the product of 4 and another factor *x*.
   (b) Express in mathematical language the sum of 5 and another addend *n*.
   (c) Express in mathematical language the fact that 5 more than 4 times some number is equal to 33.
   (d) Solve the equation of part (c).

3. Eight more than twice a certain number is equal to 26. Write and solve an equation for this problem.

4. Five less than 7 times a certain rational number is equal to 15. Find the number.

5. Six more than 3 times a certain number is equal to 7 minus the number. What is the solution for this problem?

6. If 7 is added to a whole number, the sum is less than 12. What whole numbers satisfy the given conditions?

7. Three times some integer is 2 less than 11. What integer satisfies this condition?

8. Two less than 5 times some integer is greater than 18. Find the solution set.

9. If the product of 3 and some *integer* is added to 6, the result is less than 17. What is the solution set?

10. If the domain of *x* is the set of integers, find the solution set for the open sentence: $|x - 2| < 5$.

11.8
Rounding Off
Decimal
Numerals

Some rational numbers are named by repeating infinite decimals, and others are represented by terminating decimals composed of many digits. We frequently approximate such numbers by using only the first few digits of their decimal representations in order to obtain decimal fractions that are convenient for computation. For example, $\frac{1}{3}$, equal to $0.\overline{3}$, may be approximated by 0.3, or by 0.33, or by 0.333, and so on. Since 0.3 is only approximately equal to $0.\overline{3}$, we should not write $0.3 = 0.\overline{3}$. The symbol "$\approx$" is used to mean "is approximately equal to," and we therefore write $0.3 \approx 0.\overline{3}$.

The difference between the approximation and the original number is equal to the number represented by the digits that have been dropped and will be referred to as the error of approximation. In the example above, if $0.\overline{3}$ is approximated by 0.3, the difference between $0.\overline{3}$ and 0.3 is $0.0\overline{3}$ since $0.\overline{3} - 0.3 = 0.0\overline{3}$. Similarly, the error in approximating $0.\overline{3}$ by 0.33 is $0.00\overline{3}$. In general, the more digits retained, the more accurate is the approximation. If a terminating decimal such as 0.32451 is approximated by 0.32, the error is 0.00451 since $0.32451 - 0.32 = 0.00451$; however, if 0.3245 is used as the approximation, the error is only 0.00001.

A decimal fraction obtained by omitting some of the ending digits of the original decimal representation is said to have been "rounded off." A convention used in rounding off a decimal numeral is to increase by 1 the last digit retained if the first digit omitted is 5 or greater ("rounding up"), and to make no change in the digits retained if the first digit omitted is 4 or less ("rounding down"). The purpose of this rule is to reduce the error of approximation. For example, if we follow convention and approximate 48.37 as 48.4 by rounding up, the error is $48.4 - 48.37 = 0.03$; but if we round down and use 48.3, the error is $48.37 - 48.3 = 0.07$.

In rounding a numeral such as 48.37 to 48.4, the situation is described by saying that the numeral has been rounded to the nearest tenth of a unit, or to one place beyond the decimal point, or to three significant digits. All digits in a decimal numeral are significant except those zeros that are used in placing the decimal point. In 0.00904, for example, the zero between the digits 9 and 4 is significant, but the other zeros are not. If a decimal such as 0.00904 is expressed in fraction form, the significant digits will be in the numerator; in this case we write $\frac{904}{100000}$ and can immediately see that there are three significant digits in 0.00904.

Example 1. Round 71.42985 to:
(a) the nearest hundredth of a unit.
(b) the nearest thousandth of a unit.
(c) three significant digits.
(d) four places beyond the decimal point.

Solution:

(a) 71.43
(b) 71.430
(c) 71.4
(d) 71.4299

Example 2. Round $0.456\overline{456}$ to:
(a) the nearest hundredth of a unit.
(b) the nearest thousandth of a unit.
(c) the nearest ten-thousandth of a unit.

Solution:

(a) 0.46
(b) 0.456
(c) 0.4565

Example 3. Express each of the following as a fraction and state the number of significant digits in each decimal fraction.
(a) 0.324
(b) 7.093
(c) 0.00032
(d) 0.0030005
(e) 9.30

Solution:

(a) $0.324 = \frac{324}{1000}$ and has 3 significant digits.
(b) $7.093 = \frac{7093}{1000}$ and has 4 significant digits.
(c) $0.00032 = \frac{32}{100000}$ and has 2 significant digits.
(d) $0.0030005 = \frac{30005}{10000000}$ and has 5 significant digits.
(e) $9.30 = \frac{930}{100}$ and has 3 significant digits.

Sometimes we approximate a whole number by replacing some of the ending digits of its numeral with zeros. For example, approximations of 93,582 are 93,580; 93,600; 94,000; and 90,000. The digits dropped must be replaced by zeros so that the digits retained will have the proper place value. Of course, if ending digits are omitted to the right of the decimal point in a numeral, no problem is encountered, and they should not be replaced by zeros.

Example 4.   Each of the following numerals is rounded to 3 significant digits.
(a) 46,259 ≈ 46,300
(b) 526,300 ≈ 526,000
(c) 8,429,400 ≈ 8,430,000

If a whole number such as 94,000 is expressed in ordinary decimal notation, we are likely to assume that the zeros are not significant, even though they may be. If the zeros are significant, this can be indicated by using scientific notation and writing 0.4000×10^4. For a review of scientific notation see Section 5.9.

EXERCISE 11.8

1. Round off the following numerals to two significant digits.
   (a) 93,422,007   (b) 239,421   (c) 607
   (d) 50,087   (e) 70,542   (f) 0.00706
   (g) 0.6706   (h) 8.96   (i) 0.00999

2. Round off the numerals in problem 1 to one significant digit.

3. Round off the following repeating decimals to four significant digits.
   (a) $0.04\overline{3}$ (b) $7.2\overline{54}$
   (c) $0.23\overline{7}$ (d) $0.4\overline{84}$
   (e) $0.\overline{27}$ (f) $4.0\overline{7}$
   (g) $5.0\overline{3}$ ✓(h) $0.3\overline{828}$

4. Round off the decimals in problem 3 to the nearest thousandth of a unit.

5. Round off the decimals in problem 3 to the nearest ten-thousandth of a unit.

6. Express the following quotients as decimals and round off to three significant digits.
   (a) 16 ÷ 7   (b) 29 ÷ 3
   (c) 64.2 ÷ 11   (d) 14.417 ÷ 2.4

7. Make up a rule for rounding off place value numerals in:
   (a) base seven
   (b) base nine
   (c) base twelve

8. (a) A piece of glass is needed for a window frame. The frame's length measures 16.38 inches. In stating the size of glass required, should 16.38 be rounded up to 16.4 or down to 16.3? Explain.

(b) A mirror has a length of 49.73 inches. In stating the size of a frame for the mirror, should 49.73 be rounded up to 49.8 or down to 49.7? Explain.

11.9
Ratio and Proportion

In Chapter 10 we showed how an ordered pair (a, b) with $b \neq 0$ may be interpreted as a fraction, or as a quotient $(a \div b)$, or simply as an element of a mathematical system. It was also mentioned that an ordered pair could be thought of as a ratio, but we did not elaborate on this idea. In this section the concept of ratio and the related topic of proportion will be developed.

Suppose there are 20 boys and 16 girls in a class of students. This situation may be described by saying that the *ratio* of boys to girls in the class is 20 to 16, or that the class has boys and girls in the ratio of 20 to 16. The expression "20 to 16" gives us a way to compare the number of boys with the number of girls. The ratio of 20 to 16 may be indicated by writing: 20 to 16, 20:16, or $\frac{20}{16}$. We shall ordinarily express ratios as fractions, but when a numeral such as $\frac{20}{16}$ is used to represent a ratio, it should be read "20 to 16" instead of "twenty-sixteenths." The form 20:16 is also read "20 to 16"; this form is less used today, although it still appears in some texts.

It is easy to see that if there are 20 boys and 16 girls in a class, then there are 10 boys for every 8 girls, or 5 boys for every 4 girls. We can, therefore, say that the ratio of boys to girls is 20 to 16, or 10 to 8, or 5 to 4, and note that:

$$\frac{20}{16} = \frac{10}{8} = \frac{5}{4} = \frac{1.25}{1}.$$

In fact, there are infinitely many ordered pairs, any one of which could be used to represent the ratio of 20 to 16. All such ordered pairs are members of a single equivalence class, and for any two members $\frac{a_1}{b_1}$ and $\frac{a_2}{b_2}$ of the equivalence class, $a_1 b_2 = b_1 a_2$.

Example 1.   If a bag contains 32 red marbles and 20 white marbles, the ratio of red marbles to white marbles is 32 to 20 or $\frac{32}{20}$. This ratio can also be expressed as 8 to 5 or $\frac{8}{5}$. We note that $\frac{32}{20} = \frac{8}{5}$ since $32(5) = 20(8)$. Similarly, the ratio of white marbles to red marbles is $\frac{20}{32}$ or $\frac{5}{8}$.

Example 2.   A photograph is $3\frac{1}{2}$ inches high and 2 inches wide.

The ratio of height to width is $\dfrac{3\frac{1}{2}}{2}$ or $\frac{7}{4}$. We see that $\dfrac{3\frac{1}{2}}{2} = \frac{7}{4}$ since $3\frac{1}{2}(4) = 2(7)$.

In some problems it is useful to compare different types of quantities through the use of ordered pairs of numbers. For example, suppose a recipe requires 2 teaspoons of salt and 5 cups of flour. Then the ratio of the number of teaspoons of salt to the number of cups of flour is 2 to 5 or $\frac{2}{5}$. Note that the ratio is an ordered pair of *numbers*, and that the fact that unlike quantities are measured in unlike units does not prevent our determining a meaningful ratio. In referring to such a pair, some authors prefer to use the term *rate pair* or *rate* rather than ratio; in this text, however, we shall not restrict ourselves in this way.

Example 3.   A certain recipe calls for 2 teaspoons of salt and 5 cups of flour. If 12 cups of flour is used, how much salt is required?

Solution: The ratio of the *number* of teaspoons of salt to the *number* of cups of flour is 2 to 5 or $\frac{2}{5}$. If this ratio is to be maintained, we have:

$$\frac{2}{5} = \frac{s}{12}$$
$$2(12) = 5s$$
$$s = \frac{2(12)}{5} = \frac{24}{5} = 4\frac{4}{5}.$$

Hence, $4\frac{4}{5}$ teaspoons of salt is required if 12 cups of flour is used.

Example 3 was solved by initially stating that two ratios were to be equal. Such a statement is called a *proportion*.

DEFINITION 11.9.1

A proportion is a statement that two ratios are equal. Thus, $\frac{a}{b} = \frac{c}{d}$ is a proportion, and a, b, c, and d are called the terms of the proportion.

A proportion such as $\frac{3}{4} = \frac{9}{12}$ is read, "3 is to 4 as 9 is to 12." Proportions are particularly useful in solving certain types of problems involving ratios. Below are typical examples. Note that in each example three of the four terms of the proportion are known, and the problem is to find the fourth term.

Example 4. If a measurement of 3 inches on an aerial photograph represents a distance of 20 miles, how many miles are represented by a measurement of $5\frac{1}{2}$ inches?

Solution:

$$\frac{3}{20} = \frac{5\frac{1}{2}}{d}$$

$$3d = 20(5\tfrac{1}{2})$$

$$3d = 20(\tfrac{11}{2}) = 110$$

$$d = \frac{110}{3} = 36.\overline{6}$$

Therefore, a measurement of $5\frac{1}{2}$ inches on an aerial photograph represents a distance of $36.\overline{6}$, or approximately 36.7, miles.

Example 5. A mixture of grass seed requires by weight 5 parts of bluegrass seed and 3 parts of clover seed. If a total of 20 pounds of seed is needed, how much bluegrass seed and how much clover seed should be in the mixture?

Solution: Each 8 pounds of mixture must contain 5 pounds of bluegrass and 3 pounds of clover. This means that the ratio of bluegrass to the total mixture will be 5 to 8 or $\frac{5}{8}$, and the ratio of clover to the total mixture will be 3 to 8 or $\frac{3}{8}$.

In finding the amount of bluegrass seed required for 20 pounds of mixture, we have:

$$\frac{b}{20} = \frac{5}{8}$$

$$b(8) = 20(5)$$

$$b = \frac{20(5)}{8} = \frac{100}{8} = 12\tfrac{1}{2}.$$

Hence, $12\frac{1}{2}$ pounds of bluegrass seed is needed.

Similarly, we may find the amount of clover seed for the 20 pounds of mixture as follows:

$$\frac{c}{20} = \frac{3}{8}$$

$$c(8) = 20(3)$$

$$c = \frac{20(3)}{8} = \frac{60}{8} = 7\tfrac{1}{2}.$$

Therefore, $7\frac{1}{2}$ pounds of clover seed is required. Of course, the amount of clover seed required could have been determined by subtraction: $20 - 12\frac{1}{2} = 7\frac{1}{2}$.

EXERCISE 11.9

1. There are 120 men and 96 women in a theater.
   (a) Express the ratio of men to women as a fraction $\frac{m}{w}$ in reduced form.
   (b) Find the number of men per woman by expressing the ratio of men to women as a quotient $\frac{m}{w}$ with $w = 1$.
   (c) Express the ratio of women to men as a fraction $\frac{w}{m}$ in reduced form.
   (d) Find the number of women per man by expressing the ratio of women to men as a quotient $\frac{w}{m}$ with $m = 1$.

2. If 2.5 inches on a map represents 50 miles, what distance is represented by 8 inches on the map?

3. An automobile travels 92 miles on 6 gallons of gasoline. At that rate, how far will it travel on 20 gallons of gasoline? Express the result to the nearest mile.

4. A cake recipe requires $\frac{3}{4}$ of a cup of sugar and 4 cups of flour. How much sugar should be used with 7 cups of flour? Express the result to the nearest fourth of a cup.

5. If 3 quarts of antifreeze will prevent an 8-quart radiator from freezing, what amount of antifreeze should be used with an 11-quart radiator?

6. A vertical 4-foot post casts a shadow 2.6 feet long and a hotel casts a shadow 165 feet long. How high is the hotel? Express the result to the nearest foot.

7. If a mixture of concrete is to have a 3 to 2 ratio of gravel to sand, how much sand should be used with 54 cubic yards of gravel?

8. It costs a farmer $640 to plant 18 acres. At this rate, what will it cost him to plant 120 acres? Express the result to the nearest dollar.

9. A mixture of paint contains 2 parts of green paint and 5 parts of white paint. How many gallons of green paint must be mixed with 16 gallons of white paint to obtain the same color? Express the result to the nearest tenth of a gallon.

10. A mixture of paint is to contain 3 parts of yellow paint and 8 parts of green paint. If 24 gallons are required to paint a house, how many gallons of each color will be needed? Express the results to the nearest tenth of a gallon.

11. If soup sells at the rate of 3 cans for 44¢, how many cans can be bought for $2? (Assume you cannot buy part of a can of soup!)

12. Oranges sell for 89¢ per dozen. At that rate how much will seven oranges cost?

13. Mr. Baker invested $8000 along with $5000 belonging to Mr. Timm. If profits are shared in proportion to the investments, how should a $20,000 profit be divided?

14. If a 3-acre field produced 3.4 bales of cotton, about how much cotton could be expected from 1200 acres under similar conditions? State the result to the nearest bale.

15. The ratio of length to width in an official United States flag is 1.9. What is the width of a flag that is 4 feet long?

16. A mixture of paint is to contain 5 parts of white paint, 3 parts of yellow, and 2 parts of green. If a total of 20 gallons of paint is required, how many gallons each of white, yellow, and green paint are needed?

17. A mixture of grass seed requires by weight 4 parts of bluegrass to 3 parts of rye to $1\frac{1}{2}$ parts of fescue. How many pounds of each should be used for 50 pounds of the mixture? Express the results to the nearest tenth of a pound.

11.10

Percent

If a ratio is expressed in such a way that the second number of the ordered pair is 100, the ratio may be called a percent. For example, $\frac{1}{2} = \frac{50}{100} = 50$ percent. The symbol % may be used in place of the word "percent," and we can write: $\frac{1}{2} = \frac{50}{100} = 50\%$.

Example 1.

(a) $\dfrac{2}{100} = 2\%$

(b) $\dfrac{3}{4} = \dfrac{75}{100} = 75\%$

(c) $\dfrac{12}{5} = \dfrac{240}{100} = 240\%$

(d) $0.24 = \dfrac{24}{100} = 24\%$

(e) $0.0734 = \dfrac{7.34}{100} = 7.34\%$

(f) $0.00048 = \dfrac{0.048}{100} = 0.048\%$

(g) $1 = \dfrac{100}{100} = 100\%$

(h) $8 = \dfrac{800}{100} = 800\%$

It is obvious that $1 = 100\%$ and that a number greater than 1 is more than 100%, while a number less than 1 is less than 100%. Example 1(f) illustrates that a number less than $\frac{1}{100}$ is less than 1%.

The word "percent" is alternatively written "per cent" since it is derived from the two Latin words *per centum,* which mean "in, to, or for every hundred." If we say that "20 percent of the apples are rotten," this means that "20 out of every 100 apples are rotten," or that "the ratio of rotten apples to the total number of apples is 20 to 100."

Any of the usual percentage problems may be expressed as a proportion in which one of the four terms of the proportion is to be found when the other three terms are known. In Example 2, a single setting is used to show how each of the different types of percentage problems may be solved by using a proportion. Note that in each proportion the term 100 is known while one of the other three terms is unknown. In the past, it was customary to classify percentage problems according to which one of the terms of the proportion was to be found.

Example 2.

(a) If 3 students out of a class of 24 are absent, what percent of the students are absent?

Solution: Let x represent the percent of students absent. Then:

$$\frac{3}{24} = \frac{x}{100}$$

$$24x = 3(100)$$

$$x = \frac{3(100)}{24} = 12.5.$$

Since $\frac{3}{24} = \frac{12.5}{100} = 12.5\%$, we see that 12.5% of the students are absent.

(b) If 12.5% of the students in a class of 24 are absent, how many students are absent?

Solution: Let a represent the number of students absent. Then:

$$\frac{12.5}{100} = \frac{a}{24}$$

$$100a = 12.5(24)$$

$$a = \frac{12.5(24)}{100} = \frac{300}{100} = 3.$$

Therefore, 3 students are absent.

(c) If 3 students are absent in a class and this is 12.5% of the class, how many students are enrolled in the class?

Solution: Let c represent the number of students enrolled in the class. Then:

$$\frac{12.5}{100} = \frac{3}{c}$$

$$12.5c = 100(3)$$

$$c = \frac{100(3)}{12.5} = \frac{300}{12.5} = 24.$$

Therefore, 24 students are enrolled in the class.

In solving percentage problems, certain techniques will be found to be more efficient than others. Below are given alternative solutions to Examples 2(a), (b), and (c). These solutions require somewhat fewer manipulations.

Example 2. (with alternative solutions)

(a) If 3 students out of a class of 24 are absent, what percent of the students are absent?

Alternative Solution:

$$\frac{3}{24} = 0.125 = 0.125\left(\frac{100}{100}\right) = \frac{12.5}{100} = 12.5\%.$$

(b) If 12.5% of the students in a class of 24 are absent, how many students are absent?

Alternative Solution:

$$12.5\% \text{ of } 24 = \frac{12.5}{100} \text{ of } 24 = 0.125(24) = 3.$$

(c) If 3 students are absent in a class and this is 12.5% of the class, how many students are enrolled in the class?

Alternative Solution: Let c represent the number of students enrolled in the class. Then:

$$12.5\% \text{ of } c = 3$$

$$\frac{12.5}{100} \text{ of } c = 3$$

$$0.125c = 3$$

$$c = \frac{3}{0.125} = 24.$$

EXERCISE 11.10

1. Express each of the following ratios as a percent by the method shown in Example 1.

   (a) $\frac{3}{5}$ (b) $\frac{7}{4}$ (c) $\frac{7}{20}$

   (d) $\frac{3}{50}$ (e) $\frac{48}{200}$ (f) $\frac{9}{75}$

2. Express each of the following ratios to the nearest tenth of a percent using division. See the alternative solution of Example 2(a).

   (a) $\frac{5}{8}$ (b) $\frac{3}{7}$ (c) $\frac{22}{3}$

   (d) $\frac{5}{12}$ (e) $\frac{7}{16}$ (f) $\frac{19}{4}$

3. Solve each of the following independently of each other
   (a) What is 15% of 20?
   (b) 3 is what percent of 20?
   (c) 15% of what number is equal to 3?

4. If a teacher earns $14,500 and receives a 7% increase in salary, what is the amount of the increase?

5. (a) If an item sells for $8.00 and the price is increased to $10.00, the increase is what percent of the original price?
   (b) If the price is then changed from $10.00 back to $8.00, what is the percent decrease?
   (c) Why is the result in part (b) different from the result in part (a)?

6. There are 16 girls and 20 boys in a class.
   (a) What percent of the class is girls?
   (b) What percent of the class is boys?

7. If 14 members of a college class wear glasses and this is 40% of the class, how many members are there in the class?

8. A man receives $5\frac{3}{4}$% interest on an investment of $12,500. What is the amount of the interest?

9. Twenty-two percent of a man's salary was paid for taxes. His taxes were $4048.00. What was his salary?

10. A boy has 25% as many black marbles as white marbles. If he has 60 white marbles, how many black marbles does he have?

11. A boy has 35% as many red marbles as yellow marbles. If he has 28 red marbles, how many yellow marbles does he have?

12. A bag contains 20 black marbles and 30 white marbles.
    (a) What percent of all the marbles are black?
    (b) What percent of all the marbles are white?
    (c) What percent of the number of white marbles is the number of black marbles?
    (d) What percent of the number of black marbles is the number of white marbles?

?   13. At the end of the day a cash register contains $1248.31. This amount includes the day's sales and a 4% sales tax.

    (a) What is the amount of the day's sales?

    (b) What is the amount of the sales tax?

11.11
Irrational and Real Numbers

In this section we shall discuss an important set of numbers called *irrational numbers*. As contrasted with the rational numbers, the irrational numbers cannot be represented as ordered pairs of integers, such as $\frac{2}{3}$, $\frac{-8}{5}$, $\frac{0}{12}$, and $\frac{432}{17}$. In studying irrational numbers we shall find it convenient to refer to the famous Pythagorean Theorem, which states a relationship among the sides of a right triangle. The Pythagorean Theorem is not proved in this section; however, a proof of the theorem is given later, in the chapter on Metric Geometry.

In a right triangle, the side opposite the right angle is called the hypotenuse and the other two sides are called the legs. The Pythagorean Theorem states that in any right triangle the square of the length of the hypotenuse is equal to the sum of the squares of the lengths of the legs. If c represents the length of the hypotenuse and if a and b represent the lengths of the legs, then $c^2 = a^2 + b^2$. For example, if the lengths of the legs are 3 and 4, then the length of the hypotenuse must equal 5 since $5^2 = 3^2 + 4^2$. Figure 11.11.1 shows the geometric relationship between

FIGURE 11.11.1

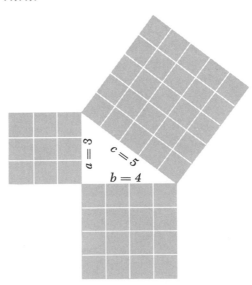

$a = 3$

$c = 5$

$b = 4$

the lengths of the sides of a 3, 4, 5 right triangle and the areas of the squares constructed on these sides; the areas are 3^2, 4^2, and 5^2.

In the above example we see that if the lengths of the legs of a right triangle are known to be 3 and 4, then the length of the hypotenuse may be determined by solving the equation $c^2 = 3^2 + 4^2 = 25$. The number c is the number that when used as a factor twice will equal 25. Such a number is called the square root of 25, and there are two such numbers: 5 and $^-5$. We are interested in the positive square root of 25 and will indicate it by writing $\sqrt{25} = 5$. The negative square root of 25 is indicated by writing $^-\sqrt{25} = {}^-5$.

Suppose each leg of a right triangle is of unit length; then $c^2 = 1^2 + 1^2 = 2$ and the length of the hypotenuse is $c = \sqrt{2}$. As we shall soon prove, the number $\sqrt{2}$ cannot be represented as an ordered pair of integers $\frac{a}{b}$ and is therefore not a rational number. This number can, however, be associated with a point on the number line. In fact, by applying the Pythagorean Theorem, the square roots of all the whole numbers can be represented geometrically as line segments and associated with points on the number line as shown in Figure 11.11.2. Some of these numbers are rational and some are not; for example, $\sqrt{4}$, $\sqrt{9}$, and $\sqrt{16}$ are rational whereas $\sqrt{2}$, $\sqrt{3}$, and $\sqrt{5}$ are not. Numbers that are not rational are called irrational numbers.

It was previously stated that $\sqrt{2}$ cannot be represented as an ordered pair of integers $\frac{a}{b}$ and hence is an irrational number. We will show that this statement is true by using an indirect proof or a proof by contradiction. The reasoning in an indirect proof is as follows: We assume as true the *negation* of the statement we wish to prove and, by the implications of this assumption, arrive at a conclusion known to be false. Since our mathematical procedures were correct, we conclude that we arrived at a contradiction because our assumption was false. Hence the original statement, rather than its negation, must be true.

FIGURE 11.11.2

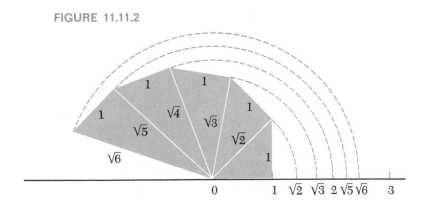

Proof that $\sqrt{2}$ *is an irrational number:* Assume that $\sqrt{2}$ is a rational number and that $\sqrt{2} = \frac{a}{b}$, where $\frac{a}{b}$ is a fraction in simplest form; that is, a and b are relatively prime and hence have no common positive integral factor other than 1. Then $2 = \dfrac{a^2}{b^2}$ and $2b^2 = a^2$. Since $2b^2$ has a factor of 2, a^2 must have a factor of 2. However, $a^2 = a \cdot a$, and each factor a must have a factor of 2 since 2 is prime and, by the Fundamental Theorem of Arithmetic, a number may be factored into primes in only one way. Since a has a factor of 2, let $a = 2k$. Then by substitution, $2b^2 = (2k)^2$ and $2b^2 = 4k^2$. Thus, $b^2 = 2k^2$. By again reasoning as above, b^2 must have a factor of 2 and hence b has a factor of 2. It has now been shown that a and b have a common factor of 2. Hence our assumption that a and b are relatively prime is contradicted, and this inconsistency leads us to conclude that $\sqrt{2}$ is not a rational number because any rational number can be represented by a fraction in simplest form. Therefore, $\sqrt{2}$ must be an irrational number.

By proofs similar to the above, it can also be shown that numbers such as $\sqrt{3}$, $\sqrt{5}$, and $\sqrt{13}$ are irrational. Other examples of irrational numbers are $\sqrt[5]{7}$, $\log_{10} 5$, and π. There are many irrational numbers. In fact, it can be proved that there are more irrational numbers than rational numbers, even though there are infinitely many elements in both sets.

The set that results from the union of the set of rational numbers and the set of irrational numbers is called the set of real numbers. The set of real numbers may be put in a one-to-one correspondence with the set of *all* points on the number line; that is, not only can every real number be associated with a unique point on the number line, but every point on the number line can also be associated with a unique real number. Thus the number line may be used as a picture of the set of real numbers in such a way that there are no "holes" in the ordering of the real numbers. The technical way of expressing this concept is to say that the real numbers are order-complete.

Since every point on the number line can be associated with some real number, this means that we can use the real numbers to measure the length of any line segment. The concept of measurement will be discussed more fully in Chapter 13.

EXERCISE 11.11

1. Prove that $\sqrt{2}$ is irrational, referring to the proof in your text if necessary.
2. Prove that $\sqrt{3}$ is irrational by a method similar to that used in problem 1.

3. Assume that $\sqrt{2}$ is known to be irrational and prove that $7 + \sqrt{2}$ is irrational. *Hint:* Assume that $7 + \sqrt{2}$ is a rational number and use an indirect proof.

4. Prove that $8 - \sqrt{3}$ is irrational if it is known that $\sqrt{3}$ is irrational.

5. (a) Find the sum $(8 - \sqrt{3}) + (8 + \sqrt{3})$. Is the sum irrational?
   (b) Find the difference $(8 - \sqrt{3}) - (8 + \sqrt{3})$. Is the difference irrational?
   (c) Find the product $(8 - \sqrt{3})(8 + \sqrt{3})$. Is the product irrational?

11.12
The Decimal Representation Real Numbers

It was shown previously that every rational number may be expressed either as a terminating or repeating decimal. In contrast, the irrational numbers may be represented by *nonrepeating infinite decimals*. Thus, every real number has a decimal representation.

Example 1. Below are listed the decimal numerals for selected real numbers. The repeating decimals represent rational numbers, and the nonrepeating decimals represent irrational numbers.

$$\sqrt{2} = 1.414214\ldots \qquad \text{irrational}$$
$$\sqrt{3} = 1.73205\ldots \qquad \text{irrational}$$
$$\sqrt{9} = 3.0000\ldots \qquad \text{rational}$$
$$\pi = 3.141592\ldots \qquad \text{irrational}$$
$$\log 7 = 0.8451\ldots \qquad \text{irrational}$$
$$\tfrac{2}{11} = 0.1818\ldots \qquad \text{rational}$$
$$\sin 45° = 0.7071\ldots \qquad \text{irrational}$$
$$\tan 45° = 1.0000\ldots \qquad \text{rational}$$
$$0.3030030003\ldots \qquad \text{irrational}$$

Just as we can approximate rational numbers by rounding off repeating decimals, we can approximate irrational numbers by rounding off nonrepeating decimals to any finite number of digits desired. Note in Example 2, which follows, that the symbol $\approx$ for "is approximately equal to" is used.

Example 2.

$$\sqrt{3} = 1.73205\ldots \approx 1.732$$
$$\pi = 3.14159\ldots \approx 3.1416$$
$$\log 7 = 0.8451\ldots \ \approx 0.85$$
$$\sin 45° = 0.7071\ldots \ \approx 0.7$$

You may be wondering how we can find the nonrepeating decimal representation of an irrational number. By using more advanced mathematical techniques than those discussed in this text, it is often possible to find an infinite sequence of terms, the sum of which is equal to a given irrational number. The sum of a sufficiently large number of terms of the infinite sequence will then result in as many digits in the nonrepeating decimal representation as may be desired. For example, $\pi = \frac{4}{1} - \frac{4}{3} + \frac{4}{5} - \frac{4}{7} + \frac{4}{9} - \frac{4}{11} + \cdots$. By using a sufficient number of terms in this sequence, any number of digits in the decimal representation of π may be found. The advantage of an electronic computer in evaluating such a series is obvious.

Ordinary arithmetic may be used to find decimal approximations of some irrational numbers such as $\sqrt{2}$, $\sqrt{3}$, $\sqrt{23}$, and $\sqrt{237}$. This may be done simply by "trial and error." In finding the decimal approximation of $\sqrt{23}$, for example, we see that $4^2 = 16$ and $5^2 = 25$. Since $16 < 23 < 25$, $4 < \sqrt{23} < 5$. However, since 23 is closer to 25 than to 16, we may guess that $\sqrt{23}$ is closer to 5 than to 4. Suppose, therefore, we make our next estimate 4.8. Since $(4.8)^2 = 23.04$, 4.8 is a little greater than $\sqrt{23}$. Our next approximation might be 4.79, and so on.

Another technique for approximating the square root of a number is the "divide and average" method. This method consists of estimating the square root of a given number and then dividing the given number by the estimate. If the estimate is smaller than the square root of the given number, then the quotient upon division will not only be larger than the divisor, but also larger than the square root of the given number; similarly, if the estimate is too large, then the quotient will be too small. Therefore, a better approximation may be found by averaging the first estimate and the quotient to obtain a second estimate. The given number is then divided by the second estimate. By averaging the second estimate with its quotient, an even better approximation of the square root is obtained. This process is continued as many times as necessary to obtain the desired degree of accuracy in the approximation. Each time the operation of division is performed, twice as many digits are kept in the quotient as in the previous approximation. In this way, each new approximation obtained by averaging will have twice as many digits as the previous approximation. This method of approximating the square root of a number sounds rather involved when described in words, but it is really quite simple, as is illustrated by Example 3.

Example 3. Approximate $\sqrt{23}$.

Solution: Since $4^2 = 16$ and $5^2 = 25$, $4 < \sqrt{23} < 5$. However, 5 appears to be a better estimate than 4. Using 5 as a first estimate, we obtain the second estimate for $\sqrt{23}$ as follows:

$$\frac{23}{5} = 4.6$$

$$\frac{5 + 4.6}{2} = \frac{9.6}{2} = 4.8 \quad \text{(second estimate)}$$

Applying the same procedure to obtain a third estimate, we have:

$$\frac{23}{4.8} = 4.792 \quad \text{(rounded to 4 significant digits)}$$

$$\frac{4.8 + 4.792}{2} = 4.796 \quad \text{(third estimate)}$$

Computing a fourth estimate, we have:

$$\frac{23}{4.796} - 4.7956631 \quad \text{(rounded to 8 significant digits)}$$

$$\frac{4.796 + 4.7956631}{2} = 4.7958316 \quad \text{(fourth estimate)}$$

In the next quotient 16 digits would be kept, then 32, and so on, until the desired degree of accuracy was obtained.

Note that the second estimate of 4.8 has no digits identical to the first estimate of 5 although 4.8 does round to 5. The third estimate of 4.796 has the same first digit as 4.8 and rounds to 4.8. The fourth estimate of 4.7958316 verifies the accuracy of 4.796 to three digits and rounds to 4.796. If we had started with some estimate other than 5 for $\sqrt{23}$ (even a poor estimate), we would still eventually obtain as many correct digits as desired in the decimal representation of $\sqrt{23}$ simply by repeating the process of dividing and averaging a sufficient number of times.

The method described above for obtaining decimal approximations for square roots may be adapted to approximate cube roots, fourth roots, and so on. Since the same techniques are applied repeatedly, the procedure lends itself quite readily to the use of modern electronic computers. As you can see, it might be less than inspiring to approximate the square roots of very many numbers by any repetitive process; it is much more stimulating to design and program a computer to carry out the task.

EXERCISE 11.12

1. Using a fairly large scale, plot the points 2, 3, and 4 on a number line. Then:
   (a) Plot π on the number line using $\pi \approx 3.14$.

(b) Given $\pi = \frac{4}{1} - \frac{4}{3} + \frac{4}{5} - \frac{4}{7} + \frac{4}{9} - \frac{4}{11} + \cdots$, plot the five numbers: $\frac{4}{1}$, $(\frac{4}{1} - \frac{4}{3})$, $(\frac{4}{1} - \frac{4}{3} + \frac{4}{5})$, $(\frac{4}{1} - \frac{4}{3} + \frac{4}{5} - \frac{4}{7})$, and $(\frac{4}{1} - \frac{4}{3} + \frac{4}{5} - \frac{4}{7} + \frac{4}{9})$.

(c) Is each of these numbers closer to π than the previous number?

2. Approximate $\sqrt{39}$ by "trial and error."

3. (a) Using 6 as a first estimate, find the second and third approximations of $\sqrt{39}$ by the "divide and average" method.

   (b) Using 7 as a first estimate, find the second and third approximations of $\sqrt{39}$ by the divide and average method.

4. Find the third approximation of $\sqrt{147}$ by the divide and average method. Use 12 as the first approximation.

5. Apply the divide and average method as many times as necessary to find $\sqrt{14}$:

   (a) rounded to 4 significant digits.

   (b) rounded to 6 significant digits.

REVIEW EXERCISES

1. The following numerals are written in a base six system of numeration. Find the terminating or repeating base six "decimal" for each.

   (a) $\frac{1}{2}$ (b) $\frac{1}{3}$ (c) $\frac{1}{4}$ (d) $\frac{1}{5}$

2. (a) How is it possible to determine without division whether a given fraction in base ten can be expressed as a terminating decimal?

   (b) How is it possible to determine without division whether a given fraction in base six can be expressed as a terminating "decimal"?

3. Express $73.49\overline{374}$ as a fraction.

4. (a) Do the decimal fractions have the property of denseness? Explain.

   (b) What decimal fraction is midway between 0.63 and 0.64?

   (c) What number is midway between $0.\overline{3}$ and 0.3? Express the result in fraction form.

5. Write $\frac{3}{11}$ as a decimal numeral and round off to the nearest:

   (a) tenth of a unit.

   (b) hundredth of a unit.

   (c) thousandth of a unit.

   (d) ten-thousandth of a unit.

6. A sample of 18 seeds was planted. Thirteen sprouted. If the 18 seeds were representative and 2000 seeds were planted, how many could be expected to germinate?

7. In order to make an off-white paint, a salesman adds 6 ounces of pigment to 20 gallons of paint. However, he gets another order for 8 more gallons

to complete the job. How much pigment should he add to the 8 gallons if it is to match the original 20 gallons?

8. A corporation's stock is currently selling at $21 per share and earning $2.40 per share. If you were to purchase the stock, how much would you be paying for each dollar of earnings?

9. If a given state has a sales tax of 4% and a merchant ends the day with $1247.36 gross receipts including the tax, what tax must be paid on the receipts of the day?

10. Apply the "divide and average" method and find $\sqrt{18}$ rounded to 4 significant digits.

Chapter Twelve

Nonmetric Geometry

12.1
Introduction

In previous chapters, we have discussed various mathematical systems that are concerned with sets of elements called numbers. Now we shall study a mathematical system that involves sets of elements called *points*. Both numbers and points are abstract mental concepts. Numbers, of course, may be represented by numerals, while points are represented by dots or in some other way. If you wish, you may think of points as locations in space, and you may think of space as the universal set of points. However, it is important to understand that the geometric concepts of point and space will be accepted as undefined. Even the concepts of line and plane will not be given explicit definitions.

The approach to geometry in this chapter will be intuitive and informal rather than axiomatic. It is hoped that as a result of this kind of treatment, the reader will have a better understanding of certain geometric concepts. The title of the chapter, "Nonmetric Geometry," implies that we shall *not* be concerned with measuring segments, regions, and spaces. Concepts of length, area, and volume will be discussed in Chapter 13, "Metric Geometry."

12.2
Points, Lines, Planes, Space

Although point, line, plane, and space are undefined terms, a few descriptive comments concerning them and their representations will be helpful.

A point may be thought of as a single exact location in space. A point has neither length, width, nor height, and it is commonly represented by a dot and named by a capital letter. In diagram (a) of Figure 12.2.1 we see a representation of the point A.

The term line will always refer to a *straight line*. A line is a particular set of points. There are infinitely many points in a line; there are also infinitely many points between any two distinct points of a line.

FIGURE 12.2.1

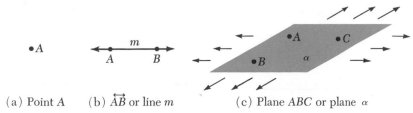

(a) Point A   (b) $\overleftrightarrow{AB}$ or line m (c) Plane ABC or plane α

A line has neither width nor thickness but is infinite in length. A taut cord or thread that is thought of as extending infinitely far in both directions may be used to represent a line. There are infinitely many lines through (or containing) a single point, but there is only one line through (or containing) any two distinct points. Hence we say "two points determine a line," and we name a line by identifying any two of its points. A representation of the line determined by the two points A and B is shown in part (b) of Figure 12.2.1. One name for this line is $\overleftrightarrow{AB}$ (read "line AB"), and another name for the same line is $\overleftrightarrow{BA}$ (read "line BA"). Since $\overleftrightarrow{AB}$ and $\overleftrightarrow{BA}$ are simply two different names for the same set of points, we state that $\overleftrightarrow{AB} = \overleftrightarrow{BA}$. Lowercase letters such as m, n, and so on, may also be used to name lines. In Figure 12.2.1, $\overleftrightarrow{AB}$, $\overleftrightarrow{BA}$, and m all name the same line.

A plane is a particular set of points that may be thought of as extending infinitely far through space. A plane has no thickness, but it is infinite in length and width. The top of a table may be used to represent a plane even though it best represents only a portion of a plane. If a plane contains any two points of a line, it will contain all the points of the line. There is only one plane through any three points that are not all on the same line; hence we say "three noncollinear points determine a plane." A plane may be named by identifying any three of its points that are noncollinear or by using some other symbol such as a Greek letter. In part (c) of Figure 12.2.1, plane ABC and plane α name the same plane; the figure may be drawn with or without the arrows.

Space may be thought of as the universal set of points. It has no beginning and no end and is infinite in extent in all directions. All points, lines, and planes are subsets of space, as are all other geometric configurations.

12.3
Line Segments,
Half-Lines,
Rays

Consider the line uniquely determined by any two distinct points A and B and identified as $\overleftrightarrow{AB}$. The set containing points A and B and all points of the line *between* these two points is called a line segment (Note that *between* is accepted here as an undefined term.) A line segment is represented in Figure 12.3.1; it is named by identifying the two

FIGURE 12.3.1

A B

endpoints A and B and writing $\overline{AB}$ (read "line segment $\overline{AB}$") or $\overline{BA}$ (read "line segment BA"). Of course, $\overline{AB} = \overline{BA}$.

A line segment is thought of as the shortest "path" between its endpoints. The shortest path between any two points on a (straight) line is the line segment determined by the two points. Although the line segment determined by any two arbitrary points A and B is a set containing infinitely many points, it is nevertheless a subset of $\overleftrightarrow{AB}$, which is also an infinite set of points.

A figure consisting of all the points of a line segment except the endpoints is called an open segment or the interior of the segment. The interior of $\overline{AB}$ is identified as $\overset{\circ}{A}\overset{\circ}{B}$ or $\overset{\circ}{B}\overset{\circ}{A}$. If only one endpoint A of $\overline{AB}$ is excluded, the figure is called a half-open segment and may be identified as $\overset{\circ}{A}B$. Similarly, we write $A\overset{\circ}{B}$ if the endpoint B is not included in the line segment.

Consider a line identified as $\overleftrightarrow{AC}$. Let B be a point between A and C (see Figure 12.3.2). The point B partitions the line into three disjoint

FIGURE 12.3.2

subsets: the singleton set containing only the point B, the set of points on the same side of B as C, and the set of points on the same side of B as A. All the points on the same side of B as C constitute a half-line and may be identified as "half-line BC" by the symbol $\overset{\circ}{B}\vec{C}$. Similarly, the half-line BA is identified by the symbol $\overset{\circ}{B}\vec{A}$. Note that the point B is not an element of either half-line. The union of the three disjoint subsets of points is the line AC; $\overset{\circ}{B}\vec{C} \cup \{B\} \cup \overset{\circ}{B}\vec{A} = \overleftrightarrow{AC}$.

Refer again to Figure 12.3.2. If the point B is included along with $\overset{\circ}{B}\vec{C}$, this set of points is called a ray—in this case $\overrightarrow{BC}$ (read "ray BC"). We see then that $\{B\} \cup \overset{\circ}{B}\vec{C} = \overrightarrow{BC}$. Similarly, $\{B\} \cup \overset{\circ}{B}\vec{A} = \overrightarrow{BA}$, and $\overrightarrow{BA} \cap \overrightarrow{BC} = \{B\}$. Note that a ray is named by identifying its endpoint and any other point of the ray distinct from the endpoint. For example, if B is the endpoint of a ray and X is some other point, then the ray may be named $\overrightarrow{BX}$.

Example 1. Consider the following diagram.

Some true statements that may be made with reference to the figure are:

(a) $\overline{AB} \cup \overline{BC} = \overline{AC}$ (b) $\overline{AB} \cap \overline{BC} = \{B\}$

(c) $\overline{AB} \cup \overrightarrow{BC} = \overrightarrow{AC}$ (d) $\overrightarrow{BC} \cup \overrightarrow{BA} = \overleftrightarrow{CA}$

(e) $\overline{BC} \cap \overleftrightarrow{BC} = \overline{BC}$ (f) $\overline{AB} \cap \overrightarrow{BC} = \{B\}$

(g) $\overline{AB} \cap \overleftarrow{BC} = \varnothing$ (h) $\overleftarrow{BA} \cap \overleftarrow{BC} = \varnothing$

(i) $\overline{AB} \cap \overrightarrow{AC} = \overline{AB}$ (j) $\overrightarrow{AB} = \overrightarrow{AC}$

EXERCISE 12.3

1. State briefly your concept of:
   (a) a point   (b) a (straight) line
   (c) a plane   (d) space

2. (a) How many planes are determined by the tips of the legs of a stool with three legs? Will the stool wobble if each of its legs is a different length?
   (b) What is the maximum number of planes that may be determined by the 4 points represented by the tips of the legs of a table?
   (c) Why do you suppose surveyors use a transit stand with 3 legs, and why do photographers use tripods for their cameras? Give a geometric interpretation.
   (d) How many planes can pass through three noncollinear points?
   (e) How many planes can pass through three collinear points?

3. Refer to the figure below and complete the statements as indicated.

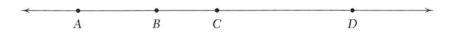

$\quad\quad A \quad\quad\quad\quad B \quad\quad\quad\quad C \quad\quad\quad\quad\quad\quad\quad\quad D$

   (a) $\overline{AB} \cup \overline{BC} = ?$ (b) $\overline{CD} \cup \overline{BC} = ?$
   (c) $\overline{CB} \cup \overline{CD} = ?$ (d) $\overline{BC} \cup \overrightarrow{CD} = ?$
   (e) $\overline{BC} \cup \overleftrightarrow{BC} = ?$ (f) $\overline{BC} \cap \overleftrightarrow{BC} = ?$
   (g) $\overrightarrow{BC} \cap \overrightarrow{CB} = ?$ (h) $\overleftrightarrow{BC} \cap \overrightarrow{CB} = ?$

4. Refer to the figure of problem 3 and tell whether each of the following statements is true or false.
   (a) $\overrightarrow{AB} = \overrightarrow{AC}$ (b) $\overrightarrow{AB} = \overrightarrow{AD}$
   (c) $\overline{AD} = \overline{DA}$ (d) $\overrightarrow{AD} = \overrightarrow{DA}$
   (e) $\overline{AB} \cap \overline{BC} = \varnothing$ (f) $\overline{BC} \cap \overline{CD} = \{C\}$
   (g) $\overline{BC} \cap \overleftarrow{BD} = \overline{BC}$ (h) $\overline{AB} \cap \overleftarrow{BA} = \overline{AB}$

As discussed in the previous section, a point on a line may be thought of as separating the line into two half-lines. In a similar way, we may think of a line in a plane as separating the plane into two *half-planes*. Consider the plane P in Figure 12.4.1.

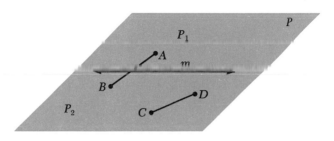

FIGURE 12.4.1

The line m in plane P partitions the plane into three disjoint subsets: the line m, the set of points in P on the A side of m, and the set of points in P on the B side of m. The set of points on the A side of m constitutes a half-plane and the set of points on the B side of m is also a half-plane; the points on the line m are in neither half-plane. If the half-plane on the A side of m is named P_1 and the half-plane on the B side of m is named P_2, it may be seen that $P_1 \cup m \cup P_2 = P$.

Intuitively, we know whether A and B are on the same side of m, but we can state explicitly the conditions under which two points are on the same or different sides of a line in a plane. If A and B are points in plane P distinct from line m, which is also in plane P, and $\overline{AB} \cap m$ is nonempty, then A and B are on different sides of m. If, however, $\overline{AB} \cap m = \varnothing$, then A and B are on the same side of m. In Figure 12.4.1, points A and B are on different sides of m. Points C and D are on the same side of m since $\overline{CD} \cap m = \varnothing$; hence points on the C side of m constitute the same set of points as those on the D side of m.

If two distinct lines (or line segments) *intersect*, their intersection is a point. If lines m and n intersect in A, as illustrated in Figure 12.4.2, we may write $m \cap n = \{A\}$.

If two distinct lines *in a plane* do not intersect, the lines are said to be parallel. However, if two distinct lines *not in the same plane* do not intersect, they are said to be skew. In Figure 12.4.3, lines r and s

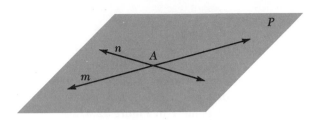

FIGURE 12.4.2

are parallel whereas line t is skew to both r and s. If lines r and s are parallel, we may write $r \parallel s$ which is read "r is parallel to s." In a similar way, if parallel lines are identified by points on the lines, we may write, for example, $\overleftrightarrow{AB} \parallel \overleftrightarrow{CD}$. Of course, if $\overleftrightarrow{AB} \parallel \overleftrightarrow{CD}$ or if $\overleftrightarrow{AB}$ and $\overleftrightarrow{CD}$ are skew, then $\overleftrightarrow{AB} \cap \overleftrightarrow{CD} = \varnothing$.

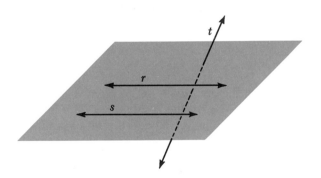

FIGURE 12.4.3

FIGURE 12.4.4

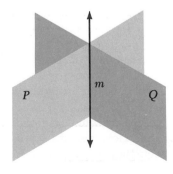

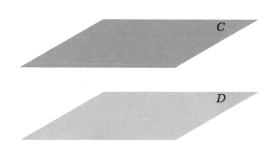

FIGURE 12.4.5

If two distinct planes *intersect*, they intersect in a line. Figure 12.4.4 illustrates the intersection of planes P and Q in line m, and we see that $P \cap Q = m$. If two distinct planes do not intersect, they are said to be parallel. Parallel planes C and D are illustrated in Figure 12.4.5, and we see that $C \cap D = \varnothing$. Figure 12.4.6 shows line n parallel to plane E, and it follows that $n \cap E = \varnothing$.

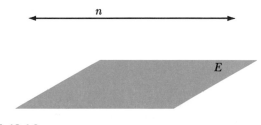

FIGURE 12.4.6

12.5
Angles

Most people probably have an intuitive concept of an angle and should have no difficulty in understanding the following statement: An angle may be defined as the union of two rays with a common endpoint. The common endpoint is called the vertex of the angle and the two rays are called the sides of the angle. An angle may be named by referring to the vertex point and two other points, one on each side of the angle. In Figure 12.5.1 the angle illustrated may be identified by writing the symbol $\angle ABC$ (read "angle ABC") or $\angle CBA$ (read "angle CBA"). Note that the vertex is always named by the middle letter of the three capital letters naming an angle; the other two letters may be interchanged. Referring again to Figure 12.5.1, we can see that, by the definition of an angle, $\overrightarrow{BA} \cup \overrightarrow{BC} = \angle ABC$.

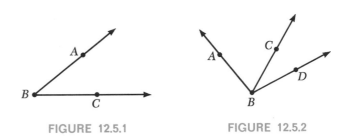

FIGURE 12.5.1　　　　　　FIGURE 12.5.2

If no ambiguity results, an angle may be named by referring only to its vertex. In Figure 12.5.1, the angle could be named "angle B" by writing $\angle B$. In Figure 12.5.2, however, $\angle B$ would not be a satisfactory name for any angle since B is the vertex of three angles: $\angle ABC$, $\angle ABD$, and $\angle CBD$.

An angle of special importance in mathematics is a *straight angle*. If the union of the sides of an angle is a line, then the angle is said to be a straight angle. In Figure 12.5.3, $\angle ABC$ represents a straight angle with B as its vertex. Observe that $\overrightarrow{BA} \cup \overrightarrow{BC} =` \angle ABC = \overleftrightarrow{AC}$.

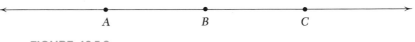

A　　　　　B　　　　　C

FIGURE 12.5.3

It is sometimes convenient to refer to the *interior* and *exterior* of an angle. In an angle such as $\angle XYZ$ in Figure 12.5.4, the interior of the angle is the intersection of the set of points on the X side of $\overleftrightarrow{YZ}$ and

FIGURE 12.5.4

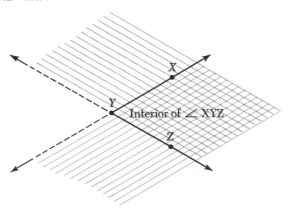

Interior of $\angle XYZ$

the set of points on the Z side of $\overleftrightarrow{YX}$. All other points that are neither in the interior of $\angle XYZ$ nor in $\angle XYZ$ itself are said to be in the exterior of $\angle XYZ$. Points in $\angle XYZ$ itself are neither interior nor exterior points but rather are boundary points between the interior and exterior points.

The method for determining the interior and the exterior of an angle as stated above applies only to angles whose measure is less than that of a straight angle. The concept may easily be extended to include larger angles after the measure of angles has been discussed in Chapter 13.

EXERCISE 12.5

1. Given a line in a plane and two points in the plane distinct from the line, how can you tell whether the two points are on the same or different sides of the line?

2. Sketch briefly a diagram showing:
   (a) a plane Q separated into two half-planes Q_1 and Q_2 by line r.
   (b) two planes P and Q intersecting in line t.
   (c) two parallel planes R and S and a line m intersecting R in point A and S in point B.
   (d) line a parallel to plane P.
   (e) parallel planes V and W with line c in V skew to line d in W.

3. Can two planes be skew? Explain.

4. Complete the following statements:
   (a) Given planes P and Q with $P \parallel Q$, $P \cap Q = ?$
   (b) Given planes P and Q with $P \nparallel Q$, $P \cap Q = ?$
   (c) Given plane P and line m with $P \parallel m$, $P \cap m = ?$
   (d) Given plane P and line m with $P \nparallel m$ and $m \not\subset P$, $P \cap m = ?$
   (e) Given lines m and n in plane R with $m \nparallel n$, $m \cap n = ?$

5. What is an angle?

6. Given $\overrightarrow{BA}$ and $\overrightarrow{BC}$:
   (a) Sketch a diagram showing $\overrightarrow{BA} \cup \overrightarrow{BC} = \angle ABC$.
   (b) Shade in the A side of $\overleftrightarrow{BC}$ and the C side of $\overleftrightarrow{BA}$.
   (c) Label the interior of $\angle ABC$.

7. If $\overrightarrow{YX} \cup \overrightarrow{YZ} = \overleftrightarrow{XZ}$, is $\overrightarrow{YX} \cup \overrightarrow{YZ} = \angle XYZ$? Explain.

12.6
Plane Curves and Regions

A curve is a set of points that may be thought of as a path through space. If a curve is a subset of the points in a plane, it is called a plane curve. In this section our discussion will be limited to plane curves, and the word "curve" will be used to mean "plane curve" just as the word "line" has been used to mean "straight line." It should be realized, however, that not all curves are plane curves.

A curve may be represented by marking a sheet of paper without lifting the pencil from the paper and without retracing portions of the drawing other than single points. This means that lines, line segments, rays, and angles are special kinds of curves. A point may also be considered a special kind of curve. With the exception of a point, all curves have infinitely many points. In Figure 12.6.1, curves are represented by diagrams (1), (2), and (3), while diagrams (4), (5), and (6) represent the union of two or more curves. Diagram (4) represents the union of 5 curves, (5) the union of 2 curves, and (6) the union of 3 curves.

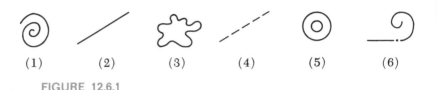

   (1)   (2)   (3)   (4)   (5)   (6)

FIGURE 12.6.1

A curve is said to be simple if it can be "traced" without tracing the same point more than once, with the exception that its endpoints may coincide. In Figure 12.6.2, curves (1), (2), and (3) are simple while curves (4), (5), and (6) are not.

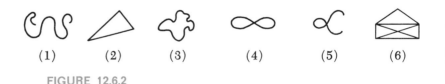

   (1)   (2)   (3)   (4)   (5)   (6)

FIGURE 12.6.2

Closed curves are of particular interest in mathematics and have many applications to the physical world. The representation of a closed curve can be drawn by starting and stopping at any single arbitrary point, and the curve may be retraced without lifting the pencil or changing direction on the curve. Examples of closed curves are shown in Figure 12.6.3. Curves (1), (2), and (3) are *simple closed curves* while (4), (5), and (6) are closed curves that are not simple.

FIGURE 12.6.3

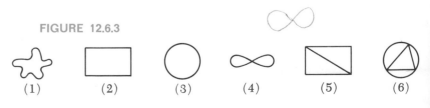

   (1)   (2)   (3)   (4)   (5)   (6)

A simple closed curve partitions a plane into three disjoint subsets: the set of points of the curve itself, the set of points called the *interior* of the curve, and the set of points called the *exterior* of the curve. The simple closed curve is the boundary between its interior and exterior points. In Figure 12.6.4, the interior of the simple closed curve has been shaded. Note that a *simple* closed curve has only one interior.

FIGURE 12.6.4

From Figure 12.6.4 we see that it is impossible for a straight line to lie entirely in the interior of a simple closed curve; however, a straight line may lie entirely in the exterior of such a curve.

The union of a simple closed curve and its interior is a region. (Some authors define a region simply as the interior of a simple closed curve.) In Chapter 13 we shall discuss the measure of the regions of selected simple closed curves, such as triangles, rectangles, trapezoids, and circles. The measure of a region is called the area of the region.

<table>
<tr><td>

12.7

Surfaces and Solids

</td><td>

Although no attempt will be made to define the word *surface,* several examples should help in formulating an intuitive notion of what is meant by a surface. Consider the plane curve *c* shown in Figure 12.7.1 and the line *m* passing through point *A*. Now consider the union of all lines passing through *c* that are parallel to *m*. The union of these lines is a surface. If the plane curve *c* were a straight line, the union of all lines through *c* parallel to *m* would be a plane surface. The outside of any object such as a ball, block, house, automobile, and so on, may be used to represent a surface.

A simple closed surface in space is analogous to a simple closed curve in a plane. A simple closed surface partitions space into three disjoint subsets: the set of points of the surface itself, the set of points called the *interior* of the surface, and the set of points called the *exterior*

</td></tr>
</table>

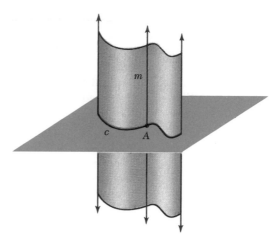

FIGURE 12.7.1

of the surface. The simple closed surface is said to be the boundary between its interior and exterior points. Examples of a few simple closed
surfaces are illustrated in Figure 12.7.2.

Simple Closed Surfaces

FIGURE 12.7.2

    The union of a simple closed surface and its interior, is called a
solid. You are probably familiar with solids determined by cones, spheres,
and pyramids. The measure of a solid is called its volume, and the measure of the surface of a solid is called its area. In Chapter 13 the volumes
and surface areas of certain selected solids will be discussed.

EXERCISE 12.7

    1. Describe briefly what is meant by the word *curve*.
    2. Which one of the following drawings represents a single curve?

(a)   (b)   (c)   (d)   (e)   (f)

3. Which of the following drawings represent simple closed curves?

(a)   (b)   (c)   (d)   (e)   (f)   (g)

4. Draw the figure in problem 3(g) without going over the same line segment more than once.

5. (a) Describe briefly what is meant by a *region* in a plane.
   (b) Sketch the diagrams of three regions.

6. A point on a line may be considered the boundary between two half-lines, and a line in a plane may be considered the boundary between two half-planes. From these statements make an analogy between a plane and space.

7. (a) Describe briefly what is meant by a *simple closed surface*.
   (b) Sketch the diagrams of three simple closed surfaces.

8. Try to formulate some method for distinguishing between the interior and the exterior of a simple closed surface.

9. (a) Why is a thin coat of paint on the outside of an object a good *representation* of a surface?
   (b) Why is it not a surface?

10. (a) What is a *solid*?
    (b) Name three physical objects that might be used to represent solids.

11. A set of points is said to be a *convex set* if, for every pair of points in the set, the line segment determined by the points is a subset of the given set. Using this definition, determine which of the following sets are convex.

   (a) a circular region   (b) a circle
   (c) a triangular region   (d) a spherical solid
   (e) the interior of   (f) the exterior of
       an angle   an angle
   (g) a line segment   (h) a ray
   (i) a square region   (j) the exterior of
                                       a circle

REVIEW EXERCISES

Define or describe briefly your concept of each of the following terms.

1. point	2. line (straight line)	3. plane
4. space	5. line segment	6. open line segment
7. half-line	8. ray	9. half-plane
10. parallel lines	11. skew lines	12. angle
13. vertex of an angle	14. curve	15. closed curve
16. simple closed curve	17. simple closed surface	18. solid

Know what they are (handwritten)

Chapter Thirteen
Metric
Geometry

13.1
Introduction

In Chapter 12, we discussed concepts concerning geometric figures such as line segments, curves, regions, surfaces, and solids. In this chapter we shall develop theory and techniques for the *measurement* of certain of these figures. This topic is called *metric geometry*. The word *metric* is derived from the Greek word for measure. As in the study of nonmetric geometry, the treatment of metric geometry will be essentially intuitive and informal rather than axiomatic.

The set of points constituting a geometric figure is measured by in some way associating the figure with a number. The association of a geometric figure with an appropriate number enables us to make statements such as, "The length of a line segment is 3," or "The area of a rectangle is 16."

A given geometric figure, such as a line segment, a circle, or a cube, is an abstract concept and may be associated with a single number called its measure. Hence the measure of a geometric figure or model is exact. However, when the theory of measurement is applied to a physical object, the measure is approximate. For example, in measuring a child's height with a ruler, the accuracy of the measurement depends upon such variables as the precision of the measuring device, the eyesight of the person doing the measuring, the temperature of the air, and so on.

The word "measure" may be used to refer to a process as well as to an end result. Used as a verb, the word "measure" refers to the process of finding the number associated with a given geometric model or physical object; used as a noun, it denotes the end result, which is a number. For example, we say, "Measure the driveway to find its length," and we also say, "The measure of the driveway in feet is 42."

13.2
The Measure of Line Segments

The *measure* of a line segment may also be called its length. If the integers are associated with points on a line, it is intuitively evident that we can then measure line segments whose lengths are 1, 2, 3, and so on. However, there are many points on the number line that are not associated with any integer, and hence there are many line segments that cannot be measured using only the integers. For example, we cannot measure any line segment whose length is greater than 3 units but less than 4 units. By associating the rational numbers with points on the number line, we can measure many more line segments than we can by using only the integers; however, there are still points on the number line that are not associated with any rational number, and therefore there are still line segments whose lengths cannot be determined. As an example, we cannot measure the hypotenuse of a right triangle whose legs are each 1 unit in length because this line segment cannot be associated with any rational number. However, the set of real numbers, which is the union of the rational numbers and the irrational numbers, can be put in a one-to-one correspondence with *all* points on a line, and by using the real numbers we are able to measure *any* line segment.

If the number a is associated with the point named A on a line and the number b is associated with the point named B, then the measure of the line segment from point A to point B is $|a - b|$. The measure of the line segment from A to B may be written $m(\overline{AB})$ or simply AB. Symbolically, $m(\overline{AB}) = AB = |a - b|$.

Example 1.

$$
\begin{array}{cccccccc}
0 & & 1 & \sqrt{2} & 2 & \frac{5}{2} & 3 & & 4 \\
\bullet & & \bullet & \bullet & \bullet & \bullet & \bullet & & \bullet \\
A & & B & C & D & E & F & & G
\end{array}
$$

Referring to the diagram, statements such as the following may be made concerning the lengths of line segments:

(a) $m(\overline{FB}) = |3 - 1| = |2| = 2.$

(b) $m(\overline{BF}) = |1 - 3| = |^-2| = 2.$

(c) $m(\overline{GA}) = |4 - 0| = |4| = 4.$

(d) $m(\overline{ED}) = |\frac{5}{2} - 2| = |\frac{1}{2}| = \frac{1}{2}.$

(e) $m(\overline{CF}) = |\sqrt{2} - 3| = 3 - \sqrt{2}.$

(f) $m(\overline{FC}) = |3 - \sqrt{2}| = 3 - \sqrt{2}.$

In Example 1 we were primarily concerned with associating a number with a given line segment and did not specifically refer to a unit of measurement. However, we tacitly assumed that $\overline{AB}$ was our unit of measurement and that the segments whose endpoints were 0 and 1, 1 and 2, 2 and 3, and 3 and 4 were exact copies or replicas of $\overline{AB}$. As a consequence, we see that $m(\overline{AB}) = 1$, $m(\overline{AD}) = 2 \cdot m(\overline{AB}) = 2$, $m(\overline{AF}) = 3 \cdot m(\overline{AB}) = 3$, and so on. The unit used in determining the measure of a line segment is arbitrary; however, the notion of comparing a line segment with a unit that is itself a line segment is implicit in the measurement of any line segment.

A measurement consists of two parts: a *measure*, which is a number, and a *unit of measurement*. For example, in the expression "A man is 70 inches tall," the measure is 70 and the unit of measurement is the inch. The measurement "70 inches" tells us that the man's height, which may be thought of as a line segment, has been compared with the "inch" line segment and found to be 70 times as great. It is important to understand that a measure is always a number and that the nature of the unit of measurement is determined by and consistent with the measurement we wish to obtain. That is, the measure of a line segment is found by comparing it with a unit that is a line segment, the measure of a region is found by comparing it with a unit that is a region, and so on.

In applying the theory of measurement to physical objects, we use *standard units of measurement*, such as the inch, foot, and meter, that are widely recognized and employed by many people. Standard units of measurement are essential in specifying the dimensions of windows, floors, automobile tires, shoes, and so on. To assist us in measuring physical objects, we manufacture measuring devices such as rulers, calipers, and micrometers which are calibrated in standard units.

Two commonly used systems of measurement are the *English* system and the *metric* system, which originated in France. Because of the advantages of the metric system, it is gradually becoming more dominant. One of its principal advantages is that its subdivisions are powers of ten; this greatly facilitates computation in our decimal system of notation. Another advantage of the metric system, particularly in scientific endeavors, involves the relationships between the units of measurement for lengths, volumes, weights, forces, and so on.

METRIC AND ENGLISH MEASUREMENTS

Length

Metric Equivalents	*English Equivalents*
1 meter = 1000 millimeters	12 inches = 1 foot
= 100 centimeters	3 feet = 1 yard
= 10 decimeters	5280 feet = 1 mile
= 0.1 dekameter	
= 0.01 hectometer	
= 0.001 kilometer	

Volume

1 liter = 1000 milliliters	2 pints = 1 quart
= 100 centiliters	4 quarts = 1 gallon
= 10 deciliters	1728 cubic inches = 1 cubic foot
= 0.1 dekaliter	27 cubic feet = 1 cubic yard
= 0.01 hectoliter	
= 0.001 kiloliter	

Note: 1 liter = 1000 cubic centimeters. This relates volume to length.

Weight

1 gram = 1000 milligrams	16 ounces = 1 pound
= 100 centigrams	2000 pounds = 1 ton
= 10 decigrams	2240 pounds = 1 long ton
= 0.1 dekagram	
= 0.01 hectogram	
= 0.001 kilogram	

Note: 1 gram = the weight of 1 cubic centimeter of water at its greatest density (4 degrees centigrade).

Approximate Equivalents

Metric–English	*English–Metric*
1 kilometer = 0.62 mile	1 mile = 1.6 kilometers
1 meter = 39.37 inches	1 yard = 0.914 meter
1 centimeter = 0.39 inch	1 inch = 2.54 centimeters
1 liter = 1.057 quarts	1 quart = 0.95 liter
1 kilogram = 2.2 pounds	1 pound = 0.45 kilogram

13.3 Congruence

Congruent geometric figures are essentially exact copies or replicas of each other. Examples of congruent figures are two circles whose diameters have the same measure, two squares whose sides have the same measure, and two line segments that have the same measure. Intuitively, we feel that if two geometric figures are congruent, their pictures should look alike, and that if we could move the points of one figure, they could be made to coincide exactly with the points of the other figure.

In constructing the number line, we stated that the line segments with endpoints 1 and 2, 2 and 3, 3 and 4, and so on, were replicas of the segment with endpoints 0 and 1. Such line segments are congruent. Similarly, the line segment on the number line with endpoints 4 and 6 is congruent to the line segment with endpoints 10 and 12.

DEFINITION 13.3.1

Two line segments are congruent if they have the same measure.

Note in the above definition that it is not necessary to know the measures of line segments to say that they are congruent; it is only necessary to know that their measures or lengths are *equal*.

The symbol used to indicate congruence is $\cong$. If $\overline{AB}$ is congruent to $\overline{CD}$, we may write "$\overline{AB} \cong \overline{CD}$." You will recall that the symbol $\cong$ was used in our study of the rational numbers to indicate an equivalence relation for ordered pairs of integers. Since congruence is reflexive, symmetric, and transitive, it too is an equivalence relation, and it should not seem unreasonable to use the same symbol for both relations. Which relation is being referred to by the symbol $\cong$ should be obvious from the context in which the symbol is used.

The congruence relation for geometric figures is not restricted to line segments. In general, any geometric figure may or may not be congruent to some other geometric figure. However, the following definition for congruent geometric figures depends upon the definition of congruence for line segments.

DEFINITION 13.3.2

Two geometric figures are congruent if and only if there exists a one-to-one correspondence between their points such that the line segment determined by any two points of one figure is congruent to the line segment determined by the corresponding points of the other figure.

Note that the definition of congruence requires more than simply being able to establish a one-to-one correspondence between the points of two figures; it is also necessary that the distance between any two points of one figure be the same as the distance between the corresponding points of the other. It is frequently easy to show a one-to-one

FIGURE 13.3.1

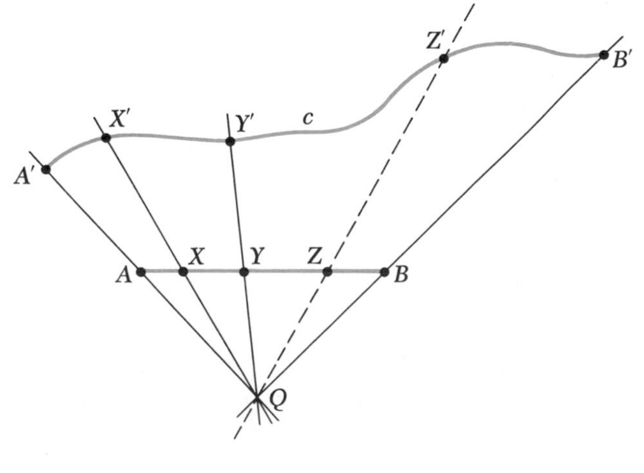

correspondence between the points of two figures even though the figures are not congruent. Consider, for example, the line segment with endpoints A and B and the curve c with endpoints A' and B' represented in Figure 13.3.1. Point Q is the intersection of $\overleftrightarrow{AA'}$ and $\overleftrightarrow{BB'}$. From the diagram it can be seen that A corresponds to A', B to B', X to X', Y to Y', and so on. Any point Z on $\overline{AB}$ will have a unique correspondent Z' on the curve c determined by the intersection of $\overleftrightarrow{QZ}$ with c. Similarly, any point on c will have a unique correspondent on $\overline{AB}$; hence a one-to-one correspondence can be established between the points of the two figures. Such a correspondence, however, does not imply that the two figures are congruent, since it has not been shown that the line segments between corresponding pairs of points in each figure are congruent.

In Figure 13.3.2, the two curves represented are congruent if for all possible correspondences, $\overline{AB} \cong \overline{A'B'}$, $\overline{AC} \cong \overline{A'C'}$, $\overline{CD} \cong \overline{C'D'}$, and so on. There are, of course, infinitely many such correspondences.

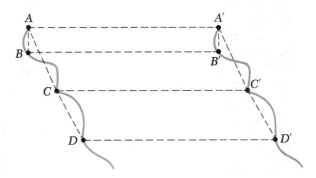

FIGURE 13.3.2

EXERCISE 13.3

1. State briefly the meaning of the term *metric geometry*.

2. (a) If two points on the number line are associated with the numbers a and b, why do we define the distance between the points to be $|a - b|$ rather than simply $a - b$?

   (b) If the distance between two points on the number line were defined to be $a - b$, what relationship would have to exist between a and b?

3. Referring to the diagram, complete statements (a) through (h).

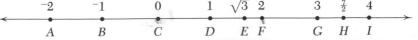

(a) $m(\overline{AD}) = ?$ (b) $m(\overline{AF}) = ?$
(c) $m(\overline{HF}) = ?$ (d) $m(\overline{FH}) = ?$
(e) $m(\overline{GB}) = ?$ (f) $m(\overline{CE}) = ?$
(g) $m(\overline{EH}) = ?$ (h) $m(\overline{HE}) = ?$

4. Why do we need *standard units of measurement*?

5. The following terms are not defined in the text. What is an appropriate definition for each?
   (a) ruler   (b) micrometer
   (c) calipers   (d) planimeter

6. Give an informal explanation of what is meant by congruent geometric figures.

7. Define *congruent line segments*.

8. Define *congruent geometric figures*.

9. (a) Using a diagram, illustrate how the points of two line segments of unequal length may be placed in a one-to-one correspondence.
   (b) Using a diagram, illustrate how the points of a semicircle and a line segment may be placed in a one-to-one correspondence.
   (c) Why are the semicircle and the line segment of part (b) not congruent?

10. Show how the points of two line segments of equal length may be placed in a one-to-one correspondence.

11. Which of the figures below appear to be congruent to the given figure?

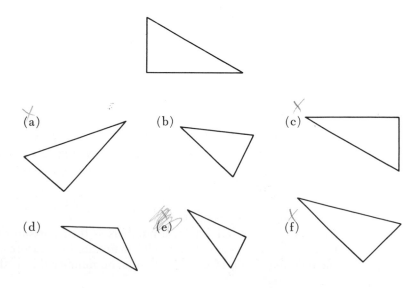

13.4

The Measure of Angles

The measure of an angle is a number, and in order to measure any given angle we must in some way associate the angle with a number. This may be done in a way similar to the way in which a line segment is associated with a number. In measuring a line segment, we compare it with an arbitrary line segment to which we assign the number 1; this arbitrary segment is our unit of measurement. Using the idea of a unit segment and assuming that a one-to-one correspondence can be established between the real numbers and the points on a line, we can associate every line segment with a real number, and hence we can measure any given line segment.

In a similar way, we shall measure an angle by comparing it with an arbitrary angle to which we assign the number 1. This arbitrary angle will be the unit of measurement. For example, let $\angle ABC$ represented in Figure 13.4.1 be a unit of measurement; then $m(\angle ABC) = 1$. If $\angle CBD$ is an "exact copy" of (is congruent to) $\angle ABC$, then $m(\angle ABD) = 2$. If $\angle DBE$ is also congruent to $\angle ABC$, then $m(\angle ABE) = 3$.

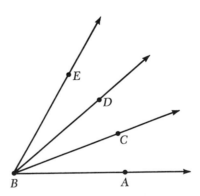

FIGURE 13.4.1

In Figure 13.4.1 we note that $\angle ABC \cap \angle CBD = \overrightarrow{BC}$. Angles such as these which have the same vertex, a common side, and nonintersecting interiors are said to be adjacent. By extending the concept of congruent adjacent angles and by establishing a process for assigning to every angle a unique positive real number, we can measure any angle. Angles are associated with real numbers as their measures in such a way that the preestablished "unit angle" maintains its measure of 1. Changing the unit angle will, of course, change the number that is the measure of any given angle, just as changing the unit line segment will change the measure of any given line segment. In saying that line segments with the same measure are congruent, it is assumed that they were measured using the same unit segment. Similarly, angles with the same measure are congruent if they are measured using the same unit angle.

In elementary mathematics, the unit of measurement most commonly used for angles is the *degree*, which may be indicated by a small circular superscript. Twenty degrees, for example, may be written 20°. A degree is a unit of measurement such that the measurement of a straight angle is 180°. (Recall that an angle is a straight angle if the union of its sides is a straight line.) Although we shall be primarily concerned with angles that measure greater than 0° and less than 180°, the theory of angular measurement may be extended to including angles greater than 180° as well as angles less than 0°.

When the theory of angular measurement is applied to physical objects or to pictorial representations of angles, a measuring device called a *protractor* is often used to find the approximate measurement of an angle. In Figure 13.4.2 the measurement of a 20° angle is illustrated.

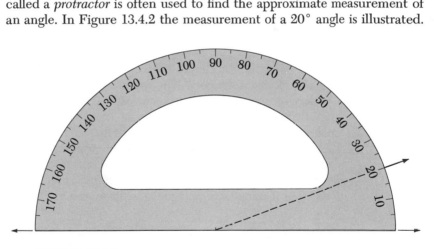

FIGURE 13.4.2

Angles are classified as a matter of convenience. An angle whose measurement is 90° is called a right angle. If two rays form an angle of 90°, the rays are said to be perpendicular to each other; similarly, line segments are said to be perpendicular if the lines they determine intersect to form right angles. An angle whose measurement is between 0° and 90° is called an acute angle, and an angle whose measurement is between 90° and 180° is called an obtuse angle. If the two rays of an angle coincide, its measurement is 0°. In Figure 13.4.3, ∠AOB is an acute angle, $\angle AOC$ is a right angle, $\angle AOD$ is an obtuse angle, and $\angle AOE$ is a straight angle. Also, $\overrightarrow{OC}$ is perpendicular to both $\overrightarrow{OA}$ and $\overrightarrow{OE}$.

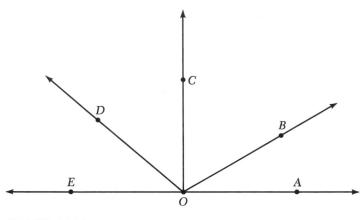

FIGURE 13.4.3

13.5
Polygons and Circles

A polygon is a simple closed curve that is the union of a finite number of line segments. The word "polygon" is derived from two Greek words meaning "many angles." Technically, a polygon has no angles since an angle is the union of two rays; however, each pair of adjacent line segments uniquely determines an angle. Hence we refer to such angles as the angles of a polygon. A polygon with three sides is called a *triangle;* with four, a *quadrilateral;* five, a *pentagon;* six, a *hexagon;* seven, a *heptagon;* eight, an *octagon;* nine, a *nonagon;* and ten, a *decagon.* Examples of polygons are illustrated in Figure 13.5.1.

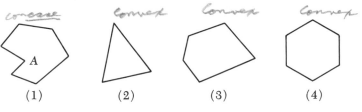

(1)　　　　(2)　　　　(3)　　　　(4)

FIGURE 13.5.1

If each interior angle determined by the line segments of a polygon is less than 180°, the polygon is said to be convex; otherwise the polygon is concave. Polygon (1) of Figure 13.5.1 is concave since the interior $\angle A$ is greater than 180°. All the other polygons illustrated are convex. If all the sides and all the angles of a convex polygon are congruent, the polygon is called a regular polygon. Polygon (4) of Figure 13.5.1 is a regular polygon.

The quadrilateral is one of the most important classifications of simple closed curves. To a large extent, the importance of the quadrilateral results from its many applications to physical objects. Quadrilaterals with certain unique properties are given special names. A *parallelogram* is a quadrilateral with both pairs of opposite sides parallel. (Line segments are said to be parallel if they lie in parallel lines.) A *rhombus* is a parallelogram with all sides congruent. A *rectangle* is a parallelogram with four right angles. A *square* is a rectangle with all sides congruent. If exactly two sides of a quadrilateral are parallel, the figure is called a *trapezoid*. If none of its sides are parallel, a quadrilateral is a *trapezium*. See Figure 13.5.2 for representative quadrilaterals.

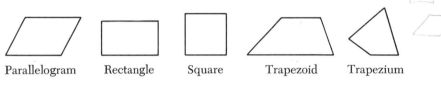

Parallelogram   Rectangle   Square   Trapezoid   Trapezium

FIGURE 13.5.2

Another important classification of simple closed curves is the *circle*. If C is a point in a plane and r is a positive real number, then a circle is the set of all points P in the plane such that $m(\overline{CP}) = r$. C is called the center of the circle and $\overline{CP}$ is a radius. A line segment whose endpoints are points of the circle is a chord, and a chord containing the center of the circle is a diameter of the circle. The measure of the diameter $d = 2r$. In Figure 13.5.3, C is the center of the circle, $\overline{CY}$ and $\overline{CX}$ are radii, $\overline{RS}$ is a chord, and $\overline{XY}$ is a diameter.

FIGURE 13.5.3

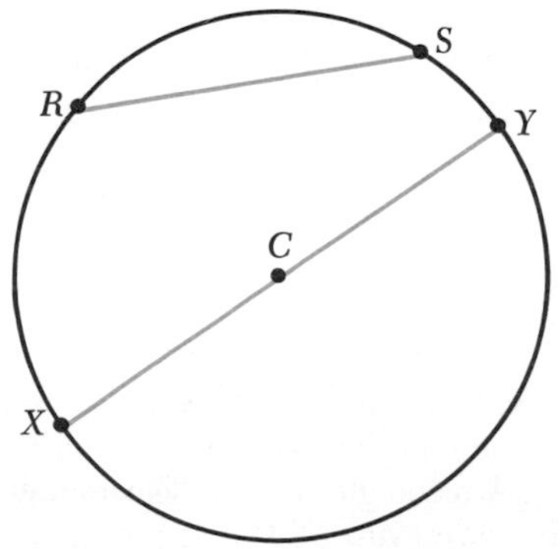

EXERCISE 13.5

1. What are *adjacent angles?*

2. Discuss the term *degree* as it is related to the measurement of angles.

3. Define and illustrate with a diagram each of the following terms.
   (a) acute angle   (b) right angle
   (c) obtuse angle   (d) straight angle

4. (a) If the degree is used as a unit of measurement, what is the measure of a straight angle?
   (b) If a right angle is used as a unit of measurement, what is the measure of a straight angle?
   (c) Discuss the statement: "Angles with different measures may be congruent."

5. What is a *protractor?*

6. (a) What is a *polygon?*
   (b) Tell what is meant by the terms *convex polygon, concave polygon,* and *regular polygon.* Illustrate with diagrams.
   (c) Using a dictionary, determine the derivation of each of the following words: triangle, quadrilateral, pentagon, and hexagon.

7. Define and illustrate with a diagram each of the following terms.
   (a) parallelogram   (b) rectangle
   (c) rhombus   (d) square
   (e) trapezoid   (f) trapezium

8. Apply the definitions of problem 7 and answer each of the following questions by responding "always," "sometimes," or "never."
   (a) Is a square a rectangle?
   (b) Is a square a parallelogram?
   (c) Is a trapezoid a parallelogram?
   (d) Is a rectangle a square?
   (e) Is a rectangle a parallelogram?
   (f) Is a square a rhombus?
   (g) Is a parallelogram a rhombus?

9. Draw a Venn diagram illustrating the relationships among quadrilaterals, parallelograms, rhombuses, rectangles, and squares.

10. Define and illustrate with a diagram each of the following terms.
    (a) circle
    (b) chord
    (c) diameter

11. Comment on the advantages and disadvantages of the following definition of a rectangle as compared with the definition in the text: A rectangle is a parallelogram with one right angle.

13.6

Perimeters of Closed Curves

The measure of a simple closed curve is called its perimeter; it is the "distance around the curve." The word "perimeter" is derived from two Greek words meaning "to measure around."

The perimeter of any polygon is simply the sum of the measures of its sides. For example, if a triangle has sides which measure 8, 10, and 12, then its perimeter is $8 + 10 + 12$, or 30. If the polygon is a regular polygon having n sides each of length s, then its perimeter is $P = ns$.

The perimeters of some simple closed curves are not easily determined. However, we can frequently approximate the perimeter of a curve by finding the perimeter of a polygon that nearly coincides with the path of the given curve. In Figure 13.6.1, for example, the perimeter of the curve is approximately equal to the perimeter of the polygon, which is $7 + 4 + 3 + 6 + 5$, or 25.

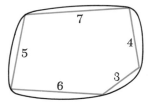

FIGURE 13.6.1

The perimeter of a circle is called its circumference and may be approximated by finding the perimeter of a regular polygon *inscribed* in the circle as shown in Figure 13.6.2. The more sides the polygon has, the closer it comes to following the path of the circle, and the better is its perimeter as an approximation of the circumference of the circle. In a similar way, the circumference of a circle may also be approximated by finding the perimeter of a polygon placed around the outside of the circle; such a polygon is said to be *circumscribed* about the circle.

An interesting property of circles is that the ratio of the circumference of any circle to the measure of its diameter is a constant irrational number which we name π. Since $\dfrac{C}{d} = \pi$, $C = \pi d$, and we may also write $C = 2\pi r$, where r is the measure of the radius of the circle. Since π is an irrational number, its decimal numeral, $3.141592\ldots$, is infinite and nonrepeating. The rational numbers 3.14 and $\frac{22}{7}$ are frequently used as approximations of π.

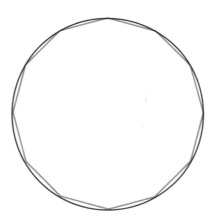

FIGURE 13.6.2

13.7
**Plane Regions
and
Their Measures**

You will recall that in Section 12.6 a *region* was defined as the union of a simple closed curve and its interior. In this section we shall discuss methods for finding the measures of regions that are determined by selected simple closed curves. The measure of a region is a number and will be referred to as the area of the particular simple closed curve that determines the region. For example, we shall speak of the area of a rectangle, the area of a trapezoid, the area of a circle, and so on.

A region can be measured by comparing it with some other arbitrary region to which we assign the number 1; this arbitrary region is, of course, a unit of measurement. It may be helpful to think of "covering" a given region with congruent regions such as triangular regions, hexagonal regions, or square regions. Several arrangements of congruent regions are illustrated in Figure 13.7.1.

From Figure 13.7.1 it is obvious that circular regions would not work very well since they do not "fit together" and part of the region to be measured would be left uncovered. Our choice will be to use a square region as the unit of measurement for area, since congruent square regions do "fit together" and since, as we shall soon see, it is relatively easy to determine how many of them are needed to "cover" a given region. If each side of a square has a measurement of one unit, the region determined by the square is called a *square unit*. If each side of a square measures an inch or a foot, then the square region is called a *square inch* or a *square foot*, and so on.

Note that the unit of measurement for a region is itself a region. This is not unexpected since the unit of measurement for line segments is a unit line segment and the unit of measurement for angles is a unit angle.

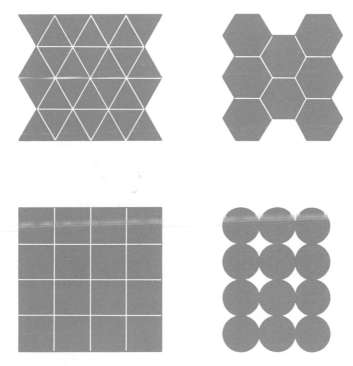

FIGURE 13.7.1

1. Rectangles and Squares

A rectangle having a length of 5 and a width of 3 is shown in Figure 13.7.2. The length and width of the rectangle are, of course, the measures of the sides.

By counting the unit squares it is easy to see that the area of the

FIGURE 13.7.2

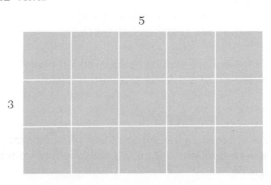

rectangle is 15. Since there are 3 square units in each of 5 columns, we can also see that the area must be 5×3, or 15. Similarly, if the dimensions of a rectangle are $3\frac{1}{2}$ and 6, then there are $3\frac{1}{2}$ square units in each of 6 columns as shown in Figure 13.7.3 and the area is $6 \times 3\frac{1}{2}$, or 21.

6

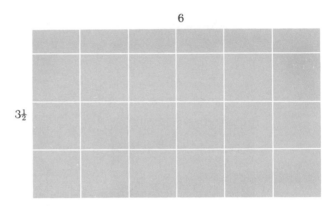

$3\frac{1}{2}$

FIGURE 13.7.3

In general, the area of a rectangle is defined as $A = lw$, where l and w represent the length and width of the rectangle; both the length and width, of course, are measured using the same unit of measurement.

Although the words "length," "width," "perimeter," "area," and so on, refer to measures that are numbers, it is common practice to also use these words to indicate measurements. Hence we could say, for example, that the area of the rectangle in Figure 13.7.3 is 21 square units rather than simply 21. In the remainder of the text we shall use these words to refer to measurements whenever it is convenient to do so.

Example 1.   Find the area of a rectangle with a length of $8\frac{1}{2}$ inches and a width of $6\frac{3}{4}$ inches.

Solution: $A = lw = 8\frac{1}{2} \cdot 6\frac{3}{4} = \frac{17}{2} \cdot \frac{27}{4} = \frac{459}{8} = 57\frac{3}{8}$. Therefore, the area is $57\frac{3}{8}$ square units.

A square may be considered a rectangle where $l = w$. If we denote the length of a side by s, then the area $A = s^2$.

2. *Parallelograms*

Figure 13.7.4 represents a parallelogram. As you will recall, both pairs of opposite sides of a parallelogram are parallel.

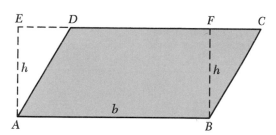

FIGURE 13.7.4

Any side of a parallelogram may be considered to be its base. An altitude of a parallelogram is a perpendicular line segment between the parallel lines in which the base and its opposite side lie. (An altitude of a geometric figure may also be called its *height;* the words altitude and height will be used interchangeably in this text.) In Figure 13.7.4, $\overline{AB}$ is considered the base, and $\overline{BF}$ and $\overline{AE}$ are altitudes since both are perpendicular to the base $\overline{AB}$. The measure of the base is $m(\overline{AB}) = b$, and the measure of the altitude or height is $m(\overline{BF}) = m(\overline{AE}) = h$.

For those who have studied geometry, it should be easy to prove that $\triangle BCF \cong \triangle ADE$; it is certainly intuitively evident that this is true. Since these two triangles are congruent, it can be seen that the area of the parallelogram $ABCD$ is the same as the area of the rectangle $ABFE$ which is equal to bh. In a similar way, any parallelogram can be associated with a rectangle of the same area, and we conclude that the area of a parallelogram is $A = bh$, where b and h represent the measures of the base and altitude of the parallelogram.

Example 2.   If the base of a parallelogram measures 9.8 feet and its altitude measures 6.2 feet, what is its area?

Solution: $A = bh = 9.8 \times 6.2 = 60.76$. Therefore, the area is 60.76 square feet.

3. Triangles

The area of a triangle will be defined in terms of its base and altitude. Any side of a triangle may be considered to be its base, and the perpendicular line segment from the vertex opposite the base to the line containing the base is the corresponding altitude. In Figure 13.7.5, several triangles have the measures of their bases and altitudes (or heights) indicated with the letters b and h. In part (2) it is necessary to extend the line segment of the base in order to indicate the altitude, and in part (3) the altitude is identical to one of the sides since the side is perpendicular to the base.

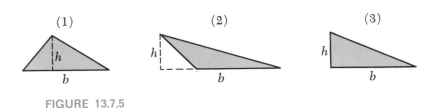

FIGURE 13.7.5

If lines are constructed parallel to two adjacent sides of a given triangle, as shown in Figure 13.7.6, a parallelogram will be formed consisting of two congruent triangles, one of which is the original triangle.

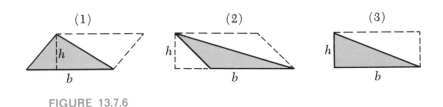

FIGURE 13.7.6

Thus the area of the original triangle will be one-half the area of the parallelogram. Since the area of the parallelogram is bh, we conclude that the area of a triangle is $A = \frac{1}{2}bh$.

Example 3. If the base of a triangle measures 3.4 inches and the altitude measures 2.7 inches, find its area.

Solution: $A = \frac{1}{2}bh = \frac{1}{2}(3.4)(2.7) = 4.59$. Therefore, the area of the triangle is 4.59 square inches.

4. Trapezoids

In discussing the area of a trapezoid, reference is made to Figure 13.7.7. The two parallel sides of a trapezoid are called the bases and their measures are indicated as b and b'. Note that $b' = x + b + y$. An

FIGURE 13.7.7

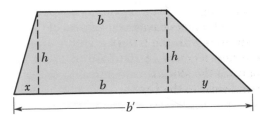

altitude of a trapezoid is a perpendicular line segment between the parallel lines in which the bases lie, and its measure is indicated as h.

The area of the trapezoid is equal to the sum of the areas of the two triangles and the rectangle shown in the figure. You should be able to justify the following statements.

$$A = \tfrac{1}{2}xh + bh + \tfrac{1}{2}yh$$

$$A = \tfrac{1}{2}xh + \frac{2bh}{2} + \tfrac{1}{2}yh$$

$$A = \left(\frac{x + 2b + y}{2}\right)h$$

$$A = \left(\frac{b + (x + b + y)}{2}\right)h$$

$$A = \left(\frac{b + b'}{2}\right)h$$

$$A = \tfrac{1}{2}(b + b')h$$

Stated in words, the area of a trapezoid is equal to the product of three factors: $\tfrac{1}{2}$, the sum of the measures of the bases, and the measure of the altitude.

Example 4. Find the area of a trapezoid with bases measuring 4.3 and 6.5 inches and a height of 3 inches.

Solution:

$$A = \tfrac{1}{2}(b + b')h$$
$$A = \tfrac{1}{2}(4.3 + 6.5)(3) = \tfrac{1}{2}(10.8)(3) = 16.2.$$

Therefore, the area of the trapezoid is 16.2 square inches.

5. *Circles*

By studying Figure 13.7.8, we can easily see that the area of the circle is greater than the area of the inscribed (shaded) square but less than the area of the circumscribed square.

The area of the inscribed square is equal to the sum of the areas of the four indicated triangles or $4(\tfrac{1}{2}r^2) = 2r^2$, where r is the measure of the radius of the circle. The area of the circumscribed square is equal to the sum of the areas of the four indicated smaller squares or $4r^2$. Therefore, we can say that the area A of the circle is such that $2r^2 < A < 4r^2$. Using a procedure similar to the one referred to below and applying

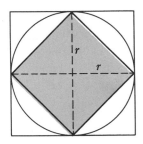

FIGURE 13.7.8

more advanced mathematical techniques, it can be shown that the area of any circle is slightly greater than $3r^2$; in fact, $A = \pi r^2$. Since the circumference of a circle is equal to πd or $2\pi r$, it should not come as a surprise to find that the area of a circle involves the number π.

It was mentioned in Section 13.6 that a good approximation of the circumference of a circle could be found by finding the perimeter of an inscribed or circumscribed regular polygon. Similarly, the area of a circle may be approximated by finding the area of such a polygon; the greater the number of sides of the polygon, the better is the approximation of the area of the circle. The area of an inscribed or circumscribed polygon may be found by subdividing it into triangles as shown in Figure 13.7.9 and finding the sum of the areas of the triangles.

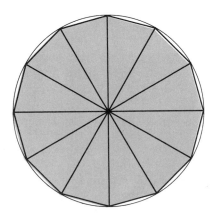

FIGURE 13.7.9

Example 5. Using 3.14 to approximate π, find the approximate area of a circle whose radius measures 5 inches.

Solution:

$$A = \pi r^2$$
$$A \approx 3.14(5)^2 - 3.14(25) = 78.5.$$

Therefore, the area of the circle is approximately 78.5 square inches.

6. *Summary of Formulas for Areas and Perimeters*

(a) Rectangle
$$A = lw$$
$$P = 2l + 2w = 2(l + w)$$

(b) Square
$$A = s^2$$
$$P = 4s$$

(c) Parallelogram
$$A = bh$$

(d) Triangle
$$A = \tfrac{1}{2}bh$$

(e) Trapezoid
$$A = \tfrac{1}{2}(b + b')h$$

(f) Circle
$$A = \pi r^2$$
$$C = 2\pi r \text{ or } \pi d$$

EXERCISE 13.7

1. (a) Define *perimeter*.
   (b) What is the perimeter of a regular pentagon if a side measures 4.3 inches?

2. (a) Define *circumference*.
   (b) What is the formula for the circumference of a circle?
   (c) Using 3.14 to approximate the number π, find the approximate circumference of a circle whose radius measures 15 inches.

3. The number π is approximately equal to 3.141592.
   (a) What is the repeating decimal for $\tfrac{22}{7}$?
   (b) How does the repeating decimal for $\tfrac{22}{7}$ rounded to four digits compare with 3.141592 rounded to 4 digits?

4. (a) What is a plane region?
   (b) What is meant by the term "area"?
   (c) Why is a square region better than a circular region as a unit of measurement for the areas of other plane regions?

5. Find the perimeter and area of a rectangle with a length of 4.6 meters and a width of 3.2 meters.

6. (a) Find the length of the side of a square if its perimeter is 24.8 inches.
   (b) What is the area of the square?

7. If a triangle has a base measuring 6 feet and a height measuring 18 inches:
   (a) What is its area measured in square inches?
   (b) What is its area measured in square feet?

8. Find the area of a trapezoid with bases of 6 and 8 units and a height of 4.2 units. Sketch the figure.

9. Compute the approximate circumference and area of a circle whose diameter measures 8 centimeters. Use 3.14 as an approximation of π.

10. (a) What is the area of a square inscribed in a circle with a radius of 3 feet? Sketch the figure.

    (b) What is the area of a square circumscribed about a circle with a radius of 3 feet? Sketch the figure.

    (c) What is the approximate area of a circle with a radius of 3 feet? Use 3.14 as an approximation of π.

11. (a) Show by a diagram that the area of a rectangle of length 7 and width 5 is $7(3 + 2) = 21 + 14$.

    (b) What property of the whole numbers is exemplified in part (a)?

12. Find the area of each of the figures illustrated below:

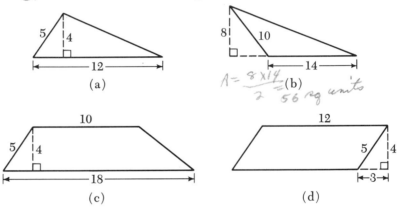

(a)

$A = \dfrac{8 \times 14}{2} = 56$ sq units (b)

(c)   (d)

13. Compute the area of a triangle with a base of 16 inches and a height of 3 feet. Sketch the figure.

13.8
Volumes and Surface Areas of Solids

In Chapter 12 a *solid* was defined as the union of a simple closed surface and its interior. The measure of a solid will be referred to as the volume of the simple closed surface that determines the solid. The measure of a simple closed surface (not including its interior) is called its surface area. Hence we shall speak of both the volume and the surface area of a cube, pyramid, sphere, and so on.

Our procedure for measuring solids will be similar to the method used in measuring line segments and regions; that is, we shall compare a given solid figure with another solid figure to which we assign the measure of 1. Our choice will be to use a solid figure determined by a cube as a unit of measurement for volume, and since a cube is a particular type of *polyhedron,* we shall give first consideration to polyhedrons.

1. Regular Polyhedrons

A polyhedron is a simple closed surface that is the union of a finite number of polygons and their interiors. Each of the plane regions determined by the polygons is called a face of the polyhedron, and each of the line segments determined by the intersections of the faces is called an edge of the polyhedron.

If the faces of a polyhedron are congruent regular polygonal regions and if the same number of edges intersect at each vertex, the polyhedron is called a regular polyhedron. When regular polyhedrons are classified according to the number of faces, exactly five classes result: the *tetrahedron* (4 faces), *hexahedron* or *cube* (6 faces), *octahedron* (8 faces), *dodecahedron* (12 faces), and *icosahedron* (20 faces). These figures are illustrated in Figure 13.8.1. Note that the faces of the tetrahedron, octahedron, and icosahedron are triangular regions, while the faces of the cube are square regions and the faces of the dodecahedron are pentagonal regions.

Some regular polyhedrons are special cases of more general types of solids. The tetrahedron is a special kind of *pyramid,* and the cube is a special kind of *prism.* The octahedron may be considered to be the union of two pyramids. The volumes and surface areas of these figures may be found by applying the same methods used in finding the volumes

FIGURE 13.8.1

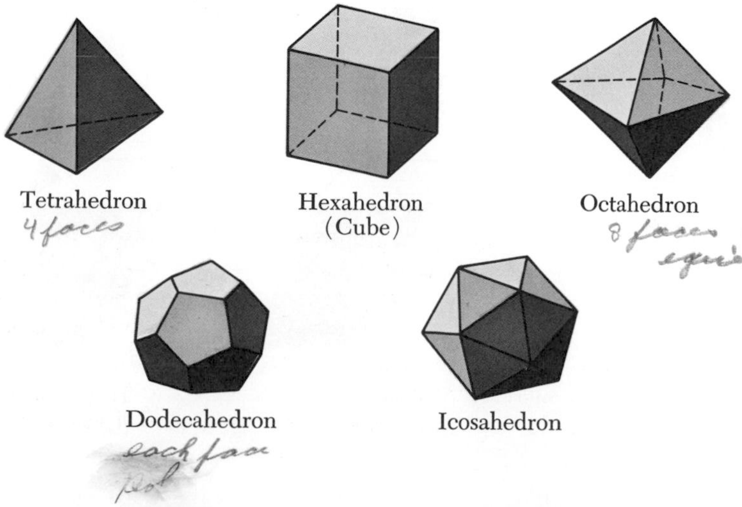

Tetrahedron

Hexahedron
(Cube)

Octahedron

Dodecahedron

Icosahedron

and surface areas of pyramids and prisms. The volumes and surface areas of the dodecahedron and the icosahedron will not be discussed in this text.

The cube (hexahedron) is of particular interest to us since, together with its interior, it is used as the unit of measurement for all solids. If each edge of a cube measures one unit, then the solid determined by the cube is *one cubic unit.* If each edge of a cube measures an inch or a foot, then the solid determined by the cube is one cubic inch or one cubic foot, and so on. We see, therefore, that the unit of measurement for solids is a cubic unit which is itself a solid. Through the use of a cubic unit of measurement, the volumes of various types of solids may be determined.

2. Prisms

A prism is a polyhedron, two faces of which are congruent polygonal regions lying in parallel planes; these two faces are called the bases. All the other faces of a prism are parallelograms and are referred to as the lateral faces. The line segments in which the lateral faces intersect are called the edges of the prism. If the edges are perpendicu-

FIGURE 13.8.2

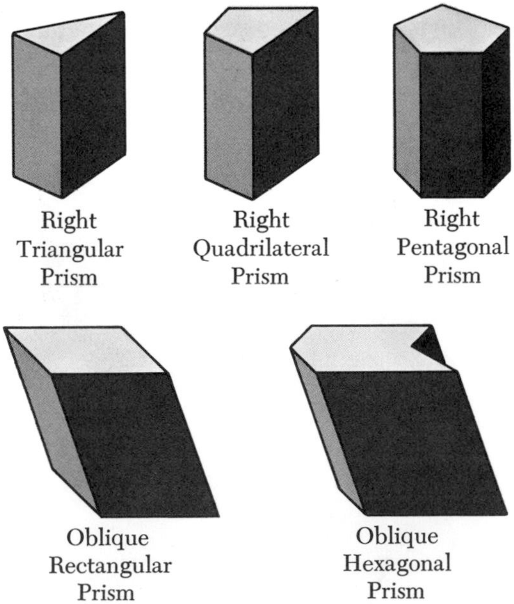

Right Triangular Prism

Right Quadrilateral Prism

Right Pentagonal Prism

Oblique Rectangular Prism

Oblique Hexagonal Prism

lar to the bases, the prism is a right prism; but if the edges are not perpendicular to the bases, the prism is oblique. A few examples of prisms are shown in Figure 13.8.2. Note that a prism may be classified as triangular, quadrilateral, pentagonal, and so on, by referring to its bases.

The surface area of any prism is, of course, equal to the sum of the areas of the bases and the lateral faces. Since any two congruent polygons can determine the bases of a prism, the specific formula for the surface area of a particular prism depends upon the polygons involved.

Before discussing the volume of a prism, it is important to understand what is meant by its altitude. The word altitude is used to name the perpendicular line segment between the parallel planes in which the bases of a prism lie. However, the term *altitude* or *height* may also be used to refer to the *measure* of such a line segment. The context in which the term is used will readily identify the meaning intended. For example, if we say, "$\overline{AB}$ is an altitude of the prism," it is obvious that we are naming a line segment; but if we say, "The altitude of the prism is 6," we are referring to the measure of a line segment. (Similarly, terms such as "side," "diameter," and "radius" are used in two different ways. For example, we may say that $\overline{CB}$ is a radius of a circle, or we may say that 8 is the radius of a circle where $8 = m(\overline{CB})$.) Since care has been taken in previous sections to clarify the distinction between a line segment and its measure, we shall now feel free to follow the common practice of using the same words to refer either to a line segment or to its length. In so doing, sentence structure is frequently simplified with no loss of meaning.

In a right prism the edges are perpendicular to the bases, as shown in diagram (1) of Figure 13.8.3, and the length of each edge is equal to the height of the prism. In an oblique prism, however, the length of each

FIGURE 13.8.3

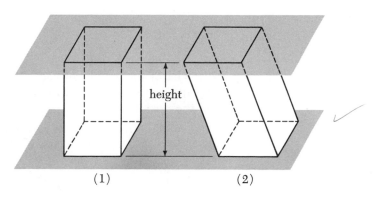

(1)　　　　　　　　(2)

edge is greater than the height of the prism, as shown in diagram (2). Both prisms, of course, have the same height since their bases lie in the same parallel planes.

To demonstrate how a unit cube may be used to determine the volume of a given solid figure, consider a right rectangular prism whose base has a length of 5 units and a width of 3 units. If the height of the prism is 1 unit, it is easy to see from Figure 13.8.4 that 15 cubic units could be used to "fill" the prism. We can also see that if the height of the prism is 2 units, 30 cubic units would fill the prism, and we can imagine that if the height were 3 units, 45 cubic units would be needed to fill the prism, and so on.

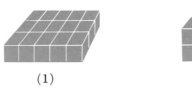

(1)   (2)

FIGURE 13.8.4

In general, the volume of any prism is defined to be $V = Bh$, where B is the area of the base and h is the height. In computing volumes, as in computing areas, it is important that the same unit of measurement be used for each dimension.

Example 1.   Find the volume of each prism indicated in Figure 13.8.4 by using the formula $V = Bh$.

Solution: Since the bases are rectangles, $B = lw$ and $V = Bh = lwh$. Referring to prism (1) we see that $V = lwh = 5(3)(1) = 15$, while in prism (2) we have $V = 5(3)(2) = 30$. Hence the volume of prism (1) is 15 cubic units, and the volume of prism (2) is 30 cubic units.

Example 2.   What is the volume of each prism in Figure 13.8.3 if the bases of both prisms are squares with each side $s = 8$, and if the height of the prisms is $h = 15$?

Solution: The volumes of the prisms are equal. In each case $V = Bh = s^2h = (8^2)(15) = 960$. Therefore, each prism has a volume of 960 cubic units.

3. Circular Cylinders

A circular cylinder is a simple closed surface which resembles a prism except that its bases are circular regions. The surface of a circular cylinder excluding the bases is called the lateral surface, and the length of a perpendicular line segment between the parallel planes in which the bases lie is called the height. The general formula for the volume of a prism also holds for the volume of a circular cylinder: $V = Bh$. In a circular cylinder, however, the bases are congruent circular regions, and the area of a base is $B = \pi r^2$. Therefore, we can write the formula for the volume of a circular cylinder in the form $V = \pi r^2 h$.

If a line segment joining the centers of the bases of a circular cylinder is perpendicular to the bases, the figure is called a right circular cylinder. The surface area of a right circular cylinder is equal to the sum of the areas of the bases and the lateral surface. The area of the two bases is, of course, $2\pi r^2$ since they are circular regions. By letting a sheet of paper represent the lateral surface of a cylinder, it is easy to see that the area of the lateral surface is equal to the area of a rectangle, as illustrated in Figure 13.8.5.

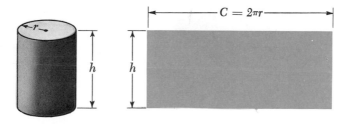

FIGURE 13.8.5

Since the circumference C of the circles that determine the bases is equal to $2\pi r$, we see from the figure that the area of the lateral surface of a cylinder is the product $Ch = 2\pi rh$. The total surface area of a right circular cylinder is, therefore, $S = $ (area of the bases) + (area of the lateral surface), or $S = 2\pi r^2 + 2\pi rh = 2\pi r(r + h)$.

Example 3.   Find the approximate volume and surface area of a right circular cylinder if the radius of the base is 4 and the height is 9. Approximate π as 3.14.

Solution:

$$V = \pi r^2 h = \pi(4^2)(9) = \pi(144) \approx 3.14(144) = 452.16.$$
$$S = 2\pi r^2 + 2\pi rh = 2\pi(4)^2 + 2\pi(4)(9) = 32\pi + 72\pi$$
$$= 104\pi \approx 104(3.14) = 326.56.$$

Therefore, the volume is approximately 452.16 cubic units, and the surface area is approximately 326.56 square units.

4. Pyramids and Circular Cones

A pyramid is a simple closed surface with a polygonal base and with triangular lateral faces having a common vertex. The common vertex of the lateral faces is called the vertex of the pyramid. A circular cone is a simple closed surface which resembles a pyramid except that its base is a circular region. A pyramid and a circular cone are illustrated in Figure 13.8.6.

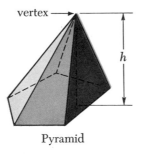
Pyramid

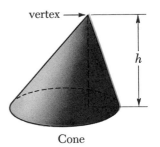
Cone

FIGURE 13.8.6

In both a pyramid and a circular cone, the vertex is joined by a line segment with each point of the simple closed curve which determines the base. The union of these line segments (which excludes the interior of the base) constitutes the lateral surface of the pyramid or cone. The height of a pyramid or cone is defined as the length of the perpendicular line segment from the vertex to the plane in which the base lies.

The volume of both a pyramid and a circular cone may be expressed as $V = \frac{1}{3}Bh$, where B is the area of the base and h is the height. The formula for the area of the base of a pyramid will, of course, depend upon the particular polygonal region involved. Since the base of a circular cone is a circular region, the volume of the cone may be written: $V = \frac{1}{3}Bh = \frac{1}{3}\pi r^2 h$. Note that the volume of a pyramid is equal to $\frac{1}{3}$ of the volume of a corresponding prism, while the volume of a cone is equal to $\frac{1}{3}$ of the volume of a corresponding cylinder.

The surface areas of pyramids and cones will not be discussed in general. However, the *lateral* surface area of a regular pyramid and the *lateral* surface area of a right circular cone will be stated. A regular pyramid is one whose base is determined by a regular polygon and whose vertex is located such that a line segment joining the vertex and the center of the base will be perpendicular to the base. Similarly, a right circular cone is a cone such that a line segment joining the vertex and the center of the base will be perpendicular to the base.

The lateral surface area of a regular pyramid is $S = \frac{1}{2} \times$ (perimeter of the base) $\times$ (slant height). The slant height of a regular pyramid is the height of any of the regular congruent triangles that determine the lateral faces. By studying the formula for the lateral surface area of a regular pyramid, we see that it is simply the sum of the areas of the triangular regions that constitute the lateral surface.

The formula for the lateral surface area of a right circular cone is $S = \pi r \sqrt{r^2 + h^2}$, where r is the radius of the base and h is the height of the cone. Note that πr is $\frac{1}{2} \times$ (perimeter of the base) and that $\sqrt{r^2 + h^2}$ is the slant height. Once again, then, a close relationship is seen to exist between a pyramid and a cone since both have the same general formula for lateral surface area.

Example 4. Find the volume and lateral surface area of the regular pyramid in the diagram.

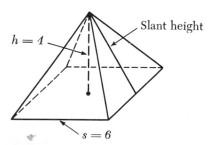

Solution:

$$V = \tfrac{1}{3}Bh = \tfrac{1}{3}s^2h = \tfrac{1}{3}(6^2)(4) = 48.$$
$$S = \tfrac{1}{2} \times \text{(perimeter of the base)} \times \text{(slant height)}$$
$$= \tfrac{1}{2}(24)(5) = 60.$$

Therefore, the volume is 48 cubic units, and the lateral surface area is 60 square units.

Example 5.   Find the approximate volume and lateral surface area of the right circular cone in the diagram.

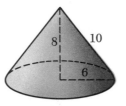

Solution:

$$V = \tfrac{1}{3}Bh = \tfrac{1}{3}\pi r^2 h \approx \tfrac{1}{3}(3.14)(6^2)(8) = 3.14(96) = 301.44.$$
$$S = \pi r\sqrt{r^2 + h^2} \approx 3.14(6)\sqrt{6^2 + 8^2} = 3.14(60) = 188.4.$$

Therefore, the approximate volume is 301.44 cubic units, and the approximate lateral surface area is 188.4 square units.

5. Spheres

Another important classification of simple closed surfaces is the *sphere*. If C is a point in space and r is a positive number, then a sphere is the set of all points P in space such that $m(\overline{PC}) = r$. C is called the center of the sphere and $\overline{PC}$ is a radius. A line segment that contains the center of the sphere and whose endpoints are points of the sphere is called a diameter of the sphere. The measure of a diameter $d = 2r$. In Figure 13.8.7, C is the center of the sphere, $\overline{CY}$ and $\overline{CX}$ are radii, and $\overleftrightarrow{XY}$ is a diameter.

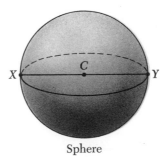

Sphere

FIGURE 13.8.7

Because of the obvious similarities between the circle as a plane figure and the sphere as a solid figure, finding the number π in the formulas for the volume and surface area of a spherical solid should not be unexpected. The formulas are $V = \frac{4}{3}\pi r^3$ and $S = 4\pi r^2$.

6. Summary of Formulas for Volumes and Surface Areas of Solids

(a) Prism

$$V = Bh$$

(b) Circular cylinder

$$V = Bh = \pi r^2 h$$

Right circular cylinder

$$S = 2\pi r^2 + 2\pi rh = 2\pi r(r + h)$$

(c) Pyramid

$$V = \frac{1}{3}Bh$$

Regular pyramid (lateral surface only)

$$S = \frac{1}{2} \times \text{(perimeter of the base)} \times \text{(slant height)}$$

(d) Circular cone

$$V = \frac{1}{3}Bh = \frac{1}{3}\pi r^2 h$$

Right circular cone (lateral surface only)

$$S = \frac{1}{2} \times \text{(perimeter of the base)} \times \text{(slant height)}$$
$$= \pi r\sqrt{r^2 + h^2}$$

(e) Sphere

$$V = \frac{4}{3}\pi r^3$$
$$S = 4\pi r^2$$

EXERCISE 13.8

1. What is the derivation of the word "polyhedron"?
2. Define:
   (a) polyhedron   (b) regular polyhedron
   (c) prism   (d) hexahedron (cube)
   (e) pyramid   (f) circular cone
3. Define:
   (a) volume   (b) unit cube
   (c) surface area   (d) unit square

4. Answer each of the following questions by responding "always," "sometimes," or "never."
   (a) Is a polyhedron a prism?
   (b) Is a pyramid a polyhedron?
   (c) Is a right circular cone a circular cone?
   (d) Is a prism a polyhedron?
   (e) Is a pyramid a regular pyramid?
   (f) Is a sphere a polyhedron?
   (g) Is a right circular cone a right circular cylinder?
   (h) Is a hexahedron a prism?
   (i) Is a hexahedron a polyhedron?
   (j) Is a hexahedron a polygon?
   (k) Is a hexahedron a regular pyramid?

5. Draw a Venn diagram showing the relationship among polyhedrons, prisms, pyramids, regular pyramids, and cubes.

6. Sketch a right rectangular prism that is 6 feet long, 2 feet wide, and 8 feet high. Find the volume and total surface area of the prism.

7. The radius of the base of a right circular cone is 5 inches and the height of the cone is 12 inches.
   (a) Sketch the figure.
   (b) Compute the approximate volume. Use 3.14 to approximate π.
   (c) Using the Pythagorean Theorem, compute the slant height.
   (d) Compute the approximate lateral surface area.
   (e) Compute the approximate total surface area.

8. Sketch a regular pyramid with a square base and find its *total* surface area if each side of the base is 6.4 feet and the slant height is 9 feet.

9. Sketch a right circular cone and find its approximate volume if the radius of the base is $3\frac{1}{2}$ meters and the height is 4 meters. Use $\frac{22}{7}$ to approximate π.

10. Prove that the slant height of a right circular cone is $\sqrt{r^2 + h^2}$ if the radius of the base is r and the height of the cone is h. (*Hint:* Use the Pythagorean Theorem.)

11. Sketch a sphere with a radius of 5 and find its approximate volume and surface area. Use $3\frac{1}{7}$ as an approximation of π.

12. What is the minimum volume of a cube that encloses a sphere whose radius measures r units?

13. If a gallon of paint will cover 250 square feet of surface, how many gallons are needed to paint the entire exterior surface of a cylindrical water tank 12 feet high with a base 20 feet in diameter? Round your answer to the nearest whole number of gallons.

14. How many cubic yards of concrete are needed for a sidewalk that is to be 147 feet long, 4 feet wide, and 4 inches thick?

15. (a) What is the effect on the volume of a cube if the length of each edge is doubled? Is tripled?

(b) What is the effect on the volume of a sphere if the length of the radius is doubled? Is tripled?

(c) What is the effect on the volume of a cone if each of its dimensions is doubled? Is tripled?

(d) What do you believe would be the effect on the volume of any solid figure if each of its dimensions is doubled? Is tripled?

13.9
The Pythagorean Theorem

The Pythagorean Theorem was stated in Section 11.11, and Figure 11.11.1 illustrates by example the relationship between the lengths of the sides of a right triangle and the areas of the squares constructed on the sides. You will recall that in a right triangle the side opposite the right angle is called the *hypotenuse* and the other two sides are called the *legs*. The reader should now review the part of Section 11.11 that concerns the Pythagorean Theorem.

THEOREM 13.9.1

The Pythagorean Theorem. If a triangle is a right triangle, then the square of the measure of the hypotenuse is equal to the sum of the squares of the measures of the legs.

The Greek philosopher and mathematician Pythagoras is usually credited with giving the first general proof for the Pythagorean Theorem in around 525 B.C. (hence its name), but there is evidence that the theorem was well known long before this time. The Chinese referred to the relationships expressed in the theorem in about 1100 B.C., and the Egyptians did so perhaps as early as 2000 B.C.

Although the exact nature of the proof by Pythagoras is not known, many proofs of the Pythagorean Theorem have been presented since his time. It seems likely that Pythagoras' proof was based on the relationship of the areas of three squares rather than simply on a numerical relationship. The proof of the Pythagorean Theorem given below depends upon the concept of area—perhaps it is similar to the proof of Pythagoras.

In Figure 13.9.1 we see a diagram of a large square, a small square, and four congruent right triangles. Each right triangle has legs with *arbitrary* measures of a and b. The object is to show that in any of the right triangles, the square of the measure of the hypotenuse c is equal to the sum of the squares of the measures of the legs, or that $c^2 = a^2 + b^2$.

By expressing the area of the large square in two different ways, we

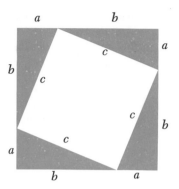

FIGURE 13.9.1

can make the following statements, which lead to the desired conclusion:

$$c^2 + 4(\tfrac{1}{2}ab) = (a + b)^2$$
$$c^2 + 2ab = a^2 + 2ab + b^2$$
$$c^2 = a^2 + b^2$$

The converse of the Pythagorean Theorem is also true; that is, if the square of the measure of one side of a triangle is equal to the sum of the squares of the measures of the other two sides, then the triangle is a right triangle.

13.10
Similar Geometric Figures

The word "similar" is often used in everyday language to mean alike in some way but not necessarily identical. For example, we may say that a boy is similar to his father. In mathematics, *similar* geometric figures may be thought of as having the same "shape" but not necessarily the same "size"; hence similar geometric figures may or may not be congruent. One of the best representations of a pair of similar figures is a photograph and its enlargement. A few examples of pairs of similar geometric figures are shown in Figure 13.10.1.

FIGURE 13.10.1

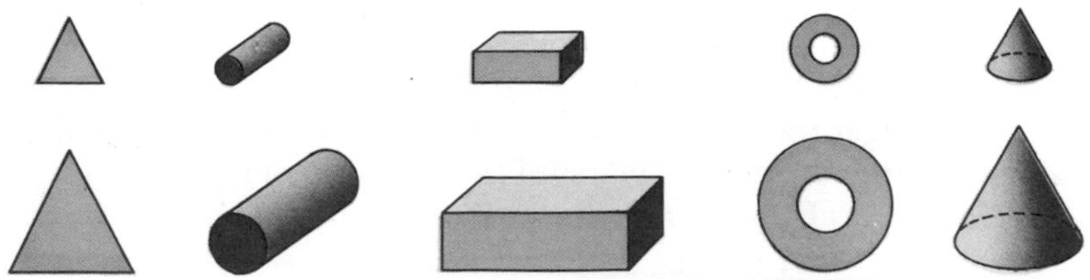

DEFINITION 13.10.1

Two geometric figures are *similar* if and only if there exists a one-to-one correspondence between their points such that the ratio of the length of the line segment between any two points of one figure to the length of the line segment between the corresponding two points of the other figure is constant.

Although Definition 13.10.1 applies to all geometric figures, we shall be concerned in particular with similar triangles and their use in making indirect measurements. For this reason, special attention is given to triangles. The following theorem, which is proved in more advanced texts, has many applications, as is illustrated by the examples.

THEOREM 13.10.1

Two triangles, $\triangle ABC$ and $\triangle A'B'C'$, are *similar* (denoted by $\triangle ABC \sim \triangle A'B'C'$) if and only if their corresponding angles are congruent and their corresponding sides are proportional in length. Symbolically, $\angle A \cong \angle A'$, $\angle B \cong \angle B'$, $\angle C \cong \angle C'$, and $\dfrac{AB}{A'B'} = \dfrac{BC}{B'C'} = \dfrac{CA}{C'A'}$.

(Note that corresponding sides in similar triangles are opposite angles whose measures are equal.)

Example 1. If $\triangle ABC$ and $\triangle ADE$ are similar, what is the height of the tree in the diagram? Measurements are given in feet.

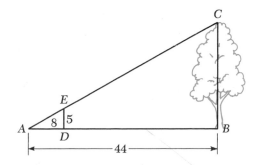

Solution: $\dfrac{AD}{AB} = \dfrac{DE}{BC}$ or $\dfrac{8}{44} = \dfrac{5}{BC}$. Then $8(BC) = 44(5)$, and $BC = \dfrac{44(5)}{8} = \dfrac{220}{8} = 27.5$. Therefore, the height of the tree is 27.5 feet.

Example 2.   A given cone with a height of 14 has a circular base with a radius of 3. If a similar cone has a height of 10, what is the radius of its base?

Solution: Since the figures are similar, the following proportion holds: $\dfrac{14}{10} = \dfrac{3}{r}$. Solving for r, we find that the radius of the base of the second cone is $2\tfrac{4}{7}$ units in length.

EXERCISE 13.10

1. Refer to Figure 13.9.1 and prove the Pythagorean Theorem. You may wish to use more steps in your proof than are given in the text. Justify each step of your proof.

2. Using the figure, prove the Pythagorean Theorem by showing that $a^2 + b^2 = c^2$. (*Hint:* Use the relation $x + a = b$.)

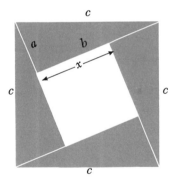

3. If the legs of a right triangle measure 9 units and 12 units, what is the length of the hypotenuse?

4. If the hypotenuse of a right triangle measures 13 feet and one of the legs measures 5 feet, what is the length of the other leg?

5. A right circular cone has a height of 8 inches and a base with a radius of 6 inches. What is the lateral surface area?

6. What is the length of the side of a square inscribed in a circle with a radius of 5 units?

7. (a) Define similar geometric figures.
   (b) How do similar figures compare if the ratio of the lengths of their corresponding line segments is equal to 1?
   (c) Are two congruent figures always similar? Explain.
   (d) Are two similar figures always congruent? Explain.

8. A rectangular photograph is 8 inches long and 6 inches wide. If an enlargement is made to measure 20 inches long, what will be its width?

9. If a 6-foot man casts a shadow 8 feet long and a hotel casts a shadow 171 feet long, how high is the hotel? Assume that the rays of the sun are parallel.

10. In making a 10-inch model of an automobile that is 17 feet long, what should be the diameter of a wheel for the model if a wheel on the automobile has a diameter of 2 feet?

11. A pyramid in Egypt has a square base with a side measuring 220 meters and a height of 70 meters. If a model is to be built using a scale of 1 inch = 20 meters, what should the height and a side of the base of the model measure?

12. In the diagram, $\triangle ABC \sim \triangle ADE$. Using Theorem 13.10.1, find $m(\overline{CE}) = x$.

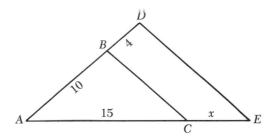

13. In order to find the distance across a river, a surveyor made the following diagram in which $\triangle ABC \sim \triangle ADE$. Using the data from the diagram and Theorem 13.10.1, find the distance across the river.

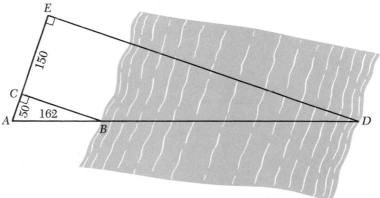

REVIEW EXERCISES

1. Contrast nonmetric geometry with metric geometry.

2. How could Definition 13.3.2 of the text be altered so that Definition 13.3.1 would be unnecessary?

3. What is:
   (a) a unit line segment?   (b) a unit angle?
   (c) a unit square?   (d) a unit cube?

4. (a) The formula for the area of a trapezoid may also be used to find the area of a square, a rectangle, a parallelogram, and a triangle. Explain why this is possible and give an example to illustrate each case.
   (b) In what respect are the formulas for the volumes of a prism and a circular cylinder similar?
   (c) In what respect are the formulas for the volumes of a cone and a pyramid similar?

5. Find the volume of a prism with a height of 8 if the base of the prism is a triangle having a base of 6 and a height of 3.

6. What is the volume of a triangular pyramid if each side of the base is 10 feet and the altitude is 20 feet?

7. What is the volume of a right circular cylinder with base of radius 5 and height of 8 units? Approximate π as 3.14.

8. How many cubic yards of concrete are needed to build a concrete walk 100 feet long, 3 feet wide, and 4 inches thick?

9. (a) What is the effect on the area of a square if the length of each side is doubled? Is tripled?
   (b) What is the effect on the area of a circle if the length of a radius is doubled? Is tripled?

10. (a) What is the effect on the volume of a cube if each of its dimensions is doubled? Is tripled?
    (b) What is the effect on the volume of a cylinder if each of its dimensions is doubled? Is tripled?

11. What is the area of a trapezoid with bases of 9 and 15 feet and a height of 6 feet? Sketch the figure.

12. Compute the approximate circumference of a circle whose diameter is 16 centimeters. Use 3.14 as an approximation of π.

13. Compute the approximate area of a circle whose diameter is 22 feet. Use 3.14 as an approximation of π.

14. Sketch a right circular cone and find its approximate volume if the radius of the base is 4.5 meters and the height is 6 meters. Use 3.14 as an approximation of π.

15. Sketch a regular pyramid with a square base and find its *total* surface area if each side of the base is 7.2 feet and the slant height is 8 feet.

16. Find the approximate lateral surface of a right circular cylinder with a base 6 feet in diameter and a height of 8 feet. Use 3.14 to approximate π.

17. Find the approximate surface area of a sphere with a diameter of 60 feet. Use 3.14 to approximate π.

18. Approximate the volume of a sphere with a radius of 5 feet. Use 3.14 to approximate π.

19. A rectangular photograph is 7 inches long and 5 inches wide. If an enlargement is made to measure 30 inches long, what will be its width?

20. If a 20 foot flagpole casts a shadow 6.5 feet long and a building casts a shadow 75 feet long, how high is the building?

Chapter Fourteen
Statistics
and Probability

14.1

Introduction

As a society becomes more complex, its members tend to collect more and more numerical data on a variety of topics and situations. Almost every facet of our culture has one or more features that are countable or measurable in some way: the weather; births, deaths, marriages, and divorces; television sets produced each year; smoking habits and lung cancer; automobile accidents; bacteria in milk and drinking water; faulty items produced on an assembly line; and so on. Statisticians are concerned not only with collecting and organizing a variety of numerical data, but also with the more difficult and more interesting task of analyzing and interpreting such data.

Predictions or conclusions involving a large number of cases can frequently be made by studying data obtained from a sample. For example, it is possible to predict with some degree of confidence who will win an election by collecting data from a sample of registered voters. The reliability of the prediction will depend upon many factors such as the size of the sample, the method of selecting the elements of the sample, the data drawn from the sample, and the ability of the statistician to analyze and interpret the collected data. A competent statistician can make useful predictions with varying degrees of confidence about such things as the possible success of a new drug if used by human beings, the number of complaints a telephone company will get with four-party lines as compared with three- or two-party lines, how effective a new spray will be in killing insects, who will be the next President of the United States of America, where one should drill for petroleum, the number of automobiles that will be sold next year, and the birth rate in 1984.

From rather modest initial applications in areas such as the social sciences, the field of statistics has grown rapidly in recent years, and its applications to the physical and biological sciences, business, economics, and education are now commonplace. Although it would take an entire text to adequately discuss even the elements of statistics and probability, a few introductory concepts are presented in this chapter. The topics selected are basic and closely related to everyday life as well as preparatory to the study of more advanced topics.

14.2

Organizing Data in Tables and Graphs

Quantitative data may be presented effectively in either *tabular* or *graphical* form. If data are recorded in a table, it is relatively easy to select and read any particular statistic in the table. In Figure 14.2.1 it is easy to see, for example, that 8 cents of every sales dollar of the XYZ Tobacco Company was used to pay income taxes.

DISTRIBUTION OF THE SALES DOLLAR
OF THE XYZ TOBACCO COMPANY

Excise taxes		36¢
Income taxes		8
Selling, administration, interest		10
Dividends		5
Earnings retained		3
Manufacturing costs		38
	Total	100¢

FIGURE 14.2.1

Although it is quite easy to find and read any single number in a statistical table, it is difficult to make comparisons. If, however, the data are presented graphically, as shown in the circle graph (pie graph) of Figure 14.2.2 and the bar graph of Figure 14.2.3, it is much easier to make comparisons because of the visual properties of the graphs. Note that the circle graph may be used to compare each part with the whole as well as to compare each part with every other part; the bar graph is essentially useful in comparing the parts with each other.

In constructing a circle graph as shown in Figure 14.2.2, the measure of the central angle of each sector of the circle must be propor-

FIGURE 14.2.2

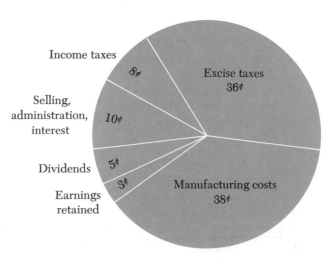

Distribution of the 1969 Sales Dollar
of the XYZ Tobacco Company

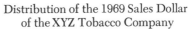

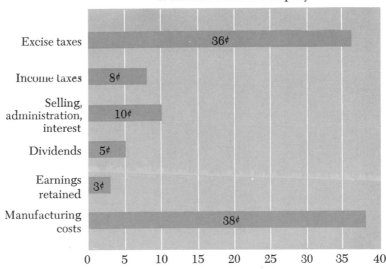

FIGURE 14.2.3

tional to that part of the whole represented by the sector. From the table in Figure 14.2.1, we see, for example, that 8 cents of each 100 cents in sales was used by the XYZ Tobacco Company to pay income taxes; therefore, the central angle of the associated sector of the circle graph must be 8 percent of 360°, or 28.8°. Similarly, 10 cents of each 100 cents was used for selling, administration, and interest; therefore, the central angle of this sector must be 10 percent of 360°, or 36°. The remaining sectors are constructed in the same manner.

Figure 14.2.3 is a *one-scale horizontal bar graph;* like the circle graph, it is used to show the distribution of the sales dollar of the XYZ Tobacco Company for a given year. If we wish to show how the sales of a company vary from year to year, a *two-scale vertical bar graph* may be used. Such a graph is shown in part (a) of Figure 14.2.4. In this graph the horizontal scale is a measure of time, while the vertical scale is a measure of the dollar value of the sales of the ABC Air Conditioning Company. In general, a two-scale graph shows the relation between two variables—in this case, sales and time. Note that the trend in sales is much more evident from the graph than it would be from a table.

Part (b) of Figure 14.2.4 is a two-scale broken-line graph which provides the same information as part (a) of the figure. Broken-line graphs are particularly effective if many closely spaced points are to be plotted.

ABC Air Conditioning Company Sales (in millions)

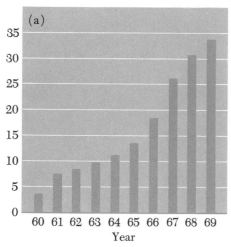
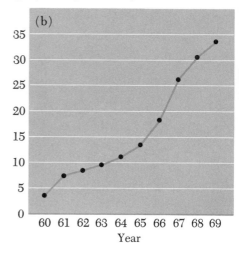

FIGURE 14.2.4

The *composite bar graph* illustrated in Figure 14.2.5 and a circle graph present information in a similar way. In both, each part may be compared with the whole as well as with every other part. A composite bar graph is probably easier to construct than a circle graph but may be somewhat less artistic.

FIGURE 14.2.5

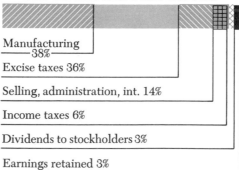

QRS Corporation
How Our 1969 Sales Dollar Was Used

Manufacturing
——38%——
Excise taxes 36%
Selling, administration, int. 14%
Income taxes 6%
Dividends to stockholders 3%
Earnings retained 3%

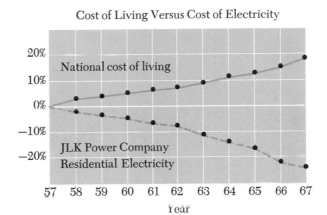

Cost of Living Versus Cost of Electricity

FIGURE 14.2.6

Many variations of tables and graphs may be found other than those illustrated above. Sometimes several types of information may be given simultaneously as shown in Figures 14.2.6, 14.2.7, and 14.2.8.

In general, a graph should be simple and direct. Attention should immediately be focused on the central idea to be conveyed to the reader, and needless details should be omitted. Data should be accurate and presented so that they can be correctly interpreted.

FIGURE 14.2.7

DEF CORPORATION

Employees' length of service	Number of employees	Percent of total
Under 5 Years	141	18
5 to 10 Years	101	13
10 to 15 Years	148	19
15 to 20 Years	137	18
20 to 30 Years	175	23
Over 30	70	9
Total on December 31	772	100

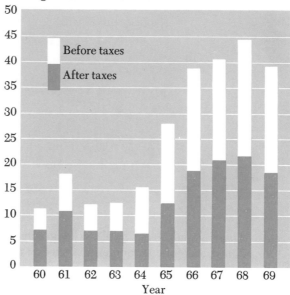

JKL Corporation

Earnings in millions of dollars

FIGURE 14.2.8

EXERCISE 14.2

1. The following table shows the approximate percentage of the earth's land surface in each principal land mass and the approximate percentage of the earth's population inhabiting each of these land masses.

Land Mass	*Area*	Population *(1966)*
Africa	22%	9%
America, North	18	9
America, South	13	5
Asia (excluding U.S.S.R.)	21	56
Europe	4	13
Oceania	6	1
U.S.S.R.	16	7
	100%	100%

(a) Make a circle graph of the area data.
(b) Make a circle graph of the population data.
(c) Make a horizontal bar graph of the area data. (Refer to Figure 14.2.3.)
(d) Make a horizontal bar graph of the population data.

2. The number of color television sets produced in the United States in each of the years from 1960 to 1966 is shown below:

COLOR TELEVISION SETS

Year	*Television Sets* *(in millions)*
1960	0.2
1961	0.4
1962	0.8
1963	1.6
1964	3.0
1965	5.0
1966	9.7

(a) Make a two-scale vertical bar graph of the data. (Refer to part (a) of Figure 14.2.4.)

(b) Make a two-scale broken-line graph of the data. (Refer to part (b) of Figure 14.2.4.)

3. Sources of revenue for the 1967–68 Federal Budget dollar are given below. Make a composite bar graph of the data similar to Figure 14.2.5.

REVENUE FOR THE FEDERAL
BUDGET DOLLAR (1967–68)

Individual income taxes	42¢
Corporation income taxes	20
Employment taxes	17
Excise taxes	8
Other revenues	11
Borrowing	2
Total	100¢

4. Expenditures of the 1967–68 Federal Budget dollar are given below. Make a composite bar graph of the data.

EXPENDITURES OF THE FEDERAL
BUDGET DOLLAR (1967–68)

National Defense	31¢
Social Security, etc.	26
Vietnam	13
Fixed interest charges	6
Veterans' benefits	4
Space	3
International	2
Agriculture	2
Other expenditures	13
Total	100¢

5. (a) In general, what are some of the advantages of presenting data in graphical form rather than in tabular form?
   (b) What advantages may a table of data have as compared with a graph of the data?

6. (a) What appears to be the central purpose of the graphs shown in Figure 14.2.6?
   (b) Why are graphs more effective than tables would be in presenting these data?

14.3
Frequency Distributions

A collection of data is of little value unless it is organized in some way. One useful method of organizing data is to classify them according to some numerical measure of magnitude. Such a classification of data is appropriately called a frequency distribution.

A frequency distribution table showing the number of students making various scores on a given test is shown in Figure 14.3.1. Each class interval indicates a given range of scores. The number of students in each class is called the frequency for that particular class. For example, the frequency for the class in the interval 100–109.9 is 26.

Class Interval	60– 69.9	70– 79.9	80– 89.9	90– 99.9	100– 109.9	110– 119.9	120– 129.9	130– 139.9	140– 149.9
Frequency	3	5	13	24	26	14	4	3	1

Scores on a Test

FIGURE 14.3.1

The size of the class interval in a frequency distribution is arbitrary, but it should be chosen in such a way that it amply displays the characteristic structure involved within a given set of data. Improperly chosen class intervals can be extremely misleading in conveying information. Ordinarily, all class intervals of a distribution are of the same *size* or *width*. Referring again to Figure 14.3.1, note that the test scores have been rounded to the nearest tenth of a unit. Therefore, the class limits are actually 59.95, 69.95, 79.95, and so on, and each class width is 10 units. The class *midpoints* are 64.95, 74.95, 84.95, and so on; however, when we have occasion to use the midpoints of class intervals such as these, we will for computational purposes round them to 65, 75, 85, and so on.

Since there are alternative ways of stating class intervals and limits, the student should study carefully the method being used by any particular author. In the above illustration, for example, we could have used class intervals of 60–70, 70–80, and so on. Using these intervals, the class midpoints would be exactly 65, 75, etc. However, since a score such as 70 is the upper limit of one interval and the lower limit of the next interval, it would be necessary to arbitrarily agree that only one of the limits belongs to each interval—either the lower limit or the upper limit.

A frequency distribution may be presented in a graphical form known as a histogram as well as in tabular form. The statistical data in the table of Figure 14.3.1 are also presented in the histogram of Figure 14.3.2. The histogram lends itself readily to the human power of visualization and from this point of view is more appealing than the frequency table.

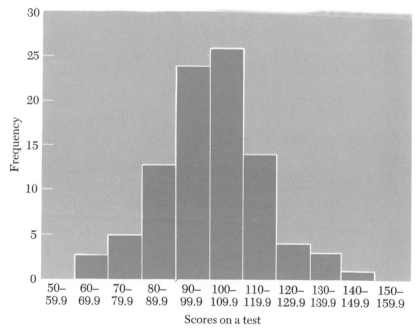

FIGURE 14.3.2

The vertical bars of the histogram are placed adjacent to each other and a scale is used such that they usually have a maximum height of about two-thirds of the base line. Note that the height and area of each vertical bar of the histogram are proportional to the frequency of scores within the particular class interval being considered.

An alternative method of graphically presenting the data shown by a histogram is to use a broken-line graph known for obvious reasons as a frequency polygon. Essentially, a frequency polygon may be constructed

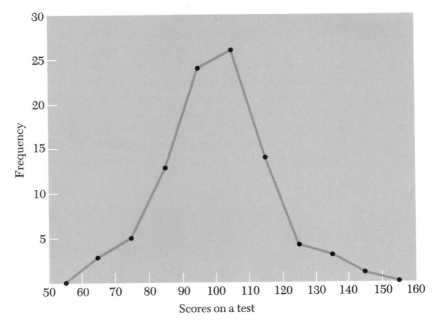

FIGURE 14.3.3

by first placing a dot above the midpoint of each class interval such that its height above the base line corresponds to the frequency for that interval and then joining the appropriate dots with line segments. Figure 14.3.3 is a frequency polygon corresponding to the table of Figure 14.3.1 and the histogram of Figure 14.3.2.

The cumulative frequency corresponding to a given class interval is the sum of the number of cases in that interval and the number of cases in all intervals that are lower on the scale. In Figure 14.3.4, the data in the table of Figure 14.3.1 are repeated, but the cumulative frequency is also shown.

FIGURE 14.3.4

Class Interval	60–69.9	70–79.9	80–89.9	90–99.9	100–109.9	110–119.9	120–129.9	130–139.9	140–149.9
Frequency	3	5	13	24	26	14	4	3	1
Cumulative Frequency	3	8	21	45	71	85	89	92	93

Scores on a Test

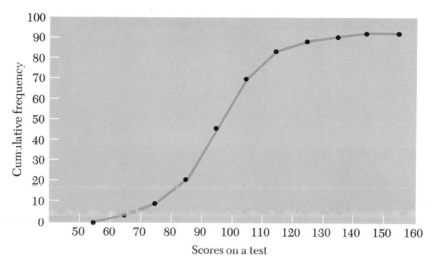

FIGURE 14.3.5

A cumulative frequency graph for the data in the table of Figure 14.3.4 is shown in Figure 14.3.5.

EXERCISE 14.3

1. The table below shows the dollar value and number of orders received on a certain day by one office of a mail-order house.

Value of Orders (in dollars)	Number of Orders
0– 9.99	9
10–19.99	18
20–29.99	29
30–39.99	50
40–49.99	12
50–59.99	3
60–69.99	1

(a) Present the data graphically in a histogram.
(b) What is the midpoint of each class interval?
(c) Construct a frequency polygon for the data.
(d) Construct a cumulative frequency graph of the data.

2. The following table shows the number of divorces in a certain city as related to the number of years of marriage.

Years of Marriage	Number of Divorces
0– 4.9	312
5– 9.9	143
10–14.9	75
15–19.9	36
20–24.9	19
25–29.9	8
30–34.9	5
35–39.9	3
40–44.9	0
45–49.9	1

(a) Present the data graphically in a histogram.
(b) What is the midpoint of each class interval?
(c) Construct a frequency polygon for the data.
(d) Construct a cumulative frequency graph of the data.

14.4 Measures of Central Tendency

A frequency distribution table is a useful and orderly means of arranging data, while the histogram and frequency polygon are aids in visualizing and understanding the data. Various other statistical techniques, such as *measures of central tendency*, are also used to extend our understanding of data. We shall discuss three measures of central tendency: the *arithmetic mean*, the *median*, and the *mode*.

1. The Arithmetic Mean

Nearly every student has computed his test average for a course at some time or other by finding the *arithmetic mean* of a set of numbers. Suppose that a student's test scores are 83, 96, 74, and 91. The arithmetic mean of these numbers is found by dividing the sum of the numbers by the number of addends. The sum of the numbers is 344 and the number of addends is 4; hence the arithmetic mean of the four test scores is $344 \div 4 = 86$, and the student can say that his test average is 86. Although the term *average* is often used to indicate the arithmetic mean, there are other measures of central tendency which are also referred to as averages. For this reason we shall use the more explicit term, arithmetic mean, rather than average.

DEFINITION 14.4.1

The arithmetic mean (denoted by m) of a set of n numbers, $x_1, x_2, \ldots, x_n$, is defined as:

$$m = \frac{x_1 + x_2 + \cdots + x_n}{n}$$

If data are presented in a frequency table, we may have no way of knowing the exact value of each of the measurements. We shall therefore assume that the data of each class are uniformly distributed about the midpoint of the class interval and use the following definition in computing the arithmetic mean from a frequency table.

DEFINITION 14.4.2

In a frequency table with k classes having midpoints of $x_1, x_2, \ldots, x_k$ and respective frequencies of $f_1, f_2, \ldots, f_k$, the arithmetic mean (denoted by m) is defined as:

$$m = \frac{x_1f_1 + x_2f_2 + \cdots + x_kf_k}{f_1 + f_2 + \cdots + f_k}$$

Example 1. Compute the arithmetic mean using the frequency table of examination scores as shown below.

DISTRIBUTION OF EXAMINATION SCORES

Class Interval	40–49.9	50–59.9	60–69.9	70–79.9	80–89.9	90–99.9
Frequency	2	0	5	8	12	6

Solution: The midpoints of each class are 45, 55, 65, and so on. By using Definition 14.4.2, we obtain:

$$\begin{aligned} m &= \frac{x_1f_1 + x_2f_2 + \cdots + x_kf_k}{f_1 + f_2 + \cdots + f_k} \\ &= \frac{45(2) + 55(0) + 65(5) + 75(8) + 85(12) + 95(6)}{2 + 0 + 5 + 8 + 12 + 6} \\ &= \frac{2605}{33} \approx 78.9 \end{aligned}$$

2. The Median

For most sets of numbers the arithmetic mean seems to be the best measure of central tendency. If, however, a set of numbers has one or more extreme measures on one side of the distribution with nothing to balance on the other side, the arithmetic mean can be quite misleading. For example, suppose the net incomes of five members of a family are $5000, $6000, $10,000, $12,000, and $200,000. The arithmetic mean is $(5000 + 6000 + 10,000 + 12,000 + 200,000) \div 5 = 46,600$. If we were to say that the average (mean) income of the members of this family is $46,600, it would be a true statement but definitely misleading without additional information. In a case such as this, the *median* is a better measure of central tendency than the arithmetic mean.

If a set of n numbers is arranged in either ascending or descending order according to magnitude, the median is the middle number if n is odd or the arithmetic mean of the two middle numbers if n is even. In the example above, there are five numbers arranged in ascending order of magnitude, and the middle number 10,000 is the median. Hence we can say that the median income of the members of the family is $10,000, while the mean income is $46,600.

DEFINITION 14.4.3

The median (denoted by m_d) of a set of n numbers, $x_1, x_2, \ldots, x_n$, is defined as:

$$m_d = x_{(n+1)/2} \text{ if } n \text{ is odd}$$

and as

$$m_d = \frac{x_{n/2} + x_{(n/2)+1}}{2} \text{ if } n \text{ is even.}$$

Example 2. The weights (in pounds) of six college girls are: 100, 106, 110, 116, 120, and 150. Find the median weight of the girls.

Solution: Since there are six addends and 6 is an even number, the median is:

$$m_d = \frac{x_{n/2} + x_{(n/2)+1}}{2}$$

$$= \frac{110 + 116}{2} = \frac{226}{2} = 113.$$

Therefore, the median weight is 113 pounds.

In Example 2, the arithmetic mean of the set is 117, which is 4 units larger than the median. We would expect the mean to be larger than the median since the number 150 is considerably larger than the other members of the set with no smaller deviates to compensate. If the number 150 is eliminated from the set, the difference between the mean and the median is small.

If data are tabulated in a frequency distribution, the *median class* may be determined by finding the lowest class for which the cumulative frequency exceeds one-half of the total number of elements in the distribution.

DEFINITION 14.4.4

The median class of a frequency distribution containing n elements is the lowest class for which the cumulative frequency exceeds $\dfrac{n}{2}$.

In the frequency distribution shown in Figure 14.4.1, the total number of elements is $3 + 2 + 19 + 17 + 8 + 2 = 51$. One-half of the number of elements in the distribution is $51 \div 2 = 25.5$. The median class of the distribution is the class in which the age range is 20–20.9. This is true since the cumulative frequency of this class $(3 + 2 + 19 + 17 = 41)$ exceeds 25.5, while the cumulative frequency of the next lower class $(3 + 2 + 19 = 24)$ does not exceed 25.5.

Ages	17–17.9	18–18.9	19–19.9	20–20.9	21–21.9	22–22.9
Frequency	3	2	19	17	8	2

Distribution of Students in a Class by Age

FIGURE 14.4.1

The median for a set of data is always a single number and may be calculated from a frequency distribution. The *median*, of course, falls within the interval of the *median class*. Referring to Figure 14.4.2, we shall compute the median for the data shown in the table.

FIGURE 14.4.2

Scores	Frequency	Cumulative Frequency
90–99.9	5	50
80–89.9	12	45
70–79.9	20	33
60–69.9	7	13
50–59.9	2	6
40–49.9	4	4

Distribution of Test Scores

Since there are a total of 50 scores, the median is the number below which there are 25 scores and above which there are 25 scores. By studying the cumulative frequency column, we see that there are only 13 scores below 70, but there are 33 scores below 80. Therefore, there must be 25 scores below some number within the 70–79.9 interval. Then, since 13 scores fall below 70, we need 12 more scores from the 70–79.9 interval for a total of 25 scores. Let us consider the scores in the interval 70–79.9 to be evenly distributed over the interval. Since there are 20 scores in the 70–79.9 interval, we multiply $\frac{12}{20} \cdot 10$, the size of the interval, and add the product 6 to 70. The sum 76 is the median of the frequency distribution.

3. The Mode

The *mode* is a term seldom used by the layman, but the concept of the mode is rather easy to understand. The mode is the number or measure that occurs most frequently in a given set of data. For example, if more families in a given city have three children than any other number of children, then the modal number of children for the families in the city is 3. If more people in a class are 19 years old than any other age, then 19 is the modal age for the class.

DEFINITION 14.4.5

The mode of a set of data is that number or measure which occurs most frequently.

If data are tabulated in classes, then the class with the most elements is called the *modal class*.

DEFINITION 14.4.6

The modal class of a frequency distribution is that class having the greatest frequency.

Since there may be more than one measure or class of measures with equal maximum frequencies, there may be more than one mode or more than one modal class in a distribution. Also, the modal class or classes may be influenced by the way that the class intervals are chosen.

EXERCISE 14.4

1. The weights of a class of college men are given in the following frequency distribution:

WEIGHTS OF A CLASS OF COLLEGE MEN

Weight (in pounds)	Frequency
100–109.9	0
110–119.9	1
120–129.9	2
130–139.9	4
140–149.9	7
150–159.9	10
160–169.9	11
170–179.9	5
180–189.9	4
190–199.9	2
200–209.9	0

(a) Present the data graphically in a histogram.

(b) Construct a frequency polygon for the data.

(c) Construct a cumulative frequency graph of the data.

(d) Assume the data of each class to be evenly distributed about the midpoint of each class interval and compute the arithmetic mean.

(e) What is the median class of the frequency distribution?

(f) What is the median of the distribution?

(g) What is the modal class of the frequency distribution?

(h) Why is it impossible to find the mode of the frequency distribution?

2. Can a frequency distribution have more than one modal class? Explain.

3. A set of test scores for a class of students is as follows: 74, 61, 67, 66, 79, 87, 97, 81, 88, 51, 73, 90, 82, 60, 72, 84, 80, 83, 76, 88, 91, 64, 73, 77, 94, 77, 56, 63, 95, 77, 68, 95, 75, 87, 71, 77, 81, 90, 75.

(a) Rearrange the scores in ascending order of magnitude.

(b) What is the arithmetic mean of the distribution?

(c) What is the median of the distribution?

(d) What is the mode of the distribution?

(e) Construct a frequency distribution table with intervals of 10 units each: 50–59.9, 60–69.9, and so on.

(f) Construct a histogram from the table of part (e).

(g) What is the median class of the distribution?

(h) What is the modal class of the distribution?

14.5
Probability

The topics of probability and statistics are closely related and supplement each other in many ways. Applications of probability and statistics to gambling are familiar to a large number of people and have been studied for years. More recently, applications to such diverse fields as physics, biology, economics, psychology, and medicine have proved most rewarding.

The concept of probability can be introduced by referring to relatively simple situations. Suppose, for example, we know that there are 50 black marbles and 50 white marbles in a jar. *Probability* tells us that if we take a sample of 10 marbles, we are likely to get about an equal number of black and white marbles. Suppose, however, that we have a jar containing 100 marbles of unknown color. If we select a sample of 10 marbles from the jar and there are 5 black marbles and 5 white marbles in the sample, *statistical inference* enables us to make a prediction concerning how many of the total of 100 marbles are likely to be black and how many are likely to be white.

Probability is a measure of "chance." Let us consider events with equally likely outcomes. For example, assume that in a deck of 52 well-shuffled cards, each card is equally likely to be selected. What is the chance that if a card is selected, it will be the ace of spades? Since there is only one ace of spades, we have 1 chance out of 52, and we say that the probability of drawing the ace of spades is $\frac{1}{52}$. What is the chance that a card selected at random will be a heart? Since there are 13 hearts, we have 13 chances out of 52; or since $\frac{13}{52} = \frac{1}{4}$, we have 1 chance out of 4, and the probability of selecting a heart is $\frac{13}{52}$ or $\frac{1}{4}$. With this rather informal introduction, let us define the probability of an event.

DEFINITION 14.5.1

If in a given situation there are n equally likely outcomes, and if a of these outcomes correspond to event A, then the probability of A is $\frac{a}{n}$. Symbolically, $P(A) = \frac{a}{n}$.

If $\bar{A}$ corresponds to *not-A*, it follows from Definition 14.5.1 that

$$P(\bar{A}) = \frac{n-a}{n} = 1 - \frac{a}{n} = 1 - P(A).$$

Example 1. If there are 25 names in a hat, 15 girls' names and 10 boys' names, what is the probability that a name drawn at random will be:

(a) a girl's name?

Solution: $P(G) = \frac{15}{25} = \frac{3}{5}$.

(b) a boy's name?

Solution: $P(B) = \frac{10}{25} = \frac{2}{5}$.

(c) not a girl's name?

Solution: $P(\bar{G}) = 1 - P(G) = 1 - \frac{3}{5} = \frac{2}{5}$.

(d) not a boy's name?

Solution: $P(\bar{B}) = 1 - P(B) = 1 - \frac{2}{5} = \frac{3}{5}$.

Example 2.   If an ordinary die is rolled having the numbers 1, 2, 3, 4, 5, and 6 on its faces, what is the probability that:

(a) the number 4 will be face up?

Solution: $P(4) = \frac{1}{6}$.

(b) an even number will be face up?

Solution: $P(\text{even number}) = \frac{3}{6} = \frac{1}{2}$.

(c) a 7 will be face up?

Solution: $P(7) = \frac{0}{6} = 0$.

(d) a number from 1 to 6 will be face up?

Solution: $P(1, 2, 3, 4, 5, \text{ or } 6) = \frac{6}{6} = 1$.

Note that the solutions to parts (c) and (d) of the above example illustrate that the probability of an event that cannot happen is 0, while the probability of an event that is certain to happen is 1.

The term *odds* is frequently used in speaking of probabilities. The relative chance that an event A will occur as compared with $\bar{A}$ (not-A) is expressed as the *odds in favor of A*.

DEFINITION 14.5.2

If in a given situation there are n equally likely outcomes, and if a of these outcomes correspond to event A, then the odds favoring A are:

$$\frac{P(A)}{P(\bar{A})} = \frac{\dfrac{a}{n}}{\dfrac{n-a}{n}} = \frac{a}{n-a}.$$

Example 3.   If there are 25 names in a hat, 15 girls' names and 10 boys' names, what are the odds favoring the random selection of a girl's name?

Solution: Odds favoring a girl's name $= \dfrac{P(G)}{P(\bar{G})} = \dfrac{\frac{15}{25}}{\frac{10}{25}} = \dfrac{15}{10} = \dfrac{3}{2}$.

We say, then, that the odds favoring the selection of a girl's name are 3 to 2. (Similarly, the odds favoring the selection of a boy's name are 2 to 3.)

Example 4.   If a penny is tossed, what are the odds in favor of its landing "heads up"?

Solution: Odds favoring $H = \dfrac{P(H)}{P(\overline{H})} = \dfrac{\frac{1}{2}}{\frac{1}{2}} = \dfrac{1}{1}$. We say, then, that the odds favoring "heads up" are 1 to 1 or that the odds are even.

Although this chapter is too brief to give an extensive insight into the nature and importance of statistics and probability, it is hoped that some students will be inspired to extend their knowledge of these subjects through further reading and study. Mathematics in general, and statistics in particular, has had a great influence in shaping the environment and lives of those living in the world today. This influence will undoubtedly continue.

EXERCISE 14.5

1. Define what is meant by the probability of an event.

2. If there are 3 red marbles, 4 white marbles, and 5 blue marbles in a box, what is the probability of selecting:
   (a) a red marble?
   (b) a white marble?
   (c) a red or blue marble?
   (d) a green marble?
   (e) a red, white, or blue marble?

3. (a) What does it mean to say that the probability that an event will occur is 0?
   (b) What does it mean if the probability of an event's occurring is 1?

4. If an ordinary die is rolled:
   (a) What is the probability that a prime number will be face up?
   (b) What is the probability that a composite number will be face up?
   (c) What are the odds in favor of rolling a prime number?
   (d) What are the odds in favor of rolling a composite number?
   (e) What are the odds that neither a prime nor a composite number will be face up?

REVIEW EXERCISES

Define or describe briefly your concept of each of the following terms.

1. statistics
2. circle graph
3. two-scale vertical bar graph
4. class interval
5. frequency
6. frequency distribution
7. histogram
8. frequency polygon
9. arithmetic mean
10. median
11. mode
12. modal class
13. probability of an event
14. odds favoring an event

Answers

to Selected Exercises

EXERCISE 1.3

1. (a) Difficult (c) Easy; $\{13, 14, 15, \ldots\}$ (e) Difficult
2. (a) $\{a, b, c, d\}$ (c) $\{5\}$ (e) The set of great living men of today is, to some extent at least, a matter of opinion and not easily determined.
3. (a) $\{a, b\}$, $\{b, a\}$ (c) $\{2, 3, 4\}$, $\{2, 4, 3\}$, $\{3, 2, 4\}$, $\{3, 4, 2\}$, $\{4, 2, 3\}$, $\{4, 3, 2\}$
4. (a) A is equal to the set whose elements are 8, 9, and 10. (c) The set of all elements x such that x is equal to a whole number. (e) B is equal to the set of all x such that x is an element of A and x is greater than 8. (g) 5 is not an element of set K.
5. (a) $C = \{5, 10, 15\}$ (c) $7 \notin C$ (e) $\{y \mid y$ is an odd number greater than $7\}$
6. (a) $\{x \mid x$ is an integer greater than 0 and less than $11\}$ (c) $\{x \mid x$ is an even integer greater than 2 and less than $14\}$ (e) $\{x \mid x$ is a letter of the alphabet coming after $r\}$

EXERCISE 1.7

1. (a) If every element of set A is an element of set B and if every element of set B is an element of set A, then set A is *equal* to set B. (c) If every element of set A is also an element of set B, then set A is a *subset* of set B.

2. $A = C = D$
3. (a) Yes (b) No (c) Yes
4. $\varnothing$ is a symbol used to indicate the empty set which contains no elements; $\{\varnothing\}$ indicates a set containing one element, the empty set.
5. The sets indicated in parts (b), (d), (e), (g), (h), and (j) are subsets of the given set; the others are not.
6. The sets indicated in parts (b), (e), (g), and (j) are proper subsets of the given set; the others are not.
7. (a) 4 (c) 2 (e) 0
8. $\{a\}$ indicates a set with a single element a as a member, while the symbol a does not indicate that a is necessarily a member of any set.
9. $A \subset B; B \supset A$

EXERCISE 1.8

1. (a) If every element of set A is also an element of set B, then set A is a *subset* of set B.
2. $3 \times 5 \times 4 = 60$
3. $2^{10} = 1024$
4. $2^6 - 1 = 63$
5. (a) $\{\{a, b, 8\}, \{a, b\}, \{a, 8\}, \{b, 8\}, \{a\}, \{b\}, \{8\}, \varnothing\}$ (c) 7
6. Statements (b), (c), (e), and (f) are true; the others are false.
7. $A = B$
8. (a) Yes. By definition of a proper subset (Definition 1.7.1) $\varnothing \subset A$.
   (c) No. The symbol 0 does not indicate a set and hence 0 cannot be a subset of A.

EXERCISE 2.4

1. If U is the universal set and if A is a subset of U, then the set of all elements of U that are not elements of A is the *complement* of A.
2. (a)   (c)

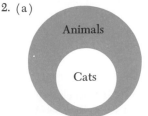

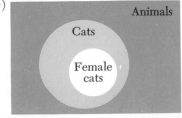

3. The sets indicated in (a), (b), (c), (d), and (f) are subsets of the given set; the others are not.

4. (a) $\{d, e\}$ (c) $\{b, c, d\}$ (e) $\{a, b, c, d, e\}$

5.

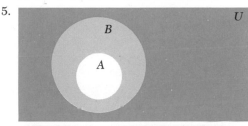

6.

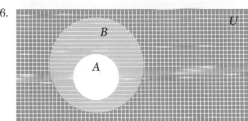

7. (a) C (c) D

EXERCISE 2.7

1. All the states are thought of as being joined to form a single entity. They may be thought of as members of a single set.

2.

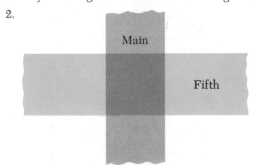

3. (a) a or b means either a or b or both.

4. (a) $\{a, b, c, d, e\}$

5. (a) The *union* of two sets A and B is the set containing all elements that belong to A or B. (c) If the intersection of two sets A and B is the empty set, then the sets are *disjoint*.

6. We mean that the operation is performed on exactly two sets (which may be equal) and, in so doing, a third set is uniquely determined.

7. (a)

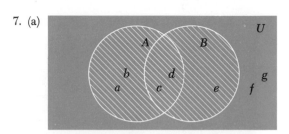

8. (a) $\{a, b, c, d, e\}$ (c) $\{e, f, g\}$ (e) $\{c, d, e, f, g\}$ (g) $\{f, g\}$

9. (a)

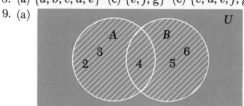

10. (a)

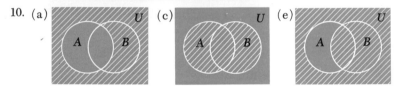

(g)

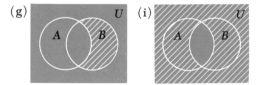

EXERCISE 2.8

1. $\{4, 5\}$
2. $\{2, 3, 4, 5, 6, 7\}$
3. (a) $A \cup B = \{a, b, c\} \cup \{c, d, e, f\} = \{a, b, c, d, e, f\}$
   $B \cup A = \{c, d, e, f\} \cup \{a, b, c\} = \{a, b, c, d, e, f\}$
   $A \cup B = B \cup A$ is verified.
   (c) $A \cap (B \cup C) = \{a, b, c\} \cap (\{c, d, e, f\} \cup \{a, e, f, g\})$
   $= \{a, b, c\} \cap \{a, c, d, e, f, g\}$
   $= \{a, c\}$
   $(A \cap B) \cup (A \cap C) = (\{a, b, c\} \cap \{c, d, e, f\}) \cup (\{a, b, c\} \cap$
   $\{a, e, f, g\})$
   $= \{c\} \cup \{a\}$
   $= \{a, c\}$
   $A \cap (B \cup C) = (A \cap B) \cup (A \cap C)$ is verified.

4. (a) A (c) $\varnothing$ (e) B (g) $\varnothing$

5.

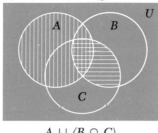

$$A \cup (B \cap C) \qquad\qquad (A \cup B) \cap (A \cup C)$$

Since all shaded regions of the left diagram correspond to the cross-hatched region of the right diagram, $A \cup (B \cap C) = (A \cup B) \cap (A \cup C)$ is verified.

6

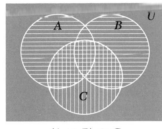 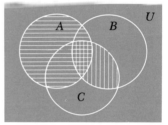

$$(A \cup B) \cap C \qquad\qquad A \cup (B \cap C)$$

Since the crosshatched region of the left diagram does not correspond to all shaded regions of the right diagram, $(A \cup B) \cap C \neq A \cup (B \cap C)$.

EXERCISE 3.2

1. The *Cartesian product* of set A and set B, denoted by $A \times B$, is the set of all ordered pairs (a, b) such that $a \in A$ and $b \in B$.
2. (a) $\{(2, 7), (2, a), (3, 7), (3, a), (4, 7), (4, a)\}$ (c) 6 (e) None or 0
3. (a) $C \times D = \{(4, 5), (4, 6), (4, 7), (5, 5), (5, 6), (5, 7), (6, 5), (6, 6), (6, 7)\}$
   (c) 9 (e) Four: $(5, 5)$, $(5, 6)$, $(6, 5)$, and $(6, 6)$
4. (a) $\{(a, f), (b, f), (c, f)\}$ (c) 3 (e) None or 0
5. (a) 3 (c) $\varnothing$ (e) None or 0
6. (a) $\{7, 8, 9, 10\}$ (c) $\{(8, 7), (8, 8), (8, 9), (8, 10), (9, 7), (9, 8), (9, 9) (9, 10)\}$ (e) $\{(8, 8), (8, 9), (9, 8), (9, 9)\}$
7. $\{(1, 1), (1, 2), (1, 3), (2, 1), (2, 2), (2, 3), (3, 1), (3, 2), (3, 3)\}$
8. (a) $\{(a, a), (a, b), (b, a), (b, b)\}$ (c) $\{(a, a), (a, b), (b, a), (b, b)\}$ (e) Because $A = B$
9. $\varnothing$

EXERCISE 3.5

1. Given two sets A and B, a relation in $A \times B$ is a subset $\mathcal{R}$ of $A \times B$.
2. (a) 12 (c) $2^{12} = 4096$

3. (a) $\{(1, 2), (1, 3), (1, 4), (1, 5), (2, 3), (2, 4), (2, 5)\}$ (c) $\{(2, 1)\}$ (e) $\{(1, 1)\}$
4. (a) $\{1, 2\}$; $\{2, 3, 4, 5\}$ (c) $\{2\}$; $\{1\}$ (e) $\{1\}$; $\{1\}$
5. $A \mathcal{R} A$; $A \mathcal{R} B$; $B \mathcal{R} B$; $C \mathcal{R} B$; $C \mathcal{R} C$; $D \mathcal{R} B$; $D \mathcal{R} C$; $D \mathcal{R} D$
6. (a) $\{(4, 1), (4, 2), (4, 3), (4, 4), (4, 5), (5, 1), (5, 2), (5, 3), (5, 4), (5, 5)\}$
   (c) $\{(4, 5)\}$ (e) $\{(5, 4)\}$
7. (a) $2^{12} = 4096$
8. $\varnothing$

EXERCISE 3.8

1. Given two sets A and B, a relation in $A \times B$ is a subset $\mathcal{R}$ of $A \times B$.
2. If a relation $\mathcal{R}$ is defined in $A \times A$ and if $a \mathcal{R} a$ for every $a \in A$, then $\mathcal{R}$ is *reflexive*.
3. If a relation $\mathcal{R}$ is defined in $A \times A$ and if $a \mathcal{R} b$ implies $b \mathcal{R} a$, then $\mathcal{R}$ is *symmetric*.
4. If a relation $\mathcal{R}$ is defined in $A \times A$ and if $a \mathcal{R} b$ and $b \mathcal{R} c$ imply $a \mathcal{R} c$, then $\mathcal{R}$ is *transitive*.
5. A relation defined in $A \times A$ with the reflexive, symmetric, and transitive properties is an *equivalence relation*.
6.

The relation	R_1	R_2	R_3	R_4	R_5
Reflexive	√		√		
Symmetric	√		√		√
Transitive	√	√	√		
Equivalence relation	√		√		

7. (a) Transitive (c) Reflexive, symmetric, transitive (e) Symmetric
8. (a) $\mathcal{R}_1 = \{(1, 9), (2, 9), (3, 9)\}$ (c) $\mathcal{R}_3 = \{(1, 1)\}$ (e) $\mathcal{R}_5 = \{(1, 1)\}$
9. (a) $\{(1, 2), (1, 3)\}$ (c) $\{(1, 1)\}$
10. $\{2, (1 + 1)\}$; $\{3, (2 + 1), \frac{6}{2}\}$; $\{\frac{1}{2}, \frac{2}{4}\}$; $\{9\}$
11. Examples are: Is less than; Is greater than; Is heavier than.
12. Examples are: Is the mother of; Is the father of; Is the square root of (defined in the whole numbers).

EXERCISE 3.10

1. $\mathcal{R}_1$, $\mathcal{R}_2$, $\mathcal{R}_3$, and $\mathcal{R}_5$ are functions.
2. $\mathcal{R}_1$, $\mathcal{R}_2$, and $\mathcal{R}_3$ are all functions.
3. (a) $\mathcal{R}_1 = \{(1, 3), (2, 6), (4, 12)\}$ (b) $\mathcal{R}_2 = \{(1, 1), (3, 9), (5, 25)\}$ (c) $\mathcal{R}_3 = \{(1, 3), (2, 4), (3, 5), \ldots, (x, x + 2), \ldots\}$

4. (a) $\mathcal{R}_1{}^{-1} = \{(6, 1), (7, 2), (8, 3), (9, 4)\}$; $\mathcal{R}_2{}^{-1} = \{(3, 2), (9, 5), (9, 6)\}$;
   $\mathcal{R}_3{}^{-1} = \{(1, 1), (2, 2), (3, 3), (4, 4)\}$; $\mathcal{R}_4{}^{-1} = \{(9, 1), (10, 1), (3, 2),$
   $(5, 4)\}$; $\mathcal{R}_5{}^{-1} = \{(7, 1), (7, 2), (7, 3), (7, 4)\}$; $\mathcal{R}_6{}^{-1} = \{(7, 8), (6, 8),$
   $(5, 8)\}$

   (b) $\mathcal{R}_1{}^{-1}$, $\mathcal{R}_3{}^{-1}$, $\mathcal{R}_4{}^{-1}$, and $\mathcal{R}_6{}^{-1}$ are functions.

5. (a) $\mathcal{R}_1{}^{-1} = \{(3, 1), (6, 2), (12, 4)\}$; $\mathcal{R}_2{}^{-1} = \{(1, 1), (9, 3), (25, 5)\}$; $\mathcal{R}_3{}^{-1} =$
   $\{(3, 1), (4, 2), (5, 3), \ldots, (x + 2, x), \ldots\}$

   (b) $\mathcal{R}_1{}^{-1}$, $\mathcal{R}_2{}^{-1}$, and $\mathcal{R}_3{}^{-1}$ are all functions.

EXERCISE 3.11

1. (a)$\mathcal{R}_1{}^{-1} = \{(2, 1), (3, 2), (5, 3), (5, 4)\}$ (c) $\mathcal{R}_3{}^{-1} = \{(1, 1), (?, ?), (3, 5)\}$
2. (a)

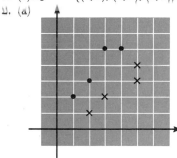

(c)

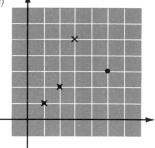

3. (a) $\mathcal{R}_1$, $\mathcal{R}_2$, and $\mathcal{R}_3$
4. $\mathcal{R}$
5. $\{(2, 3), (a, 7)\}$
6. The components of any given element are either equal or for each element (a, b) there is also an element (b, a).
7. The inverse of a given function will also be a function if for each element of the range of the given function there is a unique element in the domain.

EXERCISE 4.3

1. The elements of two sets A and B are said to be in a *one-to-one correspondence* if each member of A is paired with exactly one member of B and if each member of B is paired with exactly one member of A in such a way that the two sets of ordered pairs are inversely related functions.
2. If the elements of two sets A and B can be placed in a one-to-one correspondence, the sets are said to be *equivalent* (or matched).
3. $\{(r, 1), (s, 2), (t, 3), (u, 4)\}$ and $\{(1, r), (2, s), (3, t), (4, u)\}$

4. Two sets are equivalent if their elements may be placed in a one-to-one correspondence, but equal sets must contain exactly the same elements.
5. (a) Yes   (b) Not necessarily
6. (a) A, B, and D (b) A, B, C, D, and E
7. $\{a, b, c, d\}$
    $\updownarrow \updownarrow \updownarrow \updownarrow$
    $\{a, b, c, d\}$
8. $\{a, b, c\}$ $\{d, e, f\}$ $\{a, b, c\}$
  If $\updownarrow \updownarrow \updownarrow$ and $\updownarrow \updownarrow \updownarrow$ then $\updownarrow \updownarrow \updownarrow$
    $\{d, e, f\}$ $\{g, h, i\}$ $\{g, h, i\}$
9. (a) $3 \times 2 \times 1 = 6$

(b) $a\,b\,c$ $a\,b\,c$ $a\,b\,c$ $a\,b\,c$ $a\,b\,c$ $a\,b\,c$
    $\updownarrow\updownarrow\updownarrow$ $\updownarrow\updownarrow\updownarrow$ $\updownarrow\updownarrow\updownarrow$ $\updownarrow\updownarrow\updownarrow$ $\updownarrow\updownarrow\updownarrow$ $\updownarrow\updownarrow\updownarrow$
    $a\,b\,c$ $a\,c\,b$ $b\,a\,c$ $b\,c\,a$ $c\,a\,b$ $c\,b\,a$
10. $5 \times 4 \times 3 \times 2 \times 1 = 120$

EXERCISE 4.6

1. The property that is possessed by all members of a class of equivalent sets is the *cardinal number* of each of the sets.
2. The cardinal number of the given set is found to be 5.
3. (a) $\{1, 2, 3\}$; 3   (c) $\{1, 2, 3, 4, 5\}$; 5   (e) $\{1, 2, 3, 4\}$; 4
4. If the elements of the given set are placed in a one-to-one correspondence with the elements of an initial subset of the natural numbers, the last-named element in the correspondence names the cardinal number of the given set. This process is called counting the elements of the given set.
5. (a) 4   (c) 3   (e) 7   (g) 12
6. (a) 4   (c) 7   (e) 3   (g) 3
7. (a) Natural numbers may have been called natural numbers because they were developed in the course of ordinary events and did not seem artificial.
8. "C if and only if D" is equivalent to two statements: (1) If D, then C, and (2) If C, then D.
9. (a) False. The fact that you are a human being does not imply that you are necessarily a woman. (c) False. The fact that a filled bucket is heavy does not imply that it is necessarily filled with lead.

EXERCISE 4.7

1. See Definition 4.7.1.
2. See Definition 4.7.2.
3. See Definition 4.7.3.

4. See Definition 4.7.4.
5. Yes. The natural numbers may be placed in a one-to-one correspondence with themselves.
6. Yes.
7. No.
8. The fact that a set is infinite does not imply that it is necessarily denumerable.
9. (a) Finite, countable (c) Infinite, denumerable, countable (e) Finite, countable (g) Finite, countable (i) Finite, countable (k) Finite, countable (m) Infinite
10. $\{10, 20, 30, \ldots, (10n), \ldots\}$
$$\updownarrow \ \updownarrow \ \updownarrow \qquad \updownarrow$$
$\{ \ 1, \ \ 2, \ \ 3, \ldots, \ \ n, \ldots\}$
11. $\{3, 6, 9, \ldots, (3n), \ldots\}$
$$\updownarrow \ \updownarrow \ \updownarrow \qquad \updownarrow$$
$\{1, 2, 3, \ldots, \ \ n, \ldots\}$
12. $\{1, 3, 5, \ldots, (2n - 1), \ldots\}$
$$\updownarrow \ \updownarrow \ \updownarrow \qquad \updownarrow$$
$\{1, 2, 3, \ldots, \ \ \ \ n, \ldots \}$
13. (a) $\{4, 8, 12, \ldots, (4n), \ldots\}$
$$\updownarrow \ \updownarrow \ \ \updownarrow \qquad \updownarrow$$
$\{1, 2, \ \ 3, \ldots, \ \ n, \ldots\}$
14. (a) No (c) An example is $\{14, 28, 42, \ldots, (14n), \ldots\}$

EXERCISE 4.10

1. 0 (zero)
2. The cardinal number of the empty set is 0 by definition.
3. $\{0, 1, 2, \ldots, (n - 1), \ldots\}$
$$\updownarrow \ \updownarrow \ \updownarrow \qquad \updownarrow$$
$\{1, 2, 3, \ldots, \ \ \ n, \ldots\}$
4. $\{10, 7, 6, 5, 4, 2\}$
$$\updownarrow \ \updownarrow \ \updownarrow \ \updownarrow \ \updownarrow \ \updownarrow$$
$\{ \ 1, 2, 3, 4, 5, 6\}$
5. $\{2, 4, 5, 6, 7, 10\}$
$$\updownarrow \ \updownarrow \ \updownarrow \ \updownarrow \ \updownarrow \ \updownarrow$$
$\{1, 2, 3, 4, 5, \ 6 \}$
6. The basketball team has 5 players.
   His hand has 5 fingers.
   One nickel equals 5 cents.
7. He was the fifth person to be chosen.
   She sits in the fifth row.
   The fifth letter in the word California is f.

8. My auto license tag number is 13898.
9. (a) 5 (c) ∅
10. (a) 3 (c) 3 (e) 1 (g) 3

EXERCISE 5.3

1. Very likely. It is an extremely simple system and it is easy to invent and use.
2. (a) ∩∩∩∩||| (c) [symbols] ℮℮℮ ∩∩∩ / ℮℮ ∩∩||
   (e) ſſſ ſſſ [symbols] |||| / [symbols] ℮ |||
3. The two numbers are equal.
4. (a) 20,063 (c) 32,347 (e) 100,603
5. (a) [symbols] ∩∩∩||||| [symbols] ℮∩∩ |||| (c) ſſſ [symbols] ℮℮∩∩ ∩∩∩ ||
6. (a) 50,366 (c) 35,254

EXERCISE 5.5

1. (a) ▼▼▼▼ ▼▼▼   (c) ⟨ ▼▼▼ ▼
2. By using commas or some other symbol to separate the units place from the 60's place, the 60's place from the 60^2 place, and so on; by simply leaving a space between groups of symbols to indicate place value.
3. The place value property.
4. (a) 24 (c) 224 (e) 2006 (g) 5280 (i) 30,559
5. (a) CCXLV (c) MLXVI (e) $\overline{\text{CXXIII}}$CDLVI
6. DCXLIX, DCL, DCLI
7. (a) CXI (c) MMMLXIV
8. (a) XLVI
9. By incorporating a place value feature into the system. (Other methods could also be used.)

EXERCISE 5.6

1. Two times.
2. (a) 32 (c) a^6 (e) 9 (g) x^{105} (i) $\frac{1}{9}$
3. (a) 8 (c) $\frac{1}{2}$ (e) 1000
4. (a) 100,000 (c) $\frac{1}{100}$ (e) 4^{12} or 16,777,216
5. (a) 800 (c) $\frac{8}{49}$ (e) $6^5 = 7776$

EXERCISE 5.7

1. Each of the ten basic symbols in our decimal system of notation is called a digit; the digits are: 0, 1, 2, 3, 4, 5, 6, 7, 8, and 9.
2. A *numeral* is a name or symbol for a number.
3. 0, 1, 2, 3, 4, 5, 6, 7, 8, 9
4. Because *decem* is the Latin word for ten and the value of each digit of a numeral is multiplied by some power of ten according to its position in the numeral.
5. The *value* of each digit is determined by its *place* (position) in the numeral.
6. The value of each digit in a numeral is multiplied by some power of ten according to its position in relation to the decimal point.
7. $643.56 = 600 + 40 + 3 + 0.5 + 0.06$
   $= 6(100) + 4(10) + 3(1) + 5(0.1) + 6(0.01)$
   $= 6 \cdot 10^2 + 4 \cdot 10^1 + 3 \cdot 10^0 + 5 \cdot 10^{-1} + 6 \cdot 10^{-2}$
8. (a) $9 \cdot 10^2 + 4 \cdot 10^1 + 3 \cdot 10^0$ (c) $1 \cdot 10^2 + 0 \cdot 10^1 + 5 \cdot 10^0$ (e) $7 \cdot 10^{-3}$
9. (a) 4376 (c) 0.0070809
10. The numeral for zero is used to properly position other digits with reference to the decimal point. Examples are 90.7, 0.0032, and 400.

EXERCISE 5.8

1. (a) 2065 (c) 15.0542 (e) 0.000116
2. Three thousand *and* fourteen ten-thousandths names the number 3000.0014 rather than the given number 0.3014.
3. (a) Five thousand, two hundred eighty.
   (c) Seven million, six thousand, five.
   (e) Sixteen and fifty-four ten-thousandths.
   (g) Five hundred and seventeen thousandths.

EXERCISE 5.9

1. (a) 7.5×10^{10} (c) 6.42×10^5 (e) 7.2×10^{-5} (g) 8×10^{-4}
2. (a) 75,000,000 (c) 0.00000043 (e) 0.00007
3. (a) 8×10^9 (c) 6×10^5

EXERCISE 5.10

1. (a) They are probably referring to the fact that twenty and thirty are multiples of the numeration base of ten.

2.   Set S $n(S)$

$\{[a\ b\ c\ d\ e\ f\ g\ h\ i\ j][k\ l\ m\ n\ o]\}$ 15_{ten}
$\{[a\ b\ c\ d\ e\ f\ g][h\ i\ j\ k\ l\ m\ n]\ o\}$ 21_{seven}

3.   Set S $n(S)$

$\{[a\ b\ c\ d][e\ f\ g\ h][i\quad j\ k\ l]\ m\ n\}$ 32_{four}
$\{[[a\ b\ c][d\ e\ f][g\ h\ i]][j\ k\ l]\ m\ n\}$ 112_{three}

4. (a) Seven (c) k
5. (a) Four sevens and three (c) Three seven-sevens, zero sevens, and four
6. 1, 2, 3, 4, 5, 6, 10, 11, 12, 13, 14, 15, 16, 20, 21
7. In base six we would not have the digit 7.
8. Because 3 is in the units place of each numeral; $3 \cdot (\text{four})^0 = 3 \cdot (\text{five})^0 = 3 \cdot (\text{six})^0$ and so on.
9. (a) 15_{twelve} (c) $11E_{\text{twelve}}$
10. (a) 19 (c) 27 (e) 412
11. (a) 3_{five} (c) 12_{five} (e) 100_{five} (g) 344_{five} (i) 1010_{five}
12. (a) 14_{seven} (c) 131_{seven}

EXERCISE 6.3

1. (a) A plan by which symbols of a given set are used separately or in combination to form numerals is called a *system of numeration*. (b) A *number system* consists of a set of elements called numbers and operations defined for these numbers.
2. *Inductive reasoning* is a method of arriving at a conclusion based on experimentation and observation of what happens in a number of similar cases.
3. In *deductive reasoning* certain basic assumptions are accepted. Assertions are made as implied by the assumptions. When the assertions lead in some logical way to a general principle, we say the principle has been proved and call it a theorem.
4. Inductive reasoning frequently serves as evidence of what might be true.
5. A *theorem* is a general statement which is proved by some method of logic.
6. (a) A proof is a convincing set of arguments establishing the truth of a general principle or statement. (b) The word *proof* is difficult to define because the methods of proof vary widely. (c) A proof is not absolute and all proved statements may be reconsidered.
7. Two numbers a and b are *equal* and we write $a = b$ if and only if a and b are names for the same number.

EXERCISE 6.5

1. See Definition 6.4.2.
2. Because $A \cap B = \{b, c\}$ and $\{b, c\} \neq \emptyset$, so our definition for the sum of two whole numbers was violated.
3. (a) $n(A \cup B) = n(A) + n(B) - n(A \cap B)$ (b) Yes
4. For any two elements a and b in the whole numbers, there exists a unique whole number $a + b$ which we call the sum.
5. *Existence* refers to the fact that there will be a whole number which is the sum of any two given whole numbers; *uniqueness* refers to the fact that there will be exactly one such number.
6. There is a whole number which is their sum, and there is exactly one such number.
7. (a) Yes (b) Yes (c) No (d) Yes

EXERCISE 6.8

1. (a) For any two elements a and b in the whole numbers, $a + b = b + a$.
   (b) $2 + 7 = 9$ and $7 + 2 = 9$; hence, $2 + 7 = 7 + 2$.
2. (a) and (b) Proofs are in Section 6.6.
3. $n(A) = 2$ 1-1 correspondence with a standard set
   $n(B) = 4$ 1-1 correspondence with a standard set
   $A \cap B = \emptyset$ A and B have no common elements
   $2 + 4 = n(A \cup B)$ Def. of add. in W
   $4 + 2 = n(B \cup A)$ Def. of add. in W
   $n(A \cup B) = n(B \cup A)$ $A \cup B = B \cup A$
   $2 + 4 = 4 + 2$ Symm. and trans. prop. of equals
4. For any elements a, b, and c in W, $(a + b) + c = a + (b + c)$.
5. $(6 + 9) + 4 = 15 + 4 = 19$, and $6 + (9 + 4) = 6 + 13 = 19$.
6. There exists a unique number 0 such that for any a in W, $a + 0 = 0 + a = a$.
7. (a) and (b) Proofs are given in Section 6.8.
8. (a) Commutative (c) Commutative (e) Associative and commutative
   (g) Additive identity

EXERCISE 6.10

1. See Definition 6.9.1.
2. See Definition 6.9.2.
3. 8

4. 8
5. $A = \{a, b, c\}$ and $B = \varnothing$ Given

    $n(A) = 3$ 1–1 correspondence with a standard set

    $n(\varnothing) = 0$ By definition

    $3 \times 0 = n(A \times B) = n(\varnothing) = 0$ Definition 6.9.2

    Therefore, $3 \times 0 = 0$.   Trans. prop. of equals

6. For any two elements a and b in W, there exists a unique whole number $a \cdot b$ which we call the product of a and b.
7. (a) Yes   (b) Yes   (c) Yes   (d) Yes   (e) Yes   (f) No
8. $a = 0$, or $b = 0$, or $a = 0$ and $b = 0$.

EXERCISE 6.12

1. For any two elements a and b in W, $a \cdot b = b \cdot a$.
2. $7 \times 35 = 245$ and $35 \times 7 = 245$. Therefore, $7 \times 35 = 35 \times 7$.
3. $A = \{a, b\}$ and $B = \{1, 2, 3\}$ Given

    $2 \cdot 3 = n(A \times B)$ Def. of mult. in W

    $n(A \times B) = n(\{(a, 1), (a, 2), (a, 3),$ Def. of $A \times B$

    $(b, 1), (b, 2), (b, 3)\}) = 6$

    $3 \cdot 2 = n(B \times A)$ Def. of mult. in W

    $n(B \times A) = n(\{(1, a), (1, b), (2, a),$ Def. of $B \times A$

    $(2, b), (3, a), (3, b)\}) = 6$

    $2 \cdot 3 = 3 \cdot 2$ Symm. and trans. prop. of equals

4. For any elements a, b, and c in W, $(a \cdot b) \cdot c = a \cdot (b \cdot c)$.
5. $A = \{a, b\}$, $B = \{k\}$, and   Given

    $C = \{1, 2, 3\}$

    $(2 \cdot 1) \cdot 3 = n[(A \times B) \times C]$ Def. of mult. in W

    $n[(A \times B) \times C] = n[\{(a, k),$ Def. of Cartesian prod.

    $(b, k)\} \times \{1, 2, 3\}] =$

    $n(\{[(a, k), 1], [(a, k), 2], [(a, k), 3],$

    $[(b, k), 1], [(b, k), 2],$

    $[(b, k), 3]\}) = 6$

    $2 \cdot (1 \cdot 3) = n[A \times (B \times C)]$ Def. of mult. in W

    $n[A \times (B \times C)] = n(\{a, b\} \times$ Def. of Cartesian prod.

    $\{(k, 1), (k, 2), (k, 3)\}) =$

    $n([a, (k, 1)], [a, (k, 2)], [a, (k, 3)],$

    $[b, (k, 1)], [b, (k, 2)], [b, (k, 3)])$

    $(2 \cdot 1) \cdot 3 = 2 \cdot (1 \cdot 3)$ Symm. and trans. prop. of equals

6. (a) Comm. prop. of add.   (c) Comm. prop. of mult.   (e) Comm. prop. of mult.   (g) Comm. prop. of add.   (i) Assoc. prop. of add.
7. $2 \times 3 \times 5 \times 4 = (2 \times 3) \times 5 \times 4 = [(2 \times 3) \times 5] \times 4 = [6 \times 5] \times 4 = 30 \times 4 = 120$.

EXERCISE 6.14

1. There exists a unique number 1 in W such that for any a in W, $a \cdot 1 = 1 \cdot a = a$.

2. (a) Proof is given in Section 6.13. (b) Suppose there is another identity element for multiplication, represented by x. Then, $x + 0 = x$ since 0 is an identity element; also, $x + 0 = 0$ since x is an identity element. But if $x = x + 0$ and $x + 0 = 0$, then $x = 0$ by the transitive property of equals. Hence, x is simply another name for 0, and 0 is unique.

3. (a) $6(8 + 3) = 6(11) = 66$, and $6 \cdot 8 + 6 \cdot 3 = 48 + 18 = 66$. Hence, $6(8 + 3) = 6 \cdot 8 + 6 \cdot 3$.

4. $a(b + c) = a \cdot b + a \cdot c$ Given
   $a(b + c) = (b + c)a$ Comm. prop. of mult.
   $(b + c)a = ab + ac$ Symm. and trans. prop. of equals
   $ab + ac = ba + ca$ Comm. prop. of mult.
   $(b + c)a = ba + ca$ Trans. prop. of equals

5. (a) $2(3 + 5) = 2 \cdot 3 + 2 \cdot 5 = 6 + 10 = 16$ (c) $2(30 + 4) = 2 \cdot 30 + 2 \cdot 4 = 60 + 8 = 68$ (e) $(40 + 3)2 = 40 \cdot 2 + 3 \cdot 2 = 80 + 6 = 86$ (g) $3[(4 + 5) + 7] = 3(4 + 5) + 3 \cdot 7 = 3 \cdot 4 + 3 \cdot 5 + 3 \cdot 7 = 12 + 15 + 21 = 48$

6. (a) $7a + 7n$ (c) $a(x + y)$ (e) $k^2(x + y)$ (g) $a(x + y) + az = a[(x + y) + z] = a(x + y + z)$ (i) $a(x + 1)$

7. (a) $7x + 3x = x \cdot 7 + x \cdot 3 = x(7 + 3) = x \cdot 10 = 10x$ (The student should justify each step.)

8. $A \times (B \cup C) = \{d, e\} \times \{f, g, h, i, j, k, l\} = \{(d, f), (d, g), (d, h), (d, i), (d, j), (d, k), (d, l)\}$, and $(A \times B) \cup (A \times C) = \{(d, f), (d, g), (d, h)\} \cup \{(d, i), (d, j), (d, k), (d, l)\} = \{(d, f), (d, g), (d, h), (d, i), (d, j), (d, k), (d, l)\}$. Hence, $A \times (B \cup C) = (A \times B) \cup (A \times C)$ is verified.

EXERCISE 6.15

1. (a) By definition of equals, a and b are names for the same number. This means that the numerals $a \cdot c$ and $b \cdot c$ represent the same product. By the closure property for multiplication in W, the product of any two whole numbers exists and is unique. Therefore, $a \cdot c = b \cdot c$. (c) By definition of equals, a and b name the same number and c and d name the same number. Hence, ac and bd are numerals for the same product. By the closure property for multiplication in W, the product of any two whole numbers exists and is unique. Therefore, $ac = bd$.

2. If a, b, and c are in W and $a + c = b + c$, then $a = b$.

3. If a, b, and c are in W, $c \neq 0$, and $ca = cb$, then $a = b$.

4. $x = 0$
5. $x = 3y + 7 = 3(4) + 7 = 12 + 7 = 19$
6. $x + 3 = 17$
   $x + 3 = 14 + 3$
   $x = 14$
7. The truth of the first statement depends upon the closure property for addition and was proved in Theorem 6.15.3. The second statement depends upon the closure property for multiplication and was proved in problem 1(c) above.
8. $3x + 4 = 52$
   $3x + 4 = 48 + 4$
   $3x = 48$
   $3x = 3(16)$
   $x = 16$
9. $x = 9$
10. 22

EXERCISE 6.16

1. See Definition 6.16.1.
2. (a) $9 - 3 = 6$ (b) $9 - 6 = 3$
3. The diagram is similar to Figure 6.16.1 and the number of elements in A that are not in B is 2. Therefore, $6 - 4 = 2$.
4. Include new numbers in the mathematical system.
5. $8 - 3 = 5$ since $8 = 3 + 5$; but $3 - 8 \neq 5$ since $3 \neq 8 + 5$. Hence, $8 - 3 \neq 3 - 8$.
6. $(8 - 5) - 2 \neq 8 - (5 - 2)$ since $(8 - 5) - 2 = 3 - 2 = 1$, while $8 - (5 - 2) = 8 - 3 = 5$.
7. Example of left distributive property: $3(8 - 2) = 3 \cdot 8 - 3 \cdot 2$ since $3(8 - 2) = 3 \cdot 6 = 18$ and $3 \cdot 8 - 3 \cdot 2 = 24 - 6 = 18$.
   Using the right distributive property: $(8 - 2)3 = 8 \cdot 3 - 2 \cdot 3$ since $(8 - 2)3 = 6 \cdot 3 = 18$ and $8 \cdot 3 - 2 \cdot 3 = 24 - 6 = 18$.

EXERCISE 6.17

1. See Definition 6.17.1.
2. (a) If $a \div 0 = q$, it is necessary by the definition of division that $a = 0 \cdot q$. But $0 \cdot q = 0$ for all values of q. Hence, $a \div 0$ is undefined for all values of $a \neq 0$.
   (c) Under no conditions.
3. "Such that" and "divides."
4. None of the given properties hold.

5. The ordered pairs of (a), (c), (d), (e), (g), and (j).
6. $a \mid a$ since $a = a \cdot 1$ for all a in N. Hence "divides" is *reflexive* in N.

   One counterexample will show that "divides" is *not symmetric* in N. $2 \mid 8$ but $8 \nmid 2$ since $2 \neq 8 \cdot c$ where $c \in W$.

   If $x \mid y$, then $y = xk_1$ and if $y \mid z$, then $z = yk_2$. But $z = yk_2 = (xk_1)k_2 = x(k_1 k_2) = xk_3$ or $z = xk_3$. Hence, $x \mid z$, and divides is *transitive* in N.
7. (a) Yes (b) No
8. $(12 + 16) \div 4 = (12 \div 4) + (16 \div 4)$. There are many other examples.
9. $(16 - 8) \div 2 = (16 \div 2) - (8 \div 2)$. There are many other examples.
10. (a) $12 \div (2 + 4) \neq (12 \div 2) + (12 \div 4)$ since $12 \div (2 + 4) = 12 \div 6 = 2$, while $(12 \div 2) + (12 \div 4) = 6 + 3 = 9$.

EXERCISE 6.18

1. A set S is said to be *closed* under the binary operation $\star$ if, for any two elements a and b in S, there exists a unique element $a \star b$ in S.
2. The binary operation $\odot$ is said to be *commutative* if $a \odot b = b \odot a$ for all a and b in S.
3. (a) For all a, b, and c in W, $a(b + c) = ab + ac$.
4. (a) There exists a number i in W such that for every a in W, $a + i = i + a = a$. (In the system of whole numbers the additive identity element is unique and we name it 0; hence, $a + 0 = 0 + a = a$.)
5. Both
6. (a) Yes (b) 0 (c) A right identity element.

EXERCISE 6.19

1. A number system consists of a set of elements called numbers and operations defined for these numbers.
2. (a) Addition and multiplication
3. See Definition 6.19.1.
4. A *numeration system* is a plan by which symbols of a given set are used separately or in combination to form numerals or names for numbers. A *number system*, however, consists of a set of numbers and operations defined for these numbers. Various numerals may be used for any given set of numbers in a number system.

EXERCISE 6.21

1. See Definition 6.21.1.
2. See Definition 6.21.2.

3. (d, e, a, b, c)
4. (c, b, a, e, d)
5. $(62, 25, 9, 7, 4)$
6. $(49, 7, 65, 43, 192)$
7. (a) Yes   (b) No; 43 and 49 have the same initial digit. Hence we can only partially order the set.
8. (a) $\{0, 1\}$ (c) $\{0, 1, 2, \ldots, 37\}$ (e) $\{0, 1, 2, \ldots, 7\}$
9. $A_1 = \{(3,3), (1,1)\}; A_2 = \{(1,3), (1,7), (4,9)\}; A_3 = \{(4,2), (7,5), (6,2)\}$
10. Only the transitive property holds.
11. 4, 5, 6, and 7.
12. Three solutions: 0, 1, and 2. Two solutions: 1 and 2.
13. (a) There is no largest whole number.
14. See proof of Theorem 6.21.1.
15. See proof of Theorem 6.21.3.
16. All four properties hold.
17. For elements a and b in S, assume that $a \, \mathcal{R} \, b$ implies $b \, \mathcal{R} \, a$. Then, by the transitive property, $a \, \mathcal{R} \, a$. But $a \, \mathcal{R} \, a$ contradicts the assumption that $a \, \mathcal{\not R} \, a$. Therefore, it must be true that if $a \, \mathcal{R} \, b$, then $b \, \mathcal{\not R} \, a$. We see, then, that the irreflexive and transitive properties of an order relation imply the asymmetric property.

EXERCISE 7.2

1. An algorithm is any particular method and symbolism used in performing an operation in mathematics.

2. (a)

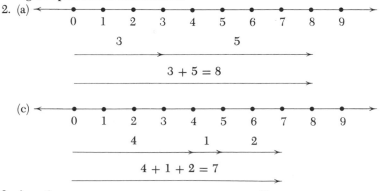

3.

Assertions	Reasons
$152 + 27 = (1 \cdot 10^2 + 5 \cdot 10^1 + 2 \cdot 10^0) + (2 \cdot 10^1 + 7 \cdot 10^0)$	System of numeration
$= 1 \cdot 10^2 + (5 \cdot 10^1 + 2 \cdot 10^1) + (2 \cdot 10^0 + 7 \cdot 10^0)$	Comm. and assoc. prop. of add.
$= 1 \cdot 10^2 + (5 + 2)10^1 + (2 + 7)10^0$	Distributive prop.
$= 1 \cdot 10^2 + 7 \cdot 10^1 + 9 \cdot 10^0$	Table of elem. facts
$= 179$	System of numeration

4. (a) By lining the numerals up on the right, digits with the same place value are in the same column. In this way the application of the distributive property is indirectly achieved. (b) 73,233
5. We may reason as indicated: $a + b + c + d = (a + b) + c + d = [(a + b) + c] + d$. In this way, we see that the binary operation of addition is performed on exactly two numbers at a time, beginning with $a + b$.

EXERCISE 7.3

1. The "take away" interpretation.
2. The "additive" interpretation.
3. Start with a given number of blocks, such as 8. See how many more blocks are needed so that the total is 12. Since 4 more are needed, the difference 12 minus 8 equals 4.
4. Begin with a given number of blocks such as 12. Take 8 from the set and see how many are left. Since 4 will remain, the difference 12 minus 8 equals 4.
5. (a) $5 - 3 = 2$

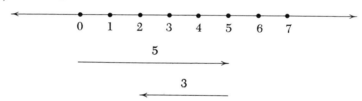

(c) $(8 - 4) - 2 = 4 - 2 = 2$

$8 - 4 = 4$ $\qquad$ $4 - 2 = 2$

(e) $(8 - 6) + 1 = 2 + 1 = 3$

$8 - 6 = 2$ $\qquad$ $2 + 1 = 3$

6. (a) 555 (c) 594,356
7. (a) $(10 - 4) - 3 = 6 - 3 = 3$ and $10 - (4 - 3) = 10 - 1 = 9$
   (b) The associative property does not hold for subtraction.

EXERCISE 7.4

1. (a) It makes it possible to find the product of any two numbers in much less time than would otherwise be possible. (c) Perhaps it was related to the fact that there are 12 inches in a foot, 12 units in a dozen, 12 months in a year, and so on.
2. (a) The new numeral represents the original number multiplied by 10. (c) The new numeral represents the original number multiplied by 10^n.
3. $100 \times 34 = 34 \times 100$ Comm. prop. of mult.
   $\quad\quad\quad = (3 \cdot 10^1 + 4 \cdot 10^0) \times 10^2$ System of numeration
   $\quad\quad\quad = 3 \cdot 10^3 + 4 \cdot 10^2$ Dist. prop.
   $\quad\quad\quad = 3400$ System of numeration
   $100 \times 34 = 3400$ Trans. prop. of equals
4. If we *annex* three zeros to 72 the result is 72,000, but if we *add* three zeros to 72 the result is $72 + 0 + 0 + 0 = 72$.
5. In base eight we would have a product eight times the original number. In base six the resulting product would be six times the original number.
6. The zeros omitted are in partial products which are to be added, and zero is the identity element for addition. Note also that when the zeros are omitted, each of the other digits maintains its proper place value.
7. (a) The product in both cases is 45,073.
8. (a) The product in both cases is 4,883,748. (c) The better choice as a multiplier is 2004 since the second and third partial products may then be omitted.

EXERCISE 7.5

1. (a) See Theorem 7.5.1.
   (b) $93 = 7(13) + 2$, and $0 \leq 2 < 7$.
2. $q = 4$ and $r = 10$.
3. With each of the three methods, $q = 242$ and $r = 23$.
4. (a) $q = 6007$ and $r = 5$ (b) $24(6007) + 5 = 144{,}173$ (c) Leaving out one or both of the zeros in the quotient.
5. $6 = 14(0) + 6$; $q = 0$ and $r = 6$.

EXERCISE 7.7

1. (a) 11 (c) 67 (e) 1378

2.

+	0	1	2	3	4	5	6
0	0	1	2	3	4	5	6
1	1	2	3	4	5	6	10
2	2	3	4	5	6	10	11
3	3	4	5	6	10	11	12
4	4	5	6	10	11	12	13
5	5	6	10	11	12	13	14
6	6	10	11	12	13	14	15

3. (a) 10 (c) 102 (e) 326
4. (a) 2 (c) 125 (e) 1003
5. (a) Three (c) Fourteen (e) Two
6. (a) Four (c) Nine
7. (a) 11 (c) 1011 (e) 110100
8. (a) 9T (c) 740 (e) 1819

EXERCISE 7.8

1.

·	0	1
0	0	0
1	0	1

·	0	1	2	3	4
0	0	0	0	0	0
1	0	1	2	3	4
2	0	2	4	11	13
3	0	3	11	14	22
4	0	4	13	22	31

3. (a) No (c) Although the multiplier 32_{five} is equal to 17_{ten}, the partial products are different because $2_{\text{five}} \neq 7_{\text{ten}}$ and $30_{\text{five}} \neq 10_{\text{ten}}$.
4. (a) 4 (c) 231 (e) 4141
5. (a) Five (c) Three (e) Eight
6. (a) 12 (c) 10 (e) 6 (g) 6

7. (a) 11; Check: $1 \times 3 = 3$. (c) 10110; Check: $2 \times 11 = 22$.
8. (a) The new numeral represents the original number multiplied by ten.
   (c) The new numeral represents the original multiplied by seven.
   (e) $23_{\text{four}} = 11$, $230_{\text{four}} = 44$, and $4 \times 11 = 44$.
9. (a) $q = 23$ and $r = 0$. Check: $3 \times 23 + 0 = 124$. (c) $q = 23$ and $r = 11$. Check: $(12 \times 23) + 11 = 342$.
10. (a) Checking base four: $30 \div 6 = 5$. Checking base five: $42 \div 7 = 6$.
    (c) Because 3 is used as a digit, and the only digits in base three are 0, 1, and 2.
11. Base six.

EXERCISE 8.2

1. $^-2$
2. $^-2$
3. $^-32$
4. $J = \{\ldots, {}^-3, {}^-2, {}^-1, 0, 1, 2, 3, \ldots\}$ or $\{\ldots, {}^-3, {}^-2, {}^-1\} \cup \{0\} \cup \{1, 2, 3, \ldots\}$.
5. The additive inverse of any integer a is the integer ^-a such that $a + {}^-a = {}^-a + a = 0$.
6. Addition in the integers is defined in such a way that $7 + {}^-7 = {}^-7 + 7 = 0$. Hence, by definition of the term *additive inverse*, $^-7$ is the additive inverse of 7.
7. The answer is analogous to the answer for problem 6.
8. (a) $^-17$ (c) $^-17$
9. (a) 25 (c) 25
10. (a) $^-7$ (c) ^-a (e) $x + y$ (g) 0
11. (a) No. Zero is neither a positive number nor a negative number.
    (c) $^-0$ and 0 are numerals for the same number and are therefore equal; $^-0 = 0$.
12. (a) $^-3$ (c) $^-7$

EXERCISE 8.4

1. Each element in J has an additive inverse.
2. (a) $^-3$ (c) 13 (e) $^-1$
3. (a) $6 + {}^-5 = (1 + 5) + {}^-5 = 1 + (5 + {}^-5) = 1 + 0 = 1$.
   $^-5 + 6 = {}^-5 + (5 + 1) = ({}^-5 + 5) + 1 = 0 + 1 = 1$.
   Therefore, $6 + {}^-5 = {}^-5 + 6$.
   The commutative property of addition is exemplified.
4. (a) $^-5$ (c) $^-15$ (e) $^-89$ (g) 3 (i) $^-8$
5. (a) 5 (c) $^-8$ (e) $3 + {}^-a$ or $3 - a$

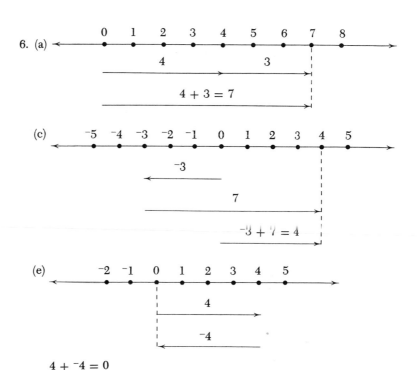

6. (a) $4 + 3 = 7$

(c) $^-3 + 7 = 4$

(e) $4 + {}^-4 = 0$

EXERCISE 8.5

1. See Definition 8.5.1.
2. (a) $^-5$ (c) $^-15$ (e) $^-10$
3. (a) $^-5$ (c) $^-15$ (e) $^-10$
4. (a) $^-2$ (c) 8 (e) $^-23$ (g) 7 (i) 1
5. $6 - {}^-4 = 6 + 4 = 10$, while $^-4 - 6 = {}^-10$. Therefore, $6 - {}^-4 \neq {}^-4 - 6$.
6. $(8 - 4) - {}^-6 = 4 + 6 = 10$, while $8 - (4 - {}^-6) = 8 - 10 = {}^-2$. Therefore, $(8 - 4) - {}^-6 \neq 8 - (4 - {}^-6)$.
7. (a) No. $7 - 5 = 2$, while $5 - 7 = {}^-2$. Subtraction is not commutative. (c) Yes. Addition is commutative.
8. (a) No. $(8 - 5) - 2 = 3 - 2 = 1$, while $8 - (5 - 2) = 8 - 3 = 5$. Subtraction is not associative. (c) Yes. Addition is associative.
9. (a) 9 (c) 0 (e) $^-8$

EXERCISE 8.6

1. (a) $^-6$ (c) $^-15$ (e) $^-12$ (g) 35 (i) 0
2. (a) $^-8$ (c) 12 (e) 0

3. (a) $^-10$ (c) 36
4. (a) 18 (c) 36 (e) 27
5. (a) $^-10$ (c) $^-4$ (e) 3

EXERCISE 8.7

1. (a) $^-4$ (c) 0 (e) 8 (g) 0 (i) 1
2. For $a = b$, $a \neq 0$ and $b \neq 0$.
3. (a) $^-2$ (b) $^-8$ (c) The associative property does not hold for division in J.
4. The quotient $7 \div 4$ does not exist in J since $7 = 4q$ has no solution in J. Therefore, J is not closed under addition.
5. $8 \div 2 = 4$, but $2 \div 8 \neq 4$. Hence, $8 \div 2 \neq 2 \div 8$ and division is not commutative.
6. (a) Yes (b) Yes (c) No (d) $(a + b) \div c = (a \div c) + (b \div c)$ *when division is possible.* Hence, use of this *right distributive property of division over addition* has limited value in J since division is frequently not possible.
7. (a) $^-5$

EXERCISE 8.9

1. *Cancellation property of addition:* If a, b, and c are in J and $a + c = b + c$, then $a = b$.
   Cancellation property of multiplication: If a, b, and c are in J, $c \neq 0$, and $ca = cb$, then $a = b$.
2. (a) *Assertions*

Assertions	*Reasons*
$a + 2 = ^-7$	Given
$(a + 2) + ^-2 = ^-7 + ^-2$	Substitution
$a + (2 + ^-2) = ^-9$	Assoc. prop. of add.
$a + 0 = ^-9$	Additive inverse
$a = ^-9$	Additive identity

3. $7x = ^-28$
   $7x = 7(^-4)$
   $x = ^-4$
4. See Definition 8.9.1.
5. (a) *Assertions*

Assertions	*Reasons*
$a < b$	Given
$a + c = b, c \in N$	Def. of $<$
$^-a + (a + c) = ^-a + b$	Substitution
$(^-a + a) + c = b + ^-a$	Assoc. and comm. prop. of add.
$0 + c = b - a$	Add. inverse and $b + ^-a = b - a$
$c = b - a$	Add. identity

6. No. Any negative integer is smaller than 0. For example, $^-5 < 0$ since
$^-5 + 5 = 0$ and 5 is a positive integer.

7. (a)
Assertions	Reasons
a, b, and c are in J and $a < b$	Given
$a + k = b$, $k \in N$	Def. of $<$
$(a + k) + c = b + c$	Substitution
$(a + c) + k = b + c$	Assoc. and comm. prop. of add.
$a + c < b + c$	Def. of $<$

8. $^-4 < {}^-3$ since $^-4 + 1 = {}^-3$ and 1 is a positive integer.

9. $^-10 < {}^-8$ since $^-10 + 2 = {}^-8$ and 2 is a positive integer.

10. (a) $x < z$ (c) $x < z$ if y is a positive integer; $x = z$ if $y = 0$; $x > z$ if y is a negative integer.

11. $\{\,3, {}^-2, {}^-1, 0, 1\}$

12. (a) $\{\ldots, {}^-3, {}^-2, {}^-1, 0, 1\}$ (c) $\{13, 14, 15, \ldots\}$

13. If a, b, and c are in J, c is a negative integer, and $a < b$, then $ca > cb$.

EXERCISE 8.10

1. See Definition 8.10.1.
2. See Definition 8.10.2.
3. (a) 7 (c) $|x - y|$ or $|y - x|$ (e) 11 (g) 0
4. (a) $\{^-2, {}^-1, 0, 1, 2\}$

(c) $\{\ldots, {}^-5, {}^-4, {}^-3, 3, 4, 5, \ldots\}$

5. (a) $\{^-5, {}^-4, {}^-3, {}^-2, {}^-1, 0, 1, 2, 3, 4, 5\}$

(c) $\{^-3, {}^-2, {}^-1, 0, 1, 2, 3\}$

6. (a) $|4 - n|$
7. (a) $|a - b| = |3 - 5| = |^-2| = {}^{--}2 = 2.$
   $|b - a| = |5 - 3| = |2| = 2.$
   Hence, $|3 - 5| = |5 - 3|$.

(c) $|a - b| = |^-8 - {}^-3| = |^-8 + 3| = |^-5| = {}^{--}5 = 5.$
$|b - a| = |^-3 - {}^-8| = |^-3 + 8| = |5| = 5.$
Hence, $|^-8 - {}^-3| = |^-3 - {}^-8|.$

8. (a) $|a \cdot b| = |5 \cdot 2| = |10| = 10.$
$|a| \cdot |b| = |5| \cdot |2| = 5 \cdot 2 = 10.$
Hence, $|5 \cdot 2| = |5| \cdot |2|.$
(c) $|a \cdot b| = |9 \cdot {}^-3| = |27| = 27.$
$|a| \cdot |b| = |^-9| \cdot |^-3| = 9 \cdot 3 = 27.$
Hence, $|^-9 \cdot {}^-3| = |^-9| \cdot |^-3|.$

9. (a) $|a + b| = |7 + 3| = |10| = 10.$
$|a| + |b| = |7| + |3| = 7 + 3 = 10.$
Since $10 \leq 10,\ |7 + 3| \leq |7| + |3|.$
(c) $|a + b| = |^-5 + {}^-8| = |^-13| = {}^{--}13 = 13.$
$|a| + |b| = |^-5| + |^-8| = 5 + 8 = 13.$
Since $13 \leq 13,\ |^-5 + {}^-8| \leq |^-5| + |^-8|.$

EXERCISE 9.3

1. See Definition 9.2.1.
2. See Definition 9.2.2.
3. (a) 2, 3, 5, 7, 11, 13, 17, 19, 23, 29, 31, 37, 41, 43, 47, 53, 59, 61, 67, 71, 73, 79, 83, 89, 97.
4. $6 = 3 + 3; 8 = 3 + 5; 10 = 3 + 7$ or $5 + 5; 12 = 5 + 7; 72 = 67 + 5$, or $59 + 13$, or $53 + 19$, or $43 + 29$, or $41 + 31; 84 = 79 + 5$, or $73 + 11$, or $71 + 13$, or $67 + 17$, or $61 + 23$, or $53 + 31$, or $47 + 37$, or $43 + 41.$
5. $22 = 3 + 19$, or $5 + 17$, or $11 + 11.$
6. $9 = 3 + 3 + 3; 11 = 3 + 3 + 5; 13 = 3 + 5 + 5; 15 = 3 + 5 + 7; 35 = 3 + 13 + 19$, or $5 + 7 + 23$, or $5 + 11 + 19$, or $5 + 13 + 17$, or $7 + 11 + 17$, or $3 + 3 + 29$, or $11 + 11 + 13.$
7. (a) $60 = 2^2 \cdot 3 \cdot 5$ (c) $51 = 3 \cdot 17$ (e) $510 = 2 \cdot 3 \cdot 5 \cdot 17$
8. (a) Only one prime factorization is possible.
9. $^-18 = {}^-1 \cdot 2 \cdot 3^2$
10. $28 = 1 + 2 + 4 + 7 + 14.$
11. $9^3 + 10^3 = 1729$

EXERCISE 9.4

1. Let a and b be members of W, then $(2a + 1)$ and $(2b + 1)$ represent any two odd numbers. The sum $(2a + 1) + (2b + 1) = 2a + 2b + 1 + 1 = 2a + 2b + 2 = 2(a + b + 1) = 2k$, where $k \in W$. But $2k$ is an even number. Hence the sum of any two odd numbers is an even number. (The appropriate reasons should be given for the various assertions in the proof.)

2. If a and b are in W, then $2a$ represents any even number and $(2b + 1)$ any odd number. The sum $2a + (2b + 1) = (2a + 2b) + 1 = 2(a + b) + 1 = (2k + 1)$, where $k \in W$. But $(2k + 1)$ is an odd number. Hence the sum of any even number and any odd number is an odd number. (The appropriate reasons should be given for the assertions in the proof.)

3. If a and b are in W, then $(2a + 1)$ and $(2b + 1)$ represent any two odd numbers. If the product $(2a + 1)(2b + 1)$ exists and is unique, the set of odd numbers is closed under multiplication. But $(2a + 1)(2b + 1) = (2a + 1)(2b) + (2a + 1)(1) = 4ab + 2b + 2a + 1 = 2(ab + b + a) + 1 = (2k + 1)$, where $k \in W$. Since $(2k + 1)$ exists and is a unique odd number, the set of odd numbers is closed under multiplication. (Reasons for each step of the proof should be given.)

4. If a and b are in W, then $2a$ represents any even number and $(2b + 1)$ any odd number. The product $(2a)(2b + 1) = 4ab + 2a = 2(2ab + a) = 2k$, where $k \in W$. But $2k$ is an even number. Hence the product of an even number and an odd number is an even number.

5. (a) $5^2 = 25$ (b) $1 + 3 + 5 + \ldots + (2n - 1) = n^2$ where n is any natural number. For example: $1 + 3 + 5 + 7 + 9 + 11 + 13 = 7^2 = 49$.

6. If a is a factor of some number n, then there must exist a number b such that $a \cdot b = n$. Hence factors occur in pairs, and there will be an even number of distinct factors of any given number n unless there is some factor c such that $c \cdot c = n$. In this case, there will be $(2k + 1)$ or an odd number of distinct factors of n. But if $c \cdot c = n$, n is a perfect square of c, and we see that a number with an odd number of distinct factors is a perfect square.

EXERCISE 9.5

1. See Definition 9.5.1.
2. (a) $D_{54} = \{1, 2, 3, 6, 9, 18, 27, 54\}$ (c) $D_{54} \cap D_{60} = \{1, 2, 3, 6\}$
3. g.c.d. $(140, 150) = 10$
4. (a) 12   (c) 12   (e) 6
5. Since every number divides 0, g.c.d. $(0, a)$ will be the greatest divisor of a. But the greatest divisor of a is a if a is positive, and ^-a if a is negative. Hence, g.c.d. $(0, a)$ is $|a|$.
6. 1
7. See Definition 9.5.2.
8. The pairs of (b), (d), and (e) are relatively prime.
9. (a) 5   (c) 7   (e) 1
10. Yes. If a and b are prime, then the factors of a are $\{a, 1\}$ and the factors of b are $\{b, 1\}$. But $\{a, 1\} \cap \{b, 1\} = 1$. Hence, a and b are relatively prime.
11. No. For example, 4 and 9 are relatively prime, but neither 4 nor 9 is a prime number.

12. (a) 6 and 35
13. (a) 5 (c) 2
14. (a) Yes. Every number is a factor of 0 while 1 has but a single distinct factor, namely 1.

EXERCISE 9.6

1. See Definition 9.6.1.
2. $\{18, 36, 54, \ldots, 18k, \ldots\}$
3. (a) 72 (c) 143 (e) 2310
4. (a) 12 (c) 1 (e) 1
5. (a) 126 (c) 2730 (e) 1200
6. If a and b are prime, then l.c.m. $(a, b) = a \cdot b$.
7. (a) ab (c) a^2bc (e) ab^2c^5
8. If a and b have no common prime factors.

EXERCISE 9.7

1. (a)

+	0	1	2
0	0	1	2
1	1	2	0
2	2	0	1

   (c) Addition is associative.

2. (a)

+	0	1	2	3	4
0	0	1	2	3	4
1	1	2	3	4	0
2	2	3	4	0	1
3	3	4	0	1	2
4	4	0	1	2	3

   (c) 0 (e) 12
3. In effect, a 24-hour clock is being used instead of a 12-hour clock. This avoids possible errors inherent in using the A.M. and P.M. symbols. The expression 0300 hours would mean 3 A.M. The expression 1620 hours means 4:20 P.M.
4. 9 A.M.
5. 1

EXERCISE 9.8

1. See Definition 9.8.1.
2. The commutative property need not necessarily hold for the defined operation of a given group. If it does, the system is a commutative group.
3. See Definition 9.8.2.
4. See Definition 9.8.3.
5. (a) The four hour clock system is a group under addition but not under multiplication. (c) The four-hour clock system is a ring under the operations of addition and multiplication.
6. (a) The five-hour clock system is a group under addition but not under multiplication. (c) The five-hour clock system is a ring under the operations of addition and multiplication.
7. (a) The element 0 must be removed from the set since it has no multiplicative inverse.
8. (a) No. (c) No.
9. The system of integers is a ring but not a field since the property concerning multiplicative inverses is not satisfied.

EXERCISE 9.9

1. See Definition 9.9.1.
2. $46 \equiv 22 \pmod 6$ since $46 - 22 = 24 = 4(6)$.
3. (a) 1 (c) 2 (e) 2 (g) 2 (i) 1
4. (a) 2 (b) $20 \equiv 2 \pmod 3$ since $20 - 1 = 18 = 6(3)$.
5. (a) 3 (mod 5) (c) 1 (mod 6) (e) 8 (mod 9) (g) 6 (mod 7) (i) 1 (mod 9)
6. (a)

+	0	1	2	3	4	5	6
0	0	1	2	3	4	5	6
1	1	2	3	4	5	6	0
2	2	3	4	5	6	0	1
3	3	4	5	6	0	1	2
4	4	5	6	0	1	2	3
5	5	6	0	1	2	3	4
6	6	0	1	2	3	4	5

(c) Yes. Every property necessary to qualify as a commutative group is satisfied. (e) Yes.

EXERCISE 9.10

1. (a) $23 \equiv 5 \pmod 9$ (c) $23{,}425 \equiv 7 \pmod 9$ (e) $823{,}429 \equiv 1 \pmod 0$
2. (a) 1462 (c) 221 (e) 144,692
3. (a) 17,782 (c) 16,005 (e) 876,042
4. (a) $q = 18$ and $r = 12$ (c) $q = 10$ and $r = 14$ (e) $q = 1857$ and $r = 2$
5. Treat the minuend as the sum of the subtrahend and the remainder. Then proceed as in checking addition by casting out nines.

EXERCISE 9.11

1. (a) 1470 is divisible by 3. (c) 235,425 is divisible by 3. (e) 23,423,535 is divisible by 3 and by 9.
2. (a) 2372 is divisible by 2 and by 4. (c) 26,428 is divisible by 2 and by 4. (e) 1,926,238 is divisible by 2.
3. The numbers of (a), (b), (c), and (d) are divisible by 11.
4. The numbers of (a), (b), (c), (e), and (f) are divisible by 7.
5. (a) 440 is divisible by 2, 4, 5, 8, 10, and 11. (c) 55,440 is divisible by 2, 3, 4, 5, 6, 7, 8, 9, 10, and 11.
6. If a number is divisible by 8, it will be divisible by 2 and by 4, but not necessarily by 16.
7. A number is divisible by 16 if and only if the number represented by its last four digits is divisible by 16. A number is divisible by 2^n if and only if the number represented by its last n digits is divisible by 2^n.
8. A number is divisible by 15 if and only if it is divisible by 3 and by 5 (the prime factors of 15).
9. A number is divisible by 25 if and only if the number represented by its last two digits is divisible by 25. The proof is similar to the proof of the test for divisibility by 4.
10. The test for divisibility by 2 in base ten works for base four since 4^1, 4^2, 4^3, and so on are divisible by 2. The proof is similar to the proof for base ten. The test fails for base three, however, since 3^1, 3^2, 3^3, and so on are not divisible by 2.
11. Not necessarily. The number 6 has a factor of 3 and hence any number divisible by 6 must be divisible by 3. If a number is divisible by 18, it must have at least two factors of 3 and at least one factor of 2.
12. Yes. Even though 4 is not prime, it has no factors of 3. Hence a number divisible by both 4 and 3 must be divisible by 4×3 or 12.

EXERCISE 10.2

1. See Definition 10.2.1.
2. (a) $\frac{4}{3} \simeq \frac{8}{6}$ since $4 \times 6 = 3 \times 8 = 24$.
   (c) $\frac{4}{9} \simeq \frac{^-4}{^-9}$ since $4 \times ^-9 = 9 \times ^-4 = ^-36$.
   (e) $\frac{^-7}{^-2} \simeq \frac{21}{6}$ since $^-7 \times 6 = ^-2 \times 21 = ^-42$.
3. (a) 6 (c) 2 (e) 0 (g) 6
4. Assume $\frac{a}{b} \simeq \frac{c}{d}$. Then $ad = bc$ by definition of the equivalence relation. By the symmetric property of equals, $bc = ad$ and since multiplication is commutative, $cb = da$. Then $\frac{c}{d} \simeq \frac{a}{b}$ by definition of $\simeq$.
5. (a) Yes. Since $0 \times 25 = 0$ and $5 \times 0 = 0$, $0 \times 25 = 5 \times 0$.
6. (a) Yes, since $2 \times 3 = 3 \times 2$. (c) Yes, since $2 \times ^-9 = 3 \times ^-6$.
7. (a) Four possible members are: $\frac{4}{1}$, $\frac{1}{4}$, $\frac{2}{8}$, and $\frac{^-4}{^-1}$. (c) Four possible members are: $\frac{^-7}{^-4}$, $\frac{^-5}{^-2}$, $\frac{^-6}{^-9}$, $\frac{0}{^-3}$.
8. $\frac{2}{3} \simeq \frac{6}{9}$ and $\frac{6}{9} \simeq \frac{12}{18}$. Hence, it should hold that $\frac{2}{3} \simeq \frac{12}{18}$. This is true since $2 \cdot 18 = 3 \cdot 12 = 36$.
9. $\frac{1}{2} \not\simeq \frac{2}{3}$ and $\frac{2}{3} \not\simeq \frac{6}{12}$, but $\frac{1}{2} \simeq \frac{6}{12}$. Hence, the relation $\not\simeq$ is not transitive.

EXERCISE 10.3

1. See Definition 10.2.1.
2. See Definition 10.3.1.
3. (a) $\frac{3}{5}$, $\frac{6}{10}$, and $\frac{9}{15}$.
4. Since $\frac{1}{2}$ and $\frac{3}{8}$ belong to the same equivalence class and since brackets indicate the entire class to which the enclosed member belongs, $[\frac{1}{2}] = [\frac{3}{8}]$.
5. See Definition 10.3.2.
6. (a) 4 and 8 are not relatively prime. (c) 6 and $^-9$ are not relatively prime and the denominator is not positive. (e) The denominator is not positive. (g) 51 and 17 are not relatively prime. (i) The denominator is not positive.
7. (a) $\frac{1}{2}$ (c) $\frac{^-2}{3}$ (e) $\frac{^-2}{3}$ (g) $\frac{3}{1}$ (i) $\frac{0}{1}$
8. $\frac{0}{2}$, $\frac{0}{3}$, $\frac{0}{4}$, $\frac{0}{5}$, and $\frac{0}{6}$.
9. No. The denominator may not be 0.
10. No. 2 and 4 are not relatively prime; hence elements such as $\frac{1}{2}$, $\frac{3}{6}$, and $\frac{5}{10}$ will not be included.
11. $\frac{a}{b} = \frac{ak}{bk}$ since $a(bk) = b(ak)$ by the associate and commutative properties of multiplication.
12. We may use $\frac{3}{4}$ to name the equivalence class to which it belongs and, from this point of view, it names a rational number.
13. (a) $\frac{3}{7}$ (c) $\frac{^-3}{2}$
14. (a) $\frac{21}{80}$ (c) $\frac{727}{1441}$

EXERCISE 10.4

1.
$\frac{3}{4}$

$\frac{6}{8}$

$\frac{9}{12}$

2. (a) If $\frac{1}{2}$ is used to represent 1 of the 2 equal parts of a unit figure while $\frac{2}{4}$ is used to represent 2 of the 4 equal parts of a unit figure, we may prefer to consider $\frac{1}{2}$ and $\frac{2}{4}$ equivalent rather than equal.

3. See Figure 10.4.2 of the text for assistance.

4. $\frac{11}{4}$, since $2\frac{3}{4} = 2 + \frac{3}{4} = \frac{8}{4} + \frac{3}{4} = \frac{11}{4}$.

5.

6. $\frac{10}{6}$, $\frac{-5}{3}$, and $\frac{25}{15}$.

7. Four

8.

EXERCISE 10.6

1. See Definition 10.5.1.

2. (a) $\frac{17}{12}$ (c) $\frac{139}{57}$ (e) $\frac{-25}{24}$ (g) $\frac{-53}{12}$ (i) $\frac{62}{15}$ (k) $\frac{-87}{91}$

3. $\dfrac{2}{7} + \dfrac{4}{5} = \dfrac{10+28}{35} = \dfrac{38}{35}$, and $\dfrac{4}{5} + \dfrac{2}{7} = \dfrac{28+10}{35} = \dfrac{38}{35}$. Hence $\dfrac{2}{7} + \dfrac{4}{5} = \dfrac{4}{5} + \dfrac{2}{7}$.

4. $\dfrac{a}{b} + \dfrac{c}{d} = \dfrac{ad+bc}{bd} = \dfrac{bc+ad}{bd} = \dfrac{cb+da}{db} = \dfrac{c}{d} + \dfrac{a}{b}$.

Hence, $\dfrac{a}{b} + \dfrac{c}{d} = \dfrac{c}{d} + \dfrac{a}{b}$. (Reasons for the steps should be given.)

5. $\left(\dfrac{2}{3} + \dfrac{4}{5}\right) + \dfrac{3}{7} = \dfrac{10 + 12}{15} + \dfrac{3}{7} = \dfrac{22}{15} + \dfrac{3}{7} = \dfrac{154 + 45}{105} = \dfrac{199}{105}$,

and

$\dfrac{2}{3} + \left(\dfrac{4}{5} + \dfrac{3}{7}\right) = \dfrac{2}{3} + \dfrac{28 + 15}{35} = \dfrac{2}{3} + \dfrac{43}{35} = \dfrac{70 + 129}{105} = \dfrac{199}{105}$.

Hence, $\left(\dfrac{2}{3} + \dfrac{4}{5}\right) + \dfrac{3}{7} = \dfrac{2}{3} + \left(\dfrac{4}{5} + \dfrac{3}{7}\right)$.

6. $\left(\dfrac{a}{b} + \dfrac{c}{d}\right) + \dfrac{e}{f} = \dfrac{ad + bc}{bd} + \dfrac{e}{f} = \dfrac{adf + bcf + bde}{bdf}$, and

$\dfrac{a}{b} + \left(\dfrac{c}{d} + \dfrac{e}{f}\right) = \dfrac{a}{b} + \dfrac{cf + de}{df} = \dfrac{adf + bcf + bde}{bdf}$. Hence,

$\left(\dfrac{a}{b} + \dfrac{c}{d}\right) + \dfrac{e}{f} = \dfrac{a}{b} + \left(\dfrac{c}{d} + \dfrac{e}{f}\right)$.

7. (a) The set S is said to contain an identity element for addition if there
is some element i such that $a + i = i + a$ for every a in S. (c) [$\frac{0}{1}$]

8. (a) Because 0 and 1 are relatively prime and 1 is positive.

9. An element a in S is said to have an additive inverse if there is an element ^-a in S such that $a + {}^-a = {}^-a + a = i$, the identity element for
addition.

10. (a) $\dfrac{-2}{5}$ (c) $\dfrac{-7}{2}$ (e) $\dfrac{2}{7}$ (g) $\dfrac{-1}{21}$ (i) $\dfrac{-7}{3}$ (k) $\dfrac{-2}{35}$

11. (a) $x = \dfrac{1}{10}$ (c) $x = \dfrac{29}{15}$ (e) $x = \dfrac{2}{3}$

12. (a) $\dfrac{17}{12}$ (c) $\dfrac{139}{57}$ (e) $\dfrac{-25}{24}$ (g) $\dfrac{-53}{12}$ (i) $\dfrac{62}{15}$ (k) $\dfrac{-87}{91}$

13. (a) $\dfrac{7}{3}$ (c) $\dfrac{-17}{5}$

14. (a) $2\frac{1}{3}$ (c) $^-2\frac{2}{3}$

15. (a) $\dfrac{67}{14} = 4\frac{11}{14}$ (c) $\dfrac{23}{8} = 2\frac{7}{8}$ (e) $\dfrac{-31}{4} = {}^-7\frac{3}{4}$

16. (a) $\dfrac{88}{15}$ (c) $\dfrac{34}{21}$ (e) $\dfrac{-509}{280}$

17. *Assertions*   *Reasons*

$\dfrac{a}{b} + \dfrac{e}{f} = \dfrac{c}{d} + \dfrac{e}{f}$ Given

$\left(\dfrac{a}{b} + \dfrac{e}{f}\right) + \dfrac{-e}{f} = \left(\dfrac{c}{d} + \dfrac{e}{f}\right) + \dfrac{-e}{f}$ Substitution

$\dfrac{a}{b} + \left(\dfrac{e}{f} + \dfrac{-e}{f}\right) = \dfrac{c}{d} + \left(\dfrac{e}{f} + \dfrac{-e}{f}\right)$ Assoc. prop. of addition

$\dfrac{a}{b} + 0 = \dfrac{c}{d} + 0$ Additive inverse

$\dfrac{a}{b} = \dfrac{c}{d}$ Additive identity

EXERCISE 10.7

1. See Definition 10.7.1.

2. (a) $\dfrac{1}{12}$ (c) $\dfrac{-43}{8}$ (e) $\dfrac{65}{24}$ (g) $\dfrac{11}{3}$

3. $\dfrac{3}{4} - \dfrac{1}{2} = \dfrac{1}{4}$, while $\dfrac{1}{2} - \dfrac{3}{4} = \dfrac{-1}{4}$. Since $\dfrac{1}{4} \neq \dfrac{-1}{4}$, $\dfrac{3}{4} - \dfrac{1}{2} \neq \dfrac{1}{2} - \dfrac{3}{4}$.

4. $\left(\dfrac{3}{4} - \dfrac{2}{3}\right) - \dfrac{1}{5} = \dfrac{-7}{60}$, while $\dfrac{3}{4} - \left(\dfrac{2}{3} - \dfrac{1}{5}\right) = \dfrac{17}{60}$.

5. (a) $\dfrac{1}{12}$ (c) $\dfrac{33}{5}$ (e) $\dfrac{19}{21}$ (g) $\dfrac{8}{7}$

6. Proof is in the text.

7. Proof is in the text.
8. (a) $\frac{11}{14}$ (c) $\frac{-5}{3}$
9. (a) $\dfrac{5}{bc}$ (c) $\dfrac{a + 3b^2}{b^3c}$

EXERCISE 10.8

1. (a) and (b) Results are analogous to Figure 10.8.1.
2. See Definition 10.8.1.
3. (a) $\frac{3}{4} \cong \frac{9}{12}$ since $3 \times 12 = 4 \times 9$. $\frac{2}{5} \cong \frac{4}{10}$ since $2 \times 10 = 5 \times 4$.
4. (a) $\frac{3}{7} \cdot \frac{4}{5} = \frac{12}{35}$ and $\frac{4}{5} \cdot \frac{3}{7} = \frac{12}{35}$. Hence, $\frac{3}{7} \cdot \frac{4}{5} = \frac{4}{5} \cdot \frac{3}{7}$.
5. (a) $(\frac{3}{4} \cdot \frac{5}{7}) \cdot \frac{2}{11} = \frac{15}{28} \cdot \frac{2}{11} = \frac{30}{308}$, and $\frac{3}{4} \cdot (\frac{5}{7} \cdot \frac{2}{11}) = \frac{3}{4} \cdot \frac{10}{77} = \frac{30}{308}$. Hence, $(\frac{3}{4} \cdot \frac{5}{7}) \cdot \frac{2}{11} = \frac{3}{4} \cdot (\frac{5}{7} \cdot \frac{2}{11})$.
6. (a) $\dfrac{a}{b} + \dfrac{0}{c} = \dfrac{a \cdot c + b \cdot 0}{b \cdot c} = \dfrac{ac}{bc} = \dfrac{a}{b}$.
7. (a) $\frac{-8}{21}$ (c) $\frac{-8}{105}$ (e) $\frac{1}{4}$ (g) $\frac{5}{6}$ (i) $\frac{19}{28}$
8. (a) $\frac{17}{14}$ (c) $\frac{5}{16}$
9. $\frac{2}{3} \cdot (\frac{3}{4} + \frac{2}{7}) = \frac{29}{42}$, and $(\frac{3}{4} + \frac{2}{7}) \cdot \frac{2}{3} = \frac{29}{42}$. Hence, $\frac{2}{3} \cdot (\frac{3}{4} + \frac{2}{7}) = (\frac{3}{4} + \frac{2}{7}) \cdot \frac{2}{3}$.
10. (a) $\frac{223}{420}$
11. (a) $\dfrac{2a}{49}$ (c) $\dfrac{ab}{x^3y^3}$ (e) $\dfrac{a}{3b}$
12. (a) $\frac{4}{3}$ (c) $\frac{-3}{2}$ (e) $\frac{-5}{6}$ (g) $\frac{-b}{2}$ (i) $\frac{y}{x}$
13. (a) $\frac{6}{5}$ (c) $\frac{-8}{15}$ (e) $\frac{8}{9}$
14. (a) $\frac{19}{40}$ (c) $\frac{39}{70}$
15. y
16. (a) 6 or $\frac{6}{1}$ (c) 4 or $\frac{4}{1}$
17. Proof is given in the text.

EXERCISE 10.9

1. See Definition 10.9.1.
2. Proof is given in the text.
3. (a) $\frac{3}{10}$ (c) $\frac{1}{4}$ (e) $\frac{14}{25}$ (g) $\frac{2}{15}$ (i) $\frac{-15}{2}$
4. $\frac{2}{3} \div \frac{5}{7} = \frac{14}{15}$, while $\frac{5}{7} \div \frac{2}{3} = \frac{15}{14}$. Hence, $\frac{2}{3} \div \frac{5}{7} \neq \frac{5}{7} \div \frac{2}{3}$.
5. $(\frac{3}{5} \div \frac{2}{3}) \div \frac{7}{2} = \frac{9}{35}$, while $\frac{3}{5} \div (\frac{2}{3} \div \frac{7}{2}) = \frac{63}{20}$. Hence, $(\frac{3}{5} \div \frac{2}{3}) \div \frac{7}{2} \neq \frac{3}{5} \div (\frac{2}{3} \div \frac{7}{2})$.
6. $\frac{3}{8}$
7. (a) $\frac{5}{6}$ (c) $\frac{33}{8}$ (e) $\frac{3}{2}$ (g) $\frac{5}{56}$ (i) $\frac{9}{8}$
8. (a) $\frac{46}{15}$ (c) 3 (e) $\frac{-12}{7}$ (g) $\frac{40}{3}$ (i) $\frac{19}{93}$
9. (a) $\frac{5}{2}$ (c) 6 (e) $^-9$
10. 20

EXERCISE 10.10

1. $\dfrac{a}{c} + \dfrac{b}{c} = \dfrac{ac + cb}{c^2} = \dfrac{c(a + b)}{c \cdot c} = \dfrac{c}{c} \cdot \dfrac{a + b}{c} = \dfrac{a + b}{c}.$

(Reasons for each step should be given.)

2. (a) c may be any positive or negative integer.

3. (a) c may be any positive or negative integer.

4. (a) $3 \cdot 3^{-1} = \frac{3}{1} \cdot \frac{1}{3} = \frac{3}{3} = 1.$ (c) $7 \cdot 7^{-1} = \frac{7}{1} \cdot \frac{1}{7} = \frac{7}{7} = 1.$

(e) $\dfrac{-5}{2} \left(\dfrac{-5}{2} \right)^{-1} = \dfrac{-5}{2} \cdot \dfrac{1}{\frac{-5}{2}} = \dfrac{-5}{2} \cdot \dfrac{2}{-5} = \dfrac{-10}{-10} = 1.$

5. (a) $\frac{-2}{-9}$

6. (a) Each element $\frac{a}{b}$ in R, $\frac{a}{b} \neq \frac{0}{1}$, has a multiplicative inverse.

EXERCISE 10.11

1. See Definition 10.11.1.

2. (a) True (c) True (e) True (g) True (i) True

3. (a) $\{x \mid x \in J \text{ and } x < 9\}$ (c) $x = 9.$

4. (a) If $\frac{a}{b} < \frac{a}{b}$, then $ab < ba$. But $ab = ba$ by the commutative property of multiplication. Hence, $\frac{a}{b} \nless \frac{a}{b}$ and the $<$ relation is irreflexive.

5. (a) $\frac{3}{4} < \frac{4}{3}$ (c) $\frac{-3}{4} < \frac{2}{3}$ (e) $\frac{16}{28} < \frac{11}{18}$

6. (a) $\{x \mid x \in R \text{ and } x < \frac{13}{12}\}$ (c) $\{x \mid x \in R \text{ and } x < \frac{3}{8}\}$ (e) $\{x \mid x \in R \text{ and } x < \frac{20}{1}\}$

EXERCISE 10.13

1. Between any two distinct rational numbers, we can always find another rational number.

2. (a) Four: 8, 9, 10, and 11. (c) 0

3. (a) Infinitely many. $\{x \mid x \in R \text{ and } \frac{3}{4} < x < \frac{4}{4}\}$. Two examples are $\frac{7}{2}$ and $\frac{11}{3}$. (c) Infinitely many. $\{x \mid x \in R \text{ and } \frac{3}{200} < x < \frac{4}{200}\}$. Two examples are $\frac{1}{60}$ and $\frac{11}{600}$.

4. (a) $\frac{19}{36}$ (c) $\frac{19}{5}$

5. $\frac{5}{12}$

6. (a) 1

7. (a) $^{-}1$

8. (a) An example is $\frac{1}{80}$.

9. (a) An example is $\frac{-1}{80}$.

10. (a) $x = \frac{3}{4}$, or $x = \frac{-3}{4}$.

11. (a) $\{x \mid x \in R \text{ and } ^{-}3 < x < 3\}$ (c) $\{x \mid x \in R \text{ and } ^{-}2 \leq x \leq 6\}$

EXERCISE 11.2

1. (a) $\frac{23}{10}$ (c) $\frac{67}{1000}$ (e) $\frac{274}{10}$ (g) $\frac{2883}{10}$ (i) $\dfrac{600,001}{1000}$

2. (a) $\frac{3}{10} + \frac{1}{100}$ (c) $\frac{42}{1} + \frac{6}{1000}$ (e) $\frac{7}{10} + \frac{3}{100} + \frac{2}{1000}$

3. (a) $2 \cdot 10^0 + 3 \cdot 10^{-1}$ (c) $6 \cdot 10^{-2} + 7 \cdot 10^{-3}$ (e) $2 \cdot 10^1 + 7 \cdot 10^0 + 4 \cdot 10^{-1}$ (g) $2 \cdot 10^2 + 8 \cdot 10^1 + 9 \cdot 10^0 + 3 \cdot 10^{-1}$ (i) $6 \cdot 10^2 + 1 \cdot 10^{-3}$

4. If the simplest fraction is used to represent a rational number and if its denominator contains only prime factors of 2's and 5's, then the number may be written as a terminating decimal.

5. (a) $\frac{1}{2} = 0.5$ (b) $\frac{2}{3}$ does not terminate. (c) $\frac{7}{21}$ does not terminate. (d) $\frac{7}{35} = 0.2$ (e) $\frac{15}{20} = 0.75$ (f) $\frac{12}{15} = 0.8$ (g) $\frac{21}{70} = 0.3$ (h) $\frac{105}{40} = 2.625$ (i) $\frac{128}{80} = 1.6$

6. (a) 0.31, 0.32, and 0.33. (c) 0.41, 0.42, and 0.43.

7. (a) $\frac{7}{9}$ (c) $\frac{59}{8}$ (e) $\frac{1715}{144}$ (g) $\frac{5}{4}$ (i) $\frac{221}{10}$

8. (a) $0.4 < 0.5$ (c) $0.007 < 0.070$ (e) $1.999 > 1.99$ (g) $34.099 < 34.19$

EXERCISE 11.5

1. (a) 7.852 (c) ⁻4.8865 (e) 2.135 (g) ⁻1.5

2. (a) 0.9282 (c) 0.67928 (e) 166.32

3. (a) $\frac{9282}{10000}$

4. (a) 6.4 (c) 2,085,000 (e) 80.03

5. (a) 0.75 (c) 0.4375 (e) 0.14

6. (a) 4.6 (c) 9.254

7. (a) 12.10_{four} (c) 1001.00_{two}

8. (a) 0.40_{five} (c) 2.13_{five} (e) 4.04_{seven}

EXERCISE 11.6

1. (a) $0.\overline{21}$ (c) 0.125 (e) $0.\overline{30}$ (g) $0.\overline{714285}$ (i) $0.2\overline{52}$

2. (a) $\frac{4}{9}$ (c) $\frac{54}{99} = \frac{6}{11}$ (e) $\frac{393}{999} = \frac{131}{333}$ (g) $\frac{889}{9}$ (i) $\frac{101}{999}$

3. (a) Twelve: 1, 2, . . . , 12. (c) Twelve

4. The reduced form of $\frac{20}{52}$ is $\frac{5}{13}$. Hence, the maximum possible number of digits in the repeating portion of the quotient is $13 - 1 = 12$.

5. (a)   Let $x = 0.44\overline{9}$ (c)   Let $x = 0.\overline{9}$
   Then $10x = 4.49\overline{9}$ Then $10x = 9.\overline{9}$
   Subtract $x = 0.44\overline{9}$ Subtract $x = 0.\overline{9}$
   ————————————   ————————
   $9x = 4.05$ $9x = 9$
   $x = 0.45$ $x = 1$

6. $\dfrac{abcd}{9999}$

EXERCISE 11.7

1. (a) {8} (c) {0, 1, 2} (e) {0, 1, 2, 3, 4} (g) Ø
2. (a) $4x$ (c) $4x + 5 = 33$.
3. $2n + 8 = 26$ and $n = 9$.
4. $\frac{20}{7}$
5. $\frac{1}{4}$
6. {0, 1, 2, 3, 4}
7. 3
8. $\{x \mid x \in J$ and $x > 4\}$
9. $\{x \mid x \subset J$ and $x < 4\}$
10. $\{x \mid x \in J$ and $^{-}3 < x < 7\}$

EXERCISE 11.8

1. (a) 93,000,000 (c) 610 (e) 71,000 (g) 0.67 (i) 0.010
2. (a) 90,000,000 (c) 600 (e) 70,000 (g) 0.7 (i) 0.01
3. (a) 0.04343 (c) 0.2378 (e) 0.2727 (g) 5.030
4. (a) 0.043 (c) 0.238 (e) 0.273 (g) 5.030
5. (a) 0.0434 (c) 0.2378 (e) 0.2727 (g) 5.0303
6. (a) 2.29 (c) 5.84
7. (a) Increase by 1 the last digit retained if the first digit omitted is 4 or greater; otherwise, make no change. (c) Increase by 1 the last digit retained if the first digit omitted is 6 or greater; otherwise, make no change.
8. (a) Round down to 16.3. Otherwise, the glass will be too large to fit into the frame.

EXERCISE 11.9

1. (a) $\frac{m}{w} = \frac{5}{4}$ (c) $\frac{w}{m} = \frac{4}{5}$
2. 160 miles
3. 307 miles
4. $1\frac{1}{4}$ cups
5. 4.125 quarts
6. 254 feet
7. 36 cubic yards
8. $4267
9. 6.4 gallons
10. 6.5 gallons yellow and 17.5 gallons green.
11. 13

12. 52 cents
13. $12,307.69 for Mr. Baker and $7,692.31 for Mr. Timm.
14. 1360 bales
15. 2.1 feet
16. 10 gallons of white, 6 of yellow, and 4 of green.
17. 23.5 pounds of bluegrass, 17.6 of rye, and 8.8 of fescue.

EXERCISE 11.10

1. (a) 60% (c) 35% (e) 24%
2. (a) 62.5% (c) 733.3% (e) 43.8%
3. (a) 3 (c) 20
4. $1,015.00
5. (a) 25% (c) In part (a) 2 is compared with 8, while in part (b) 2 is compared with 10.
6. (a) 44.$\overline{4}$%
7. 35
8. $718.75
9. $18,400.00
10. 15
11. 80
12. (a) 40% (c) 66.$\overline{6}$%
13. $1200.30

EXERCISE 11.11

1. Proof is in the text.
2. Assume $\sqrt{3}$ is a rational number indicated by $\dfrac{a}{b}$ in simplest form. Then $3 = \dfrac{a^2}{b^2}$ and $3b^2 = a^2$. Since $3b^2$ has a factor of 3, a^2 must have a factor of 3. Hence, a must have a factor of 3 since 3 is prime, and we may let $a = 3k$. Then $3b^2 = (3k)^2$, or $3b^2 = 9k^2$. Thus, $b^2 = 3k^2$. By again reasoning as above, b^2 must have a factor of 3 and hence b has a factor of 3. But if both a and b have a factor of 3, our assumption that $\dfrac{a}{b}$ is in simplest form is contradicted. Since any rational number can be represented by a fraction in simplest form, $\sqrt{3}$ must be irrational.
3. Assume $7 + \sqrt{2} = r_1$, a rational number. Then, $\sqrt{2} = r_1 - 7$. But the rationals have closure for subtraction; hence, we conclude that $r_1 - 7$ is a rational number r_2. Then $\sqrt{2} = r_2$, a rational number. However, since we know $\sqrt{2}$ is irrational, our assumption that $7 + \sqrt{2}$ is rational must be false.
4. Proof is analogous to problem 3.
5. (a) 16. No. (c) $-2\sqrt{3}$. Yes. (e) 61. No.

EXERCISE 11.12

1. (a) and (b)

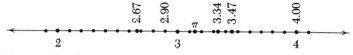

$(\tfrac{4}{1}) = 4$; $(\tfrac{4}{1} - \tfrac{4}{3}) \approx 2.67$; $(\tfrac{4}{1} - \tfrac{4}{3} + \tfrac{4}{5}) \approx 3.47$; $(\tfrac{4}{1} - \tfrac{4}{3} + \tfrac{4}{5} - \tfrac{4}{7}) \approx 2.90$;
$(\tfrac{4}{1} - \tfrac{4}{3} + \tfrac{4}{5} - \tfrac{4}{7} + \tfrac{4}{9}) \approx 3.34$.
(c) Yes.
2. $\sqrt{39}$ ... 0.24
3. (a) Second approximation: 6.3. Third approximation: 0.245.
4. 12.124357
5. (a) 3.742

EXERCISE 12.3

1. Answers may vary somewhat. See text for assistance.
2. (a) 1. No. (c) Three points determine at most only one plane. Hence, a stand with three legs will not wobble. (e) Infinitely many.
3. (a) $\overleftrightarrow{AC}$ (c) $\overline{BD}$ (e) $\overrightarrow{BC}$ (g) $\overline{BC}$
4. (a) True (c) True (e) False (g) False

EXERCISE 12.5

1. Let A and B name the given points of the plane, and let m name the given line. Then, if $\overline{AB} \cap m$ is nonempty, A and B are on different sides of m; but if $\overline{AB} \cap m = \varnothing$, then A and B are on the same side of m.
2. (a) See Figure 12.4.1 for assistance. (b) See Figure 12.4.4 for assistance. (c) See Figures 12.4.3 and 12.4.5 for assistance. (d) See Figure 12.4.6 for assistance. (e) Begin with a figure similar to Figure 12.4.5.
3. No. The planes are either parallel or they intersect.
4. (a) $\varnothing$ (c) $\varnothing$ (e) A set consisting of a single point.
5. An *angle* is the union of two rays with a common endpoint.
6. See Figure 12.5.4 for assistance.
7. Yes; $\angle XYZ$ is a straight angle.

EXERCISE 12.7

1. Answers may vary somewhat. See the text for assistance.
2. (a) and (c).

3. (a), (e), and (f).
4. Draw the segments in the indicated sequence beginning at A, proceeding to B, and so on:

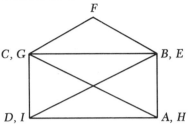

5. (a) The union of a simple closed curve and its interior is a *region*. (Some authors include only the interior of the curve.) (b) Answers may vary. See Figure 12.6.4.
6. A plane may be considered to be the boundary between two half-spaces.
7. (a) Answers may vary somewhat. See the text for assistance. (b) See Figure 12.7.2 for assistance.
8. A line may lie entirely in the exterior of a simple closed surface, but not entirely in the interior of the simple closed surface.
9. (a) Because the thickness of the paint is relatively small. (b) Because the paint has a thickness and we think of a surface as having no thickness.
10. (a) The union of a simple closed surface and its interior is a *solid*. (b) A golf ball, automobile, hammer, and so on.
11. (a), (c), (d), (e), (g), (h), and (i).

EXERCISE 13.3

1. *Metric geometry* refers to the theory and techniques involved in the measurement of geometric figures.
2. (a) Using $|a - b|$, all measurements will be non-negative. (b) It would be necessary that a be greater than or equal to b for measurements to be non-negative.
3. (a) 3 (c) $\frac{3}{2}$ (e) 4 (g) $\frac{7}{2} - \sqrt{3}$
4. Standard units of measurement are necessary for purposes of communication, especially when the measurement of physical objects is involved.
5. See dictionary or other references.
6. On the intuitive level, congruent figures may be thought of as having the same size and shape; they are exact copies of each other.
7. See Definition 13.3.1.
8. See Definition 13.3.2.
9. (a) and (b) See Figure 13.3.1 for assistance. (c) The figures are not congruent because the line segment determined by any two points on the

semicircle is not congruent to the line segment determined by the corresponding points of the given line segment.

10. See Figure 13.3.1 for assistance.
11. (a), (c), and (f).

EXERCISE 13.5

1. If two angles have a common vertex, a common side, and nonintersecting interiors, they are *adjacent angles*.
2. A degree is a unit of measurement such that the measurement of a straight angle is 180°.
3. See Figure 13.4.3 for assistance.
4. (a) 180 (b) 2 (c) If different units of measurement are used, then it is possible for two given angles with different measures to be congruent. If the same unit of measurement is used, of course, then angles having the same measure will be congruent.
5. A *protractor* is an instrument for measuring or drawing angles.
6. (a) A *polygon* is a simple closed curve which is the union of a finite number of line segments. (c) See dictionary.
7. Definitions are clearly stated in Section 13.5.
8. (a) Always (c) Never (e) Always (g) Sometimes.
9. Q = Quadrilaterals
   P = Parallelograms
   Rho = Rhombuses
   Rec = Rectangles
   S = Squares

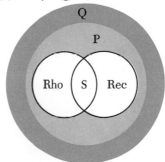

10. See Figure 13.5.3.
11. The definition of the text states more properties than necessary; it is only necessary to mention that a rectangle has one right angle since we may prove that the other angles are right angles. The definition of the text, however, is more meaningful to the reader with limited mathematical experience than the alternative definition.

EXERCISE 13.7

1. (a) The measure of a simple closed curve is called its *perimeter*. (b) 21.5 inches.

2. (a) The perimeter of a circle is called its *circumference*.   (b) $c = 2\pi r$ or πd (c) 94.2 inches
3. (a) $3.\overline{142857}$ (b) The difference is $3.143 - 3.142 = 0.001$.
4. (a) A *plane region* is the union of a simple closed curve and its interior.
   (b) The measure of a region is called its *area*.   (c) It is easier to cover the region with unit squares than with unit circles since unit squares "fit together."
5. $P = 15.6$ meters. $A = 14.72$ square meters.
6. (a) 6.2 inches   (b) $= 38.44$ square inches
7. (a) 648 square inches   (b) 4.5 square feet
8. 29.4 square units
9. $C = 25.12$ centimeters. $A = 50.24$ square centimeters
10. (a) 18 square feet   (b) 36 square feet   (c) 28.26 square feet
11. (a) See Figure 13.7.2 for assistance.   (b) The distributive property.
12. (a) 24   (b) 56   (c) 56   (d) 48
13. 2 square feet or 288 square inches

EXERCISE 13.8

1. Consult dictionary.
2. See definitions in the text.
3. (a) The measure of a solid is called its *volume*. (c) The measure of a simple closed surface (not including its interior) is called its *surface area*.
4. (a) Sometimes (c) Always (e) Sometimes (g) Never (i) Always (k) Never
5. Reg. pyr. = Regular pyramids

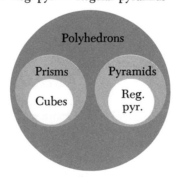

6. $V = 96$ cubic feet. $S = 152$ square feet
7. (a) For assistance see the figure in Example 5 of Section 13.8.   (c) 13 inches (e) 282.6 square inches
8. 156.16 square feet (including the base)
9. $51\frac{1}{3}$ cubic meters
10. No assistance should be necessary.

11. $V = 523\frac{17}{21}$. $S = 314\frac{2}{7}$.
12. $8r^3$
13. 6 gallons
14. 7.3 cubic yards
15. (a) The volume is multiplied by 8; by 27. (c) The volume is multiplied by 8; by 27.

EXERCISE 13.10

1. Proof is given in the text.
2. $c^2 = x^2 + 4[\frac{a}{2}(x + a)]$
   $c^2 = x^2 + 2a(x + a)$
   $c^2 = x^2 + 2ax + 2a^2$
   $c^2 = x^2 + 2ax + a^2 + a^2$
   $c^2 = (x + a)^2 + a^2$
   $c^2 = b^2 + a^2$
3. 15 units
4. 12 feet
5. 60π square inches ≈ 188.4 square inches
6. $5\sqrt{2}$ inches
7. (a) See Definition 13.10.1. (b) The figures are congruent. (c) Yes; if two figures are congruent, Definition 13.10.1 (concerning similarity) is satisfied. (d) No; similar figures are congruent if and only if the ratio of the lengths of their corresponding line segments is equal to 1.
8. 15 inches
9. 128.25 feet
10. $\frac{20}{17}$ inches ≈ 1.18 inches
11. $h = 3.5$ inches and $s = 11$ inches
12. $x = 6$
13. 486

EXERCISE 14.2

1. (a) and (b) See Figure 14.2.2 for assistance. (c) and (d) See Figure 14.2.3 for assistance.
2. (a) and (b) See Figure 14.2.4 for assistance.
3. See Figure 14.2.5 for assistance.
4. See Figure 14.2.5 for assistance.
5. (a) Graphs may be used to help compare each part with every other part as well as each part with the whole. (b) Tables of data make it easy to select any particular statistic and to read it accurately.
6. (a) The graphs compare the changes in the cost of living with the changes in the cost of electricity from 1957 to 1967. (b) The visual

properties of the graph convey almost immediately the rate at which
the cost of living has increased as compared with the rate at which the
cost of electricity has decreased.

EXERCISE 14.3

1. (a) See Figure 14.3.2 for assistance. (b) The midpoints of the class intervals are, when rounded, 5, 15, 25, 35, 45, 55, and 65. (c) See Figure
   14.3.3 for assistance. (d) See Figures 14.3.4 and 14.3.5 for assistance.
2. (a) See Figure 14.3.2 for assistance. (b) The midpoints of the class intervals are, when rounded, 2.5, 7.5, 12.5, 17.5, 22.5, 27.5, 32.5, 37.5,
   42.5, and 47.5. (c) See Figure 14.3.3 for assistance. (d) See Figures
   14.3.4 and 14.3.5 for assistance.

EXERCISE 14.4

1. (a) See Figure 14.3.2 for assistance. (b) See Figure 14.3.3 for assistance.
   (c) See Figures 14.3.4 and 14.3.5 for assistance. (d) 158.5 pounds (e)
   150–159.9 (f) 159 (g) 160–169.9 (h) Since the frequencies are tabulated into classes, the weight occurring most frequently, the mode,
   cannot be found from the table.
2. Yes; any of the selected classes may have the same frequency.
3. (a) 51, 56, 60, 61, 63, 64, 66, 67, 68, 71, 72, 73, 73, 74, 75, 75, 76, 77,
   77, 77, 77, 79, 80, 81, 81, 82, 83, 84, 87, 87, 88, 88, 90, 90, 91, 94, 95,
   95, 97. (b) 77.6 (c) 77 (d) 77 (e) See Figure 14.3.1 for assistance. (f)
   See Figure 14.3.2 for assistance. (g) 70–79.9 (h) 70–79.9

EXERCISE 14.5

1. See Definition 14.5.1.
2. (a) $\frac{1}{4}$ (c) $\frac{2}{3}$ (e) 1
3. (a) It means the event cannot occur.
4. (a) $\frac{1}{2}$ (c) $\frac{1}{1}$, or 1 to 1. (e) $\frac{1}{5}$, or 1 to 5.

Index

B 0
C 1
D 2
E 3
F 4
G 5
H 6
I 7
J 8
  9

List of Symbols

Symbol	Meaning
$\{a, b, c, \ldots\}$	The set whose elements are $a, b, c, \ldots$
$x \in A$	x is an element of set A
$x \notin A$	x is not an element of set A
$\mid$	Such that; divides
$\nmid$	Does not divide
$=$	Is equal to
$\neq$	Is not equal to
$\{ \ \}$ or $\varnothing$	The empty set
$A \subseteq B$	A is a subset of B
$A \subset B$	A is a proper subset of B
A'	The complement of set A
$S \vee T$	Statement S *or* statement T
$S \wedge T$	Statement S *and* statement T
$A \cup B$	The union of sets A and B
$A \cap B$	The intersection of sets A and B
(a, b)	Ordered pair
$A \times B$	The Cartesian product of sets A and B
$a \, \mathcal{R} \, b$	a has relation $\mathcal{R}$ to b
$\mathcal{R}^{-1}$	The inverse relation of $\mathcal{R}$
$[a]$	The equivalence class of a
$1\text{--}1$	One-to-one correspondence
$n(A)$	The cardinal number of set A
$N = \{1, 2, 3, \ldots\}$	The set of natural numbers
iff	If and only if
$W = \{0, 1, 2, 3, \ldots\}$	The set of whole numbers
$a + b$	The sum of a and b
$a \cdot b,\ a \times b,\ (a)(b),\ ab$	The product of a and b
$(a, b, c, \ldots)$	The ordered set whose elements are $a, b, c, \ldots$
$<$	Is less than
$\nless$	Is not less than
$\leq$	Is less than or equal to